Springer Series: FOCUS ON WOMEN

Violet Franks, Ph.D., Series Editor

Confronting the major psychological, medical, and social issues of today and tomorrow. *Focus on Women* provides a wide range of books on the changing concerns of women.

VOLUME 1
THE SAFETY OF FERTILITY CONTROL
Editor-in-Chief: Louis G. Keith, M.D.; Associate Editors: Deryck R. Kent, M.D.; Gary S. Berger, M.D., and Janelle R. Brittain, M.B.A.

VOLUME 2
THERAPY WITH WOMEN: A Feminist Philosophy of Treatment
Susan Sturdivant, Ph.D.

VOLUME 3
SHELTERING BATTERED WOMEN
A National Study and Service Guide
Albert R. Roberts, D.S.W.

VOLUME 4
WOMEN OVER FORTY: Visions and Realities
Jean D. Grambs, Ed.D.

VOLUME 5
THE STEREOTYPING OF WOMEN: Its Effects on Mental Health
Violet Franks, Ph.D., and Esther D. Rothblum, Ph.D.

VOLUME 6
THE BATTERED WOMAN SYNDROME
Lenore E. Walker, Ed.D.

VOLUME 7
WOMEN THERAPISTS WORKING WITH WOMEN
New Theory and Process of Feminist Therapy
Claire M. Brody, Ph.D., Editor

VOLUME 8
CAREER GUIDE FOR WOMEN SCHOLARS
Suzanna Rose, Ph.D.

VOLUME 9
A MOTE IN FREUD'S EYE: From Psychoanalysis to the Psychology of Women
Hannah Lerman, Ph.D

VOLUME 10
WOMEN'S THERAPY GROUPS: Paradigms of Feminist Treatment
Claire M. Brody, Ph.D, Editor

VOLUME 11
WOMEN AND DEPRESSION: A Lifespan Perspective
Ruth Formanek, Ph.D., and Anita Gurian, Ph.D., Editors

VOLUME 12
TRANSITIONS IN A WOMAN'S LIFE: Major Life Events in Developmental Context
Ramona T. Mercer, Ph.D., F.A.A.N., Elizabeth G. Nichols, D.N.S., F.A.A.N., Gillen C. Doyle, Ed.D., R.N.

VOLUME 13
NEW DIRECTIONS IN FEMINIST PSYCHOLOGY: Practice, Theory, and Research
Joan C. Chrisler, Ph.D., and Doris Howard, Ph.D.

VOLUME 14
THE EMPLOYED MOTHER AND THE FAMILY CONTEXT
Judith Frankel, Ph.D., Editor

VOLUME 15
WOMEN AND ANGER
Sandra P. Thomas, Ph.D., R.N., Editor

Sandra P. Thomas, PhD, RN, is Director, Center for Nursing Research, University of Tennessee, Knoxville, and teaches in the master's and doctor's programs in the College of Nursing. She holds bachelor's, master's, and doctorate degrees in education as well as a master's in nursing, with specialization in community mental health. During her doctoral program she majored in educational psychology, with a supporting emphasis in preventive mental health, and a cognate in child and family studies. She has extensive clinical experience, primarily in psychiatric/mental health nursing of adults. She is a member of the American Nurses' Association, the American Psychological Association (Health Psychology and Psychology of Women Divisions), Sigma Theta Tau International, and the Society of Behavioral Medicine. She serves on the Board of Directors of the International Council on Women's Health Issues. Dr. Thomas is associate editor of *Issues in Mental Health Nursing* and serves as a reviewer for four other professional journals. Her research has focused primarily on stress and the potentially modifiable attitudinal, emotional, and behavioral variables which affect health. She has presented her research at numerous national and international conferences and has also published extensively.

WOMEN AND ANGER

Sandra P. Thomas, PhD, RN
Editor

 Springer Publishing Company • *New York*

Springer Publishing Company, Inc
536 Broadway
New York, NY 10012-3955

93 94 95 96 97 / 5 4 3 2 1

Library of Congress Cataloging-in-Publication Data

Thomas, Sandra P.
   Women and anger / Sandra P. Thomas and contributors.
     p.   cm. — (Focus on women series ; v. 15)
   Includes bibliographical references and index.
   ISBN 0-8261-8100-7
    1. Anger.   2. Women—Psychology.   I. Series: Springer series,
focus on women ; v. 15.
   BF575.A5T48 1993
   155.6'33—dc20
                                        92-44878
                                           CIP

Stanzas from poems numbers 341 and 1123 by Emily Dickinson
were used by permission of Little, Brown and Company. These
poems appear in *The Complete Poems of Emily Dickinson* edited
by Thomas H. Johnson, copyright 1929 © by Martha Dickinson
Bianchi; copyright © renewed 1957 by Mary L. Hampson.

Printed in the United States of America

Contents

Contributors

Kaye Bultemeier, MSN, RN, is a doctoral candidate at the University of Tennessee, College of Nursing. Her professional career, as a family nurse practitioner, has focused on the health care of women. A private practice in obstetrics and gynecology affords her opportunity to care for women during a multiplicity of health care situations.

Gayle Denham, MSN, RN, is an assistant professor at Eastern Kentucky University and a doctoral student at the University of Tennessee, Knoxville, College of Nursing. Her BA degree was obtained from Eastern Kentucky University and her MSN from the University of Kentucky. She has eight years of clinical experience. Her research areas are in self-esteem and anger.

Madge M. Donnellan, PhD, RN, is nursing systems division chairperson at the Nell Hodgson Woodruff School of Nursing, Emory University, Atlanta, Georgia. She coordinates and teaches in the nurse practitioner program and directs the school's nursing center, where she is currently evaluating the quality and costs of the primary care services which are provided. Dr. Donnellan received her BSN and MS from the State University of New York, Buffalo, and a PhD in health education at the University of Tennessee, Knoxville.

Patricia G. Droppleman, PhD, RN, attended college at the Catholic University of America and the University of Tennessee, Knoxville, where she completed her doctoral work in 1979. She is an associate professor in the College of Nursing at the University of Tennessee and is the coordinator of the parent–child graduate track, which includes women's health issues. Dr. Droppleman has practiced primarily in obstetrical and pediatric settings in hospitals, in public health, in private settings, and in rural primary care clinics, but she has also worked in medical-surgical and geriatric nursing.

June Martin, MSN, RN, has 15 years clinical experience in emergency room nursing. She recently attained her MSN in mental health nursing from the University of Tennessee, Knoxville. She is currently employed as Director of the Medication Clinic at a psychiatric hospital in Knoxville.

Mary Anne Modrcin-McCarthy, MSN, RN, is currently completing her dissertation in the doctoral program at the University of Tennessee, Knoxville. She attained her MSN from Boston University, and received her BSN from the University of Kansas, Kansas City. She has been a clinical specialist/ nurse educator and has 14 years of clinical experience and 10 years of teaching at various levels of nursing.

Sheryl S. Russell, MSN, RN, CCRN, is a doctoral student in nursing at the University of Tennessee, Knoxville. She also received her master's degree from the University of Tennessee, with a clinical focus on endocrinology and a functional focus in teaching. Her research areas of interest are addiction and eating disorders.

Margaret (Pegge) Saylor, PhD, RNC, received her PhD from the University of Michigan, where her dissertation was titled, "Anger Experience, Anger Expression, Hostility, Hardiness, Social Support and Health." Currently, Dr. Saylor is associate professor of nursing at University of North Carolina–Charlotte, teaching in the outreach MSN program in Asheville. She remains active in clinical practice as an adult nurse practitioner, in addition to teaching and research activities, finding that each role gives added meaning to the others.

Elizabeth G. Seabrook, MMSc, MS, is a graduate of Southern Methodist University and holds a master's degree in counseling psychology from Georgia State University, where she completed an internship in the field of addiction. She is currently a doctoral candidate in counseling psychology at the University of Tennessee, Knoxville. Ms. Seabrook's research pursuits developed from her interest in gender issues related to the treatment of codependency and alcoholism in women.

Barbara Shirk, RN, MS, has 40 years of experience in nursing. The past 12 years were devoted to developing and conducting weight management programs in a private internal medicine practice. A graduate of the University of Illinois, College of Nursing, her master's thesis explored a behavioral weight-loss program for people with high blood pressure.

Carol J. Smucker, RN, MA, is a nursing doctoral student at the University of Tennessee, Knoxville. Her predissertation focus has been spirituality. She is particularly interested in contributing to the development of the nursing diagnosis, spiritual distress. She received her master's in nursing from the University of Iowa and was subsequently a member of the nursing faculty there before she began her doctoral work.

Jane Tollett, MSN, RN, is a doctoral candidate at the University of Tennessee, Knoxville, College of Nursing. She has clinical experience in a variety of settings, including public health and long-term and acute care. For the past 15 years she has worked in management roles as director of nursing service and, most recently, as a director/clinical nurse specialist in a homeless veterans program.

Dorothy L. Wilt, BSN, MSN, was educated at Marquette University and the University of Tennessee. She is an assistant professor at the University of Tennessee. She is also a nurse psychotherapist. In private practice she has provided individual, family, and group therapy for the last 12 years. She is a clinical member of the American Association of Marriage and Family Therapists and is a certified family therapist in the state of Tennessee.

Preface

The study reported in this volume is the first large-scale, comprehensive, empirical investigation of women's anger. The project involved three years of work by an all-female research group at the University of Tennessee, Knoxville. A brief explanation of the modus operandi of our group is in order. Formed in the fall of 1989 under the leadership of Sandra Thomas, the group brought together faculty and graduate students interested in women's mental health. The project reported in this book was conceptualized and data collection subsequently proceeded with assistance from collaborators at several other universities, including the University of North Carolina at Charlotte, Emory University, and East Tennessee State University. There were two waves of data collection, with an expanded test battery used in the second phase (1990–1991). In the summer of 1991 opportunities to participate in the preparation of this manuscript were offered to members of the group. At that time claims were staked for various chapters and the book prospectus was submitted. We agreed that we would strive to write this book so that students as well as practicing professionals would find it clear and useful.

The content should be of interest to academicians and practitioners in a variety of disciplines, including nursing, medicine, psychology, social work, and other health care or counseling fields. To avoid confusion on the part of the reader, we point out here that all chapter authors worked with the same data set (with one exception—see Chapter 12). Individual authors developed their topics, conducted necessary data analyses, and prepared initial drafts that were circulated to all members of the group. The process of critiquing each other's work and incorporating feedback from peers has been at various times stimulating, painful, or tedious, but generally indispensable. And we have managed to accomplish the compilation of the final manuscript without becoming angry! As in most research projects, new questions have been generated that can take future investigators in several directions. Even though we take pride in the information we have contributed to the burgeoning literature on human emotions and emotion-health linkages, we are fully cognizant that we have mapped only a portion of the vast territory yet to be explored.

Foreword

This book's consideration of anger is part of a paradigm shift that has taken place since Betty Friedan published her landmark book, *The Feminine Mystique* (1963), discussing "The Problem That Has No Name"—the terrible tiredness that took so many American women to physicians in the 1950s. Since that time, a new conceptualization of women's health emerged that focuses on women's dis-eases—e.g., the health ramifications of anger—and not just their diseases (Stevenson, 1977). This is a view that moves women's health away from gynecology, synonymous more or less with a concern for feminine plumbing, to GYN-ecology, meaning by the latter a study of the positive fit between a woman's well-being and her environment (Rosser, 1991).

In the quarter century that has seen women's health evolve into a distinct and important subset of women's studies, the emphasis has largely been on critiquing the ways in which the health of women has been constrained by contextual factors (McBride & McBride, 1981). Some of these factors are the extent to which females have not been included as subjects in health research (e.g., studies of alcoholism and coronary disease) and the disregard for some of their major health problems (e.g., violence against women and poverty). One of the major issues being raised by the women's health movement is whether the larger society supports "healthy choices being the easy choices," for example, Does the environment promote breastfeeding? Are girls encouraged to be active in sports? It is only recently, however, that the move has been beyond critique to assertion, meaning by the latter an in-depth exploration of new ways of describing health and its absence.

The authors of this volume have taken women's anger seriously as a phenomenon for study and in the process have moved beyond stereotyped thinking towards some emerging, often counter-intuitive recognitions, e.g., that women juggling the most roles may be least prone to anger; that women's reasoning may be more influenced by considerations of justice than once thought given the extent to which blame-proneness may be associated with anger; that crying may be a manifestation of anger. In this process of exploration, both the just anger traditionally accorded the patriarch and the total acceptance expected of his female counterpart have been called seriously into question.

Anger and its health consequences is an enormously important subject in women's lives. Women are continually in situations of subordination that produce anger (e.g., often not having control over their bodies; making less money than men with the same education, responsibilities, and experience; being the recipients of abuse 10 times more frequently than are men), but the culture still largely denies them direct expression of that emotion. Expressions of anger get women labeled pejoratively—bitch, virago, shrew, harpy. Because they are not expected to express anger forthrightly, women choke back such feelings, then often release them when pressure-cooker levels of emotional steam have been reached. Since the resulting explosion has been so long in the making the response inevitably seems disproportionate to the stimulus provoking it (i.e., unreasonable or irrational), which only serves to make women redouble their efforts at sealing over their anger once the sparks have been dampened, thus setting the stage for the very same behavior pattern to unfold once more–a pattern which on the face of it seems "mad" and not just angry.

Lazarus (1991) places all considerations of emotion within changing person–environment relationships. For him, anger is shorthand for "a demeaning offense against me and mine" (p. 222). This contextual conceptualization, which is further described in this book by Sandra P. Thomas and her colleagues, makes sense out of why anger is a special health problem for women, with their historic second-class status, and why anger is an excellent example of a dis-ease in need of study when considering the evolution of a new health paradigm focusing on the fit between person and environment. The highest praise I can offer this book is to acknowledge that it has made me think that how a person handles anger should be a part of every health professional's assessment of a new patient.

Angela Barron McBride, PhD
—Distinguished Professor and University Dean, Indiana University School of Nursing,
—Adjunct Professor, Purdue University School of Science at Indianapolis, Indiana University School of Medicine, and Indiana University-Purdue University at Indianapolis

REFERENCES

Friedan, B. (1963). *The feminine mystique*. New York: Dell Publishing.

Lazarus, R. S. (1991). *Emotion and adaptation*. New York: Oxford University Press.

McBride, A. B., & McBride, W. L. (1981). Theoretical underpinnings for women's health. *Women & Health, 6*(1/2), 37–55.

Rosser, S. V. (1991). Eco-feminism. Lessons for feminism from ecology. *Women's Studies International Forum, 14,* 143–151.

Stevenson, J. S. (1977). Women's health research. Why, what and so what? *CNR Voice* (The Ohio State University School of Nursing), *21,* 1–2.

Acknowledgments

The Women's Anger Study was supported by a Faculty Research Award, University of Tennessee, Knoxville, and by a grant from the associate vice-provost for research for doctoral research assistantships for Jane Tollett and Mary Anne Modrcin-McCarthy. Additional support was received from the discretionary fund of the Dean, College of Nursing, Dr. Sylvia Hart. Countless hours were donated by our data collectors, who included Dr. Pegge Saylor at the University of North Carolina at Charlotte, Dr. Madge Donnellan at Emory University, Dr. Susan Grover at East Tennessee State University, Dr. Damaris Young, a counseling psychologist in private practice in Tennessee, and Barbara Shirk, a clinical specialist in an internal medicine practice in Illinois, as well as several University of Tennessee master's and doctoral students in nursing. Among the master's students, special recognition must be given to Carol Fong-Jui Tsai, Becky Fields, Darneta Brown, and Risa Schwartz. Among the doctoral students, we acknowledge the assistance of Joan Wagner. Accuracy of computer data entry can largely be attributed to Mary Anne Modrcin-McCarthy, although several other individuals contributed time to this tedious but vitally important task. We are grateful to Jean Hunt, David Wilt, Sally Blowers, and Joan Wagner for reading drafts of various chapters. We appreciated the assistance of Noel Kuck and Michael Lusk with graphics. Our word-processing specialist Linda Dalton was essential to the successful completion of this undertaking; revision after revision was speedily and efficiently finished. Momentum for the project over the years, from 1989 to 1992, was provided by the Women's Mental Health Research Group at the University of Tennessee. Although the group has been comprised primarily of nurses, we have benefited by input from faculty and students in psychology and education. The contributions of Dr. Kathleen Bennett DeMarrais deserve special mention. Ongoing discussions of concepts, methodological issues, clinical experiences, and sometimes very personal anger experiences, kept enthusiasm high. We acknowledge our debt to those members of the group who shared in our early discussions but were unable to continue with the project. The initial encouragement of Barbara Watkins at Springer and the subsequent support of Dr. Ursula Springer were deeply appreciated. Finally, we acknowledge the women who participated in the study. By sharing their anger experiences they have provided the foundational data on which future studies can build. For their time, candor, and insightful comments we express our profound gratitude.

■ 1
Introduction

Sandra P. Thomas

This is a book about women's anger, written *by* women, *for* women. Why have we written a book on women's anger? Because we have new information, grounded in research data, that we believe will be helpful to health care providers and to their female clients. Although some excellent books about anger have appeared in recent years, this one differs in several ways. This is not a self-help book, like Harriet Lerner's (1985) *The Dance of Anger*. Nor is this a critique of research findings for the general public like *Anger: The Misunderstood Emotion* by Carol Tavris (1989). Nor do we write to make a political statement about women's oppression in American society. We write to share the perceptions and words of more than 500 women, our research participants, who told us about the power and the pain of their anger.

This book addresses the anger experience of all types of women. The women in our study are ordinary women, partnered and unpartnered, employed and unemployed, affluent and poor, mothers and nonmothers. They live in cities as well as smaller towns and rural areas. They range in age from 25 to 66. Occupations of the women include real estate agent, export representative, office manager, teacher, electrical designer, social worker, homemaker, speech pathologist, masseuse, psychotherapist, hairdresser, registered nurse, technical editor, secretary, travel agent, decorator, rural mail carrier, factory worker, nutritionist, bank executive, school bus driver, scientist, day care director, business owner, insurance agent, and computer analyst—and this is not an exhaustive list! Most women in the sample were presently healthy (i.e., not hospitalized at the time of data collection and contacted in community settings). However, we also collected data from some groups with medi-

1

cal or psychiatric problems to permit comparisons in terms of anger expression styles, stress, and other factors.

There is a shocking lack of research about anger experience in women. In fact, Harriet Lerner wondered if women's anger could be a taboo topic when she undertook her first search of the literature, finding nothing within the vast resources of the Menninger Clinic library. Psychoanalyst Jean Baker Miller (1991) has pointed out that "One topic most people really do not want to hear about is women's anger!" (p. 182). She attributes the profound cultural fear of women's anger to women's assignment as principal caretakers. Men do not make commitments to look after each other; in fact, their interactions are often competitive or confrontational. Therefore, women must be there to attend to their needs. According to Miller's argument, it is unthinkable that the ever-nurturing caretaker could experience *anger*.

If Miller is correct, then what do women *do* with the anger that is generated in their daily interactions—given a cultural climate in which expression of this emotion would be improper, even alarming? Miller contends "there is only one way women's anger could go: into indirection and confusion" (p. 187)—with disastrous psychological consequences for women. Does the research evidence support Miller's contention?

When we turned to the literature, we found two early studies (Anastasi, Cohen, & Spatz, 1948; Gates, 1926) that focused on women's anger in small samples of college students. In both investigations, women recorded anger incidents for a week. The average number of incidents ranged from 3 per week in the Gates study to 16 per week in Anastasi's; some women reported as many as 42. Thus, anger was a rather common occurrence. The chief cause of anger in both studies was termed "thwarting" (of *self-assertion* in the Gates study, of *plans* in the Anastasi study). In the severer anger episodes, the primary cause was a "domineering attitude of others" (Gates, 1926). The Gates project report included richly detailed descriptions of the women's subjective experience including impulses to injure the offender by slapping, pinching, shaking, scratching, tearing to pieces, and choking, as well as responding verbally.

Despite these interesting preliminary findings, apparently there was no continuing line of research. Presumably few rewards existed for investigators focusing on women's issues within predominately male psychology departments during the first half of the century. During those years researchers displayed little interest in the study of *anyone's* subjective experience; they were mainly interested in the physiology of emotion or in behavior that could be readily observed. Rapaport (1971) noted that the physiological changes that occur during emotional states have been well described in the literature, whereas the "emotion felt" has received scant attention. Although the emotion system has been termed the primary motivational system throughout the human life-span (Malatesta & Izard, 1984a), the role of emotions has been ignored in many major motivation theories; this neglect of emotions has been attributed to difficulties in defining them (K. B. Hoyenga & K. T. Hoyenga, 1984). Richard Lazarus (1991b) pointed out that between 1920 and 1960, only an occasional monograph on emotion appeared in the social science literature. But the lack of research on women's anger in more recent years is indeed puzzling, given the upsurge of interest in emotion by scientists—and the centrality of emotional experience in life as a whole. According to Zajonc (1984) people are always in *some* emotional state. Who would argue that emotions are among the brightest threads in the intricate tapestry of a life? Memories of events are always colored by their emotional component, bringing us to tears, laughter, or anger, years later. In fact, anger proved to be the predominant emotion in a longitudinal study of important events (and the feelings generated by them) across 19 years of women's lives (Malatesta & Culver, 1984). Anger is also proving to be important in the etiology and progression of health problems such as coronary heart disease (Williams & Barefoot, 1988). This powerful and poorly understood emotion obviously needs to be studied.

And behavioral health researchers *are* studying anger now—but all too often the study participants are exclusively male. For example, an Israeli study on the relationship of anger and blood pressure involved 10,000 male civil service workers (Kahn, Medalie, Neufeld, Riss, & Goldbourt, 1972). A more recent report on anger expression styles and blood pressure also focused exclusively on men (Harburg, Gleiberman, Russell, & Cooper, 1991). Only men were used in a study of relationships between anger expression styles and cardiovascular reactivity conducted by Engebretson, Matthews, and Scheier (1989). In angiographic studies examining suppressed anger's connection with coronary atherosclerosis, only men were included (MacDougall, Dembroski, Dimsdale, & Hackett, 1985). Male samples were used in the Western Collaborative Group Study (well known for establishing the link between the anger-prone Type A personality and coronary heart disease [CHD]) as well as the Multiple Risk Factor Intervention Trial (equally well known for its *failure* to show a link between global Type A and heart disease—although the *antagonistic hostility component* of Type A did increase the risk for CHD). Many other Type A studies (e.g., the French-Belgian Cooperative Heart study, the Belgian Heart Disease Prevention Trial, the Honolulu Heart Program and the Recurrent Coronary Prevention Project) were conducted only with male subjects (Fischman, 1987). In most cases, no rationale was provided for the omission of female subjects. Certainly, both the Type A pattern and CHD occur in women! And high blood pressure is more prevalent in women than in men (Strickland, 1988).

When studies of anger variables *do* include women as well as men, quite often the researcher's hypotheses are not supported for the female participants. The discrepant findings are dutifully noted but rarely discussed in the summary sections of articles; the researchers emphasize their important findings regarding males. Here is an example of this tendency. In a recent book chapter, Smith and Christensen (1992) reviewed several studies that examined hostility in both men and women. Hostility was assessed by the Cook-Medley Ho Scale, which will be discussed later in the chapter. The following statements were made (emphasis added):

- "Interestingly, Ho scores were only weakly related to overt behaviors and reported affect among wives" (p. 37).
- "Ho scores of the wives were unrelated to blood pressure reactivity in either condition" (p. 39).
- "Hostile persons also report interpersonal conflict at work, in their families of origin, and in their marriages, *although the latter effect has been found for men but not women*" (p. 40).

In the summary section of this book chapter, there is no further mention of gender differences nor any suggestion for further study of women. Smith and Christensen probably should not be singled out for criticism; their book chapter is just one example of a phenomenon that is all too prevalent in the literature. We will not belabor the point by offering additional examples. Obviously it is time for some careful attention to women who have been overlooked or termed "deviant cases" or "outliers" in so many previous studies. Psychologist Bernice Lott asserted, "The lives of women provide rich sources of information for study; psychology must focus on human beings, not just men, college students, heterosexuals, or middle-class European Americans" (Lott, 1991, p. 510).

MYTHS ABOUT WOMEN'S ANGER

There are several myths and untested theories about women's anger. Because women's anger has been neglected by researchers, there is no empirical evidence to refute myths, folk wisdom, and misinformation. Let us review some prevalent myths. Perhaps the most widely circulated allegation is that women have difficulty acknowledging and expressing their anger. Judith Bardwick (1979) contended: "Women are not entitled to anger. Anger, except in some girlish tantrum, is unfeminine. Direct, bold, eyeball-to-eyeball, confronting, dominating, resisting, insisting anger has been traditionally forbidden to women" (p. 48). Various reasons for inhibition of anger have been given. In an argument similar to Miller's, Bernardez (1987) asserted that women must conform to the feminine ideal of the selfless, ever-nurturing, "perfect mother"; venting anger would conjure up the opposite image of "bad mother." Women are said to fear and suppress anger because of its potential for disruption of relationships with men (Bernardez-Bonesatti, 1978). According to Bernardez-Bonesatti, women's anger toward men is allegedly redirected against the self or other women, displaced onto children or other less powerful persons, or vented in futile outbursts that accomplish nothing.

Women are also said to use passive-aggressive forms of anger expression such as pouting, whining, manipulating, backbiting, or gossiping instead of direct, forthright anger messages (Mueller & Leidig, 1976, cited in Tavris, 1989). Because men have been dominant and women subordinate in our society, women have allegedly adopted beliefs that are culturally sanctioned: (a) I am weak, (b) I am unworthy, and (c) I have no right or cause to be angry (Miller, 1983). The ultimate consequence of denied or suppressed anger is depression, according to several theorists (Bernardez, 1987; Freud, 1917/1961; Klauber, 1966; White, 1977). Women's suppressed anger has also been linked to frigidity, hysteria, phobias, and a variety of other problems (Chesler, 1971).

A major problem with much of this theorizing is that the theorists (usually psychologists and psychiatrists) derived their ideas about women's anger mainly from clinical work with clients who had serious problems expressing anger appropriately and effectively. Clinical case reports clearly document that many women in therapy have anger-related problems, and there is valuable information for clinicians in the articles and books that address inhibited, displaced, or unduly militant forms of anger. However, conclusions about anger phenomena based on troubled women in therapy may not be valid for all women. For example, Lerner's (1985) book is based on her work with clients at the Menninger clinic. With no intent to disparage this important contribution to the literature, women in therapy at Menninger's probably do not represent typical American women. Women receiving psychotherapy often have devastating traumas such as rape, incest, battering, abandonment, or other life-shattering events in their history. The deep-seated anger and rage produced by such events, although a grave problem both to the victims and to society at large, is not the everyday anger the present study seeks to understand. Recent research, including our own, raises questions about the validity of some of the anger theories developed by clinicians—at least, when the formulations are generalized without modification to nonclinical samples. For example, several writers claim that women don't even *know* when they are angry. Although this may be true for some profoundly oppressed women, only a small percentage of our subjects failed to fill out the "typical anger experience" page of our questionnaire. Women *do* know when they are angry—they told us about it.

Another problem with the clinical literature is its preoccupation with women's anger that is generated within their intimate relationships. Obviously, women have an enormous investment in their relationships with parents, spouses, and children, and strong feelings are evoked when such important relationships are disrupted. But today's women are not confined to home and hearth; most are also employed. What information is available in the literature about women's anger on the job? Despite the huge increase in women's workforce participation since the 1970s, there is almost no research on the anger of female workers at their supervisors, colleagues, and subordinates. Women are also angry about poverty, sexism, and a host of issues much larger and in some ways more difficult to address than those within the immediate family or workplace. For example, one of our research subjects said she became angry about "political decisions that I do not agree with in all levels of life experiences." Another participant in our study listed such diverse triggers of her anger as

- World situation
- Abuse of power
- War
- Problems in America such as education, the economy, violence, homelessness, rape, campus problems, lack of gun control
- Unfairness to others or myself

Concern beyond the personal self, with a strong moral connotation, is evident in these responses. Anger is not confined to situations in which women are directly affected. Injustices that violate our deepest values or spiritual beliefs can produce a very constructive form of anger—one that may eventually lead to crusading for social change. In our research, we did not ask women to confine their anger descriptions to particular situations or circumstances; they could write whatever came to mind. Thus, we can broadly examine the subjects about which women in the 1990s are angry.

Women themselves have seldom been questioned by researchers about their anger. Within the scientific establishment there has been mistrust, even disparagement, of self-report data. It has been assumed that people will not or cannot honestly report their experience. Deception of subjects has been quite common in both experiments and surveys. In contrast, this book was undertaken from the premise that each woman is an expert on her own self. Gordon Allport once said, "If you want to know something about a person, ask." We as researchers trust the validity of women's accounts of their own feelings, and we will use quotes liberally to illustrate the richness of their descriptions of anger experiences. Together, we dispel myths and misinformation about women's anger.

WHY IS ANGER IMPORTANT?

The authors of this book are nurses and counselors. We are interested in (a) how often women are provoked to anger and (b) how they express (or suppress) it, because anger—if excessive or managed inappropriately—can play an important role in many kinds of mental or physical illnesses. The influence of emotions on health has been recognized since the early Greek civilization, although American medicine has been slow to acknowledge the connection. Early psychodynamic formulations associating specific emotions with particular physical or mental disorders generally failed to receive empirical support. However, the amazing discoveries in the past two decades of linkages among the central nervous system (origin of thoughts and emotions), the endocrine system (origin of hormones), and the immune system (origin of our defenses against disease) have forced even reluctant individuals to reconsider emotion-health interconnectedness. The discipline studying the messengers that unite the three systems is called "psychoneuroimmunology" (PNI), and its research findings on messenger substances (such as neurotransmitters, hormones, peptides, and lymphokines) are being shared in the popular press as well as with scientific audiences. The basic premise of PNI is "an assumption . . . that *all* disease (including mental illness and also medical conditions not ordinarily considered "psychosomatic") is multifactorial in origin, the result of interrelationships among the genetic, endocrine, nervous and immune systems, and behavioral-emotional factors" (Solomon, 1985, p. 7). It is no longer a radical or far-fetched notion that emotions can have considerable impact on health—and research has shown that the two most powerful emotions in the United States are love and anger (Heider, cited in Adler, 1989).

Let us review some health problems of women in which anger may be implicated. Women predominate in diagnoses of major depression, dysthymia, anxiety disorders, somatoform pain disorder, and several other emotional or mental conditions (McGrath, Keita, Strickland, & Russo, 1990; Robins et al., 1984); they are more likely than men to use mental health facilities (Strickland, 1988). Biomedical models have failed to explain the greater prevalence of these mental disorders in women. Women also have higher rates for most acute diseases and most nonfatal chronic conditions than do men (Verbrugge, 1985). For example, hypertension, rheumatoid arthritis, and lupus erythematosis are more prevalent in women (Strickland, 1988). Higher proportions of women than men have respiratory and gastrointestinal problems (Rodin & Ickovics, 1990). Migraine headaches are also more frequent in women than in men; Witkin (1991) has presented case material linking migraine attacks to situations in which rage was aroused but not expressed. Although more men die of CHD, women are also at risk; CHD is the leading cause of death for women just as it is for men (Centers for Disease Control, 1989). The incidence of angina pectoris has increased by 69 percent for women during the past 15 years compared with an increase of 31 percent for men (Witkin, 1991). Obesity and diabetes incidence rates are higher for women than men in most studies (Rodin & Ickovics, 1990) and women's death rate from strokes is higher (Strickland, 1988). Breast cancer, which affects one in nine women, is only one type of cancer that afflicts women; a growing body of evidence implicates emotional factors in the development of breast cancer as well as other malignant tumors (Greer & Morris, 1975; Greer & Morris, 1978; C. Thomas, 1988).

It is also well known that women, although they live longer, are sick more often than men. This has been true in the United States for as long as vital statistics have been compiled. Women restrict their activities for health problems about 25 percent more days each year than men do, and they spend about 40 percent more days in bed per year (Verbrugge, 1985). Rates of hospitalization are higher for women than men (even when obstetrical conditions are excluded), and more prescription and nonprescription medications are taken by women (Nathanson, 1977). Despite this array of statistics—which clearly documents the need for more research on women's health—many studies funded by the National Institutes of Health (NIH) have examined only men. Overall, NIH spends only 13 percent of its $7.7 billion budget on women's health issues (Purvis, 1990). Women are responsible for spending two of every three health care dollars, yet the bulk of research dollars has been spent on male diseases (Wentz & Haseltine, 1992). Although the Office on Women's Health was established within the Public Health Service in 1991, and the new "PHS Action Plan for Women's Health" calls for more biomedical and behavioral research on women, significant knowledge deficits will remain for several years. One puzzling issue is the decline in women's mortality advantage. Although women still live longer than men, women's mortality advantage has begun to decline in recent years, for reasons that are unclear. The death rates for heart disease and cancer have decreased for men during the past few decades, but the picture is not as positive for women. Cancer rates for women have not declined as rapidly as for men, and cardiac mortality has stayed the same (Rodin & Ickovics, 1990). Some authorities have suggested that the increased stress of women's lives contributes to the declining mortality advantage as well as to many of the illnesses we have enumerated (cf. Verbrugge, 1989).

STRESS IN WOMEN'S LIVES

According to Verbrugge (1985), women feel more daily and long-term emotional distress, and they are less happy about life and less satisfied with their roles than are men. Stress research has focused mainly on stressors of men in their work roles, as if the home were a stress-free sanctuary. However, women are often greatly stressed by their family roles. Women must cope with a high level of demands from spouses, children, and others in the home, although they have a low level of control over the behavior of these individuals. Women report lower levels of marital happiness and are less satisfied with the companionship and expressive interaction in marriage than are men; married women also report more mental health problems than married men (Bernard,

1982). Women who work outside the home often have little autonomy and control in their jobs and few outlets for their stress. After the workday is finished, the second shift of work begins in the home (the daily cooking, cleaning, and laundry) rather than relaxation and respite from tasks. As Mary Catherine Bateson (1990) astutely observed, "relaxing at home" is an *oxymoron* for most women.

The joint effects of family and work roles produce role overload, role conflict, and role strain in many women. Employed women average 15 hours more work per week and one-half hour less sleep each night than housewives (Pleck & Rustad, 1980). Almost 70% of employed women have children under age 18 (McBride, 1988). The total workload (combined demands of paid and unpaid work) of women with two children was 80 hours per week (with three or more children, 90 hours per week) in a study of white-collar workers conducted by Frankenhaeuser, Lundberg, and Mardberg (1990). Being a mother in itself increases psychological distress for women, whether or not they work outside the home (Thoits, 1986). Another potential contributor to a woman's stress level is caregiving responsibility for elderly parents or other individuals. Bernardy (1987) stated, "Of the eight million Americans who provide some level of care to an elderly relative or friend, most are daughters" (p. 4).

A phenomenon called "vicarious stress" is also reported by women. Kessler and McLeod (1984) found that for women, stress is due not only to the number of events occurring in their own lives, but also to the misfortunes of their friends and relatives. In other words, they take on the burdens of others. Women tend to have larger social networks than men, requiring greater energy in nurturing the various individuals to whom they are connected. There are costs as well as benefits of large social networks. It is difficult trying to be everything to everybody. Sometimes women end up giving more support to others than they are getting in return (Turkington, 1985).

Witkin (1991) claims that women's stress is greater in the 1990s than in previous decades. In addition to events long known to be stressful, such as divorce, participants in Witkin's study reported new sources of stress such as the "refilled-nest syndrome" (in which adult children return home because of personal or economic crises) and increases in crime victimization, time pressures, job and money changes. According to Witkin, life in the 1990s has become unpredictable; few women have the life they expected while growing up.

LINK OF STRESS AND ANGER

What does stress have to do with anger? Stress produces emotional arousal and dysphoria including feelings such as anger (Caplan, 1981). If women are more stressed in the 1990s, might they consequently be more angry? Several recent studies have shown significant relationships between higher levels of life stress and greater anger or hostility in both men and women (Adams et al., 1986; Hardy & Smith, 1988; Scherwitz, Perkins, Chesney, & Hughes, 1991; Smith & Frohm, 1985; S. Thomas & Donnellan, 1991; S. Thomas & Williams, 1991). Emotions can play a role at any point in the stress process, from the initial recognition of the stressful event to the stage of developing a coping strategy. In an interesting series of studies, Stone and colleagues first established that stressful daily events were associated with negative moods. Then they examined the relation between daily fluctuations of mood and immune system competence. In their 8-week study of dental students, secretory IgA antibody response was lower on negative mood days and higher on days with more positive mood (Stone, 1981; Stone & Neale, 1984; Stone, Cox, Valdimarsdottir, Jandorf, & Neale, 1987).

Some individuals may experience more stress than circumstances warrant because they have ineffective coping strategies. Novaco (1985) contends that the person who is chronically or frequently angry may have learned to cope with stressful life demands by becoming angry. The problem with this coping style is that stress may be increased, not decreased, by the anger. And the anger generated by the stressors may become an *additional* stressor to the body. Julius, Harburg, Cottington, and Johnson (1986) view disruptive anger coping responses as specific stressors that could alter the body's biochemical balance, precipitating disease.

Both stress and anger have been linked to a variety of diseases such as arthritis, cancer, and heart disease. The coronary-prone highly stressed and overtly angry Type A individual epitomizes the reciprocal relationships of stress and anger. In this syndrome, hostile, competitive behavior is both the reaction to stressful environmental challenges and the creator of additional stresses for Type A personalities. Research on the coronary-prone behavior pattern has prompted a plethora of newspaper and magazine articles with sensational titles such as "The Deadly Emotions," "The Hostile Heart," "Temper Those Tantrums," and "Is Anger Killing You?" In one such article, anger is termed "a poison." The advice given to readers is sometimes as simplistic as "Avoid feeling angry."

POSITIVE FUNCTIONS OF ANGER

Despite its recent bad press, anger is not entirely unhealthy, a thing to be eradicated. Anger certainly can have negative effects, such as disrupting our ability to think clearly and behave sensibly. Anger can instigate reckless driving, excessive eating or drinking, and other behaviors that are directly or indirectly deleterious to health. However, anger also has many positive functions. In some situations expression of anger actually *promotes* health. For example, women who openly express anger about having cancer live longer than do those who express no anger (Derogatis, Abeloff, & Mellisaratos, 1979). Expression of anger may actually result in greater attention or better medical care than that received by a more passive patient (Appel, Holroyd, & Gorkin, 1983). Further, anger can mobilize energy to fight the assaults of disease or other threats to the integrity of the self. It is quite possible that this health-promoting anger has different physiological concomitants than the "poisonous" anger emphasized in recent literature.

Averill (1982) argues that anger would not have been a central feature of Western civilization for well over 2,500 years if it did not serve a valuable social function. Anger can serve as a useful warning signal that stressors are exceeding our resources (Taylor, 1988). As Tomkins (1991) puts it, anger tells us that our experience is "too much, too dense, and too punishing, whatever else it may be in its particulars" (p. 117). Anger is an entirely natural, legitimate response in many situations. As Lerner (1985) pointed out, anger can be a signal that our rights or values are being compromised, that others are doing too much or too little for us, that something is wrong and should be corrected. Unless the anger is expressed, the offending party has no opportunity to make needed changes in behavior. In Averill's (1983) research, 76% of the targets of someone's anger said they came to realize their own faults because of the other person's anger. Furthermore, the relationship with the angry person was more often strengthened than weakened. Rothenberg asserted that "when anger is accompanied by clear communication, it is a sign of basic respect for a loved person" (1971, p. 90). Bernardez (1987) speaks of anger in terms of self-love as well. She defines a positive kind of anger called "liberating," wherein a woman decides to stop being silent about injustices and begins to construct a new future for herself.

Thus, it seems worthwhile to investigate anger management styles that may be *adaptive* or *health enhancing* as well as styles that may have a negative effect on physical or mental health. We do not believe that it is possible to eliminate anger arousal. However, individuals can learn to reduce their reactivity to minor frustrations (or avoid some people and places) if they are becoming angry too frequently. Irrational thoughts that fuel anger can be replaced with more logical, realistic, ones. And it is possible to change habitual anger expression methods if one becomes aware that they are ineffective or harmful. At present, there is insufficient information in the literature to guide women in selecting appropriate anger expression methods. As we will see, both holding anger in and venting it outwardly have been blamed for health problems—which leaves the average person wondering what to do.

WHAT THIS BOOK IS ABOUT

The material in this book is based on the first large-scale descriptive study of women's anger. In view of the paucity of research on the phenomenon, our aim was to *describe* what occurs in the natural settings where women enact their social roles; no experimental manipulations were introduced. This project is consistent with Averill's (1983) recommendation that scholars examine emotional phenomena such as anger "as they are experienced and conceptualized in everyday affairs" (p. 1156). We questioned women about their typical day-to-day experiences of anger. We asked them to tell us about situations or circumstances that would trigger their anger and people with whom they might become angry. We also asked to whom they would express their anger, how they would express it, and how long typical anger episodes would last. To explore constraints that prevent or limit women's anger expression, we asked the study participants about individuals to whom they would *not* express their anger. Anger cognitions (such as thinking about unfairness of others' actions) and physical manifestations of anger (such as a knotted feeling in stomach, pounding heart, flushing, breathing changes) were also assessed. Realizing that some people are temperamentally more fiery and easily triggered, we asked the women how "hotheaded" or easily annoyed they considered themselves. Reactivity to criticism or frustration was also measured.

Both quantitative and qualitative methods were used in the study. Thus, although we used structured tests that yield numeric scores to examine some anger dimensions, we also provided space for women to write descriptions of stressful and anger-producing situations. Focus groups were used by two members of the research team to explore women's eating behaviors when they are angry. We wanted to get at the *meaning* of anger incidents in women's lives, not just the superficial aspects. Because some of the questionnaires had been developed by male researchers, we wondered if there were things women do while angry that would not be tapped by the questionnaire items; we asked for written descriptions. Responses to the open-ended questions proved to be some of our most intriguing data.

Anger is an extremely complex emotion. Many factors influence the causes, manifestations, and consequences of women's anger. One research project cannot consider all of them. We selected significant factors in women's lives for inclusion in this research: stress, self-esteem, social support, values/spirituality, and role responsibilities. We also looked at the relationships of anger variables with obesity, substance use, depression, and health habits/health status. In subsequent chapters we include an in-depth examination of each of these topics along with our study's findings.

Obviously, women are not a monolithic, homogeneous group. Despite the common factor of gender, women's life experiences differ tremendously according to their marital status, education, occupation, age, ethnicity, and other factors. These disparate life experiences could affect anger expression styles. Therefore, we will be discussing differences between selected subgroups of women as well as general themes and commonalities found across groups. Although we could not investigate the anger behaviors of *all* of America's racial and ethnocultural minority groups, we devote special attention to African-American and Chinese-American women in an attempt to discover differences shaped by their unique cultural origins.

WHAT THIS BOOK IS NOT ABOUT

This book is *not* about aggression, hostility, or violence. Instead, our focus is on the anger women feel in their everyday home and work situations. We will spend a few minutes distinguishing anger from aggression, hostility, and violence before we go on. With the exception of violence, these terms often have been used interchangeably in the literature. Although some may argue that precise distinctions among the terms cannot be made, we believe that each phenomenon has unique attributes. Establishing distinctions is important, given the confusion evident in much of the literature. *Anger* is a strong feeling of distress or displeasure in response to a specific provocation of some kind (a threat, an insult, an injustice), whereas *hostility* implies a more pervasive and enduring antagonistic mental attitude. *Aggression* involves an actual or impending physical or verbal attack on someone, and *violence* is a forceful assault that violates the rights of others. Anger and aggression are usually considered to be synonymous in the clinical literature; no distinction is made between the two. Another problem is the use of a continuum conceptualization of these emotions. In other words, a pole is described, with mild anger at one end and aggression at the other. The continuum concept implies that if anger is unchecked, it may escalate to aggressive action. However, this idea is not substantiated by the research evidence. Aggressive behavior can occur in the absence of anger and vice versa. Averill calls aggression a product of biological evolution, whereas anger is termed a product of social evolution (Averill, 1982).

Aggression seldom occurs in normal everyday anger episodes. In a study by Averill (1983), one of the few studies on non–student community samples of men and women, the most frequent responses of angry subjects were nonaggressive (e.g., engaging in calming activities or talking about the incident with the instigator). When aggression did occur, it usually took the verbal or symbolic form. Direct physical aggression occurred in only 10% of episodes.

Laboratory experiments on aggression have dominated the scientific literature. We do not deny that aggression is a serious social problem that deserves the attention of researchers. However, in our opinion, contrived experiments with lower animals or undergraduate psychology students have only remote relevance to aggression in the world outside the laboratory. In a typical experiment, a college student is provoked or insulted by another person and then provided a chance to respond aggressively by administering shocks (Averill, 1982). Participants in a Berkowitz experiment had to keep their hands in painfully cold water as they administered rewards and punishments to fellow students (Berkowitz, 1990). There are several reasons why laboratory experiments of this type may not yield credible findings or may fail to inform about everyday emotional experience in the real world. College students are hardly typical of the American population because of their youth, intelligence, and privilege. Further, when they are recruited to participate in experiments, they are usually paid or given course credit. Incentives such as these may cause students to alter their customary behavior. Students also could behave differently in the laboratory to receive professor approval (or, in the case of a disliked professor, to "screw up" the experiment). We will see an example of deliberately altered student behavior in the Schachter and Singer (1962) experiment described in chapter 2. Student behavior could also be influenced by the anxiety of being observed, audiotaped, or videotaped; the wariness produced by elaborate deceptions; the artificial nature of the laboratory setting; and conditions such as the painful cold water in the Berkowitz study. A final flaw, from our perspective, is that many of the laboratory studies have used male subjects exclusively.

The research focus on aggression has given anger a bad reputation. Stearns and Stearns (1986) stated, "we all know that violence is a bad thing, and if violence comes from aggression, and if anger is also somehow aggressive, then anger must be bad" (p. 248). Another result of the research emphasis on aggression is a dearth of information about anger. We suspect that most people are angered (whether or not they choose to express the feeling) many times each day. Gaylin (1984) claimed that the dangers and frustrations of modern American urban life generate diffuse anger. We are angry not only at the traffic, noise, and crowding, but also at rude strangers and maddening bureaucracies. Yet, we do not usually resort to aggression. The strains of relationship intimacy also produce considerable anger. Not surprisingly, Averill's research showed that the typical target of anger is a friend or loved one. But even in the most provoking circumstances when spouses or children have acted thoughtlessly or let us down, actual aggression does not routinely occur. The workplace is another arena where egos bump, rules chafe, and conflict over issues cannot always remain cordial. We need research on the behavior of ordinary people who become angry, but not aggressive, in these various arenas. In contrast to the hundreds of laboratory studies on aggression, Averill (1982) noted that surveys of everyday anger could be counted on the fingers of one hand. The scarcity of research on anger served as one impetus for the present study.

Having established that this book is not about aggression, we also state at the outset that this book is *not* about *cynical hostility*. Cynical hostility is a kind of pathological mistrust of people that currently receives a great deal of attention in the behavioral medicine literature. Cynical hostility is clearly important to health, given research evidence linking it to adverse health outcomes such as high blood pressure, heart disease, and premature death (Dembroski & Costa, 1987; Shekelle, Gale, Ostfeld, & Paul, 1983; Williams & Barefoot, 1988). Thus, this is an important line of research. However, in many of these studies only male subjects were used. Therefore, the picture is less clear regarding women.

We wonder if the cynical hostility concept is really pertinent to the normal, average woman. Persons who score high on the questionnaire most commonly used to measure cynical hostility (the Cook-Medley Ho Scale) are described as having little confidence in people, viewing others as dishonest and mean. Such individuals often believe others are out to get them or will treat them unfairly. Greenglass and Julkunen (1989) even used the term "chronic hate." This kind of hostility involves an attitude of superior self-righteousness along with indignant condemnation of other persons (Costa, Zonderman, McCrae, & Williams, 1986). Understandably, social isolation is a correlate of cynical hostility (Scherwitz, Perkins, Chesney, & Hughes, 1991; Smith & Frohm, 1985), and the family or work relationships that hostile individuals *do* have are conflictual (Smith, Pope, Sanders, Allred, & O'Keeffe, 1988). However, the latter finding by Smith's research group did *not* hold true for women.

Recent research on a large national sample (ages 18–90) showed that men scored higher than women on cynical hostility at all ages. Women were less cynical in their thinking about people than were men and less likely to use aggressive behaviors as a means of coping with problems (Barefoot et al., 1991). In another large study (N = 5,115) focusing on young adults (ages 18–30), cynical hostility scores were also significantly higher in young men than in young women (p < .001) (Scherwitz, Perkins, Chesney, & Hughes, 1991). Thus, it does not seem appropriate to use the cynical hostility questionnaire for a study of the day-to-day anger of women.

To delimit our topic further, we do not explore the life histories of our study participants. Anger behaviors are learned in a particular sociocultural context, initially within the family of origin. However, any attempt to explore family-of-origin issues or early memories with our subjects would have required extensive in-depth interviewing, which is not possible when conducting such a large survey. Thus, we simply report the typical anger experiences of adult women, as described to us, without speculation about the preceding or underlying factors. Our research design is cross-sectional; we present a snapshot made at a particular time of the woman's life. As we will see, the picture is fascinating in its shades of color and detail.

Finally, no attempt is made in this book to *prove* that women's anger is different from that of men. Although some researchers have found few gender differences (Averill, 1982; Kopper & Epperson, 1991), it makes sense to us that women's anger would have unique aspects. Women and men are biologically different and socialized differently as well; women's life roles (wife, mother, daughter) are substantially different from those of men. Jessie Bernard (1981) wrote of "women's world" with its love and duty ethos prescribing that women care for others. The most pervasive function of women, according to Bernard, is "stroking," which means helping, rewarding, agreeing, complying, understanding, and passively accepting. Expressing anger could be viewed as inconsistent with agreeing, complying, and passively accepting.

An interesting gender difference found in one of Averill's (1982) studies was greater intensity of women's anger episodes; women also were more likely than men to acknowledge that their anger may have been greater than the incidents warranted. For men, there was only a modest correlation between intensity of anger and the duration of the anger episode, whereas for women there was a substantial correlation between intensity and duration. Fujita, Diener, and Sandvik (1991) have proposed that women experience *all* emotions more vividly than do men. Women are also said to be better than men at receiving and projecting emotional signals (K. B. Hoyenga & K. T. Hoyenga, 1979). Our own previous studies have shown differences between men and women in terms of some (but not all) of the anger expression modes (S. Thomas, 1989; S. Thomas & Williams, 1991). Despite the temptation to make additional comparisons based on gender, our research group decided to confine this investigation of anger to women. We did not collect data from men in this project. Our task is simply to be faithful interpreters of *women's* anger experience, as revealed to us by our research subjects. As Voydanoff noted, "The female world has remained relatively invisible and unexamined" (1988, p. 271). An in-depth examination of men's anger would be a welcome contribution to the literature, but we leave this work to other investigators.

METHOD OF THE STUDY

Data included in the present report were derived from a two-stage data collection effort conducted by the authors, other members of the Women's Mental Health Research Group, and graduate students at the University of Tennessee, Knoxville. The project was framed within the research strategy that Coward (1990) has described as *critical multiplism* (i.e., use of multiple stakeholders to develop the research questions, probes of many different types of issues within a single investigation, and multiple modes of data collection and analysis). Although the strategy has commonalities with triangulation, Coward contends that critical multiplism is "more than" triangulation. Benefits of the strategy include reconciliation of quantitative and qualitative research methods as well as ongoing dialogue among multiple data analysts with different perspectives. The diversity of perspectives among members of the research group will be evident in succeeding chapters. Some authors term themselves feminists; some do not. Some have traditional religious orientations; others do not. We view our diversity as an asset rather than a limitation.

A combination of network and purposive sampling was used by the data collectors to obtain subjects from a variety of community sources such as work sites, educational settings, women's groups, and social clubs. Although initially we had focused on midlife women (defined as ages 35–55), to build on our previous studies (cf. S. Thomas & Donnellan, 1991), the research group members later decided to broaden the age parameters to include all adult women. Another extension of the study occurred when we realized that, despite our main objective of describing anger experiences of "normal" or "average" women, comparisons with clinical groups would be very useful. Therefore, permission was obtained from several health care providers in private practice to approach their clients regarding study participation, and we received access to women hospitalized in two inpatient psychiatric facilities. Women in the "medical" group had chronic conditions such as diabetes, obesity, and hypertension; acutely ill individuals were not recruited for the study. Women in the "psychiatric" group were all nonpsychotic and had sought treatment voluntarily. The majority (63%) were depressed according to scoring criteria for the Beck Depression Inventory. Additional information about all of the groups will be presented in chapter 3.

Although there were more participants from small- to medium-sized cities and rural areas in the southeastern United States, several members of the research team used their contacts in western and northern regions of the country to recruit additional subjects. Data collection in Atlanta provided access to women residing in a large metropolitan area. The resultant sample of 535 women was quite diverse. Demographic characteristics of the aggregated sample are presented in Tables 1 and 2 (see Appendix). How similar are the demographic characteristics of our sample to "average" American women? This is an important question because of the nonprobability sampling method we used. Most of our research participants are married, mothers, and working outside the home; in these respects, the sample is consistent with current national norms. The average number of children was two; only 14% of the women were childless. According to a recent compendium of statistics on women (Taeuber, 1991), the fertility rate (average number of lifetime births per woman) in the United States in 1988 was 1.9 births per woman; again, our sample is congruent with the norm. In terms of education, Taeuber (1991) reports that 23% of American women have completed 4 or more years of college. Educational attainment of the present sample is significantly higher: 46% have achieved this level. However, there was a sizable proportion of women (36%) who had less than 4 years of college (e.g., 2-year associate degrees or diplomas from technical programs), and 18% had only high school or less than 12 years of education. Although a variety of occupations was represented in the sample, including the professions and entrepreneurial ventures, the preponderance of women were in traditional female areas such as clerical work and human services; percentages in various occupational categories were not inconsistent with national statistics. Homemakers (10% of the sample) were perhaps slightly underrepresented, but the full-time homemaker is truly a vanishing breed; each new set of statistics reveals fewer women in this category. In terms of racial composition the sample corresponds to figures reported by Taeuber (1991) with the exception of fewer Hispanics: In a representative group of 100 American women, there would be 84 whites, 13 blacks, 8 Hispanics, and 3 of other races. In summary, the sample closely approximates national norms on most characteristics, with the exception of education.

Income levels of study participants varied considerably, with extremes of both poverty and affluence; however, the preponderance of women could probably be categorized as middle class. Of the women who were married, 77% had been continuously married to the same partner, whereas 23% reported previous marriages. The average length of marriage was 19 years (SD, 9.5; range, 1–44 years). Although we did not ask questions about same-sex partnerships, some women volunteered this information. One fifth of the sample had caretaking responsibilities for individuals other than children; 60% of these women were caring for parents, and the remainder for other relatives (such as siblings, aunts or uncles, grandparents, grandchildren) or for friends. These caretaking obligations were reported to be stressful by the majority (70%) of respondents. Of the women who had divorced or separated, 69% were the initiators of the process (by filing for divorce or requesting the separation). This statistic is consistent with the literature; wives are the plaintiffs in most American divorce actions (cf. Levinger, 1976).

The test battery was comprised of well-known questionnaires with established reliability and validity. To ascertain reliability of the scales for the present sample, Cronbach's alpha was used (see Table 3, Appendix, for alpha values). Detailed information on the instruments and their psychometric properties will be given at appropriate points in the text (e.g., the self-esteem tool will be described in the chapter on anger's connection with self-esteem). Phase II testing (1990–1991) included some instruments that had not been administered in Phase I (1989-1990); in the real world of research (as opposed to the textbook picture) we sometimes realize omissions midstream and move to correct them. A copy of the complete test battery is available from the authors on request. Two hundred sixty women completed the Phase I battery, and 275 women participated in Phase II.

Regardless of the setting, data collection procedures were the same. Members of the research team provided both written and verbal explanations of the study to potential participants, obtained their written consent (on a form subsequently filed separately from the test packet), and distributed the packet of self-report instruments. Recruitment of the African-American and Chinese-American subjects was accomplished by data collectors indigenous to these groups. Most women completed the questionnaires in the privacy of their homes or other settings of their choice and returned the completed forms in sealed envelopes. Subjects did not identify themselves by name on the questionnaires; code numbers were used. Although quoted material is used throughout the book to illustrate important themes and patterns, privacy of the research subjects is protected through the use of names created by the authors and omission of unique descriptors that might permit identification.

Most of the variables examined in this study were continuous, permitting analyses by linear correlation, multiple regression, t tests, analysis of variance, and other standard parametric procedures. Two-tailed tests of statistical significance were used throughout the analyses. Persons with missing data were excluded from analyses involving the missing variables; thus, the number of subjects used in various procedures differs slightly. The nonclinical sample (n = 387) is used in all instances when we are describing the "normal" or "average" woman; the psychiatric (n = 52) and medical (n = 40) samples are used mainly in selected comparative procedures. When we refer to the "total sample," we mean all women (whether nonclinical or clinical), with the exception of the Chinese Americans (n = 56) whose data were used only for some cross-cultural comparisons. Because the Chinese-American women were immigrants from Taiwan, it was inappropriate to combine their data with that of the women who had resided in America all of their lives. To avoid disruption of the narrative, most of our findings are presented without cluttering the text with F, r, t, and p values; these values can be found in statistical tables provided in the Appendix.

CONCLUSION

In this chapter we established the rationale for the study, delineated the parameters and methodology of the project, and introduced the sample. In the next chapter we review pertinent literature on emotions and how they develop, with special emphasis on theories and research that shed light on the emotion of anger.

■2
Emotions and How They Develop

Sandra P. Thomas

Understanding our emotions is not extraneous to wisdom but its
very essence.
> —*R. C. Solomon*, **Emotions in Ideal Human Development**

Before we present the findings of our investigation of women's anger, we need
to lay the groundwork for a thorough understanding of this complex emotion.
We begin with a review (of necessity, a very brief one) of the general emotion literature to provide some background information. Our selective glimpses
of this literature will be primarily confined to current theories and research,
although the pioneers within each major theoretical tradition will be recognized. Some emotion researchers study nonhuman primates, but here we
consider only investigations of humans. Throughout this review, we highlight
the emotion of anger and the perspectives of various theories on its etiology
and manifestations.

What are emotions and how do they develop? The word "emotion" comes
from the Latin word "emovere," which means "to move out." De Rivera (cited
in Zegans, 1983) pointed out that "the word captures an important feature of
emotion—that we experience ourselves or the other as being moved" (p. 240).
The emotional system is one of several subsystems of the personality. Three
aspects of the emotional system have been defined (Malatesta & Izard, 1984a).

- Physiological (including faster heart rate, sugar being
  released into the blood, muscles tensing, and so on)
- Behavioral (including facial expression, changes in voice
  tone, movements of our bodies)
- Subjective (what the person privately feels inside)

20

In the literature, more attention has been devoted to the physiological and behavioral components of emotion than to the subjective elements. Theories of emotion have tended to focus their spotlights on one dark corner of the stage. Each theory illuminates a particular *aspect* of the emotion phenomenon, while failing to shed light on other aspects.

PSYCHOPHYSIOLOGICAL THEORIES

William James (1884) focused on visceral and other bodily changes associated with emotion; our experience of these changes as they occur *is* the emotion. For James, the body was the core of experience and the origin of reality. The body reacts to a stimulus and the body's reaction causes the emotional experience. In the words of James, "The body changes follow directly the perception of the exciting fact . . . we feel sorry because we cry, angry because we strike, afraid because we tremble, and not that we cry, strike, or tremble because we are sorry, angry, or fearful, as the case may be" (James, 1890, pp. 449–450).

One of the major traditions in the study of emotion, the psychophysiological, originated with James and Walter Cannon (1932), who proposed and tested central-neural theories. Researchers within this tradition have examined brain structures involved in emotion (e.g., the amygdala, the hippocampus) as well as autonomic, cardiovascular, and neuroendocrine changes connected with emotional experiences. We now know that the entire brain is involved in emotional experience and expression (Pribram, 1980), and there is an explosion of new knowledge in neuroscience about neurotransmitters (e.g., epinephrine, norepinephrine, serotonin, dopamine), peptides (e.g., endorphins, substance P, vasoactive intestinal peptide), and interactions between the nervous system and the immune system. We know that anger activates the sympathetic nervous system as well as the adrenal medulla and cortex. Because of space constraints, we cannot cover the vast psychophysiological literature, but it is appropriate to briefly mention some classic studies. Anger, fear, and depression are the emotions studied most often in the laboratory.

One line of research sought to differentiate emotional states such as fear and anger using measures of electrodermal, cardiovascular, respiratory, and muscular activity. In the early 1950s, Ax conducted a study that has been termed the "grandfather study of the physiology of anger," in which subjects were deceived regarding a "high-voltage short circuit" (inducing fear) and then insulted by a research assistant (inducing anger) (Tavris, 1989). Although Ax (1953) found differences on 7 of 14 measures (e.g., anger produced higher overall muscle tension, whereas fear produced intermittent tension), his methodology and conclusions have been criticized. In the 1960s and early 1970s several researchers (cf. Fine & Sweeney, 1968; Frankenhaeuser, 1971) focused on secretion of epinephrine (adrenalin) and norepinephrine (noradrenalin) by the adrenal medulla during experiences of anger and fear. As Tavris (1989) points out, "Epinephrine and norepinephrine are what provide the *feeling* of a feeling: that tingle, arousal, excitement, energy" (p. 89). These early studies showed that epinephrine was associated with fear and the "flight response," while norepinephrine was associated with anger and the "fight response." Norepinephrine is associated with increases in cardiac output, blood pressure, and peripheral resistance, whereas epinephrine has a biphasic effect on blood pressure and less effect on peripheral resistance (although it also increases cardiac output). Greatly elevated urinary norepinephrine levels were found in Type A individuals in response to the activities of the normal workday in an early study by Friedman and colleagues (Friedman, St. George, Byers, & Rosenman, 1960); the reader will recall from chapter 1 that frequent anger is the chief toxic component of the coronary-prone Type A behavior pattern. In a study that assessed men and women managers at home as well as during the workday, men's norepinephrine levels dropped sharply on arrival at home—but norepinephrine excretion continued to rise in the evening for women as they dealt with demands of the family and their "second job" of household chores (Frankenhaeuser, Lundberg, & Fredrikson, 1989).

Some recent studies have demonstrated that anger responses apparently involve *both* epinephrine and norepinephrine with rise of both cardiac output and peripheral vascular resistance (Schwartz, Weinberger, & Singer, 1981). The study by Schwartz and his colleagues also showed that anger evoked the greatest overall cardiovascular responses (i.e., heart rate, blood pressure) of any of the four emotions they examined (fear, happiness, sadness, and anger). Hokanson's work (Hokanson & Burgess, 1962; Hokanson, Burgess, & Cohen, 1963; Hokanson & Edelman, 1966) suggested that different cardiovascular responses occurred when anger was expressed in the subjects' *preferred* style than when this expression was prohibited. More recent work by Engebretson, Matthews, and Scheier (1989) supported Hokanson's findings. Generally, cardiovascular reactivity is greater when individuals are *prevented* from using their customary mode of anger expression. This research has implications for women and minorities because of the many situations in which forthright anger expression is forbidden.

Researchers also have examined cortisol, a secretion of the adrenal cortex, in situations of anger, and it is now believed that the increased secretion of cortisol that occurs during anger experiences may play a causal role in atherogenesis (Williams, Barefoot, & Shekelle, 1985). Cortisol potentiates both cardiovascular and metabolic effects of catecholamines; increased plasma levels of catecholamines and cortisol have been associated with atherosclerosis. Thus, we have evidence of a linkage between anger and one of the major health problems in the Western world.

DARWINIAN EVOLUTIONARY THEORIES

Another theoretical tradition, derived from Darwinian evolutionary theory, emphasizes the legacy of our prehistoric ancestors (Izard, 1971; Plutchik, 1980). Darwin's theory, introduced in 1872, included several key elements: (a) humans are genetically programmed with a set of basic emotions; (b) emotional expression, in terms of facial and postural indicators, is universal, not culture specific; and (c) mechanisms of emotional expression evolved because of the selection pressures in the species, thus having adaptive value for survival. Survival involved recognizing and responding appropriately to behavioral expressions of emotions in other members of the species (e.g., in anger, animals bare their teeth—the better to bite with) (K. B. Hoyenga & K. T. Hoyenga, 1984). Darwin supported his theory through observations across species and cultures (Darwin, 1872). However, there was no further research with the theory for almost 100 years. A contemporary line of research following Darwinian theory examines changes in facial expression during emotion (e.g., Ekman, 1972; Tomkins, 1963). Using a set of photographs displaying primary emotions, Ekman found that people in both Eastern and Western countries could accurately identify which emotions were depicted. Even individuals in preliterate cultures (e.g., New Guinea) correctly categorized the facial expressions, supporting the universality of anger as well as fear, sadness, surprise, disgust, and joy. Ekman concluded that Darwin's formulation had held up well.

Facial expression is a central focus of Izard's (1980) emotion theory also, playing a key role in generating subjective experience of emotion. The activation of an emotion involves (a) an internal or external event (memory, image, impulse or interpersonal communication) that changes the level of electrochemical activity in the nervous system; (b) occurrence of the innately determined facial expression; and (c) sensory feedback from the face leading to the emotion, which is then amplified or regulated by the cardiovascular, respiratory, and other systems (Izard & Buechler, 1980). Electromyography (EMG) is currently used in facial expression research. Coding systems specify the facial muscles involved in each particular emotion; electrodes are placed accordingly. According to Izard (1990) substantial evidence has been collected regarding congruence among facial behavior, physiological function, and individuals' self-reports of their emotion experiences. Debate at present centers on a chicken-and-egg question: Does facial behavior *cause* emotion or is it simply a readout of underlying experience, playing no causal role? The "facial feedback hypothesis" (attributed variously to Darwin, James, and Tomkins) has been tested in approximately 20 studies, with diverse results (Izard, 1990). Based on their series of studies, Zajonc and colleagues concluded that facial movements do elicit or alter feeling states; the effects of these facial muscle movements on affective experiences are said to be mediated by changes in vascular blood flow to the brain, with consequent changes in hormones and neurotransmitters (Zajonc, Murphy, & Inglehart, cited in Izard, 1990).

Another theorist within the Darwinian tradition, Silvan Tomkins, views the *skin* of the face as more essential than its musculature in providing feedback for emotions. Among Tomkins's (1980) propositions are the following: (a) affects are muscular and glandular responses triggered by innate mechanisms; (b) affect is primarily facial behavior, and secondly bodily behavior and inner visceral behavior; (c) when individuals become aware of their facial or visceral responses, they are aware of their affects; (d) individuals learn to generate from memory images of these responses; (e) affect amplifies not only its activator (e.g., increased neural firing) but also the response both to the activator and to itself. Tomkins (1980) proposed nine "innate affects" (anger being one of the nine) and their facial indicators. Anger is recognizable to observers by a red face, frown, and clenched jaw. According to Tomkins (1991), anger is the most urgent of all affects and the most problematic in social interactions. No society permits unrestrained cries of anger, so humans learn to press their lips together tightly and clench their jaws. Interestingly, Tomkins contends that "a substantial quantity of the affect we experience as adults is pseudo, backed-up affect" (1980, p. 146), a view that may be of particular interest to investigators of psychosomatic disorders.

Building on Darwin's notion of the *adaptive* role of emotions, Plutchik (1980) defined the *origin* and *function* of each of the eight emotions he terms "primary." For example, the origin of fear is a threatening stimulus; anger results from meeting an obstacle termed "enemy." The function of *fear* is protection of oneself, while the function of *anger* is destruction of one's enemy. Plutchik views anger and fear as opposites, as the former implies attack and the latter flight; both emotions lead to behaviors with survival value. Thus, in Plutchik's theory (described by its originator as a "general psychoevolutionary theory of emotion"), emotion is conceptualized as a signaling system and a homeostatic process.

EMOTIONS AS JUDGMENTS: A MODERN VERSION OF ARISTOTLE

Although the research on physiological aspects of emotion and changes in facial musculature is fascinating, some very important elements of the emotion construct are not addressed by this research. Emotions involve the whole person, not just his or her hormones or bodily sensations. Karl Pribram once articulated his dissatisfaction with emotion research as follows:

> It was not so very long ago that I attended a symposium on "emotion" at an international congress in Montreal. The participants discussed factor analysis, limbic

neuroanatomy, and operant conditioning. Somewhere in the agenda emotions were hidden from view, lurking in the dark alleys of our ignorance. No one even dared to use the term, and certainly no one discussed emotions as would the man in the street. (Pribram, 1980, p. 246)

What, then, *is* emotion, beyond physiological arousal and expressive behavior? Philosopher Robert Solomon (1989) says it with flair: "Thousands of years before undergraduates and epinephrine were available for experimentation, Aristotle saw that the understanding of emotion was essentially the analysis of certain kinds of judgments concerning the self" (p. 137). Consistent with the Aristotelian formulation, Solomon defines every emotion as "a basic judgment about ourselves and our place in the world, the projection of the values and ideals, structures and mythologies, according to which we live and through which we experience our lives" (Solomon, 1976, p. 187). Solomon's model of emotion emphasizes the active role of an individual in *creating* emotions such as anger; he claimed that "it is obvious that we make ourselves angry" (1976, p. 193). Anger is construed as a judgment of personal offense. In contrast to some theorists who contend that emotion *interferes* with purposive action, Solomon insisted that emotions *motivate* us to act "to change the world and change our selves" (p. 190). For example, anger demands that someone be punished, that injustice be corrected. Solomon even called emotions *strategies* that we use purposefully.

For Solomon's depiction of emotion to be credible, we must accept the underlying assumption that human beings are rational and make objective judgments about situations. Weiner (1991) speaks of the "person as judge" metaphor that is evident in this type of theory. The person as judge makes inferences about the intentions of others. For example, anger is generated when a negative event is judged as *intentionally* caused by other people. Empirical support for Solomon's conceptualization of anger has been provided by Averill's (1983) finding that the typical instigation to anger is a judgment, an attribution of blame.

PSYCHODYNAMIC VIEWS OF EMOTION

Both professionals and laypersons are probably most familiar with the psychodynamic tradition that began with Sigmund Freud, in which emotions are drive-related primitive forces that can make us do things we don't even *want* to do. In this biologically grounded view, we cannot really be held responsible because powerful passions overtake us. The human psyche is a "caldron of pressures demanding their release" (Solomon, 1976, p. 143). According to Weiner (1991), the metaphor of *machine* is discernible in Freud's explanations of human behavior. The machine is endowed with a fixed amount of energy; if energy is spent performing one function, it is unavailable for others. The language of hydraulics is evident in terms such as *cathexis* (filling) and *catharsis* (flow, release). Viewing anger within the hydraulic model, we might speak of a person *filled* with anger who needs to get the anger *out* of his or her system. Holding anger back is unhealthy; it must be discharged in some way. Although Freud himself did not recommend catharsis for the management of anger and aggression, others within the psychodynamic tradition (cf. Bach & Goldberg, 1974) have done so. Ethologist Konrad Lorenz (1966) contended that athletic activities serve such a purpose; however, riots after soccer games and other sporting events suggest that aggression has been heightened, not lessened. Research has failed to support catharsis for reduction of angry affect (Baron, 1983).

Freud's (1921/1946) version of the hydraulic model particularly emphasized pressures from the unconscious mind threatening to enter consciousness to obtain discharge. Carl Jung pointed out how *easily* consciousness succumbs to unconscious influences. Under the influence of strong emotion, Jung thought the ego and the unconscious may "change places." In one paper, he defined emotions as "instinctive, involuntary reactions which upset the rational order of consciousness by their elemental outbursts. Affects are not 'made' or willfully produced; they simply happen" (cited in Storr, 1983, p. 215). In another explanation of emotion, Jung (1940) termed it "the intrusion of an unconscious personality" (p. 19). By this, he meant that the person had been seized by a *complex* (the nucleus of a complex being an archetype, such as the demon or the trickster). In popular parlance, we still hear echoes of this notion in statements such as "I don't know what got into me," or "I was not myself," or "The devil made me do it."

The involuntary nature of emotion depicted by early versions of the "hydraulic model" is still evident in more contemporary theories. For example, Frijda (1988) asserted that "the laws of emotion are grounded in mechanisms that are not of a voluntary nature and that are only partially under voluntary control. . . . We are subject to our emotions, and we cannot engender emotions at will" (p. 349). Viewing anger in this light, it is an opponent with whom we struggle. Here are some sentences taken from a book by Kövecses (1990, p. 61) that exemplify anger as an opponent.

- I'm *struggling* with my anger.
- He was *battling* his anger.
- She *fought back* her anger.
- He *lost control over* his anger.
- He *surrendered* to his anger.
- I was *overcome* by anger.

An important contribution of the dynamic tradition was elucidation of the role of defense mechanisms in regulation of emotions. For example, if ventilation of anger is construed as dangerous, an individual may use the mechanism of displacement to "dump" the emotion on a weaker scapegoat. Psychotherapy frequently involves assessment of the client's repertoire of defenses and subsequent modification of those mechanisms that do not serve him or her well (e.g., suppression or displacement of anger). As Tavris (1989) notes, therapists are "continually 'uprooting' anger or 'unearthing' it, as if it were a turnip" (p. 23). However, defenses should not be challenged prematurely. Little research is available regarding the efficacy of some techniques presumed to be therapeutic. Mishandling of anger by therapists recently received attention from Meyer (1988) and Wilt (1989).

HUMANISTIC VIEWS OF EMOTION

In the view of humanistic psychotherapists, feelings are considered a valued aspect of human experience; they are not to be expelled or discharged but used as "orienting information." For example, within the Gestalt school, emotion is regarded as "the organism's direct, evaluative, immediate experience of the organism/environment field, furnishing the basis of awareness of what is important to the organism and organizing action" (Greenberg & Safran, 1989, p. 20). Thus, increasing awareness of emotion is a therapeutic objective. Becoming aware of anger might alert persons to violations of their rights, to situations in which too much of the self is being given to another (i.e., when one is being used), or to circumstances in which significant others are doing too much for them (i.e., stifling them). Outcomes of the increased awareness are (a) growth-promoting motivation to change and (b) subsequent constructive actions. One of the most well known theorists-practitioners within the humanistic tradition was Carl Rogers. Rogerian theory emphasized the facilitation of client awareness of emotions that had been distorted or denied in the past. The ability to experience feelings fully was shown by Rogers and others to be predictive of positive psychotherapy outcomes (Rogers, 1959).

COGNITIVE THEORIES OF EMOTION

Another group of emotion theories places heavy emphasis on cognition and cognitive appraisals. In contrast to depictions of emotions as primitive forces that may seize us unawares, many cognitive theorists see an emotion like anger arising only after our brains have processed a situation sufficiently to recognize a wrong or slight. As Lazarus puts it, "Emotion without thought would be mere activation without the directionally distinctive impulses of attacking in anger or fleeing in fear" (1991a, p. 353). This assertion by Lazarus is a clear refutation of Izard and Buechler's claim that "The entire experience of an emotion, from its neural activation through its behavioral expression, can occur without cognitive mediation" (1980, p. 180). Within the cognitive tradition, beliefs regarding the meaning of an event are crucial determinants of emotional experience. The cognitive emphasis is relatively new, arising in the 1960s after a long tradition of noncognitive theories of emotion (cf. James, 1884), although the pioneering work of Carl Stumpf (1848–1936) has generally been overlooked. Stumpf developed a cognitive-evaluative theory of emotion in 1899 in which beliefs were deemed as *necessary causal conditions* for emotions; Reisenzein and Schönpflug (1992) claim that Stumpf's views are still worthy of contemporary scholars' attention. Certainly his views are consistent with more recent formulations, whether or not we agree with Reisenzein and Schönpflug that Stumpf goes beyond them.

Magda Arnold (1960) is considered the first modern theorist to propose that appraisals determine the particular emotion that a person will experience. In Arnold's conceptualization anger is generated when a harmful object is present and appraised as difficult to overcome. Newer theories focusing on appraisals and emotion have been posited by Scherer (1982, 1984, 1988) and by Roseman (1979, 1983, 1984, 1990). A thorough review of all of this material would take us too far afield, but a 1990 investigation by Roseman and colleagues deserves attention. The study (Roseman, Spindel, & Jose, 1990) tested hypotheses derived from Arnold's and Scherer's theories as well as Roseman's. Subjects wrote narratives about emotional experiences that had actually occurred. They responded to questions about their appraisals of (a) motivational state (was the motive to avoid punishment or obtain reward?), (b) situational state (was the event unwanted by the person or consistent with motives?), (c) probability (was the event predictable?), (d) power (did you feel strong or powerless?), (e) legitimacy (was the event an injustice or deserved?), and (f) agency (whether the event was caused by someone else or by self) at the time of the emotion-generating events. The researchers sought to specify the appraisals that elicit 16 discrete emotions, one of which was anger. Among the general findings that are germane to this discussion are the following: (a) appraisals clearly differed from emotion to emotion; (b) appraisal of situational state had the most predictive power, distinguishing negative from positive emotions; (c) there was some support for each of the theories. Regarding the appraisals made in experiences of anger, key elements appeared to be situations that were *unwanted* (motive-inconsistent) and *caused by someone else*; anger situations were also characterized by *low power* and *beliefs that a more positive outcome was deserved*.

Schachter and Singer (1962) proposed that emotional states are a function of the interaction between the physiological component (arousal) and the cognitive component (thinking about the *cause* of the arousal). They contended that *intensity* of emotion is determined by level of arousal, whereas *quality* of emotional state hinges on the cognitive appraisal. Cognition exerts a "steering function," determining how a person labels his or her state of arousal.

Schachter and Singer's classic experiment (1962) also revealed *social* determinants of emotion. Groups of college students were exposed to conditions that would elicit anger or euphoria. Consistent with predictions, subjects described themselves as happy in the "euphoria" condition. However, contrary to investigator expectations, subjects also reported that they were happy in the *anger* condition. During postexperiment debriefing, the researchers learned that students in the anger condition had indeed *felt* angry while in the angry condition but had been afraid to say so. As an incentive for research participation, the students had been promised extra points on their final examination; they feared jeopardizing their grades by revealing anger to the experimenter.

More recently, Berkowitz (1990) proposed a model of anger formation (termed cognitive-neoassociationistic) that integrates the relatively automatic arousal processes and higher-order cognitive concepts such as appraisals. He described a series of stages in the formation of anger; first, associative processes are dominant and then more complicated cognitive processes become involved. A broad range of unpleasant circumstances may induce the initial, rudimentary anger reaction. The angry person then considers possible causes of the anger ("What's happening here? Why is this pushing my button?") and alternative courses of action ("I won't give her the satisfaction of seeing that she got my goat.") The person may think the provocation is too trivial to warrant anger, deciding to modulate the arousal ("This is not worth getting mad about"). Or the person may engage in cognitive evaluations that escalate or perpetuate the initial arousal ("I can't believe he did that! This is really the last straw. I am not going to take another day of this. I don't deserve to be treated this way. I have given that man the best years of my life").

The reader should keep in mind that the cognitive theorists do not imply *rationality* or accuracy of interpretation; thoughts and beliefs can be *irrational*. At least one cognitive theorist (Lazarus, 1991a) has also made it clear that appraisals take place at the unconscious and preconscious levels of the mind as well as the conscious. Aaron Beck's (1976) chief contribution to the present discussion is his emphasis on *faulty* or *distorted* thinking that may lead to *inappropriate* emotion. Normal, appropriate anger is generated when there is an assault on one's domain, values, or moral code; the degree of anger is proportionate to the cognitive appraisal of the offense. In the case of an offense we appraise as *intentional, malicious,* or *unjustified,* anger is heightened accordingly. It is easy to see that appraisals could be erroneous, however. Take the case of a salesperson whose rudeness we find unacceptable; we are angry. Perhaps the salesperson who was short with us "didn't mean anything personal," but was absorbed in her own concerns, overloaded with caffeine, and weary from being on her feet for hours. Perhaps our expectation that we would be waited on promptly by the salesperson was unrealistic, given the number of aisles and counters that she must cover. Perhaps the other customer really approached the cash register with his purchase first.

And perhaps it was a lousy idea in the first place for us to schedule a series of shopping errands when we were hurrying home from work. At any rate, anger has been generated in a situation meriting only mild annoyance. We have not been seriously inconvenienced or harmed. In contrast to this example where faulty appraisal of "rudeness" caused inappropriate anger, let's consider a case of justified anger. A graduate student has discovered considerable plagiarism of her work by another student; there was neither permission to cite the work nor credit to the original author. Clearly, the act was intentional and reprehensible. A moral issue is involved. The original author is understandably offended and wants the thief of her ideas and words to be punished.

RELATIONAL ASPECTS OF EMOTIONS

Lazarus (1991b) says that emotions are always *relational*, meaning that we must take into account both the person (with his or her unique perceptions) and the situation (with its provoking stimulus). One of the key premises of the newest version of Lazarus's theory is that each emotion has its unique *relational* theme. For example, Lazarus says that "Anger is defined relationally as being unfairly slighted or demeaned, which in turn depends on there being an external agent that is held blameworthy for the harmful action" (1991b, p. 528). In essence, we have not been treated in the way we like to be treated and we want to retaliate in some way.

De Rivera (1984) is another theorist who emphasizes that emotion is not just a response to an external event but a transaction between person and situation. The person may choose to *allow* one emotion or another. Personal development is promoted when the chosen emotion is appropriate to the circumstances and hindered when the wrong emotion is selected (De Rivera, 1984). According to De Rivera, some emotions are aimed at transforming a relationship with another person, whereas others are directed at transforming the self.

Averill (1982) defines emotion from a social-constructivist point of view, that is, emotions are *socially constituted syndromes* (transitory social roles). He emphasizes the social origins and current functions of emotions such as anger. Averill makes the case that "ultimately, the functional significance of anger—if it has any—must be found on the level of everyday affairs" (p. 147). Most people become angry daily and also quite frequently bear the brunt of angry expressions from others in their interpersonal networks. Averill acknowledges that anger may be *related* to one or more biological systems, but he contends that it is nevertheless a *social* construction. His own program of research demonstrated that anger is a highly interpersonal emotion that cannot be understood without consideration of the social context.

CULTURAL ASPECTS OF EMOTION

The influence of culture on emotion is profound. Although Ekman's work (1972) demonstrated the universality of primary emotions, the *performance rules* differ greatly from culture to culture. Both Tavris (1989) and Averill (1982) have provided fascinating glimpses of angry behaviors in other cultures including mad dances, ritual bickering, haranguing, and running amok; there are also cultures where outward display of anger is prohibited or severely constrained. As strange as it may seem to us, anger may be subtly expressed by a Japanese wife through a disorderly flower arrangement, which her husband will interpret as an indicator that she is upset (Averill, 1982). Utku Eskimos discourage the expression of anger by cultivating acceptance of situations as they are (in the case of a snowstorm that blocks their plans, they accept the fact and build an igloo). However, the Utku man erupts in sporadic violence (beating his dogs), which raises questions about the success of Utku cultural rules in truly controlling anger (De Rivera, 1984).

Americans live in a culture where anger is freely expressed, at least by individuals in positions of power and dominance. There is no particular virtue in being prudent, civil, restrained. There is a degree of pride in announcing "I told her off," or "I punched him out." Several of the authors of this book have observed physicians who regularly have temper tantrums during their hospital rounds or surgery, sometimes involving hurling surgical instruments. In one case still vivid to the author after many years, a doctor actually threw a bedpan out the window of a patient's room. Loud cursing is the norm in many business settings, not only between peers but also directed at secretaries, receptionists, and messengers.

Tavris (1989) blames American individualism (the imperial "I") for the currently prevailing philosophy of emotional ventilationism. She points out that in Eastern cultures, emotion is subdued to preserve relationships; in contrast, Americans express emotion even at the *expense* of relationships. It seems that we feel *entitled* to reciprocate when somebody provokes us. Perhaps we have something to learn from other cultures. However, it is possible that Tavris's assertion is more applicable to American men than to women. Containing anger to prevent hurting another is a familiar tactic to most women.

SUMMARY

We have reviewed a diverse sampling of theories in which emotions were variously conceptualized as remnants of our phylogenetic past, uncontrollable primitive forces, bodily sensations, social constructions, purposeful strategies, and so forth. What can we possibly say in the way of summary comments? Perhaps that we find no theory fully satisfying. Newer theories are more integrative, considering cognitive processing and interpretation of the personal meaning of events along with biological underpinnings. So much prominence is now accorded to cognition that Tomkins (1991) warned, "We are now in danger of rewriting affect as though it were a form of cognition or a dependent variable of cognition" (p. 47). Perhaps Tomkins is correct that "Affect can determine cognition at one time, be determined by cognition at another time, and also be interdependent under other circumstances" (p. 72). It seems clear that despite our evolutionary heritage, we are not passive recipients of emotional states such as anger. The emotions of human beings are not just instincts or drives like hunger, thirst, or sex. Research is providing support for the contention of Tavris (1989) that "we need not be hostages to our emotions" (p. 100).

Anger is undoubtedly one of the most complex emotional experiences. Ortony and his colleagues call anger a "compound" emotion because it involves both *reproach* (disapproving of someone's blameworthy action) and being displeased or *distressed* about an undesirable outcome (Ortony, Clore, & Collins, 1988). In our review of the literature we have seen that theorists emphasize different elements of the anger experience such as interference with goals or plans, affront to personal dignity or beliefs, or physiological changes such as increased heart rate, skin temperature, and muscular tension. Some theorists acknowledge the limitations of their formulations; for example, Berkowitz (1990) admitted that his model had nothing to say about interpersonal relationships as elicitors of anger. Obviously, it is not necessary that each theory address all facets of a multifaceted phenomenon. One area of clear agreement among theorists is that anger is a basic emotion; it is included in all lists of "primary," "fundamental," or "basic" emotions (Arnold, 1960; Ekman, Friesen, & Ellsworth, 1982; Frijda, 1987; Izard, 1972; McDougall, 1926; Oatley & Johnson-Laird, 1987; Plutchik, 1980; Tomkins, 1984). Further, no one disputes that anger is a powerful "high arousal" emotion in terms of physiological alterations. The need for further research on people's everyday experiences with this emotion is evident.

DEVELOPMENT OF EMOTIONS:
ORIGINS IN INFANCY

We turn our attention now to the development of emotions and the changes that occur across the life cycle. Again, we provide as much information as possible about the emotion of anger. Emotions arise in response to a person's goals or concerns (Fridja, 1988). Obviously, our goals and concerns change throughout life. The needs of infants are pretty limited (to be warm, dry, fed, cuddled a bit, and so forth) and their emotions are relatively simple. In infancy, emotions are elicited by physical stimuli more so than by psychological stimuli, but the types (and diversity) of emotion-producing events increase rapidly during growth and development (Malatesta & Izard, 1984a). Emotions become more complex as the infant's world widens and information processing becomes more sophisticated. A series of experiments on anger expression in infancy (Stenberg & Campos, 1990) illustrates what we mean. At 3 months of age, babies react with an undifferentiated emotional distress to restraint by a researcher's arm. By 4 months, the same frustrating stimulus produces marked *anger,* and the baby looks at the hand that is restraining its movement. By 7 months, the infant looks at the face of the person restraining him, or at the mother if she is in the vicinity.

Some infants, from the time of birth, seem to be more emotional than others. Buss (1987) uses the term "emotionality" to include distress, fear, and anger, and he claims that emotionality is, in part, inherited. Evidence has been found in studies of twins. He explains, "what is inherited appears to be how the sympathetic division of the autonomic nervous system reacts in the face of stressful life situations. Greater emotionality is reflected in a more intense physiological reaction to stress" (p. 27). There is some evidence of prenatal influences on emotionality. In studies by Stott, maternal stress during pregnancy appeared to have adverse effects on babies; the most damaging type of maternal stress was produced by chronic arguments with the father. Effects observed in the babies immediately after birth included fear of loud noises and propensity to startle easily. Hyperactivity or excessive timidity were also found (Stott, 1973; Stott & Latchford, 1976).

An interesting new line of research looks at the expression of emotion in interactions between mothers and their young infants. Psychologist Edward Tronick wondered how some children become sad and withdrawn or angry, whereas others become self-confident and happy, and he began to study emotions in infants. Infant emotions and emotional communications are far more organized than we once realized. Babies are capable of discriminating the facial expressions of others. For example, they look more at facial expressions of joy than anger. Babies also react to their mothers' emotional expressions with emotions of their own (Tronick, 1989). There is a reciprocity or synchrony between the emotions of mothers and their babies when things are going well. In normal interactions an infant's experiences of negative emotions are brief. In abnormal interactions, such as with a depressed, irritable mother, the infant may experience prolonged negative emotion (Tronick, 1989). Hamilton (1989) found that 3-month-old infants whose mothers reported more anger expressed more anger. Lest we interpret this finding in a way that increases mother-guilt (already epidemic in our society), other research shows that the infant's own basic temperament causes differences in the parents' responses.

Scarr (1987) points out that a smiling, good-natured baby elicits more social stimulation than a fussy, difficult infant. She argues that the baby's genetic heritage causes the baby to evoke different experiences from environments. Logically, irritable infants cause their mothers to feel inept and frustrated in attempts to pacify them. Thus, not surprisingly, researchers have found that infant expressions of anger or sadness produce emotional responses of anger or sadness in their mothers (Malatesta & Izard, 1984b).

Actually, we have known since the 1960s that babies have unique temperaments from birth. Pioneers in this research area were Carey (1970), Chess, Thomas, and Birch (1965), and Brazelton (1976). The word *temperament* refers to "psychological qualities that display considerable variation among infants and, in addition, have a relatively, but not indefinitely, stable biological basis in the organism's genotype, even though the inherited physiological processes mediate different phenotypic displays as the child grows" (Kagan, 1989, p. 668). According to Kagan and Snidman (1991), temperamental constructs are currently experiencing a renaissance, fueled in part by the dramatic advances in neuroscience. We now know that some temperaments *predispose* a child to display certain emotions in certain circumstances (e.g., novel or challenging events). For example, Kagan and Snidman (1991) examined babies at 4 months in terms of their responses to unfamiliar stimuli, finding distinct patterns (inhibited and uninhibited) that remained stable through their second year. Other studies conducted in Kagan's laboratory showed continued stability of the patterns through the 8th year (Kagan, 1989).

Obviously, the emotions of infants and small children cannot be considered equivalent to adult emotions. Nevertheless, early childhood experience is undoubtedly of critical importance in the development of personality and emotional habits. Chronically miscoordinated interactions with primary caregivers may hamper the ability to regulate emotions or communicate emotions in later life. Temperament mismatches between caregivers and their babies have been studied using mother-son pairs and mother-daughter pairs. In a recent project conducted when babies were 6 and 9 months old, mother-son pairs were in well-coordinated interactive states about 50% more often than were mother-daughter pairs (Tronick & Cohn, 1989). Thus, mother and daughters were more often "out of synch." The full meaning of such research findings is unclear, and further studies are needed.

EMOTIONAL DEVELOPMENT IN CHILDHOOD

Although children have emotions before they are able to verbalize them, complex emotional capacity develops in conjunction with thinking and language. As children learn the proper use of emotion words such as "anger" or "love," they learn what the terms imply and how to discriminate between the concepts; by age 5, children have a good grasp of many emotional concepts (Averill, 1982, 1984). Averill (1980) points out that children "play at being angry, fearful, in love, etc., just as they play at being doctors, parents, garbage collectors, and the like" (p. 321). As growing children become increasingly aware of their emotional behavior, they also learn to modify behavior to conform to parental injunctions, social rules, and a variety of changing external circumstances (Malatesta & Izard, 1984a). Children receive subtle messages as well as more direct feedback when they express their emotions. With respect to anger, parents are more accepting of anger expression by sons than daughters (Birnbaum & Croll, 1984). Miller (1983) pointed out that boys are stimulated to aggressive action by their fathers from ages as young as 1½ to 2 years.

Rewards and punishments for anger outbursts help to determine whether the child will repeat them. If the child feels powerful and satisfied because a tantrum resulted in the provision of goodies, the next time he wants another child's toy or a treat in the grocery store he will behave the same way (as most mothers know). If the child is forced to squelch anger because it is unacceptable in the family, she may feel guilt or shame even when anger is a legitimate response to provocation. Several researchers have found that parents' use of physical punishments fostered the development of aggression (W. McCord, J. McCord, & Howard; Olweus, 1980).

Research on incidents that trigger young children's anger is sparse, but an early 1980s Canadian study (Rotenberg, 1983) provided some information. The research surveyed children from first, third, fifth, and seventh grades. Parents, siblings, and peers were the three major sources of the children's anger, as expected, with siblings topping the list. Physical assault, verbal insult, and prevention of goal achievement were the main precipitants of angry episodes. According to Rotenberg, anger became more constructive with age. Thus, older children were more likely to say that the purpose of their anger was to make someone else see their viewpoint. Older children were less likely to retaliate aggressively (i.e., by hitting), preferring nonretaliation or indirect retaliation.

Children imitate the emotional behavior of their parents and other significant adults such as teachers. Children also refine their emotional habits because of interactions with siblings and playmates. Lever (1976) noted that boys' play and girls' differed in several respects. Boys played competitive games, "quarrelling all the time" (p. 482), whereas girls played cooperative games— and terminated their play when quarrels occurred. Thus, boys had greater opportunity to practice anger behaviors during childhood play than did girls. Males continue to use and channel aggression in the games of business, politics, and war, whereas females never learn to play these games well (Miller, 1983).

ADOLESCENT EMOTIONAL DEVELOPMENT

Discussions of emotional development are usually restricted to the early years of life, probably because of the influence of psychoanalytic theorists who believe everything is "jelled" by age 5 or 6. However, emotional development continues throughout a person's life. During adolescence, there are tremendous changes in physical, cognitive, social, and emotional characteristics, with changes in one area interdependent on changes in another area (Newman & Newman, 1979). A key influence on the adolescent's emotional behavior is the feedback received from peers, especially intimate partners. Harry Stack Sullivan (1953) was the first to recognize the importance of a close same-sex relationship during preadolescence, wherein the youngster begins to develop sensitivity regarding another person's happiness. Most of us can remember who our "best friend" was at about age 11 or 12, and the intense emotions of this friendship. In early adolescence, interest shifts to experimentation with opposite-sex relationships. A little later on, the teenager can become totally engrossed in the strong emotionality of "first love," with its traumatic fights as well as its heady euphoria.

In addition to the shaping of emotional habits that is occurring in intimate partnerships, further change occurs as adolescents begin to sharply diverge in their gender roles. During adolescence, traditional sex-typed expectations of the adolescent by parents, teachers, and peers become more pronounced. Both the public display of emotions and the meaning or interpretation of emotions are affected by gender role socialization (Haviland & Malatesta, 1981). A phenomenon called *invalidation* can be a powerful mechanism in discouraging anger expression in young girls. Invalidation means that the girl's anger is not recognized or is labeled as inappropriate by a powerful other (parent, teacher, or boyfriend). In situations in which she is provoked by teasing, she is told to be a good sport rather than make a fuss. In situations in which she angrily confronts a boyfriend, he may negate the anger by responding with some version of the "you're so cute when you're angry" line. Consequently, the girl feels misunderstood; her emotion has been denied or trivialized. She may question her own judgment of the original incident or become ashamed of her outburst. A group of female Australian theorists recently provided several compelling examples of such invalidation from their own memories of girlhood experiences (Crawford, Kippax, Onyx, Gault, & Benton, 1990).

Carol Gilligan (cited in Moses, 1990) attributed girls' losses in ability to express anger in the teenage years to "enormous pressure to be perfect girls —who are always quiet, calm and kind" (p. 26). During Gilligan's five-year study, girls were interviewed yearly. When the girls were younger, they spoke openly about their anger and other feelings; their voices were clear and honest. However, in adolescence the girls (with few exceptions) stopped expressing their real feelings (especially anger) because they wanted to be popular. Gilligan concluded that, "The coming of age of girls in this society is accompanied by a falling away of self" (p. 26). These research findings led Gilligan to speculate that adolescent girls' repression of their real selves and emotions may contribute to their propensity to be more depressed and stressed than adolescent boys. In our own studies, we have found adolescent girls to be more stressed than boys both as high school freshmen (S. Thomas, Shoffner, & Groër, 1988) and as seniors (Groër, S. Thomas, & Shoffner, 1992).

In a recent study of adolescents' emotional experiences by Stapley and Haviland (1989), there were several gender differences. Anger was the most salient negative emotion for both boys and girls. However, boys and girls differed in *causes* of anger as well as *direction* of anger expression. Adolescent females were angry because of interpersonal experiences and directed their anger inwardly; males were angry in situations in which performance was evaluated and directed anger outwardly. Another group of researchers corroborated the interpersonal source of girls' anger. For example, the girls were more likely to respond angrily to unfair treatment and being taken advantage of by others. Situations of property damage or personal damage generated boys' anger arousal (Lohr, Hamberger, & Bonge, 1988).

We conducted a longitudinal study in which we measured students' anger with Siegel's Anger Index (1984) when they were high school freshmen and then again when they were seniors (Kollar, Groër, Thomas, & Cunningham, 1991). Both developmental and gender differences were found. To wit, the adolescents appeared to view some situations differently over time. For example, restriction of their freedom created more anger in the senior year than in the freshman year. This finding is understandable from a developmental perspective, given the seniors' need to attain independence from their families. Females and males differed in several ways. On the majority of individual items on the Anger Index females scored higher than males. Girls were more likely than boys to get angry when frustrated or when someone blocked their plans or tried to take advantage of their friendship. Girls reported raising their voices when they got angry, whereas boys were more likely to initiate a motor response such as throwing or breaking things.

Several studies have revealed progress toward emotional maturity in adolescents studied over time. In a project assessing boys and girls at 12, 15, and 18, Torestad (1990a, 1990b) found that in most anger-provoking situations, the subject himself or herself was wronged (egocentric anger). However, with increasing age, adolescents developed the capacity to be angry in situations in which other people were badly treated rather than themselves (unselfish or altruistic anger). This change makes sense in terms of adolescents' increased moral reasoning ability and decreased egocentrism as they move toward adulthood. Another study of high school students measured at two points in time (first when they were 13–16 and then two years later) showed an increasing ability of adolescents to understand and empathize with people with whom they were angry (Freeman, Csikszentmihalyi, & Larsen, 1986). This is an important aspect of emotional maturity.

ADULT EMOTIONAL DEVELOPMENT

The concept of *adult* emotional development is fairly new—and to us, exciting, because there is recognition that individuals can overcome negative effects of earlier experiences and discard old habits. Many women have learned less-than-ideal ways of dealing with strong emotions during their childhood or adolescent years. As Malatesta and Izard noted, most people have "mixed feelings about feelings" (1984a, p. 15) because emotions can be very troublesome as well as pleasant or exciting. Anger is one of the emotions many individuals consider troublesome, for anger episodes leave them miserable, drained, guilty, depressed, even sick. But we can learn new ways of managing anger. The members of our research group at the University of Tennessee espouse a holistic philosophy that emphasizes forward movement of the person toward wholeness throughout life.

Adulthood is not some vast unremarkable plateau between the turbulent adolescent period and the achievement of senior citizen status. Averill (1984), De Rivera (1984), and Malatesta and Izard (1984a) have contributed to our understanding of adult emotional development, which involves both the acquisition of new emotions and the abandonment (or diminished use) of old ones. Frijda (1988) pointed out that "Emotions change when meanings change. Emotions are changed when events are viewed differently" (p. 350). There can be amazing transformations in an emotion such as anger. The authors of this book can attest to such transformations from our clinical experience in health care and psychotherapeutic settings. Among the factors that produce such changes are life crises (illness, moving, changing jobs), revisions in values or spiritual orientations, and the day-to-day give and take of significant relationships. Spouses, children, and friends provoke us, gladden us, urge us to express (or inhibit) our feelings. We learn about emotions in every important relationship. An emotion that was previously denied can become accessible through psychotherapy. A practice such as meditation can facilitate "letting go" of emotion (De Rivera, 1984). What would optimal emotional development involve? There are two key elements: (a) developing a wide repertoire of emotional behaviors; and (b) allowing oneself to express whatever emotion is appropriate to the situation—bearing in mind that some emotional patterns adversely affect physical and mental health. We reiterate that one of the purposes of this book is to distinguish between health-promoting and health-damaging anger.

CONCLUSION

In this chapter we have reviewed major theoretical formulations of emotion, focusing on anger when theorists made specific references to anger. As yet, there are few theories specific to anger and none entirely satisfactory for illuminating the unique experiences of women. We have also devoted attention to the development of emotional habits and to points during development when gender role socialization has particularly powerful effects on girls' behavior. This chapter provides a foundation for the remainder of the book.

■ 3
Anger and Its Manifestations in Women

Sandra P. Thomas

Throughout the literature, we find anger described as a "multidimensional" construct. As an amalgam of cognitions, behaviors, and somatic sensations, anger has presented a formidable challenge to researchers. Several dimensions of anger were measured in the Women's Anger Project. We now introduce terms and clarify distinctions among the various anger dimensions. Later in the chapter, we present the scoring patterns of the sample as a whole on each of the components of anger, followed by examination of scores for selected subgroups.

According to psychologist Charles Spielberger, anger is both an emotional state (a transient condition consisting of subjective feelings that vary in intensity) and a personality trait (one's general proneness to perceive situations as anger provoking and to respond with angry feelings) (Spielberger, Jacobs, Russell, & Crane, 1983). Before Spielberger's work, the state-trait distinction was not usually considered by researchers. We view the distinction as important because emotional behavior has both consistency *and* variability over time and across diverse situations. Because our subjects were adult women whose emotional habits were presumed to have some stability, we were particularly interested in "trait anger," the aspect that is relatively stable over time.

TRAIT ANGER: GENERAL PRONENESS TO BECOME ANGRY

Scoring high on trait anger indicates that there is a general tendency to get angry more frequently and in a wider range of situations, in contrast to individuals who score low. Further, persons high in trait anger experience more intense levels of anger when annoying and frustrating conditions are encountered (Spielberger, Jacobs, Russell, & Crane, 1983). It seems that some people bring their anger readiness with them to the various environments in which they enact their roles. As Averill (1983) pointed out, individual episodes of anger may not be particularly dramatic or noteworthy, but the cumulative effects of many bursts of anger are significant, especially in terms of health consequences and interpersonal relationships. Why are some people more hotheaded and easily provoked to anger? Several explanations have been offered. One group of researchers proposed that there is a genetic component of trait anger; in their study of female twins, the data supported this hypothesis (Cates, Houston, Vavak, Crawford, & Utley, 1990). Some babies appear to have a lower threshold to display negative emotion, and there is interesting research on asymmetry of the brain's frontal lobe in such infants (Fox, 1991). As we have seen in the general discussion of emotional development, experiences during infancy and childhood further shape innate temperamental characteristics. The family environment is a critical influence on trait anger, as demonstrated in a recent study by Woodall and Matthews (1989). The researchers investigated trait anger and other variables in boys and girls (grades 2–12) from 114 suburban families. Children who were higher in trait anger came from families where the emotional climate was not as warm and cohesive. Family members of the angrier children were not as supportive or open to emotional expression. In distressed families studied by Reid (cited in Patterson, 1985), mothers rated their daily discipline confrontations with children as significantly more angry than did mothers in normal families. Overt conflict among the adult members of the family is another stimulus known to elicit anger and distress in young children (Cummings, 1987; Cummings, Zahn-Waxler, & Radke-Yarrow, 1981; El-Sheikh, Cummings, & Goetsch, 1989). Tensions between parents are believed to stimulate conflict between siblings as well (Ewart, 1991). There has been a considerable amount of research on aggressive children, with well-established findings regarding their marked attributional bias to infer hostile intentions on the part of others. Because they interpret others' intentions in this manner, they engage in retaliatory aggression (Nasby, Hayden, & DePaulo, 1980). Based on the available evidence, we conclude that an equation involving both a temperamental predisposition to be angry and a reaction style learned in a contentious family atmosphere is predictive of trait anger in adults.

Trait anger has been studied in thousands of subjects by Spielberger who developed the questionnaire we used. During the development and validation of Spielberger's Trait Anger Scale, factor analysis revealed two dimensions of trait anger (Spielberger, Jacobs, Russell, & Crane, 1983). The first is called "angry temperament," which refers to individual differences in the tendency to express anger, without any consideration of provoking circumstances.

Typical items are "I am a hot-headed person," and "I fly off the handle." The items in this subscale seem to measure the genetic component we described earlier. The second dimension is termed "angry reaction," which refers to situational circumstances that trigger anger (e.g., "It makes me furious when I am criticized in front of others"). Although Spielberger does not speculate about the origins of this readiness to respond angrily to criticism, it stands to reason that earlier life experiences of criticism may have eroded the self-concept. Thus, the individual reacts defensively to protect the self. The two-factor structure of the Trait Anger Scale has been supported in a study of Dutch army draftees (Van der Ploeg, 1988).

We selected Spielberger's instrument not only because of the extensive validation work on the tool but also because it has been used in well-known studies such as the San Francisco Life-Style Heart Trial (Scherwitz & Rugulies, 1992). The Trait Anger Scale was initially given to more than 3,000 students in junior and senior high schools in Florida as well as to 2,500 military recruits, more than 1,600 college students, and more than 1,200 working adults who ranged in age from 18 to 63. The junior and senior high school students scored substantially higher on trait anger than the other groups, and the younger working adults scored higher than their older counterparts (Spielberger, Jacobs, Russell, & Crane, 1983). This finding suggests that age may be a factor in the tendency to be angry on a frequent basis.

Researchers have found relationships between trait anger and several other personal characteristics and health indicators. Trait anger was correlated with trait anxiety (general proneness to be anxious and apprehensive) in studies by Spielberger's group (Spielberger et al., 1979) and by Israeli researchers (Ben-Zur & Zeidner, 1988). In college women, higher trait anger was related to lower levels of (a) optimism, (b) purpose in life, (c) self-efficacy and (d) life satisfaction, as well as to beliefs that life's rewards are controlled by fate, chance, or luck (rather than by one's personal efforts) (Thomas & Williams, unpublished data). Trait anger was found to be associated with higher blood pressure in women in a study by Durel and associates (1989). The study involved monitoring of blood pressure while the women were at work, at rest, and during laboratory tasks. Both systolic and diastolic blood pressure were related to trait anger. In women who were already diagnosed with hypertension, Rickman and Spielberger (1990) found higher scores on the Angry Reaction Subscale of Trait Anger (in comparison with a control group with normal blood pressure). Spielberger and colleagues (1983) found relatively high correlations (.43–.59) between trait anger and hostility (measured by the Ho Scale) in college students and Navy recruits, suggesting that persons with a hostile attitudinal set experience the emotion of anger more frequently. This connection between the two constructs has been discussed by Williams, Barefoot, and Shekelle (1985).

In the present study the 10-item form of the Trait Anger Scale was used; previous work by Spielberger demonstrated that this version provided the same information as a longer 15-item version. An additional advantage of this form of the test is that items correlating highly with anxiety have been eliminated (Spielberger, Jacobs, Russell, & Crane, 1983). Subjects rate each item on a scale from 1 to 4 with response options ranging from "almost never" to "almost always."

MODES OF ANGER EXPRESSION

Having discussed anger arousal as a relatively stable personality characteristic, let us examine modes or ways of *expressing* the emotion once it has been aroused. Obviously, we have a repertoire of behaviors that can be called on when anger is aroused. We do not always express anger the same way. Sometimes we dare not let it out because we might be harmed, punished, or scorned. We may hastily hurl a frying pan or slam a door. At other times we choose to confront the offender to preserve our dignity. And the list of possible responses could go on. Unlike other mammals, humans can choose to control and direct emotion rather than behave reflexively. When threatened or provoked, the response we select depends on several factors including cognitions, situational factors, and cultural rules for behavior. Frijda (1988) contends that "every emotional impulse elicits a secondary impulse that tends to modify it in view of its possible consequences" (p. 355).

As nurses and counselors, we were particularly interested in the modes of anger expression because they may have different consequences for physical and mental health. In 1954, experiments by Funkenstein, King, and Drolette showed that the physiological component of anger is mediated by the *direction* of anger expression. In other words, the bodily changes (e.g., cardiovascular reactions, muscle changes) that occur during anger arousal differ according to the responses we select. Anger can be suppressed (termed "anger-in" in current research literature), directed outwardly in an unhealthy way (termed "anger-out"), directed outwardly in a healthy way (through discussion of the incident with a supportive listener), or expressed in physical symptoms like headache. Most previous studies have examined just two modes of anger expression: anger-in and anger-out. Interestingly, there is not only a large body of research showing that anger-in is associated with greater cardiovascular reactivity or other disease risk indicators (Funkenstein, King, & Drolette, 1954; Gentry, Chesney, Gary, Hall, & Harburg, 1982; Haynes, Feinleib, & Kannel, 1980; Julius, Harburg, Cottington, & Johnson, 1986; Waldstein, Manuck, Bachen, Muldoon, & Bricker, 1990), but also considerable evidence that anger-out is harmful as well (Johnson & Broman, 1987; Matthews, Glass, Rosenman, & Bortner, 1977; Van Egeren, Abelson, & Thornton, 1978; Williams, Haney, Lee, Kong, Blumenthal, & Whalen, 1980). In a study of women who developed breast cancer, both the "extreme suppressors" (who had not openly shown anger more than once or twice in their lives) and the "exploders" (who had frequent temper outbursts) had higher rates of diagnosed breast cancer than women with less extreme anger expression styles (Greer & Morris, 1975).

Our research project not only examined women's use of anger-in and anger-out, but also the likelihood of using other modes of expressing anger. We used the Framingham Anger Scales developed for the famous prospective study of coronary heart disease risk in Framingham, Massachusetts (Haynes, Levine, Scotch, Feinleib, & Kannel, 1978). These scales assess what you do with anger once you feel it. Using a 3-point response format, respondents indicate how likely they are to behave in each of the specified ways "when really angry or annoyed." Scores between zero and one were assigned by the Framingham researchers; in the present study, scores of one to three were assigned to the responses of "not too likely," "somewhat likely," and "very likely." Thus mean scores are not directly comparable with the Framingham study. Items for the Framingham test battery were selected from an initial 300-item pool by expert judges and evaluated by both item analysis and factor analysis (Haynes et al., 1978). Although reliability of the scales was not entirely satisfactory in a study by Durel and colleagues (1989), coefficient alphas for the present sample were generally acceptable (see Appendix). The Framingham scales were selected because no other tools include both adaptive and nonadaptive anger expression modes. For example, the Anger Expression (AX) Scale (Spielberger et al., 1985) and the Multidimensional Anger Inventory (Siegel, 1985) include only anger-in and anger-out behaviors. Riley and Treiber (1989) included three of the Framingham scales in a study assessing convergent and discriminant validity of multiple measures of anger and hostility. They concluded that each scale was a valid measure of the mode of anger expression it purported to measure, with the possible exception of the anger-out scale. The researchers questioned the validity of the anger-out scale because it correlated with other measures of anger experience and hostility, but not with other measures of anger expression. Further validity examination would be useful. However, the items of the anger-out scale clearly have content validity. The respondent is acknowledging that when really angry or annoyed, she takes it out on others and blames someone else. We will now describe each of the four expression modes assessed by the Framingham scales in greater detail.

Anger Suppression (Anger-In)

This mode of expression involves keeping angry feelings to oneself. Behaviors assessed by the Framingham Anger-In Scale include "try to act as though nothing much happened." If asked to speculate, most readers would predict high scores for women on the anger suppression questionnaire. When the anger-in scale was administered to Framingham study participants, women scored significantly higher than men (Haynes, Levine, Scotch, Feinleib, Kannel, 1978). As Lerner points out, "nice ladies" have been discouraged from forthright expression of their anger. Women who express anger are called unfeminine, shrews, bitches, man-haters, and other uncomplimentary or derogatory epithets (Lerner, 1985). Gender role socialization in America is said to discourage anger expression in girls, while stimulating boys to be aggressive, to refuse to "take it lying down," to "fight it out," and so on. As we have seen in chapter 2, powerful socialization agents (parents and the media) inculcate the rules of emotional display, that is, parents are more accepting of anger in sons than in daughters, and on television male characters display significantly more anger than do females (Birnbaum & Croll, 1984).

Control of anger was actually the ideal in civilized nations during much of recorded history—for both men and women. In an article in *Issues in Mental Health Nursing* (Thomas, 1990), I reviewed conceptualizations of anger through history, noting that for centuries anger was considered a sin, a weakness, or a madness that was to be avoided or contained. Suppression of anger was seen as the hallmark of a civilized person. The following quotations (taken from Seldes, 1985) are typical of early views:

- "Lust, anger and greed, these three are the soul-destroying gates of hell" (Hindu Bhagavad-Gita, 2nd-century B.C., p. 4).
- "Hesitation is the best cure for anger" (Seneca, Roman philosopher born in 4 B.C., p. 378).
- "Master anger" (Periander of Corinth, Greece, p. 168).
- "Envy, mockery, contempt, anger, revenge, and the other affects which are related to hatred or arise from it, are evil" (Spinoza, 17th-century Dutch philosopher, p. 395).
- "Five great enemies to peace inhabit within us: avarice, ambition, envy, anger, and pride. If those enemies were to be banished, we should infallibly enjoy perpetual peace" (Petrarch, 14th-century Italian poet, p. 328).

Stearns and Stearns (1986), a psychiatrist-historian writing team, reviewed American cultural ideas about anger from the 18th through the 20th century. The dominant theme was control of this negatively viewed emotion. Until the mid-19th century, the anger-free family was promoted as the ideal. Behavior of husbands and wives was emphasized during this period; marital quarreling was to be avoided at all costs. During the Victorian period, a minister quoted by Stearns and Stearns (1986) advised wives that quarreling is "death to happiness" and admonished husbands, "If you become angry with her . . . she will never forget it" (p. 40). To produce anger-free adults, parenting manuals began to promote child-rearing practices that suppressed anger. Anger control efforts later extended into school and work arenas as well.

The prevailing view of anger is quite different today. What happened to alter the American cultural attitude about anger? Influenced by (a) Darwinian evolutionary theory, (b) the research of ethologists such as Lorenz, who studied aggression in animals, and (c) the revelations by Freud regarding the unconscious mind, a new approach to anger, sometimes called the "ventilationist" or "let-it-all-hang-out" approach, was recommended. Anger was considered a powerful instinctive drive; holding it back or bottling it up was deemed unhealthy because it would eventually erupt in some form or contribute to development of psychological or physical illnesses. This brings us to the second mode of anger expression: anger-out.

Anger-Out

This way of expressing anger involves ventilation in an attacking or blaming way. The individual takes it out on others. In a recent study by Hart (1992), subjects scoring high on anger-out made *external* attributions for the cause of provoking incidents, whereas individuals scoring low on anger-out were more likely to make *internal* attributions (i.e., take personal responsibility for the anger incident). Use of this mode of anger expression may damage interpersonal relationships. The person who has followed Bach and Goldberg's (1974) advice to insult, scold, and scream at other people may feel some momentary satisfaction or release, but the recipients of the barrage may retaliate, withdraw, or even sever their association with the attacker. It is also doubtful that anger ventilation benefits the individual. Pop psychology advice about punching pillows, fighting with foam rubber bats, throwing darts or beanbags, screaming loudly, or cursing may be useless or even harmful in some cases. Venting anger may actually cause escalation of the anger arousal rather than relief. Tavris (1989) claims that those who vent their anger get angrier, not less angry. A bizarre new anger-out phenomenon, "vending machine madness," was reported in the 1988 *Journal of the American Medical Association (JAMA)* (Tavris, 1989). The article described crushing injuries and fatalities of men so enraged by the machines' failure to dispense sodas that they had kicked them until they overturned. Although the report in *JAMA* referred only to men, women are joining the ranks of those who have succumbed to "vending machine madness." A 19-year-old woman recently sustained serious internal injuries ("Soda vending machine falls on woman after she kicks it," *Knoxville News-Sentinel*, January 1, 1992, p. A12).

Subjects in a study done by Kaplan in 1975 who expressed anger became more hostile than those who (a) expressed the opposite of their angry feelings or (b) maintained neutrality. Siegman and his colleagues (1990) have done experiments in which men and women talked about anger-arousing events that had recently happened to them. They were instructed to speak in each of three different ways about these events: fast and loud, slow and soft, and normally. Their blood pressures and heart rates were monitored, and their subjective feelings of anger were assessed after each style of speaking. When the subjects spoke fast and loud (as most people do when ventilating anger to another person), there were greater blood pressure and heart rate increases. Further, the subjects felt more angry than they had felt discussing the episodes in a normal voice or in the slow-soft style. Thus, both physiological arousal and subjective anger experience were affected by loud verbalization.

Before we leave the topic of outward ventilation of anger, we must assure the reader that we are not speaking here of healthy outlets like physical exercise. There might even be occasions when it is healthy to scream privately to reduce extreme tension. However, the anger-out expression mode, as currently measured by researchers, has almost no positive aspects. The questionnaire we used assesses the likelihood of attacking and blaming others when angry. Thus, when we talk about anger-out, we mean an unhealthy sort of displacing or "dumping."

Anger-Discuss

Another way of getting anger off one's chest involves discussion of the incident with a friend or relative. Less is known about this mode of anger expression because of its omission from most questionnaires. However, Riley and Treiber (1989) found that the Framingham Anger-Discuss Scale loaded on a factor titled Verbal/Adaptive Anger Expression in their factor analysis of several anger measures. Discussion of one's anger appears to be a healthy choice that deserves investigation. In fact, the only anger expression style found to relate *positively* to general physical health in our previous studies was anger-discuss (Thomas & Williams, 1991). *Not* discussing anger (i.e., scoring low on anger-discuss) was a significant predictor of coronary heart disease in females aged 45 to 64 at their eighth or ninth biennial medical examination in the Framingham study (Haynes, Feinleib, & Kannel, 1980).

Available evidence indicates that when the anger-discuss mode is included in the tests researchers administer, women score higher than men (Riley, Treiber, & Woods, 1989; Thomas, 1989; Thomas & Williams, 1991). Similarly, Averill (1982) found that women, more so than men, wanted to talk about angry incidents, either with the instigator or a third party. Along the same lines, Harburg, Blakelock, and Roeper (1979) described a reflective anger coping style that was more characteristic of the women in their sample than of the men. Women said they used this style to handle an angry boss, for example. Individuals who used this method had lower blood pressure compared with those who held anger in or expressed it outwardly. The greater propensity of females to discuss anger with a confidant has been documented as early as the 4th grade. In a study of boys and girls from 4th, 8th, and 12th grades, Brondolo (1992) found that girls at all ages were more willing than boys to confide in someone about their angry feelings.

In the Framingham study, a subsample of female clerical workers were selected for close scrutiny because they had a greater risk of CHD than other workers or housewives. In multiple logistic regression analyses, *inability* to *discuss anger* was an independent predictor of CHD (along with lack of support from boss and greater family responsibility) (Haynes & Feinleib, 1980). In summary, discussion of anger appears to be a health-promoting choice that women actually prefer, but situational constraints of some occupations (or other factors) may prevent this style of anger expression.

Anger Symptoms

The final anger expression mode is called "Anger Symptoms," which means that rather intense physical symptoms are experienced in reaction to anger arousal. For example, some people feel a lot of tension, develop a severe headache, or get very shaky. In traditional explanations of the mechanism of somatization, it is presumed that people who are prone to have symptoms when angry are unable to properly verbalize their feelings—hence, the physical expression ensues. However, in an earlier study of women's anger (Thomas & Donnellan, 1991), we found that those who scored high on somatic symptoms were not more likely to suppress anger than low scorers; they were significantly more likely to vent the anger outwardly in the attacking, blaming way we previously mentioned. Similarly, another group of researchers (Armstead et al., 1989) found that black college students who coped with racism by expressing anger outwardly scored higher on anger symptoms than students who held anger in when responding to racism. Along the same lines, scores on the Framingham anger symptoms scale have been correlated with Type A behavior pattern, which is characterized by overt anger expression rather than inhibition (Haynes, Levine, Scotch, Feinleib, & Kannel, 1978).

Persons who score high on anger symptoms have been found to have health problems. In the Framingham study, middle-aged women with CHD had higher scores on anger symptoms than disease-free subjects (Haynes, Feinleib, Levine, Scotch, & Kannel, 1978). Another research group found relationships between high levels of somatic anger and diagnosis of hypertension (Contrada et al., 1986). Inverse relationships between anger symptoms and general health status were found for women in our previous studies (Thomas, 1989; Thomas & Williams, 1991). Causality cannot be inferred in cross-sectional studies, so the reader is cautioned not to assume that all of these studies show that disease is a *consequence* of using this mode of anger expression. However, there is one prospective relationship that deserves mention here. Housewives in Framingham who initially scored higher on anger symptoms were more likely to develop CHD during the 8-year follow-up period than were housewives who scored lower on the scale when enrolled in the longitudinal study (Haynes, Feinleib, & Kannel, 1980).

In studies where both men and women have been assessed, women scored higher on anger symptoms than men (Durel et al., 1989; Haynes et al., 1978; Thomas, 1989; Thomas & Williams, 1991). Reasons for this are unclear. Are women simply more aware of, or willing to acknowledge, their bodily reactions to anger than men? Do they experience anger more intensely as proposed by Fujita, Diener, and Sandvik (1991)? Because somatic expression of anger appears to be more characteristic of women, we wanted to examine this mode thoroughly; we used two different scales to measure it. In addition to the 5-item Framingham anger symptoms scale, we used the 10-item Somatic Anger Scale developed by Contrada and associates (1986). Respondents are asked to describe themselves when angry in terms of statements such as "My whole body is keyed up," and "There is a tight knotted feeling in my stomach." The Contrada scale taps several bodily reactions to anger that are not assessed by the Framingham scale, such as pulse quickening, fists clenching, and faster respirations. A 4-point Likert response format is used.

ANGER COGNITIONS

A final element of anger experience is the type of thinking in which one customarily engages. The reader will recall our review (chapter 2) of the effects of faulty or irrational thinking on emotion. Believing that someone *deliberately* provoked you produces a different response than interpreting a provocation as unintentional. Construing a situation as *unfair* may generate more anger or influence the way in which the anger is expressed. Obsessing or *ruminating* about an incident can prevent termination of emotional arousal and complicate or delay the process of reconciliation with the offender. High levels of cognitions such as these are associated with systolic blood pressure reactivity to laboratory tasks (Contrada et al., 1986) and with both systolic and diastolic blood pressure reactivity in women at work (Durel et al., 1989). We suspected that more enduring negative cognitions (as in the case of a woman in a perpetually conflictual marriage or work situation) could have substantial effects on blood pressure and other physiological parameters as well as mental health. Therefore, we included the Cognitive Anger Scale during our second wave of data collection. This 10-item instrument (Contrada et al., 1986) includes items such as "My mind seems to be caught up and overwhelmed with the feeling," "I keep thinking about what happened over and over again," and "I keep thinking of getting even" as well as items pertaining to the faulty attributions described earlier. As in the Somatic Anger Scale, subjects are asked to indicate how characteristic such cognitions are on a 4-point scale ("almost never" to "almost always"). The respondent is instructed to circle the number that best describes how she *generally* acts or feels when angry or furious; higher scores indicate greater propensity to engage in unhealthy thinking and ruminating about angry incidents.

Summary

We have now described the major dimensions of anger included in this investigation: personality-trait anger (and its subscales of anger temperament and angry reactivity), four modes of anger expression, and anger cognitions. The reader may wonder how all of these dimensions mesh, or clash, in an individual woman's behavioral repertoire. The following case profiles demonstrate the importance of considering each individual dimension as well as the woman's pattern of scores across the dimensions. The relationships of anger scores to other variables of the study (such as stress, self-esteem, social support, and values) are mentioned briefly, although further discussion of these variables will be postponed until their respective chapters.

Marcia: A High Scorer on Angry Temperament

When angry, Marcia said "I scream, rant, rave, throw things and drive my car too fast!" Marcia is one of the women in our study who scored high on the part of the Trait Anger questionnaire measuring "angry temperament," the general proneness to respond angrily regardless of situational circumstances. Thus, Marcia describes herself as "hot-headed," "quick-tempered," and "fiery." Instead of keeping her anger to herself, she vents it outwardly. Sometimes she expresses the anger in a healthy way (discussing with a friend or relative), but she also admits taking the anger out on others: "When I get mad, I say nasty things." When asked to whom she would be likely to express anger, Marcia replied, "My husband, my sister-in-law, and I all too often yell at my kids when I'm not even angry at them." She went on to disclose, "Actually, I'll vent on whoever is handy." Interestingly, the ventilation apparently does not necessarily diminish the anger or produce a sense of relief. Marcia reports that "I can sometimes be mad all day—or even for days." Apparently, a variety of things trigger Marcia's anger. Like many women in our sample, she mentions both family and work situations. In response to the question "When are you likely to become angry?" she says, "if my husband is thoughtless," or "when someone does something stupid that interferes with me or my family." When asked with whom she might become angry, she mentions the management of the institution where she works and insurance companies with which she must deal in her daily job responsibilities.

Marcia also scores high on the "Angry reaction" test items. Both criticism and lack of recognition produce anger. Marcia reports, "It makes me furious when I am criticized in front of others," "I feel infuriated when I do a good job and get a poor evaluation," and "I feel annoyed when I am not given recognition for doing good work." There is an element of the time urgency and impatience that characterizes Type A personalities: "I get angry when I'm slowed down by others' mistakes."

Marcia's anger episodes involve both thoughts of revenge and physical symptoms. On the cognitive scale we administered, Marcia reported that she "almost always" has the following thoughts when angry: I keep thinking about what happened over and over again, I keep thinking of getting even, I can only think of what caused the feeling, My mind seems to be caught up and overwhelmed with the feeling, I keep thinking how unfair the situation is, I think "nobody has a right to act that way," and In my mind, I call the other person names (in the margin, Marcia added that she calls the other person names "out loud too"). On the somatic scales, Marcia reported that these physical symptoms frequently occur when she is angry: face and mouth tight, tense and hard; quickened pulse; tight, knotted feeling in stomach; clenched fists, pounding heart, faster breathing, and whole body keyed up.

Who is Marcia? She is a 30-year-old mother of two young children, married for 13 years, and working full time in one of the health professions. High occupational stress is characteristic of her field, although we have no direct assessment of the factors that may be unique to Marcia's position. Marcia says her greatest stress right now is "money." She would like to have a more prosperous life. Notably, she lists only two people in her social support network, the same two with whom she is usually angry. She has no church involvement, although she does espouse belief in a higher power. On the Value Survey, she indicated that her values were "not clear at all." Her physical health is good, but she scores in the mildly depressed range on the depression test we used. One of the most striking aspects of Marcia's pattern of test scores is her low score on self-esteem. She agrees with test items such as "At times I think I am no good at all," and "I certainly feel useless at times." She wishes she could have more respect for herself. She volunteered the following rather pessimistic forecast, "I don't think my self-respect is ever going to improve." Self-esteem was one of three factors clearly differentiating women scoring high and low on the angry temperament scale in this study. The high scorers, like Marcia, tend to have lower self-esteem. They also tend to be more stressed and depressed. In the chapters on self-esteem, stress, and depression, we explore these relationships further.

Barbara: A High Scorer on Angry Reaction

At first glance Barbara, a high scorer on the Angry Reaction section of the Trait Anger questionnaire, seems very different from Marcia, whom we profiled for high Angry Temperament. For example, Barbara is older, divorced, and parenting teenagers rather than young children. In contrast with Marcia's low self-esteem, Barbara scores high. In comparison with Marcia's limited social support network, Barbara has an extensive network of relatives and friends who affirm her. Unlike Marcia, Barbara is regularly involved in church activities. She asserts that she is "very clear" about her values. Barbara's physical health is good, and she scored low on our measures of stress and depression. After 15 years of marriage, she was the initiator of her divorce 11 years ago. "Freedom" is one of Barbara's top-ranked values. She does acknowledge, "[It] would be nice to have someone nice (but not "clingy") to grow old with." Barbara receives child support, and with her teaching salary she has adequate income. On the scales measuring anger expression modes, Barbara scored right at the sample mean on three of the four modes, and just a bit below the mean on anger suppression (indicating she is not as likely to hold her anger in).

Despite some obvious assets when compared with Marcia, Barbara scored the highest possible score on Angry Reaction. Thus, she endorsed questionnaire items about becoming furious when criticized or poorly evaluated, and annoyed when her good work is not recognized. Examining Barbara's choices on the Values Survey provided a clue to help understand her intense reaction to criticism or lack of recognition. Self-respect, social recognition, and a sense of accomplishment were among Barbara's top four values. Thus her angry reactions may be related, at least in part, to infringements on these values. For example, when criticized, she may feel that she is not receiving the recognition she deserves from others. Barbara considered work as her greatest stress, although she scored low on our overall stress questionnaire. She mentions "one particular coworker" with whom she is likely to become angry, although she would not express anger to coworkers. She used the term "pettiness" to describe some situations that provoke her anger. When asked to whom she would be likely to express anger, Barbara replies "secretary," pointing out that the anger is not about the *secretary's* behavior. Instead, the secretary is apparently someone to whom anger expression is safe, comfortable, or convenient.

Like Marcia, there is an element of time urgency in Barbara's angry reactivity. "Not having enough time" triggers her anger, and she becomes angry when slowed down by others' mistakes. Perhaps this impatience could be connected with her valuing of accomplishment; others' errors interfere with her task completion. Barbara also reports that she gets angry at her children, although she provides no further details about the circumstances.

Those of us who have teenaged children have no difficulty imagining typical scenarios, but we will not insert our speculations into the data!

Barbara's profile is very similar to Marcia's in terms of cognitive and somatic anger scale scores. Barbara's scores were in the top 25% on both of these scales. Thus, Barbara has intense thoughts and physical symptoms when her anger is aroused. She admits that her mind gets "caught up and overwhelmed with the feeling," and she "keeps thinking how unfair the situation is." In her mind, she calls the other person names. She acknowledges that her "whole body is keyed up." Lump in throat, shaky voice, tightness in stomach, rapid breathing, and flushing are often experienced. Interestingly, despite the intensity of Barbara's angry reactions, she reports that typical day-to-day anger episodes only last a few minutes. In this respect, she is very different from Marcia who sometimes retains anger for days.

In summary, there is no suggestion in Barbara's pattern of scores that she is a *globally angry* sort of person. However, certain situations involving performance evaluation (particularly when it is unfair) or impediments to performance (slowness or mistakes of others) trigger a very intense, although brief, anger. The anger is not expressed to Barbara's peers, but to a subordinate, the secretary. The secretary's view of all of this is unknown.

In subsequent chapters, you will meet other women who participated in our research. Although the size of the sample precludes in-depth profiles of all subjects, we share with you the words of women themselves whenever possible, with contextual detail of their anger episodes and glimpses of their multifaceted lives as mothers, workers, partners, friends; the collective wisdom of more than 500 women informs and inspires.

SCORING PATTERNS OF THE SAMPLE ON ANGER DIMENSIONS

In this section of the chapter, we review the descriptive statistics for the sample on each of the anger dimensions we measured. Initial examination of the data revealed that the distribution of scores was relatively normal for every anger variable, with no problematic skewness. Thus, there was no evidence supporting myths such as women's alleged greater propensity to suppress the emotion of anger (see Table 4, Appendix). If most women were suppressors, there would have been skewed distributions on expression modes such as anger-in and anger-out; such was not the case. The full range of possible scores was observed for all anger variables except cognitive anger, for which the scores ranged from 10 to 35 (possible maximum score was 40). The slightly attenuated range on cognitive anger may be attributed to the preponderance of "normal" healthy women in the sample; perhaps only certain types of psychiatric patients would make extremely high scores on this test of unhealthy cognitions.

Analyses of subgroups of the sample according to various demographic characteristics were performed next. Comparisons of subjects in terms of education (see Table 5, Appendix) revealed significant differences in only two anger dimensions. To conduct these comparisons, we selected the upper 25% ($n = 135$) and the lower 25% ($n = 133$) of the sample; t tests were used for the analyses. Mean scores on anger-in and anger symptoms were higher for women with less education (≤ 13 years) than for women in the top quartile (≥ 17 years). It is likely that education levels sort women into different social roles with different rules for emotional expression. Although some women in the lower quartile had achieved high school education or high school plus a year of technical school or college, women in this group do not have access to the wide range of occupations open to women with graduate preparation. Instead, they tend to be concentrated in clerical jobs (or comparable positions of low autonomy and control) where anger must be inhibited. Physical symptoms such as headache could be the result of anger suppression on the job.

Occupational Analysis

Results of the analyses on education led us to compare the anger of women in occupations grouped according to prestige, autonomy, and control. In the "high" category we placed subjects in professional practice, management-executive positions, and owners of their own businesses ($n = 69$). In the "medium" category we placed teachers, nurses, social workers, and other human service workers ($n = 163$). Clerical workers and homemakers constitute the "low" category ($n = 133$), although we hasten to assure the reader that this "low" categorization is not meant to offend women who perform these vital services; unfortunately, society accords little prestige to these occupations and our categorization simply reflects that. Using analysis of variance, we found significant differences between the three groups on *anger-in*, with the "low" group scoring higher and the remaining two groups not different from each other. This finding corroborates the previously discussed results of education comparisons; undoubtedly, many of the women categorized as "low" in occupational prestige were the same women in the "low" group on education. Reasons for suppression of their anger deserve attention in future investigations.

There were two other significant differences: on *trait anger* and the *angry reaction subscale* of the Spielberger tool, the "medium" occupational group scored *highest*. This group of women—the teachers, nurses, social workers, and other professional helpers—must deal with the restrictions of bureaucratic organizations, the multifaceted needs of diverse clients, and other occupational frustrations that are well documented in the literature. A common element is inadequate recognition for their work; women in these occupations receive neither high monetary compensation nor high levels of appreciation from supervisors. Many of these women are supervised by men. For example, in most school systems the principals and higher level administrators are males, although the preponderance of teachers are women. Considering these factors, it is easy to understand their greater anger propensity and greater reactivity to the situations described in the Spielberger questionnaire (e.g., "I feel annoyed when I am not given recognition for doing good work.")

Comparisons of Married and Unmarried Women

Comparisons were also made based on marital status, with the sample dichotomously categorized for these analyses as married or unmarried. There were no significant differences on any anger dimensions except anger-in. Married women scored *lower* than unmarried women, indicating *less* likelihood of holding their anger in. Given the power imbalance between wives and husbands posited in some contemporary marriage literature, it seems that the opposite tendency would be evident (i.e., married women, possessing less power than their partners, would suppress anger). There are several plausible explanations for our contrary finding. Perhaps such power imbalances are less common today than in the past, a more egalitarian marital relationship having become the norm. It is also possible that married women in our sample are somewhat atypical, in that so many are well educated and work outside the home (imbuing them with greater power). Perhaps a benefit of having a committed relationship is freedom to express one's anger (or other strong emotions), trusting that the partnership will endure.

Comparisons By Age of Youngest Child

Inasmuch as interactions with children are a potential source of anger in the daily lives of women who are mothers, we examined scores on anger variables for subjects grouped according to age of their youngest child. There were 136 mothers of preschoolers (age 5 or younger), 76 mothers of elementary school-aged children (6–12), 75 mothers of adolescents (ages 13–18), and 120 mothers of adult children (older than 18). Analysis of variance revealed significant differences between groups on anger-in, anger-out, trait anger, and the angry temperament subscale of trait anger. Let us examine these differences more closely. In terms of anger suppression, women who had adult children were the most likely to be suppressors; mean scores on anger-in of the other three groups were lower. One interpretation of this finding is that women may feel more constrained from telling adult children that they are angry with them (not wishing to appear intrusive or meddlesome), whereas with younger children it is more permissible to express anger. Supportive of this interpretation is the complementary finding that mothers of elementary school–aged children scored highest on *anger-out*. Children in this stage of development frequently question parental authority and test limits as their social world enlarges and they begin to emulate peers. Consequently, their mothers are frequently provoked to anger and, according to these research results, vent it freely in a blaming way. Examples of triggering events appear in our qualitative data (presented in chapter 4). Overall propensity to be angry (trait anger) and angry temperament were higher in *all* groups of mothers with preadult children (< 18) than in the mothers whose children were older than age 18.

Comparisons by Age of Participants

We wondered if the findings we have just reviewed could be attributed at least in part to the age of the mothers rather than the age of their children. There is some evidence in the literature that scores on anger instruments vary according to age (cf. Spielberger et al., 1983). Therefore, after creating six age categories, we compared women's mean scores on anger dimensions using analysis of variance. There were significant differences on seven of the nine dimensions (see Table 6, Appendix), indicating that age is an important demographic characteristic to consider in anger research. The most striking differences between groups were found on trait anger and its two subscales. On both the overall trait anger scale and the angry reaction subscale, the youngest group (age 34 or less) had the highest mean, followed by successively decreasing means for the other groups; with the oldest group (age 55 or older) scoring lowest of all. On the angry temperament subscale, younger women also scored higher than older, although the means were not ordered in perfect "stairstep" fashion. Similar patterns were observed for several other variables: anger-out was highest for the youngest women, as was cognitive anger; scores on both of these dimensions decreased with increasing age. Conversely, women age 55 and older scored highest on anger-in. What could account for these remarkably consistent findings? It is reasonable to assume that the youngest and oldest cohorts of women had very different socialization experiences. Women in their late 20s and early 30s at the time of our survey were born in the late 1950s and early 1960s, thus they were impressionable adolescents during the turbulent 1970s when the feminist movement called attention to the devastating consequences of sexism and sex role stereotyping. Many of their role models were speaking out, no longer denying their anger. In contrast, the women in our oldest group (age 55 and up) were born in the 1930s; they were adolescents during the very conservative postwar period. It appears that they learned well to be "nice ladies."

Because women's anger is related to their current life stresses and many other factors, we do not suggest that socialization influences during development are the only explanation for our findings. Lacking longitudinal data, we do not know if older women scoring low on anger dimensions in the 1990s are behaving much the same way they always have (decades of ladylike behavior?) or if they are in a life stage of "mellowing," no longer provoked to anger in their daily lives by recalcitrant children or thoughtless spouses. There are many unanswered questions and implications for further research.

One other interesting age difference deserves mention. *Anger symptoms* were highest in midlife women (40s and early 50s), somewhat lower in younger women, and lowest in the age 55-and-older group. Middle adulthood is known to be one of the most stressful life stages for women, which may account for the high level of anger symptoms. In our previous study of midlife women, frequency and severity of daily hassles were significantly correlated with anger symptoms (Thomas & Donnellan, 1991). There could be a linkage to menopausal phenomena as well. In her study of midlife women, Atakan (1989) found that menopausal women reporting emotional symptoms (nervousness, irritability) were significantly higher in anger symptoms than those who only had physical complaints like hot flashes and night sweats. It is currently believed that menopause does not *cause* psychological distress but it may *intensify* preexisting problems.

Comparisons of Clinical and Nonclinical Groups

The next set of comparisons examined differences among the psychiatric patients ($n = 52$), the medical patients ($n = 40$), and the nonclinical sample (a randomly selected subsample of 50 was drawn from the 387 women in this group to use in these analyses). Results of analysis of variance (ANOVA) procedures may be found in Table 7 (see Appendix). The most significant differences between groups were on trait anger, the angry reaction subscale of trait anger, and anger symptoms, with the psychiatric patients scoring higher than the other two groups on each of these anger dimensions; medical and nonclinical groups did not differ from each other. Women in the psychiatric group also scored higher on anger-out, but there were no differences between these women and the other groups on anger-in, anger discussion, or angry temperament. The medical group did not score differently from the nonclinical group on any measures. Given that the women in the psychiatric group were currently in treatment, and thus probably in varying stages of exploring anger-provoking issues with their therapists, we do not suggest that too much be made of these findings. We do not have data on premorbid personalities and certainly do not claim to have established any causal connections between style of anger management and psychiatric conditions. What, then, is the potential value of these comparisons? If Spielberger (1983, 1985) is correct, one aspect of an individual's anger proneness in adulthood is a basic personality factor, the relatively stable "temperament" aspect that probably has a genetic component. As we have seen earlier, babies display unique temperaments from birth (cf. Chess, Thomas, & Birch, 1965). What the present findings tell us is that women in the psychiatric group are *no different* from the other women on this basic personality factor. The significant difference we found on overall trait anger was apparently due to the influence of the angry *reaction* items that pertain more directly to current life circumstances. These findings suggest that researchers using Spielberger's Trait Anger Scale should examine (and report) subscale scores as well as total scores. Examination of scores on perceived stress revealed that the psychiatric patients, not surprisingly, were significantly more stressed than were the other two groups. At the time we tested them, their anger was being vented outwardly, accompanied by somatic symptoms such as shakiness and weakness. Through the process of psychotherapy, they will presumably learn healthier anger management techniques. In chapter 12, a therapist shares her strategies for assisting female clients to deal with their anger.

Racial Comparisons

The final set of subgroup comparisons was undertaken to explore scoring patterns on anger dimensions in three nonclinical groups of women with different racial-cultural heritages; there were 63 African Americans, 56 Chinese Americans, and 312 Caucasian Americans in these analyses. Culture is the crucible in which emotional habits are shaped. Too often, researchers have considered only the dominant white culture (see chapter 1 regarding studies using convenience samples of college students who are usually white, middle-to-upper class, etc.). African Americans were of particular interest to us because they constitute the largest minority group in this country (Taeuber, 1991). An extensive literature review by the African-American member of our research group revealed no studies on the everyday experience of anger in black women. Chinese Americans were selected for the study for two reasons: (a) they come to this country with a radically different orientation toward emotional experience and expression; and (b) a Chinese-American member of our research group had a wealth of information about her culture as well as access to potential participants. Taeuber (1991) notes that the Asian population in the United States is growing at a very high rate because of immigration, and the Chinese constitute the largest group of Asian Americans. The Chinese participants in our study were immigrants from Taiwan who came to the United States as adults, either as wives of students or to pursue their own advanced studies. Fluency in English was ascertained by our data collector prior to recruitment for the study. Although space limitations preclude a thorough examination of each culture, we had predicted higher anger levels in African-American women (based on their disadvantaged status within the predominantly white culture) and inhibition of anger by Chinese-American women (based on the Oriental tradition of restraint of strong emotions). Neither prediction was confirmed by the data.

Literature Review and Findings

African-American Women

In the CARDIA study, a prospective epidemiological study involving 5,115 individuals, hostility scores were significantly higher in blacks than in whites (Scherwitz & Rugulies, 1992). Similarly, *hostility* scores were higher for blacks than for whites in the study by Durel et al. (1989), although *trait anger* scores of blacks were *lower*. The researchers interpreted this to mean that blacks, although more resentful and distrustful than whites, were less likely to acknowledge anger openly because of fears of counteraggression from whites. In a symposium on anger in people of color at the 1989 American Psychological Association convention, Maxine Rawlins pointed out, "It's difficult to be Black in America and not be angry. The history of Blacks in America is a very painful one and it's very difficult to discuss it in a dispassionate way" (cited in Watson, 1989, p. 31). In contrast to other settlers of the "new world," Blacks were brought to this country involuntarily. Slavery shaped the social, psychological, economic, and political development of all black people, and its legacy is with us today. It is not news to the readers of this book that many African Americans remain disenfranchised in myriad ways: education, income, housing, opportunities for employment and advancement, political power, and other basic elements of America's "good life." The ugliness of racism is a daily stressor that produces both anger and elevated blood pressure (Armstead et al., 1989). In her American Psychological Association (APA) presentation, Rawlins spoke of inner-directed anger that contributes to self-destructive behaviors (e.g., taking drugs) as well as outwardly directed anger that results in rioting in black neighborhoods. As this book was being written, the rioting in Los Angeles confirmed Rawlins's words: "We tend to burn our own stores and destroy our own homes" (cited in Watson, 1989, p. 30).

Given the powerful rationale for black anger, the reader will initially be puzzled, as we were, by the results of ANOVA comparisons between racial groups shown in Table 8 (see Appendix). The significant F's were all due to differences between the Chinese-Americans and the other groups. Mean scores on all anger variables were virtually the same for white and black women; there were no significant differences between these two groups. Although it was surprising that there were no differences between African-American and Caucasian-American women in this study, at least one other research team reported the same thing. In a study of blacks and whites using multiple anger and hostility measures, there were no significant differences for race on any of the measures (Riley & Treiber, 1989). Because we found no differences, blacks and whites were not separated for the various analyses discussed in the remainder of the book.

What could explain the similarity in anger scores of our samples of black and white women? Examination of demographic characteristics provided one clue; the black women who participated in our study could be categorized as middle class, based on their educational attainment (mean = 15.9 years), their occupations (primarily "medium" prestige, that is, teaching, nursing, other human services) and their household incomes (mean = $35,000). Thus, in some ways they share at least a part of the same world as whites (i.e., the work world) and perhaps some of the same middle-class values. The black middle class has received little attention in the literature, although this is a rapidly burgeoning group. Presently 40% of blacks are middle class (Sue & Sue, 1990), and the percentage is expected to increase to 56% by the end of the next decade. Like the white women, the majority of blacks were mothers and full-time workers; however, fewer were married at the time of data collection. More black women were never married, divorced, or widowed; less than half were married (compared with 77% of whites).

One other notable aspect of demographic comparisons between blacks and whites was the level of religious involvement. Only 3% of black women were uninvolved in church activities; 71% were regular attenders, and the remaining 26% had at least some church involvement. In contrast, 20% of white women reported no church involvement, 24% "some," and 56% "regular." The black church has a powerful impact not only on its members but on the culture; the church has been a symbol of liberation during the Civil Rights movement and a place of solace during times of crisis. Boyd (1981) contended that it is in the church that the black woman obtains a unique sense of strength and power, enabling her to manage anger and conflict.

Perusal of black women's write-in responses about precipitants of anger revealed nothing unusual that would shed light on the quantitative findings. If racism or tension owing to racial differences is frequently encountered by our respondents, they did not choose to describe it explicitly—with one exception. One African-American woman responded to our question about situations or circumstances that trigger daily anger in terms of "the first White person I see in the morning at work except M____." It is probable that interview methodology (using well-trained, culturally sensitive data collectors) would be a useful approach in further explorations of black women's anger. Obviously, black culture is not homogeneous, containing many subcultures;

we have provided only the briefest glimpse of one aspect (the anger experience) of the middle-class black woman's life-world. Results of these analyses may not be generalizable to other black women. Much remains to be done by researchers in this area.

Chinese-American Women

According to Yeung and Schwartz (1986) 20,000 Chinese people have immigrated to the U.S. from Taiwan since 1982; some of these individuals are among the participants in the present study. They bring with them cultural traditions influenced by the teachings of Confucius, Laotze, and Buddha (Ryan, 1985), which vastly differ from the American valuing of individualism, self-reliance, and freedom. Chinese society emphasizes interdependence, harmony in family relationships, and filial piety (Rawl, 1992). In Taiwan, most married women live with their mothers-in-law and have much contact with the extended family, whereas the usual living arrangement for our respondents in the United States was with husband and children only. In Chinese culture, the husband's wishes (and those of his mother and family) are paramount, and Chinese women have little status until they become elders. Ryan (1985) cites an old saying in which daughters are described as "spilled water" (i.e., a waste) because they move to their husband's family after marriage. In Ryan's view, "Chinese-American women face grave conflicts when they or their daughters attempt to take on the more flexible role of the American woman. They may find it almost impossible to reconcile the differing expectations and demands" (Ryan, 1985, p. 336). In a Canadian study of four ethnocultural groups of immigrant women, the Chinese women were found to be depressed (as were women of Portuguese; Vietnamese, and Latin-American origin); in regression analyses, perceived stress was the primary contributor to the level of depression in the Chinese group (Franks & Faux, 1990).

Regarding emotional expression, Chinese culture downplays individual feelings; avoidance of strong emotionalism is necessary to preserve family harmony. Chinese children are taught that strong and negative feelings are not to be openly expressed (Rawl, 1992). Therefore, we had predicted that Chinese-American women would score higher on anger suppression and lower on scales measuring outward expression. As depicted in Table 8 (see Appendix), our findings were just the opposite. *White* women were highest on anger-in, significantly higher than Chinese (although not different from blacks). Chinese-Americans scored highest on *trait anger*, the *angry temperament subscale* of Spielberger's trait anger tool, and *anger-out*. There were no differences among the three groups on angry reaction, anger symptoms, or any other anger dimensions.

Immigration forces biculturism (identification with the ethnic culture *and* with the majority society), or a loss of one's old identity and the development of a new one. The individuals who participated in our study are undoubtedly in varying stages of assimilation, acculturation, or culture conflict. Sue and Sue (1990) assert that Asian Americans may find it quite difficult to reconcile their loyalties to two different cultural traditions: "Bombarded on all sides by peers, schools, and the mass media upholding Western standards as better than their own, Asian Americans are frequently placed in situations of extreme culture conflict that may lead to much pain and agony" (Sue & Sue, 1990, p. 201). Three coping strategies have been identified: (a) remaining loyal to the ethnic group norms and values; (b) becoming "overwesternized," rejecting the traditional values; and (c) adopting a stance of militancy with regard to racist treatment and civil rights (the "Yellow Power Movement"). We propose that the higher scores of our Chinese-American sample on anger propensity and outwardly vented anger may be related to the phenomenon of "overwesternization" described in the literature. Although this interpretation is tentative, our cultural informant believes that many of her peers are indeed rejecting their own culture and teaching their children to be like Americans. She also pointed out the greater *freedom* to express emotions for these women who do not have to live with their mothers-in-law and extended families.

There are other possible explanations for our findings. In view of the study by Franks and Faux (1990), we examined stress and depression scores to ascertain if we had measured a highly distressed group of Chinese-American women; if that were the case, the high anger levels would not be attributable to "overwesternization" but to profound disequilibrium. On perceived stress, the Chinese mean was 23.8, virtually identical to the mean for the nonclinical white group used in these comparisons. On depression, the Chinese mean was 7.55 (within the nondepressed range), although there were a few women with scores that indicated depression. Self-esteem, physical health, and social support were on par with the remainder of our subjects. We also examined demographic characteristics, finding educational level comparable with the rest of the sample (almost 16 years), occupations generally more prestigious (largely professional), and income very close to the overall sample mean. Most of the Chinese-American women were married (82%), and most had children (75%). A higher percentage were students (11%) than in the other racial groups; as stated previously, pursuit of educational goals was a primary reason for immigration to the U.S. Examination of the qualitative data revealed that precipitants of anger were similar to those reported by other respondents, and the primary targets of the anger were husbands. In summary, the Chinese-American women appear comparable with other subjects in many respects. Their anger proneness is not attributable to greater stress or economic hardship.

Clearly, the findings reported here should be viewed with caution. Characteristics not assessed by any of our measures could have accounted for the high anger scores of the Chinese-American women. We are cognizant of the uniqueness of this sample of Taiwanese women, and do not suggest that our findings can be generalized to other groups of women of Chinese origin. We did find one study that provided some support for our findings. In a study of American, Greek, Chinese, and West Indian students attending U.S. universities, Sommers (1984) found that no Chinese subjects dreaded having anger, and only 20% preferred to hide their anger. Further, most (60%) Chinese students asserted that the emotion of anger was useful and constructive to experience. In contrast, Americans differed significantly from all other cultural groups in preference for hiding anger. Sommers did not do any gender-specific analyses because of her small samples of students. We conclude this section of the chapter by reiterating the suggestion we made for further exploration of anger in blacks: interviewing members of the cultural group. However, the anonymity of the questionnaire format may have allowed Chinese women to disclose their anger in a way that face-to-face interviewing would not permit. There are many issues that must be carefully considered by future investigators.

ARE THERE RELATIONSHIPS AMONG ANGER DIMENSIONS?

In the early period of research on anger expression, a unidimensional conceptualization dominated; anger expression was depicted on a continuum with low scores indicating anger-in and high scores indicating anger-out. This depiction is evident in papers by Funkenstein et al. (1954), Harburg et al. (1973), and Gentry et al. (1982). However, subsequent research by Spielberger et al. (1985) demonstrated that anger-in and anger-out are independent dimensions. Our own previous studies have supported the independence of these dimensions; correlations between anger-in and anger-out were essentially zero for both males and females in studies of midlife subjects (Thomas, 1989) and college students (Thomas & Williams, 1991). In the present sample of women, these findings were replicated; the correlation between anger-in and anger-out was –0.06 (correlations among all anger dimensions appear in Table 9, Appendix).

Are there any anger dimensions that do relate to each other? Miller (1983) proposed that women's suppressed anger is often expressed via somatic symptoms. Our correlational analyses support Miller's hypothesized linkage of anger-in and somatic symptoms (Framingham measure); however, anger symptoms are also related to anger-out and *every other anger variable*, with the exception of anger discussion. Thus, anger symptoms are likely to occur when women are venting anger *outwardly* as well as when *inhibiting* its expression. At first, this finding appears paradoxical. We will attempt to resolve the confusion. Anger symptoms are strongly related to unhealthy anger cognitions, providing a helpful clue. Women who score high on the cognitive anger scale have acknowledged that they generally have a very intense experience when angry; they endorsed items such as "I can't pay attention to anything else," and "My mind seems to be caught up and overwhelmed with the feeling." They also indicated that they do not easily let go of the angry feeling (i.e., "I keep thinking about what happened over and over again"). Thus, it is logical to assume that the actual mode of anger expression makes little difference; the arousal is apparently intense and prolonged even when ventilation has occurred. The somatic symptoms may be generated or maintained by the *intensity* of the emotion.

The two somatic measures (Contrada & Framingham scales) used in our study were correlated with each other, as expected, but not so strongly as to suggest redundancy; each scale does contain a different list of bodily reactions. Both somatic measures relate similarly to other anger dimensions, in that they are positively associated with virtually every variable but anger discussion.

Other interesting relationships among anger dimensions were found in the correlational analyses. *Trait anger* (general propensity to become aroused to anger) was strongly linked to higher scores on the *cognitive scale*. Thus, anger-prone individuals are likely to think that the situations that evoke their anger are unfair, that they have been *deliberately* provoked, and so forth. They are attributing responsibility externally, which may account for their greater tendency to use the anger-out expression mode (to attack and blame the perceived source of the problems).

Our findings regarding the linkage between trait anger and faulty cognitions are consistent with studies conducted by Hazaleus and Deffenbacher (1985) and Lohr, Hamberger, and Bonge (1988). In both of these studies, anger proneness was measured by Novaco's (1975) Anger Inventory and irrational cognitions were assessed by Jones's (1969) Irrational Beliefs Test; subjects in both were introductory psychology students who received course credit for participation. Propensity to be aroused to anger was shown to be related to endorsement of specific irrational beliefs (e.g., anxious overconcern that negative events may occur), and gender differences were noted by both sets of researchers. The cognitive mediation of anger arousal was termed "more complex for women" by Hazaleus and Deffenbacher because four irrational cognitions (compared with one for men) entered a discriminant function performed to discriminate between high anger and low anger groups. There was an interesting inverse relationship for *dependency* (the belief that one must have someone to depend on), indicating that women higher in anger scored *lower* on this irrational belief. *Blame proneness* (believing people should be blamed and punished when they do wrong) was predictive of women's anger in both studies in regression analysis. Further exploration of associations between irrational beliefs and anger in women is warranted.

Anger discussion appears to be the most independent dimension, unrelated to anger cognitions, anger-out, and somatic measures, and only weakly related to trait anger and its subscales. The only sizable correlation was an inverse relationship with anger-in (greater anger discussion associated with lesser anger inhibition), which obviously makes sense. A final comment about the interrelationships among anger variables shown in Table 9 is that most correlations were moderate, not substantial. Despite some linkages, the different concepts do not seem to be overlapping. Therefore, there appears to be some value in using multiple measures to assess the relatively distinct aspects of women's anger experience.

DO WOMEN REPORT ANGER EXPRESSION MODES NOT ASSESSED BY THE STRUCTURED TESTS?

Our research team had selected well-known, established tests to measure anger dimensions, so that our findings could be easily understood and applied by other researchers and health care professionals. However, we wondered if women have other ways of expressing their anger that would not be captured by the structured tests. Therefore, in the second phase of data collection we included in our test packet a request for women to provide written descriptions of other anger expression modes: "If there is anything else you do when angry that has not been mentioned on our questionnaires, please describe." Eighty-three subjects wrote descriptions of their responses. Many of the women listed several different anger management strategies. These responses were categorized by two independent raters.

Crying was the most frequently reported experience. One woman wrote, "[I] almost always cry at some point before resolution." The relationship between anger and crying has received little attention in the literature. However, one group of authors (Hoover-Dempsey, Plas, & Wallston, 1986) in a paper on crying among adult professional women at work, proposed two interesting mechanisms: (a) an initial response of anger during interpersonal conflicts, followed by tears; and (b) crying followed by anger, owing to the crier's perception that she had lost control of herself and the situation. Most of the women who shared anecdotes with Hoover-Dempsey and colleagues were ashamed of crying, but could not imagine themselves arguing or "telling someone off" in the work setting; thus, the crying provided a release for the aborted anger. Further research on this mode of anger expression is warranted. However, crying is not included in any of the anger expression tools known to the author. Averill (1982) found that women were more likely than men to cry when angry (34% of women compared with 9% of men). In his sample, approximately 80% of the women who reported crying said that this occurred near the beginning of an anger episode or in the middle, not toward the end, suggesting that crying was not usually a means of bringing the anger episode to a close.

Anger and physical activity seem to go together for some women. Walking, jogging, exercising, keeping oneself occupied, doing housework or yardwork, keeping busy in general with activities such as shopping or playing the piano, were some of the ways that these women said they responded to or managed their anger. These physical activities were helpful in that they decreased angry feelings, relieved frustration, and helped the person calm down; one woman wrote, "I walk it [the anger] off." Eating, smoking, and other consumptive behaviors were also mentioned by some respondents; linkages between anger and these behaviors will be explored in later chapters.

The response of many women to angry situations is to *reflect* on various aspects of the situation, such as what caused them to feel angry, or to look at the situation from the other person's perspective. The words these women used to describe their actions imply a rational or cognitive approach: "I try to look at a situation rationally . . . ; [I] try to think things through"; "[I] . . . try to understand the situation or the other person's motivation." Apparently the purpose of such thoughtful analysis is to help the woman decide on what to do about her anger.

Some responses described activities we labeled "planning," as they involved rehearsal for confronting the offender or solving the problem. One woman said "I roleplay in my head dealing with the situation." Another said "I plan what I need to do to resolve." Another response of some women to anger episodes was to go somewhere to be alone, or to remove themselves physically from the place or person associated with the angry episode. Removal of oneself from a situation was a deliberate action; the woman walked away, or let time pass before deciding on an action. Once the anger subsided or was brought under control, and a plan of some kind developed, the woman approached the other person in the situation.

Less frequently reported responses to anger used by some women included prayer and writing. Prayer is not the reflection or meditation described earlier, but a religious activity; "I go to a quiet place and talk with God and ask Him to help me to deal with the problem." Writing was used in very specific ways. One woman wrote that the memos that she penned while angry were deliberately destroyed after 24 hours had passed; this action kept her from acting impulsively. "Writing is my way of venting" wrote another.

Some women described the physical sensations they experienced as part of the angry episode, although many of these sensations were included in the somatic scales in the test battery. These included clenched teeth, knot in the stomach, heartburn, stiff neck, sleep disturbances, and feeling like "pulling my hair out." Other individual responses included a general feeling of anxiety for the rest of the day, ignoring the person who caused the anger, and feeling guilty about the anger. Overall, with the exception of anxiety and somatic symptoms, the anger responses described by study participants appeared to be adaptive and health promoting. Developers of instruments have focused on maladaptive expression of anger, preventing exploration of these healthier methods. Crying, an emotional behavior sanctioned only for women and children in our society, deserves special attention. The only major study on crying in adults (Frey & Langseth, 1981) was devoted to a chemical analysis of tears and the physiological function of tears. Interestingly, *emotional* tears were chemically different than *irritant* tears (e.g., tears caused by air pollution or cutting up onions), in that they were found to contain chemicals which may mediate the immune system's response to stress. This finding raises an intriguing question: by stifling their tears, are some people depriving themselves of the benefits of a natural mechanism that could combat the ill effects of angry, stressful situations?

CONCLUSION

In this chapter we have examined data for the full sample, and for various subgroups of women, concerning anger arousal and the manifestations of anger when it is experienced. However, we have not yet examined *why* women become angry as they enact the routines of their daily lives. We turn now to examination of precipitants of anger in chapter four.

■ 4
Anger: Targets and Triggers

Gayle Denham and Kaye Bultemeier

How might it have been different for you, if, early in your life, the first time you as a tiny child felt your anger coming together inside yourself, someone, a parent or grandparent, or older sister or brother, had said, "Bravo! Yes, that's it! You're feeling it!"

If, the first time you had experienced that sharp awareness of ego, of "me, I'm me, not you" . . . you had been received and hugged and affirmed, instead of shamed and isolated.

If someone had been able to see that you were taking the first tiny baby step toward feeling your own feelings, of knowing that you saw life differently from those around you. If you had been helped to experience your own uniqueness, to feel the excitement of sensing, for the very first time, your own awareness of life. What if someone had helped you to own all of this . . . to own your own life?

—Judith Duerk, Circle of Stones: Woman's Journey to Herself

In this chapter, we examine precipitants of women's anger in their daily lives. As Lazarus (1991c) pointed out, recurring emotions such as anger provide clues about a person's characteristic way of appraising encounters, and life itself. Words of the women experiencing anger provided the data for qualitative exploration of the emotion anger. What was the situation, how did the woman perceive what was real, what was her response, and how did she describe the experience that culminated in the very real feeling of anger? A

68

clearer understanding of this emotion was constructed through listening to women as they told their stories of anger situations. Thus, the researchers began with the words of women themselves as they recalled situations, persons, places, and things involved in anger episodes. Descriptions of women's anger experiences were obtained through an open-ended questionnaire added during the second phase of data collection. One hundred eighty-five women responded to the following five questions about their typical day-to-day experience of feeling angry:

1. *When* are you likely to become angry? In other words, *what* situations or circumstances would *usually* trigger anger?
2. With *whom* are you be likely to become angry?
3. To *whom* would you be likely to *express* the anger?
4. To *whom* would you *not* express anger?
5. How long does a *typical day-to-day* anger episode usually last for you?

Analysis of these everyday anger precipitants yielded two global categories, *triggers* of anger and *targets* of anger. An anger trigger is defined as a person, object, situation, or circumstance that results in anger. An anger target is defined as an object, person, or situation that emerges as the recipient of the woman's anger.

DATA ANALYSIS

Conceptualization of anger experiences within the categories of targets and triggers provided a rich array of data that led to a clearer understanding of women's anger. Using the qualitative data analysis approach of Miles and Huberman (1984), the two researchers independently examined the responses from women with respect to anger in their daily lives. Our process involved the following phases:

1. All data were transcribed into the computer software program "Hyperqual." (One researcher used the computer software for her analysis; the other researcher used hand tabulation.)
2. Responses were sorted by question.
3. Each response was coded for major ideas and thoughts.
4. Collaboratively the data for each question were sorted into three realms:
   a. Intrapersonal: occurring within the individual self.
   b. Interpersonal: involving relations between people.
   c. Extrapersonal: involving all other relationships including societal and environmental.
5. The data were subsorted by idea or thought within each realm.

6. The subsorted data sets were independently analyzed thematically.
7. Themes identified by each coder were compared, resulting in the findings in this chapter.
8. Numerical tabulations were completed for each theme.
9. Exemplars depicting each theme and subtheme were selected.
10. After identifying themes, a literature review was completed.

A descriptive approach, with emphasis on sensitization of the reader to the content as outlined by Knafl and Howard, was followed in reporting results of the analysis. Sensitization is emphasized for this study based upon the following (Knafl & Howard, 1986): (a) it is appropriate for reporting results of a descriptive study; (b) few studies have been done on women's everyday experiences of anger, therefore a knowledge base that accurately reflects their experiences is absent; and (c) the purpose of this study is to sensitize the reader to women's anger experiences. The results of this analysis provided a variety of subthemes that depicted the complexity of anger-producing situations and individuals involved in the anger situations. Themes and subthemes that emerged provided the classification system for reporting women's responses. A summary of emerging themes and subthemes is presented next. The model depicted in Figure 4.1 emerged from analysis of the data and illustrates women's typical anger experiences.

An umbrella theme of *personal ideology* emerged as the overriding pattern. Ideologies set standards from which women evaluate all life experiences. Ideology is defined as "a systematic body of concepts, esp. about human life or culture" (Webster, 1989, p. 597). Women held ideologies about roles and behavior involving themselves (the intrapersonal realm), their family and work interactions (interpersonal realm), and society in general (extrapersonal realm). Anger did not occur if events occurring within each realm were congruent with ideologies. But if an event was not congruent, anger was triggered. Women seemed to make moral ethical decisions about anger expression; in other words, moral reasoning was implicated. Gilligan (1982) suggests that relationships heavily influence moral reasoning and that ethical dilemmas arise from conflicting responsibilities more than from violated rights. Additionally, moral ethical decisions vary depending on the situation. Gilligan's (1982) theory includes key concepts such as caring, self-sacrifice to ensure care for others, goodness, an injunction against hurting self or others, and logic of relationships. It was obvious that women carefully decided when and to whom they would express their anger based on ethical foundations aimed at achieving the most good for all in the situation.

This conceptual model of women's anger is illustrated by accounts of anger experiences from our respondents. For example, one women wrote that anger was usually triggered in the following situations:

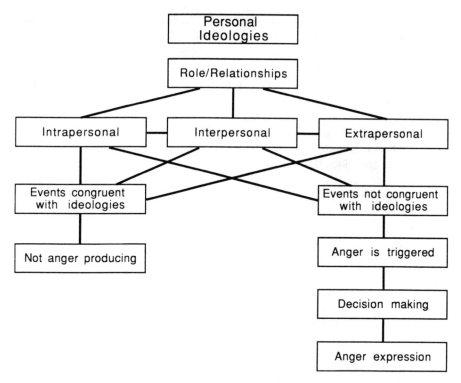

FIGURE 4.1 Model of women's anger experience.

"Employees not carrying their workload"
"Continued belligerence or disrespect from children"
"The stronger taking advantage of the weaker"
"Power hungry people"
"Unfaithfulness"

She responded that she was most likely to become angry at "People involved in all above situations." It seems she held ideologies that employees should be responsible in the area of job performance, that children should be respectful, that the strong should not take advantage of the weak, and that people should not be power hungry or unfaithful. When people behaved incongruently with these ideologies, anger was aroused. At this point it seemed that this woman made a decision about expressing her anger, for she identified that she would likely express her anger "to those people or internalize anger if unable to express to those people." She identified that she would not express anger "to those I'm not able to reach." These data suggest that she made a decision about anger expression—either express it to the people who could be reached or internalize and suppress it.

In another example one woman responded that anger was triggered in the following situations:

"When my husband/children don't help around the house"
"When husband/children won't leave appropriate messages"
"Half-done jobs that I must re-do"

She responded that she was most likely to become angry at

"Husband/children" and "co-workers"

She expresses that anger to her

"Husband/children" and "co-workers"

However, she indicated that she would *not* express anger to her

"Boss"

In these examples, we see that women hold ideologies or expectations about roles and behavior that guide their actions. The role that expectations play in anger has been mentioned in chapter 2. Solomon described the importance of beliefs in emotions beautifully in stating: "An emotion is a basic judgment about our Selves and our place in our world, the projection of the values and ideals, structures and mythologies, according to which we live and through which we experience life. This is why emotions are so dependent upon our opinions and beliefs" (Solomon, 1976, p. 187). He continues that emotions provide an avenue on which all that is meaningful in our life surfaces. Solomon could be interpreted to state that emotions reflect a judgment of what is occurring in our lives; an opinion of ourselves, plus an opinion of others around us. The emotion of anger is therefore a powerful way to express what is meaningful in a woman's life. Solomon noted that most of our emotions do involve other people; trust, betrayal, and the opinion of others are very important aspects of what surfaces through emotions. "Anger is usually direct and explicit in its projection of our personal values and expectations on the world" (Solomon, p. 287). Anger can be a way to show our disappointment in the world. Solomon contends that anger has a component of wanting to punish the other person(s) involved. The data from this study did not support a contention of wanting to punish rather an inclination to want to *make right.* Solomon also contends that anger has a component of self-righteousness, but our data did not support a self-righteous stance in the anger experiences.

ANGER TRIGGERS

Women were asked, *"When* are you likely to become angry?" In other words, what situations or circumstances would usually trigger anger? A total of 179 different responses were reported for question 1. These responses indicated that as long as events within the world were congruent with personal ideologies, emotions of anger were not aroused. Experienced events such as behaviors, relationships, and lived experiences within the world must be congruent with ideologies held by all persons interacting. If they are not congruent, anger is triggered. This group of women indicated that ideologies concerning *power* issues, *justice* and *responsibility* were often incongruent with events encountered within their lived experiences. And so ideologies surrounding power, justice and responsibility that were found within the realms of women's lived experiences (intrapersonal, interpersonal, and extrapersonal) became themes for this set of data (see Table 10, Appendix).

As shown in Figure 4.2, the largest realm represented was the interpersonal realm. This was followed by anger at self and finally anger at society. One could conclude women believed that those closest to them would share and live consistent with their basic ideations. Regarding the themes of power, justice and responsibility, *power* was the primary theme associated with

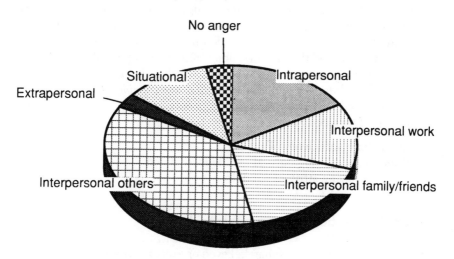

FIGURE 4.2 Frequency with which women reported anger situations.

anger as illustrated below (respondents typically identified > 1 anger-producing situation within each realm):

Power	274/421 responses
Justice	93/421 responses
Responsibility	54/421 responses

The prominence of the interpersonal realm is congruent with Averill's (1982) viewpoint that anger has a social component, occurring daily as people interact in their interpersonal network. Moreover, gender studies of emotions indicated that adolescent females were most likely to become angry as a result of interpersonal experiences, whereas males became angry in situations where performance was evaluated (Stapley & Haviland, 1989).

Our findings are also consistent with a study by Roseman and colleagues (1990) that identified key appraisal elements surrounding anger experiences: the situations were unwanted (could have been attributed to a lack of responsibility or powerlessness); were caused by someone else (another person was responsible for the situation); were characterized by low power and a belief that different, more positive outcomes were deserved (could apply to injustice situations).

POWER

Power as defined by Bush (1988) is "the capability of one social actor to overcome resistance in another social actor in achieving a desired objective." Goodrich (1991) defines power as "the capacity to gain whatever resources are necessary to remove oneself from a condition of oppression, to guarantee one's ability to perform, and to affect not only one's own circumstances but also more general circumstances outside one's intimate surroundings." The role of power, or lack thereof, in women's anger arousal will become very clear as our discussion proceeds. Within this analysis the concept of power is defined by the subthemes *competent, effective,* and *capable.* These subthemes of power were extricated as ideological concepts, which, when not met, triggered anger. Definitions of the three key terms are

Competent: sufficiency of means
Effective: producing desired or intended effects
Capable: having attributes required

Power Within the Intrapersonal Realm

Within the personal realm women believed or expected certain behavior from themselves. The women believed that they would be capable, competent, and effective (listed in order of frequency of responses). When they identified themselves as breaching this expectation, anger ensued. We will now provide examples of women's responses to illustrate each subtheme.

Capable/Energy

Personal unmet expectations were reported with respect to physical functioning. The women were angry when they were physically unable to do all that they expected of themselves, for they reported "I become angry more often when I have not had enough rest" and "when I am exhausted, I become angry easily." They conveyed a disappointment with the fact that their bodies did not respond as they thought they should or could. It became apparent that women expected of themselves that they would have energy and strength, for they identified anger being triggered "when I'm tired and I have a lot of work to do," "when I can't function in ways I was able to two years ago," and "occurs most frequently when I am very physically fatigued." During times when their body fails to support this ideation, anger is identified. A major source of anger within the personal realm related to physical exhaustion. When the subjects were exhausted, anger ensued. Women appeared to believe that they would always have the energy or strength for what was needed, as the following examples of anger triggers depicted:

"When I am sick I am more angry"
"When I haven't had enough rest"
"When I'm tired or feeling overwhelmed"
"When I am tired"
"When I'm extremely tired"
"Usually, when I'm tired"
"When I am tired I get angry easy"

Premenstrual syndrome (PMS) was mentioned by some subjects to specify further when they were not as capable as they expected to be and anger resulted. For example, women reported the following anger triggers:

"PMS time I am shorter of temper, less patient."
"When I'm tired and premenstrual."
"My children can upset me and I usually overreact if I am PMS."

Anger triggers resulting from PMS could be attributed to monthly hormonal changes. The phenomenon of "shifting the focus" is an alternative explanation. One way to overlook a woman's lack of power is to shift the focus to physical problems (Hare-Mustin, 1991). Women's anger triggered by fatigue or even exhaustion could stem from lacking a well-developed sense of personal authority. According to Rampage (1991), personal authority is the ability to know one's own needs and meet them, even when there is pressure from others to conform to their expectations for you. Personal authority means a woman may have to put her needs above those of others around her. She may have to say "no" to demands that deplete her energy.

Capable/Work

Women believe that they should be able to change a situation at work to make it more consistent with their ideations. Subjects reported anger when they lacked the necessary resources or power to change frustrating situations. These responses are illustrative:

> "My anger occurs usually in the work place when adequate staff is not assigned."
> "When work assignments are late."
> "When I'm over-worked, appointments overbooked and short of help."
> "Work. When I am unable to control circumstances re: patient care and staffing situations."
> "Situations which slow down my progress in reaching my goals, ex. dashing to the bank and finding the teller line 15 people long."
> "When asked to do something I really do not want to do but do anyway."
> "Not being offered a choice when I feel I should be, about something which affects me."

Competent/Finances

The second major category within the intrapersonal realm related to financial concerns. For many women the expectation that they would have resources to provide for themselves and their families was evident. Financial concerns were identified as precipitators of anger. Money, or lack thereof, was frequently mentioned as women reported anger "when money becomes very tight" or "when I don't have money to do the things I want to do." One can conclude that women become angry when they do not have financial resources to do what is necessary. Incongruent ideologies regarding competencies in managing money could also trigger anger, as evidenced by women reporting anger with "financial problems, husband not acting responsibly about financial matters"; "finances not taken care of, no money"; "when a bill comes in I can't pay"; and "unexpected financial problems." Their anger was triggered when "managing the checking account and finances"; "concerning money, bills" and "situations involving money, finances." Most people would agree that it is a frustrating and potentially anger-triggering situation to lack money for items needed or strongly desired.

Effective

Other situations of intrapersonal anger triggering emerged. The women expected that they would be able to manage or have control of situations. Women evidenced the belief that they should be effective or possess the ability to produce the desired effects. Perhaps contemporary American society has set women up to believe they should possess superhuman qualities. An inability to effect power according to this definition seemed to trigger anger for women as they described situations in which they, themselves, did *not* produce the desired effects. The following anger-producing situations are illustrative:

"I feel angry when I don't accomplish the goals I've set for myself."
"I become angry when I have little input in what happens to me and sometimes in situations which are beyond my control. Basically when I lose 'control' I am angry and stressed."
"When the situation is out of my control."
"When my words are ignored, one-sided conversations."
"I always run late, not meeting deadlines."
"I become angry when I am afraid I can't control a situation."
"When I feel overwhelmed and out of control."
"I want to get a lot of things done and people poke around and hinder me from doing them."
"Fear, loss of control."

There are many reasons why women perceive lack of control. Goodrich (1991) comments that patriarchy has done a superb job instilling an unequal privilege between husband and wife. So effectively has this been accomplished that many times women do not even recognize the full degree of unfairness. Children grow up expecting certain behaviors from their mother, and as adults they continue the expectation that those behaviors will be passed on to the next generation. Thus it seems natural that women abide by the rules of patriarchy. Because our women were mostly married, with two children and working outside of the home, it could be that their internal expectations for fulfilling their many roles were set too high. The role of a mother is quite demanding all by itself. Even if there is an equal sharing of duties by both parents, there exists the burden of helping children to grow up as responsible humans. According to Asplund (1988) a mother's role has inherent demands that call for constant attention and continual effort. One woman manager that Asplund (1988) interviewed commented that finding time to visit her parents, stay in touch with friends and attend her children's school functions was the most difficult aspect in life; she felt she never had enough time. Perhaps the women in our study felt these same pressures and identified them as an inability to control situations.

Power Within the Interpersonal Realm

Within the interpersonal realm, women expected certain behavior from significant people in their lives. This realm comprised the largest number of responses. Subgroups of family/friends and work associates were identified within the interpersonal realm.

Family/Friends

Family members are identified as frequent precipitators of anger. Spouse, significant others, and children are the predominant sources of anger. Averill (1982) listed several reasons why most people become angry at loved ones, as opposed to strangers: (a) close, continual contact; (b) cumulative transgressions; (c) stronger motivation to get loved ones to change their ways; and (d) confidence that the expression of anger will be tolerated. Several subthemes emerged within the interpersonal/family realm as significant factors. A continuum emerges from what the woman believes can be expected and how much power the woman has to affect the situation. It appears that women are quite aware of ideation which they hold with respect to the actions and behaviors of others. Family and friends are identified as the individual(s) who do not function congruent with the woman's ideation.

Competent. Significant others are expected to be competent; when this is not realized, anger is described:

"Uncooperative family members."
"After a hard day's work; when everyone (the family) comes home and I have to cook and serve my family."
"Twenty-one-year old son not showing any ambition or initiative. Deplorable home situation with alcoholic brother-in-law and his mother."
"When my children consistently disobey—particularly away from home with or in front of other people."
"I feel angry when my husband 'forgets' something I feel is important. I feel angry when my sons are 'late' or 'slow' to act."
"When I'm trying to get my children to help around the house."
"Family members' expectations are sometimes more than I want them to be and cause anger."

"I am most likely to become angry in situations that involve my children. I have little time to myself and the constant power struggles are draining."

Work

Powerlessness in the work force stems from the same gender stereotypes that occur within the family. A qualitative synthesis of literature on women's work found that American women workers exhibited characteristics of high energy, creativity, persistence, and skill while at the same time experiencing discrimination (Needleman & Nelson, 1988). The undervaluing of women's work is evidenced by wage discrimination and job discrimination (Goldin, 1990). Women that manage to break into higher management positions all too often find that they are judged by their ability to perform like a man and not given proper credit for their abilities stemming from a female perspective (Collins, 1988; Statham, 1988). In a study of 40 corporate women holding manager positions, women reported that their gender was associated with discrimination, the need to prove oneself, availability of support and being a minority among the group of managers (Freeman, 1990). Furthermore Freeman (1990) found that the ideology that women are not supposed to work outside the home still exists. Given the combination of conflicting ideologies and a predominantly male authoritative workforce it was little wonder that women identified anger-producing situations at work. Themes of *competent and effective* were used to organize women's reports of anger triggers related to power issues at work.

Competent. Working women identified a belief that others would be able to manage a situation. They additionally believed that others would support and believe in them in the work setting. Situations in which the subjects lacked support from coworkers, supervisors, or subordinates were identified as anger precipitators.

"When I feel I'm being taken advantage of. When I feel I have no control over a situation."
"When there are a lot of things that need to be done and people are taking it easy."
"Sometimes when people try to boss me and I feel I do what I need to do without anyone 'bossing me.'"
"When my subordinates didn't follow my instruction."
"I . . . get upset when my abilities aren't utilized or recognized at times by coworkers."
"When I have to hold my own and then one of my co-workers because they aren't capable of doing their job."
"If somebody tries to manipulate me or dump their work or responsibility on me."

Effective. Women believe that coworkers will be effective and useful. One can conclude from the data that women have clear beliefs about what is appropriate, effective action on the part of coworkers. Situations wherein coworkers are not producing the intended or proper results can lead to anger situations.

> "Disorganized employer."
> "When I am constantly interrupted. When people demand I help them or take on another task, when I already have too much to do."
> "Co-workers make me angry when they complain about work load, census, etc. But are unwilling to work toward situations to make the work more manageable."
> "Procrastination: poor work performance: not meeting deadlines."
> "Students who come to class to socialize and not to learn."
> "Lack of follow-through by others."
> "When someone does not do what is expected of them professionally—when someone can not think for themselves."

Power Within the Extrapersonal Realm

Power issues outside the intrapersonal and interpersonal realm of women also trigger anger. Within the extrapersonal realm women expected global events to be congruent with their personal ideology. Subthemes of *effective and capable* emerged within the extrapersonal realm.

Effective. A subtheme emerged regarding effectiveness of the behavior of people within our society. Women hold expectations regarding society. When an unexpected or unwanted behavior or happening occurs, anger is described.

> "When someone won't listen to me because I'm a woman. When I'm minding my own business and some man says something harassing or threatening."
> "People using me."
> "Other people trying to tell me what to do. Especially what I should do.
> "Everyone expects me to handle everything."
> "Demanding, arrogant people can make me instantly angry."
> "When a person I talk with is always right and I'm wrong, or when I try to tell something that's happened which is really important to me and no one listens."
> "I would say my worst anger is vented at other drivers. I have little tolerance for stupidity-slowness-indecisiveness."

Capable. This group of responses supports an ideation that one would be capable of accomplishing what is demanded but external pressure is so strong that the task cannot be completed. This pressure is not assigned to any particular source but is noted in the following responses:

"When under pressure and requested to change plans without notice."
"Unexpected demands on my time."
"Generally time pressure and/or lack of time makes me feel pushed."
"Things that affect me but are out of my control."
"Something happens unexpectedly and you can't control it."
"When decisions that affect me are made without consulting me."

JUSTICE

The second most frequent theme that precipitated anger was *justice*. The theme of justice is defined as fair, trustworthy, respecting, considerate and correct. Kohlberg's moral development theory (1969), which conceptualizes morality around a core concept of justice, is particularly relevant regarding this theme. According to this theory moral development occurs on three levels, each with two stages. As one progresses through each level, the core concept of justice increases in complexity (Parker, 1990). Women in this study could be identified as operating within levels 2 and 3. The second level of development is characterized by an emphasis on maintaining interpersonal concordance (pleasing others and maintaining interpersonal relationships), and maintaining law and order (performing one's duty and maintaining social order). The third level seeks to maintain social consensus and universal ethical principles. For this level the emphasis is on justice, fairness, and adherence to self-chosen principles (Kohlberg, 1984).

Justice Within the Interpersonal Realm

Within the interpersonal realm women expected to be treated justly by the significant people in their lives. Once again a distinction is made between the subgroups of family/friends and work.

Family/Friends

A betrayal of trust or unfair treatment emerged as significant in precipitating anger toward the family. The subjects give numerous examples of anger precipitated by their family or loved ones not respecting them. Once again, the belief is that one will be treated with respect and dignity, and if reality does not support this belief, then anger results. Typical responses were

"Husband staying out late."
"Son telling lies."
"When boyfriend doesn't show up or doesn't call."
"When my husband spends a lot of money without telling me."
"When my children act hateful."
"Stupidity, disrespect, dishonesty."
"When someone close, especially family, doesn't show me respect."
"Recently a friend that I trusted lied to me and recalling that makes me angry."
"I get mad when husband and son are what I consider inconsiderate."
"When my husband tells me "there you go again" or compares me to my mother!"

Work

Women in this sample believe that the work world should be "just." The women cited numerous examples of disrespect and disregard among coworkers which precipitated anger. The women expected that a certain level of regard would exist between coworkers; when this was absent, anger ensued.

"Untrue accusations by doctors in work setting."
"Being unjustly accused of mistakes on the job."
"When people act ugly toward me."
"When someone talks down to me as if I were stupid."
"Those that involve injustice, that involve situations that I think have been clarified previously—especially when I put time and energy into that clarification, and now here's the problem again."
"Being put down or yelled at in front of a bunch of people. Especially if you are around people you don't know well enough to understand the circumstances."
"When someone uses me as an excuse to lie or lies to me."
"Certain situations at work: being blamed for something I didn't do or being ignored."
"When someone at work tries to prove me wrong in front of others."

Justice Within the Extrapersonal Realm

Factors that were outside of the personal realm of the subjects were also identified as precipitators of anger. Within the extrapersonal realm it emerges that women have expectations and beliefs about what the world should be. If the world does not exemplify the values that the subjects expect, anger is identified. The anger precipitators vary, ranging from careless drivers to the world situation. Women believe that the world will be just and fair, that a moral code exists dictating what exists in the world. This belief includes the belief that the world will be safe and not harm. Illustrative responses included:

"Sexist behaviors."
"Political decisions that I do not agree with in all levels of life experiences."
"War, problems in America, education, gun control (rather lack of), the economy, violence, homelessness, rape, campus problems."
"Violence toward women."
"Threat of harm to me or immediate family, near auto accident, robbery."
"The world situation, war, abuse of power."
"Being used for others' gains."
"When a child takes advantage of my child or hurts her in some way."
"When someone has pushed me too far about a particular stand I have taken or a moral conviction I have."

RESPONSIBILITY

Responsibility was the third theme that emerged as an anger trigger. Events that were incongruent with ideologies of responsibility were identified only within the interpersonal realms of family/friends and work. Women expected the significant people in their lives to act responsibly. They identified numerous situations of irresponsible behavior involving family/friends and work associates. These situations were further delineated as anger triggering.

Responsibility Within the Interpersonal Realm

Family/Friends

The belief that others will be responsible within the family is a major subtheme. Women expect commitment and a certain level of performance from family and friends. One can conclude women expect that their significant others will be reliable and accountable for behavior and share responsibilities. Papp (1991) writes that "There is one issue that cuts across all national boundaries, indeed, all boundaries of race, color, and creed—that is the issue of gender which exists in every country in the world where there are families. It is impossible to talk about love, marriage, sex, intimacy, and childbearing without taking into account gender inequalities." In attempts to equalize household responsibilities Papp (1991) found that oftentimes women and their spouses would get hung up on whose turn it was to do the dishes, instead of tackling their basic attitudes and beliefs about gender roles. Resentment related to the unfair burden of "double duty" colors every aspect of the family relationship. Spouses may pay lip service to equality while their behaviors fail to support their professed commitment. If, for example, the spouse considers mowing the average lawn a few months out of the year equal to the wife's doing laundry for a family of four all year, he should hardly consider this an equal exchange. The realization that others may not share or support the women's expectations of equal duty could be disquieting and anger provoking. Thomas, Albrecht, and White (1984) investigated marital satisfaction in dual-career couples. Their study supported the findings reported by Papp. Spouses reported discrepant perceptions of the amount of involvement the husband had in household and child-rearing activities. Husbands rated themselves as more helpful with chores and child care than their wives perceived them to be. The researchers concluded that clarification and modification of expectations by each partner is necessary to decrease the dissatisfaction resulting from discrepancy between expectations and reality.

The women in our sample expected responsible behavior, and when it did not occur they identified this as anger provoking:

"Husband not doing his share in our home."
"Not getting help around the house."
"Children not sharing in household chores."
"My children don't do as they're told or else being exceedingly difficult (more than usual)."
"Husband not acting responsibly about financial matters."
"When children are not responsible, children misbehave, husband doesn't show love and care, finances not taken care of, no money, ugly words spoken, things not taken care of properly in business, etc."

These findings are congruent with those of Lohr, Hamberger, and Bonge (1988) regarding women's anger arousal in interactions with "insensitive others," usually within one-sided, but familiar, relationships. In contrast, men in their sample were more likely to react angrily to inconsiderate behavior of strangers.

Work

A theme that emerged is the expectation that coworkers should be responsible, and when they fail to be responsible, anger results. Women expect a level of commitment and a certain level of performance from coworkers.

"When at work you've done your job and they put more work on you, while some others get away with doing nothing all day."
"To have to assume responsibility for a task that a person has shirked that have the same capabilities as I have."
"When people are irresponsible on their job or don't care."
"When others do not, or I perceive they do not, take care of their 'fair share' of the day to day responsibilities."
"Co-workers not doing what they are responsible for."
"When other people have "bright ideas" for someone else (me) to do rather than doing it themselves."

NO ANGER

An unexpected finding in this analysis was that some women denied anger experiences. These women could not identify any situations that were not congruent with personal ideations. A total of five women responded that they did not get angry. One respondent left this space blank, and she was added to the "no anger" subgroup. From their words the reader can sense a feeling of pride on the part of these subjects that they do not experience anger. Does this support the notion that anger is construed as negative rather than as a healthy emotion? Or is anger suppressed or repressed so that it is not within the women's conscious awareness?

"Normally do not get angry"
"Rarely feel angry"
"Do not get angry"
"As a personal challenge I do not allow anger to present itself"
"Not angered very often"

TARGETS OF WOMEN'S ANGER

Who are the targets of women's anger experiences? A total of 349 responses to the question "With whom are you likely to become angry?" were identified (see Table 11, Appendix). The interpersonal realm emerges as the largest group which incite anger feelings. More specifically, members of the woman's family are identified. Responses to this question were mainly one word, such as husband or coworker. The subgroup *family* is the highest, closely followed by the subgroup of work. Husband was identified 49 times, closely followed by children 44 times. Consequently, the anger target is someone very close to the woman herself. Women appear to identify a particular person that is the target of the anger situation. Within the work setting, 38 identified

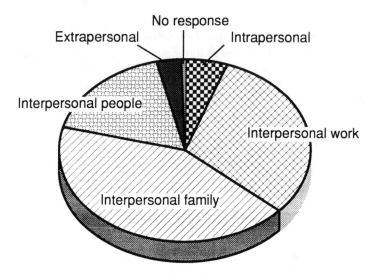

FIGURE 4.3 Targets of women's anger.

coworkers as the anger precipitator, and employees were identified 34 times. The boss or employer only accounted for 9 responses. The targets of anger for women emerge as mainly interpersonal with a small percentage representing anger at self and at society. Occasionally, a respondent would speak of groups of people rather than individuals.

> "Administrators who perceive women or nurses as less capable than their peers in other professions"
> "Controlling men (and women) who appear to be threatened by assertive behaviors, particularly physicians, lawyers, politicians"

Figure 4.3 depicts the distribution of subjects' responses. These findings are consistent with Averill's (1982) report of anger in a community sample.

RECIPIENTS OF WOMEN'S ANGER EXPRESSION

Women were asked, "To whom would you be likely to express the anger?" There were a total of 323 responses (see Figure 4.4; percentages are reported in Table 12, Appendix). The major person with whom anger was shared was identified as a family member. Women reported being more likely to express anger to their family than to anyone else and to their husband more than any other family member. As noted in chapter 3, the freedom to express one's

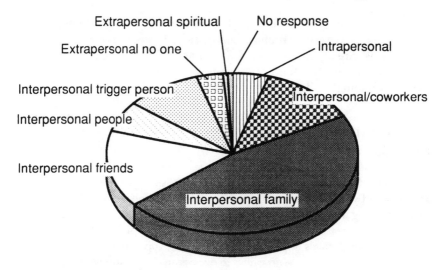

FIGURE 4.4 Anger expression.

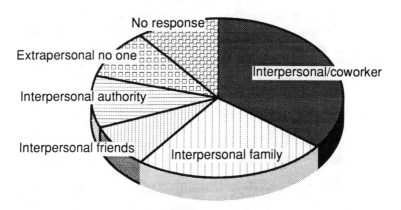

FIGURE 4.5 To whom women would not express anger.

anger may be a benefit of a committed relationship. Children, family, husband, and parents were the subcategories within the code of family. Many respondents identified coworkers as the individual to whom they would express the anger. The identified coworkers included administrative staff, associates, and boss. Additionally friends were identified as persons to whom anger would be expressed. The remaining 20 responses were categorized as "people." This subgroup included all responses that identified people other than family, coworkers, or friends. Importantly, 31 women reported that they would speak directly to the person who triggered their anger. Conceptually we would consider this the healthiest response to an anger situation; however, it was found to depict only 9.6% of the responses.

TO WHOM WOMEN WOULD NOT
EXPRESS ANGER

To explore barriers or constraints on anger expression, women were asked, "To whom would you *not* express anger?" The typical response was a single- word answer naming a person by their relationship to the women. Two hundred nine responses were recorded. Results of these analyses are presented graphically in Figure 4.5; percentages appear in Table 13 (see Appendix). Most women responded that they would be unwilling to discuss anger situations with family and coworkers. In an earlier part of the chapter we reported that situations involving family and friends were frequently identified as anger *triggers*, yet some women (obviously not all, given the findings in the previous section) reported being *unwilling to discuss* the anger situations with them. This finding has several implications for further research. Is the unwillingness to express anger because of fear of alienating family members, lack of assertiveness, gender role socialization, or other factors? Given Averill's (1982) finding that lack of communication often *prolongs* anger, women who fail to express this powerful emotion may be more likely to ruminate about episodes. It would be interesting to follow this group of women in terms of eventual health consequences.

Other individuals were identified in addition to coworkers, family, authority figures, and friends, and were simply categorized as "people." A variety of constraints may prevent anger expression to these individuals. For example, one woman said that she would not express anger ". . . to those that might jeopardize my husband's or my employment, for example, my husband's boss, those in positions of authority several levels *above* my boss, for example, board of governance, or those where jumping levels in the line of authority is inappropriate." This type of constraint is obviously a pragmatic one. The moral ethical aspect of women's decision making about anger expression is evident in the following summary of people to whom one respondent would not express anger:

"Poorly educated or vulnerable individuals"
"Those who do not have authority to change outcome"

Significantly, 22 women did not complete this question. Sixteen women left the space blank and six marked this question with a question mark. This could indicate that the question was confusing for some respondents. Another

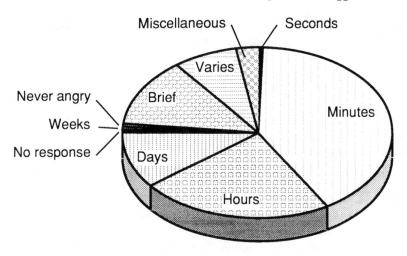

FIGURE 4.6 Duration of women's anger.

possibility is that the question was situation dependent and therefore difficult to answer. In retrospect, asking subjects to describe specific situational constraints would have been valuable.

DURATION OF ANGER EPISODES

Women were asked, "How long does a typical day-to-day anger episode usually last for you?" Although responses ranged from "just a few seconds" to "indefinitely," most women reported anger episodes lasting from minutes to hours (see Figure 4.6; percentages are reported in Table 14, Appendix). Most women move through the anger relatively quickly (41% in a matter of minutes and 64% in less than one day). In the words of one respondent, "I get over my angers quickly and do not hold grudges. I can go on with my life once I've thrown my fit." Twenty responses fell under the category of days. Only one subject reported holding on to anger for weeks. One woman reported a range of days to years. These data indicate that women generally do process their anger rapidly despite its origin within personal ideology. Some responses did not include a numerical measurement of time but instead described episodes as *brief* or *varying*. These responses are reported under the heading "miscellaneous." Nine women report that it depends on the situation. Duration was defined as "the length of time it takes to find a solution to the situation" by one respondent. Another study participant described the duration of her anger as "few minutes—except for husband. Occasionally he stays on my list for days." Another respondent reported considerable variability in the length of anger episodes: "depends on issue and seriousness of etiology of anger. May be minutes, hours, or in one situation where individual prevented meaningful job opportunity, anger continues in a repressed manner."

CONCLUSION

The proposed model of women's anger experience asserts that their anger reflects situations of incongruence between personal ideation and lived experience. These situations have a role/relationship component identified within the intrapersonal, interpersonal, or extrapersonal realms. Once anger is triggered, the woman determines if, when, and to whom she will express the anger. The health significance of this process requires further investigation. The model provides a structure for describing the phenomenon of women's anger.

From the data it emerges that the typical woman feels anger in a situation involving others, either within the family or at work; she will share this feeling with her family, chiefly her husband; and the anger will persist for less than 1 hour. Conversely, the person she is *least* likely to share the situation with is her family. Importantly, only about 9% of women reported that they would express their anger to the person they identified as the trigger of anger. The family emerges as a critical component of the anger experience for women. A paradox becomes apparent in that women reported *the family* as the most frequent response to all the questions asked about anger episodes. Anger episodes emerge from the family dynamics, and evolve within the family realm, however, apparently not in direct dialogue with the family member who is the target of the anger. Further research is needed to determine (a) the precise avenue by which anger experiences evolve within the realm in which they originated and (b) what factors inhibit or facilitate successful resolution of angry incidents—from the woman's viewpoint. Additionally, situations involving friends and coworkers are significant.

Women have firm expectations about themselves, those they care about, and society. These expectations provide the parameters from which women evaluate their life experiences. When they, those they love, or society fail to concur with their ideation, a basic belief is threatened. Anger can then be viewed as reflecting a disappointment in the fact that life is not what women believed it would be. One can conclude that anger reflects a threat to the very core of a woman's life. Perhaps it is an attempt to try to separate from what is not congruent with the woman's belief about life. We believe that the power and health of this emotion must be realized. Women through their anger depictions disclose their beliefs about living, loving, working, and raising children. The results of this data analysis indicate that anger is an important emotion which reflects the essence of the woman involved in the anger experience. Women need to embrace their anger and explore it for what it has to teach them about themselves and what they value most in life.

■5
Women's Anger and Self-Esteem

Margaret Saylor and Gayle Denham

Self-esteem is something probably everyone wants and which everyone definitely needs. We want self-esteem because it increases our chance of finding happiness in life and makes it possible to cope with life's disappointments and changes. We need self-esteem because nothing is as important to psychological well-being. Our level of self-esteem affects virtually everything we think, say and do.

—**L. T. Sanford and M. E. Donovan, Women and Self-Esteem**

SIGNIFICANCE AND DEFINITION OF SELF-ESTEEM

Although there are many definitions of self-esteem, we begin with one of the simplest: having confidence or satisfaction in oneself (Webster, 1976). Self-esteem is widely regarded as the most important of psychological needs (Branden, 1971; M. Rosenberg, 1979; Steffenhagen & Burns, 1987). Over the years students of human nature have asserted that maintaining and enhancing self-esteem provides a driving motivation for how one interprets the world, reacts emotionally, and behaves (Allport, 1961; James, 1890/1950; Kaplan, 1975; Sanford & Donovan, 1985; Snygg & Combs, 1949). The state of California considered self-esteem so crucial that it funded a task force to study self-esteem and social problems, with the goal of finding ways to decrease social problems by increasing self-esteem (Mecca, Smelser, & Vasconellos, 1989). The success of this task force has led not only to similar initiatives in other states but also to the establishment of an International Council for Self-Esteem (Steinem, 1991a).

Self-esteem has been variously defined by such phrases as the "evaluation of the self," "the estimate passed on the self," "evaluative attitudes
toward the self," or "the experience of one's personal self-worth." Self-esteem
has been likened to self-attitudes, self-affection, self-regard, self-worth, self-
respect, self-confidence and self-acceptance. According to Morris Rosenberg
(1979), self-esteem is a component of our self-concept, but differs in that self-
concept relates to the totality of thoughts and feelings about ourselves, our
identity, whereas self-esteem refers to the positive or negative evaluation we
have of that identity.

High self-esteem, then, means a positive evaluation of oneself: an appreciation of one's inherent significance and worth, a positive attitude toward
one's own qualities, and a sense of one's ability to do what one wants (Coopersmith, 1967). In general, self-esteem is proposed to consist of two interrelated
aspects: a sense that one is competent to do what needs to be done, and a
sense of oneself as worthy of love and respect (Branden, 1987; M. Rosenberg,
1979; Smelser, 1989). Sanford and Donovan (1985) propose that in women
self-esteem requires "a sense of significance, a sense of competence, a sense
of connectedness to others balanced by a sense of separateness from them, a
sense of realism about ourselves and the world, and a coherent set of ethics
and values" (p. 38). The sense of being competent, a widely recognized part
of self-esteem, implies an awareness that we have choices and the ability to
choose for ourselves. It reflects the notion of a sense of being in control of
one's own actions and reactions, and of being able to attain goals one has laid
out (Steffenhagen & Burns, 1983). Some people negate the value of self-
esteem, mistakenly confusing it with feelings of superiority, arrogance, and/
or contempt for others. However, a person with a genuine sense of self-worth,
while appreciating personal merits, can also recognize faults. Though not
always "right," a person with high self-esteem can still feel competent to think,
evaluate, and learn from mistakes.

Persons with low self-esteem, on the other hand, have a lack of respect
for themselves, and consider themselves unworthy, inadequate, and seriously
deficient as human beings. They are often characterized by self-depreciation,
helplessness, powerlessness, and depression. Steffenhagen and Burns (1983)
claim that all deviant behavior has its basis in low self-esteem. The California
Task Force on Self-Esteem was founded on the premise that low levels of
self-esteem may lead to self-defeating deviant behavior such as adolescent
pregnancy, substance abuse, or criminal activity (Smelser, 1989). Earlier,
M. Rosenberg (1979) had found social isolation, depression, and anxiety to
be associated with low self-esteem. (It could be proposed in turn that the
socially isolated individual has less opportunity for experiences that enhance
self-esteem.)

Opinions vary as to the *stability* or *variability* of self-esteem. Obviously
high and low self-esteem are not absolutes, but exist along a continuum. Once

formed, the level of global self-esteem seems to remain fairly constant (Crouch & Straub, 1983). Branden (1971) describes self-esteem as a constantly experienced feeling that is part of every other feeling, that is, it is involved in every emotional response. Congruent with this line of thinking are the assertions of Kaplan, Robbins and Martin (1983) that a tendency toward self denigration leads to increased stress, and Hobfoll (1988), who describes self-esteem as an ongoing resource helpful in resisting stress. Conversely, life events and situations can certainly cause fluctuations in self-esteem. Daily experience tells us we feel better about ourselves on some days more than others, and fluctuating self-esteem has been documented in research subjects (Kernis, Grannemann, & Barclay, 1989). The general consensus seems to be that both stability and change characterize self-esteem, with a global self-esteem laid down in childhood serving as a fairly constant baseline from which fluctuations occur (Crouch & Straub 1983; Demo, 1985; Kernis et al., 1989; M. Rosenberg, 1986; Schaefer, 1990). Experiences in which persons perceive themselves responding less than optimally to opportunities, or as unable to control or influence situations important to them, often lead to decreased self-esteem, whereas experiences that produce a sense of competence or significance tend to increase self-esteem. Paradoxically, it seems that self-esteem influences how situations are experienced, and one's response to situations influences self-esteem. Campbell (1990) asserts that persons with low self-esteem are more likely to have unstable self concepts. They think they are valuable sometimes and of low worth at other times. A recent study found some decline in self-esteem during adolescence, a trend more marked in girls (Folkenberg, 1991). After early adulthood, Knox (1977) claims that self-esteem tends to increase until middle age and that it tends to stabilize then, with a single event having less power to increase or decrease self-esteem to any great degree.

Before we move to special considerations of women's self-esteem or the relationship of anger dimensions and self-esteem, practical questions about self-esteem deserve at least a brief mention: Where does self-esteem come from? How does it develop? The following section will look at answers to these questions.

WHERE DOES SELF-ESTEEM COME FROM?

Self-esteem is an attitude or feeling about the self based on all of life experiences and is developed through interaction with the environment in which the experiences occur. Of all environments the home environment has the greatest impact on the development of self-esteem. This is because self-esteem undergoes its greatest development during the first 5 years (Hayes & Fors, 1990). The crucial role of parents in determining children's self-esteem was demonstrated by Coopersmith (1967) in a study of white boys aged 10 to 12. He found that children with high self-esteem had parents who demonstrated concern, attentiveness, and nearly total acceptance of them. Clearly defined and enforced limits, combined with respect and room for individuality within those limits, were also associated with high self-esteem. Not surprisingly, these characteristics were observed primarily in parents with high self-esteem. Both perception of favorable attitudes and treatment by significant others and attainment of valued goals characterized subjects with high self-esteem. Subjects whose parents stressed values of being acceptable and pleasing others were more likely to experience low self-esteem, whereas children whose parents stressed achievement and self-competence were more likely to experience high self-esteem.

Morris Rosenberg (1965, 1979), who also studied self-esteem in children and adolescents, was highly influenced by the work of George Mead (1934); Mead had theorized that social interactions have a major impact on how we think and feel about ourselves. As previously mentioned, M. Rosenberg proposed that self-esteem is the evaluative stance toward the self-concept. He described self-esteem as being developed from reflected appraisals (seeing the self as seen by others), social comparison, and self-attribution regarding one's own behavior, moderated by the *importance* to the individual of the various appraisals, comparisons, and attributions. Like Coopersmith (1967), M. Rosenberg found that parents who placed value on their children (as evidenced by parental interest in their child's activity) were more likely to have children with high self-esteem.

In both the Coopersmith and Rosenberg studies, there was no predictable relationship between social status and self-esteem. One explanation is that children are not held responsible for their social standing, whereas adults are. When M. Rosenberg (1979) used data from a large study by Leonard Pearlin to explore social status and self-esteem in adults, he found moderately positive associations between self-esteem and income, education, and occupation.

SELF-ESTEEM AND GENDER

M. Rosenberg found a general tendency for only children to have higher self-esteem. But when looking at only children by gender, he found that it was boys, not girls, who were especially likely to have high self-esteem. The self-esteem of boys was enhanced if surrounded by female siblings. However, girls' self-esteem was not enhanced if surrounded by male siblings. Another gender difference documented by Rosenberg was a difference in value systems. Rosenberg (1965) assessed the top three values for adolescent boys and girls. Boys listed (a) good at working with hands, (b) good at many things, and

(c) knows many things. Girls listed (a) likeable; (b) friendly, sociable, and pleasant; and (c) kind and considerate. Even though boys also cared about being liked by others, girls gave that characteristic a much higher rating than did boys. In keeping with Rosenberg's proposition that centrality of a value determines how much it influences self-esteem, it would appear that self-esteem might be related more to perceptions of competence in boys and to being liked or loved in girls.

Feminist authors assert that women are more prone to low self-esteem than are men. For instance, in 1971 Bardwick proposed that self-esteem reflects how well persons perform in the roles of their lives and how well their capabilities are used in these roles. She claimed that women are brought up to value a feminine role that focuses on interpersonal interaction and care-taking. However, she saw society valuing achievement activities that tradition-ally have been expected of and pursued by men. Thus low self-esteem in women could be caused by (a) investing themselves in a role devalued by society, a role that does not permit them to use the full range of their poten-tial, or (b) focusing on occupational success (despite the "natural" motivation to focus on nurturing relationships with significant others), a choice that creates self doubt and sometimes guilt (Bardwick, 1971; Bernardez, 1988). In this view, women were doomed to low self-esteem no matter which path they chose.

The preceding theory was first advanced more than 20 years ago, and role expectations for both genders have been undergoing great shifts since that time. Bardwick's (1979) later work proposed that being employed may logically produce higher self-esteem because employment and productivity are culturally valued in our society. Women's need to have mastery or a sense of competence may be more important than has been previously realized. In a study of midlife women, Coleman and Antonucci (1983) found working out-side the home to be the only significant predictor of self-esteem. And Baruch, Barnett, and Rivers (1983), in a study of 300 New England women, found higher self-esteem in employed women than in homemakers, with occupa-tional prestige incrementally associated with higher self-esteem.

There are different perspectives on interpersonal relationships as the basis of women's self-esteem. Hockett (1989) emphasized women's own perceived competence in initiating and maintaining relationships, whereas others have emphasized women's perceptions of how they are viewed by people impor-tant to them (Bardwick, 1979; Baruch et al., 1983; Miller, 1976; Surrey, 1984). In response to the question: "Who am I?" Mulford and Salisbury (1964) found that women with children were more likely to reply in terms of being moth-ers and wives than men were to reply in terms of being fathers and husbands, which supports the notion of relationships being more central to women. In fact, one study found perception of husbands' regard to be the most impor-tant predictor of women's self-esteem. However, for employed women this factor only accounted for 10% of the variability in self-esteem scores; for homemakers, the influence of husband's regard increased to 28% (Meisenhelder, 1986). This finding is congruent with the discovery by Baruch et al. (1983), that husband's approval was much more important for homemakers than for women who were employed. Employed women and homemakers did not differ in self-esteem in the Meisenhelder (1986) study. However, there was greater self-esteem in those employed full time than those employed part time. This unexplored finding might be related to earning power or to high expectations of homemaking tasks for those working only part time. As noted earlier, the major difference was in the degree of influence on self-esteem provided by perceptions of husband's regard. Yet the small amount of women's self-esteem accounted for by this variable indicates that many other factors must be involved. Other factors such as regard from coworkers and a sense of competence in performing the job help contribute to self-esteem for the employed woman.

In the group of women studied by Baruch et al. (1983) homemakers in general had lower self-esteem than those who were employed. However, those who had made a conscious decision that being in the home met their own needs, as well as the needs of others, and who enjoyed and felt competent in the work of homemaking, also exhibited self-esteem. This finding is consistent with the findings for the whole sample that self-esteem was strongly associated with a sense of control over one's life. In the final analysis the woman's own unique pattern of needs and values as well as values of those close to her may influence how employment outside the home impacts self-esteem. The sense of control involved in choosing one's activities is predicted to be accompanied by a sense of mastery and competence. However, it is shocking that one of the major feminist leaders of our time recently revealed her own low self-esteem (Steinem, 1991b).

The literature on self-esteem includes several studies done on male subjects only, as in Coopersmith (1967), and treatises on self-esteem using totally male pronouns and examples, as in Branden (1971). Studies drawn from populations including both sexes have shown inconsistent results, with such investigators as F. Rosenberg and Simmons (1975) and Bush, Simmons, Hutchinson and Blyth (1977–78) reporting lower self-esteem in women, whereas Maccoby and Jacklin (1974) and M. Rosenberg (1965) found minimal differences by gender. Although F. Rosenberg and Simmons (1975) found somewhat lower self-esteem in adolescent girls than in boys, their more striking findings were (a) a markedly higher *instability* of girl's self-concept and (b) much greater self-consciousness regarding how they *appeared* to others. These findings suggest that low self-esteem is associated with greater variability in how one views the self and that females are more responsive to the viewpoint of others than are males.

The fact that women suffer from depression, which typically involves low self-esteem, in much greater numbers than do men might suggest that women are more prone to low self-esteem. But the occurrence of low self-esteem in this clinical syndrome may not be typical of the general population. That is, the fact than an illness more common in women involves low self-esteem does not necessarily mean that low self-esteem is more characteristic of women. However, it can be argued that numerous reasons for low self-esteem in women as a group abound in the social fabric of our lives. Until recently, when groups of people have been referred to, male pronouns have been used, implying that males are the important persons; in marriage a woman has traditionally taken the name of the man. Women have been grossly underrepresented in studies of development and in medical investigations (Gilligan, 1982; Purvis, 1990). Work at which women have traditionally excelled (e.g., child care, teaching, nursing, and other particularly nurturant activities) has been, and remains, undervalued both in terms of financial rewards and of status. When women enter other areas of work we encounter such experiences as being addressed by our first names (when the men around us are addressed as "Mister ____" or "Doctor"), and being expected to take the minutes or bring the coffee. More important, across all work classifications we find lower pay and fewer opportunities for advancement. According to a recently released United Nations report, "The World's Women 1970–1990," worldwide women's pay averages 30% to 40% less than men's, and women hold only 10% to 20% of managerial positions. Likewise, fewer than 10% of legislators were women ("U.N. finds women lag in power, opportunity," 1991).

It is disappointing that a recent survey sponsored by the American Association of University Women revealed that today's high school girls have a poorer self-image than do their male counterparts. These findings were especially significant regarding self-perception of competence in math and science courses (Shearer, 1991), which are courses viewed by many as requiring greater intelligence and having greater potential for lucrative careers. This state of affairs may be due in part to the way teachers respond to boys and to girls. When girls have failure experiences in school, teachers tend to accept failure as though that is the best the girls can do. Boys, conversely, are told that they could do better if they would just try. The message received by the children who observe these differential responses is that boys have more control over their lives than do girls (Pines, 1984).

Comparisons are said to be offensive, and we have little interest in pitting women's self-esteem against that of men. In our opinion the world would be a better place if all persons esteemed themselves highly. We do, however, hope to shed some light on women's self-esteem and how it relates to various aspects of daily life, as well as to the experience and expression of anger. We turn now to consideration of the relationship between self-esteem and anger.

SELF-ESTEEM AND ANGER

One theorist proposes that "our emotions, to put the matter bluntly, are nothing other than our attempts to establish and defend our self-esteem" (Solomon, 1976, p. 100). This notion certainly seems to fit when applied to anger. As is mentioned numerous times in this book, anger is a complex emotion. One of the major mechanisms of anger is a response to threats—to us, to those we love, to our possessions. One of the greatest threats we experience is threat to our self-esteem, which produces anxiety with anger often quickly following. As uncomfortable as anger is for many of us, it can be preferable to anxiety, as it lays the blame outside ourselves. Gormley and Gormley (1984) found in college age (18–25) women that situations associated with anger, in descending order, were characterized by

1. Failing to achieve success in situations in which success was expected
2. Feeling treated disrespectfully by someone significant
3. Perceiving social rejection
4. Experiencing disagreement from others

Each of these situations is related to self-esteem; in each, anger could be seen as warding off anxiety. These findings are congruent with findings from an exploratory study of anger in a community sample, in which loss of self-esteem was cited by 65% of participants as a major instigator of anger (Averill, 1982). In the same vein, restoring status and power (and thus presumably, self-esteem) in an experimental situation has been shown to lower hostility (Worchel, 1961).

In a study of college students designed to investigate both level and stability of self-esteem as predictors of anger arousal and hostility, persons with a high level of self-esteem that was relatively *stable* were the least prone to experience anger. However, those who were high in self-esteem but who had large short-term *fluctuations* in self-esteem were the most likely to experience anger. Persons scoring low on self-esteem fell some place between these two extremes. The tendency of these low self-esteem individuals to be prone to anger was not related to fluctuations in self-esteem (Kernis et al., 1989). Wide fluctuations in self-esteem may reflect a high degree of sensitivity to feedback from others, with the self-esteem of the moment greatly dependent on the latest social interactions. For those who are sensitive in this manner but manage to attain periodic higher self-esteem, there is conceivably more to lose when a threat is encountered than for those who never achieve a high level. The generalizability of the Kernis et al. (1989) study is limited because of its college student sample, with payment for participation.

Averill (1982) proposed that those with both high *and* low extremes of self-esteem may have less tendency to experience anger in response to a threat:

high self-esteem persons because they do not perceive the experience as a threat and low self-esteem individuals because they accept the negative evaluation as deserved. In contrast to this contention the preponderance of literature suggests that persons low in self-esteem tend to become angry easily in comparison to those with high self-esteem (Hockett, 1989; Houston & Vavak, 1991; Rosenbaum & de Charms, 1961; Worchel, 1961). Thomas (1991) proposed that when self-esteem is low, we may have a global tendency to interpret events in a manner that produces anger, that is, be high in what is called "trait anger." This is an alternative explanation for Hockett's (1989) finding of higher awareness of anger in women with low self-esteem, which she attributes to anger *causing* low self-esteem rather than low self-esteem being a predisposition to anger. Indeed, a complicating factor in the self-esteem anger linkage for women is that many of us were brought up to believe that anger is an unacceptable emotion; therefore, when we are angry, diminished self-esteem results (Bernardez, 1987; Bernardez-Bonesatti, 1978; Miller, 1983). It is possible that a vicious cycle can be set up in this manner, for example, low self-esteem predisposes to feeling angry, which predisposes to low self-esteem.

In the study by Hockett (1989), women with high self-esteem reported higher levels of verbal expression of anger (but not of physical expression) than those with low self-esteem. Interpretation of this finding is difficult because of some confounding of anger and aggression, and of the terms "expression" and "aggression," so that it is unclear what kind of expression of anger was considered. Hockett's (1989) analysis used anger and its expression as predictors of self-esteem, a view in keeping with the popular tradition that holds that suppressing anger or inhibiting its expression leads to turning anger against oneself, thus producing low self-esteem and depression. This same school of thought holds that venting one's anger leads to increased self-esteem. A popular 1970s example of this school of thought is portrayed in *The Angry Book* by Theodore Rubin (1970).

However, another school of thought (typified by Harriet Lerner's *Dance of Anger*, 1983) proposes that venting anger does not solve underlying problems and in fact leads to lowered self-esteem. This view has been substantiated in Brown's study (1976, cited in Tavris, 1989) of women after divorce in which the researcher found that expressing anger did not lead to increased self-esteem or to feeling better. Lerner (1983) specifically differentiated between "venting" anger and discussing conflicts in a constructive problem-solving manner that establishes one's boundaries. To the extent that expressing one's anger would foster control over the situation, we might expect that it *could* lead to increased self-esteem, given the relationship of feelings of competence to self-esteem. In our view, directionality may proceed both ways, with self-esteem and the experience and expression of anger continually affecting each other.

Study Findings

We now turn to the findings from our sample of women regarding relationships of anger and self-esteem. We measured self-esteem with the Rosenberg Self-Esteem Scale (RES), a 10-item scale to which the respondent indicates "strongly agree," "agree," "disagree," or "strongly disagree." These responses are scaled on a 1 to 4 scale; thus scores range from 10 (lowest self-esteem) to 40 (highest self-esteem). To avoid response bias, half of the items are worded in such a way as to require reverse scoring. M. Rosenberg (1965) reported construct validity of the RES based on clear (negative) relationships between depression and self-esteem, and positive relationship with peer evaluations. Convergent and discriminant validity were established via the multitrait multi-method framework proposed by Campbell and Fiske (1959); correlations of two comparisons of the Coopersmith Self-Esteem Inventory with the RES were .55 and .65, which Wylie (1989) judged to be adequate. Rosenberg developed the scale to be a unidimensional measure of self-esteem, assuming that a person weighs the varying personal importance of her own unique set of attributes in arriving at a response reflecting overall self-esteem (Wylie, 1989). The RES has been widely used across ages, nationalities, sexes, self-esteem levels, ethnicity, and psychological conditions. Of these studies several have used factor analysis to explore if self-esteem, as measured by the RES, is truly unidimensional or is composed of various factors. Results are mixed, with some investigators finding it unidimensional and others explicating two: one factor consisting of self-derogation, negative self-esteem, and self-depreciation; the second factor consisting of defense of self-worth, self-confidence, and positive self-esteem (Wylie, 1989). Carmines and Zeller (1974), who found two factors, characterized them as "positive self-esteem" and "negative self-esteem" factors. On further investigation, including correlations with criterion variables, they concluded that their factors actually "seem to tap the same rather than different dimensions." For our study, we considered self-esteem, as measured by the RES, to be unidimensional, existing on a continuum of high to low.

Our research questions regarding the complex interrelationships of anger and self-esteem were

1. What is the relationship between level of self-esteem and overall tendency to experience anger (trait anger)?
2. What are the relationships between self-esteem and the other anger variables?
3. How do relationships between self-esteem and anger dimensions vary among nonclinical, medical, and psychiatric groups?
4. How do those women very high and very low on self-esteem compare on anger dimensions?

We first sought to answer the question: What is the relationship of self-esteem and overall tendency to become angry? Congruent with Thomas's (1991) formulation that self-esteem is a factor in general propensity to become angry, we found lower self-esteem to be related to a higher level of trait anger in this sample (see Table 15, Appendix). This finding conflicts with Averill's (1982) proposal that persons lower in self-esteem may be less apt to become angry, but supports the model proposed by Thomas (1991) and is congruent with previous studies (Hockett, 1989; Houston & Vavak, 1991; Rosenbaum & deCharms, 1961; Worchel, 1961). For instance, Rosenbaum and deCharms (1960) found that persons with high self-esteem became angry less easily. Their interpretation was that persons high in self-esteem might have a certain lack of sensitivity to negative comments of others or have a tendency to interpret events in a way that does not instigate anger. Although the Rosenbaum and deCharms study was performed on college students, a recent study of employed adult women supports the same notion. Women with high self-esteem reported significantly less awareness of anger than did women with low self-esteem (Hockett, 1989).

What are the relationships between self-esteem and various dimensions of anger, once experienced? Using the full sample, negative correlations with self-esteem were found for all anger variables, with the exception of anger-discuss (see Table 15, Appendix). The negative relationship of self-esteem with anger symptoms was by far the most significant finding, that is, women with higher self-esteem reported fewer physical symptoms in response to anger. High self-esteem women in our sample also reported less of a tendency to brood or ruminate over anger incidents as reflected by scores on the cognitive anger scale, less tendency to vent their anger outwardly in a blaming way, and slightly less tendency to hold anger in. The one positive relationship was that women with higher self-esteem were more likely to discuss their anger.

In summary, for our total sample of women, higher self-esteem was related to less of a tendency to become angry, as well as to a lower likelihood of converting anger into physical symptoms, or ruminating over anger producing events. Self-esteem was positively associated with a tendency to discuss anger in a nonblaming way. Interestingly, lower self-esteem was related to both venting anger *and* keeping it in, and the relationship was stronger for self-esteem and anger out (venting). To further explore these relationships, regression analyses were performed to discover the strongest predictive relationships (see Tables 16 and 17, Appendix). Using anger variables as the dependent variables, lower self-esteem was found to be strongly predictive of anger symptoms and somewhat less strongly associated with anger cognitions. In descending order of amount of variance accounted for, low self-esteem was also predictive of trait anger, anger-out, and angry temperament, and all of these relationships were significant. When self-esteem was used as the dependent variable in a regression including other study variables, most of the explained variance was due to depression and perceived stress. However both anger symptoms and anger-out added to the prediction.

How do relationships between self-esteem and anger dimensions vary among the nonclinical, medical, and psychiatric groups in our sample? The findings for the nonclinical group were all congruent with (and very close to) the relationships for the aggregate sample, reflecting the large proportion of respondents who fit in this category (see Table 15, Appendix). The one finding consistent across all groups was the negative relationship of self-esteem with anger symptoms. For women in the psychiatric group, as for those in the nonclinical group, lower self-esteem was also related to a greater tendency to (a) brood or ruminate over anger incidents, (b) experience somatic symptoms, and (c) keep anger in. (Although these correlations were of greater magnitude for the psychiatric group, statistical significance was less, because of the smaller sample size.) The cluster and strength of these relationships, combined with the absence of relationship between anger-out and self-esteem in the psychiatric group, may help explain the focus in clinical literature on anger-in as detrimental. Earlier theories and studies focused mainly on people who presented themselves for psychological help. It is probable that many of those individuals did have difficulty managing anger and needed to learn how to deal with it in an effective way. The negative association of anger-in with self-esteem could lead one to think self-esteem might be enhanced by helping people learn to get their anger expressed. However, the finding that low self-esteem was also related to *venting* anger in the nonclinical group gives support to the notion that neither "stuffing it" nor "shouting it" is the answer to handling anger in a way that promotes self-esteem.

It is of note that when the groups were examined separately, the relationship of lower self-esteem to higher trait anger showed up only in the nonclinical group; for the psychiatric and medical groups, correlations were nonsignificant. In other words, in *healthy* women, the higher the self-esteem, the less the tendency to become angry in response to provocation. The meaning of these differences is not clear. It may be that women who are receiving care for a medical or psychiatric condition feel justified in venting anger, and it thus does not lower their self-esteem.

The medical group differed from both the nonclinical and psychiatric groups in the lack of significant relationship between self-esteem and unhealthy anger cognitions, a finding for which we have no current explanation. Conversely, the magnitude of the positive correlation between discussing anger and self-esteem was greater for the medical group than for the nonclinical group. It may be that being able to discuss negative emotions, especially anger, in the midst of medical problems serves a positive function in maintaining self-esteem. No significant relationship between anger discuss and self-esteem was found in the psychiatric group.

Finally, how do those women very high and very low on self-esteem compare on anger dimensions? To answer this question we compared scores using *t* tests, on trait anger and its two subscales, anger cognitions, anger-in, anger-out, anger symptoms, and discussion of anger for the groups of women highest and lowest on the Rosenberg scale, that is, the upper and lower quartiles (25%) (see Table 18, Appendix). The tests were run on both the nonclinical sample and the entire aggregated sample to see if findings were comparable. When these high and low scorers on self-esteem were compared, the results were illuminating. There were highly significant differences on anger dimensions between women high and low on self-esteem, with similar findings for the full sample and the nonclinical sample. Those with high self-esteem were much less likely to convert their anger into physical symptoms (the greatest difference) or to continue thinking angry thoughts. They were also less likely to use either suppression of anger or venting of anger as a mode of anger expression. Significant differences between high and low self-esteem groups for both the nonclinical sample and the entire sample, for the anger variables tested, were congruent with the total sample correlations and gave added strength to the findings. In theory, hypersensitivity to criticism, opinions, and behaviors of others may make persons with low self-esteem more susceptible to unhealthy anger cognitions. Examples of anger cognitions, as mentioned in chapter 3, are thinking about what happened over and over again; thinking the provocation was deliberate; becoming overwhelmed with the feeling; calling the other person names; and thinking how unfair the situation is. The woman with low self-esteem may increase her anger and further lower her self-esteem by such cognitions as thinking that the situation "proves" someone does not regard her positively or that she is powerless in the situation or that her worth has been attacked. If she suppresses her anger and depends on her own interpretation of the event via anger cognitions, there is no opportunity for her perceptions to be validated or invalidated from other sources. If, on the other hand, her cognitions involve calling the other person names and concentrating on unfairness, she may vent her anger outwardly but still keep the angry situation alive by continuing the same thought process.

Indeed, in our sample, women with low self-esteem also tended to have specific thoughts about their anger experience. They tended to think that people deliberately provoked them and were unfair, or they continuously replayed the event in their mind to the point of obsession. We have no way of knowing whether their perceptions were faulty or accurate. Faulty perception in this instance would be the mistaken thought that something someone said or did was intended as a put-down. Perception is influenced by self-esteem (Allport, 1961; Kaplan, 1975). As suggested earlier, low self-esteem can presumably result in faulty perceptions that indicate threat when none is intended. Continuing to think thoughts related to these perceptions can set up a vicious cycle of increased anger and lower self-esteem.

As we have seen, study participants with low self-esteem typically used unhealthy modes of expression for anger. Compared with women with higher evaluations of their self-worth, these subjects suppressed their anger (held it in), or they expressed it in an attacking or blaming way (vented it). Unfortunately these modes of expression could potentially lower self-esteem even further. Keeping anger in prevents communication and problem solving, and keeps a woman feeling powerless. Venting may result in the person who was blamed or attacked by the woman responding by withdrawing love, avoiding her, or counterattacking, invoking cultural prohibitions against women acting in such a manner. Either of these instances can be internalized as signals that her worth is low and be perceived as further threats to self-esteem. A summary of these relationships is presented in the model in Figure 5.1.

Conversely, women with high self-esteem were more likely to discuss their anger rationally. This choice of expressing anger has been shown by several investigators to be more prevalent in women (Averill, 1982; Harburg, Blakelock, & Roeper, 1979; Riley, Treiber, & Woods, 1989; Thomas, 1989; Thomas & Williams, 1991). Now it appears that in women it is even more prevalent in those higher in self-esteem. Evidently the woman with high self-esteem does not have to busy herself with protecting a fragile sense of self, but can identify the salient aspects of the anger producing situation and approach it from a problem-solving stance.

CASE STUDIES OF WOMEN LOW AND HIGH IN SELF-ESTEEM

Physical symptoms such as headache, shakiness, and tension can result when emotions of anger are ignited. In this study women with low self-esteem were not only more likely to become angry but also were *highly* likely to experience physical symptoms.

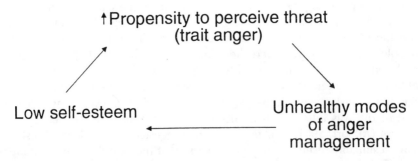

FIGURE 5.1 Relationships of self-esteem and anger dimensions in women.

Susan

Susan, a 36-year-old woman in this study, scored very low on self-esteem. She has been divorced for 11 years and has one 18-year-old child who just left home. Susan is likely to become angry when people put pressure on her. She typically stays angry for several hours and is not likely to tell anyone, even her family, about her anger. Anger symptoms she reported being likely to experience included getting shaky or nervous, feeling her heart pounding, feeling tense, getting a choking feeling or lump in the throat, breathing faster and deeper, feeling weak, and getting a headache. She was also very likely to act as though nothing happened, keep it to herself, apologize even though she was right, and feel depressed. She definitely suppressed her anger. Susan was hospitalized in a psychiatric unit when she participated in the study. She was depressed and felt sad, hopeless, guilty, and generally unable to complete even simple typical day-to-day activities successfully. Susan reported that she almost always kept thinking about anger events over and over again, kept thinking of getting even, seemed to get caught up and overwhelmed with feeling anger, and lost the ability to pay attention to anything else. These angry cognitions in a woman with low self-esteem illustrate well findings previously identified.

Not all women with low self-esteem who report multiple anger symptoms suppress their anger. Some express their anger by attacking or blaming others. This is what the next case demonstrates.

Jodi

Jodi, a 35-year-old single parent of an 8-year-old, has been married four times and is currently divorced. She initiated the divorce process. She has seen a doctor more than 30 times in the past year and takes many prescribed drugs, smokes one-and-a-half packs of cigarettes a day, and has about 10 drinks of alcoholic beverages a week. Her self-esteem was very low, and like Susan she was a patient in a psychiatric unit at the time of this study. She described herself as a hot-headed, quick-tempered person with a fiery temper who said nasty things when angry. She was very likely to get things off her chest and take it out on others when angered, and also somewhat likely to blame someone else. She felt symptoms of tension, headache, weakness, nervousness, and shakiness. She also felt depressed, in poor health, irritated, worried, extremely sad, hopeless, and guilty. Unlike Susan, Jodi let her anger out; like Susan, however, Jodi reported many anger symptoms and had a very low self-esteem score.

Now let's examine a high scorer on self-esteem.

Lana

Lana, a 36-year-old white female, had been married to the same partner for 11 years, and had two sets of twins ages 18 months and 4½ years. Her career as a social worker had been put on hold to stay home with the children. In addition to caring for the four preschoolers, her husband had a son from a previous marriage for whom she was responsible at intervals—a task she considered stressful at times. Lana's change in roles from paid worker to homemaker and the never-ending energy requirements involved in being major caretaker for four preschoolers (as well as shouldering stepmothering responsibilities) indicate that her life was inherently stressful. The most frequent objects of Lana's anger were her children. The anger was usually triggered when she was "tired" coupled with the children "being exceedingly difficult" or failing to "do as they're told." She was most likely to express anger to children and spouse, but cited no one to whom she would *not* express anger. In her angry episodes, which usually lasted about 10 minutes, Lana was not very likely to hold her anger in; however, while "flying off the handle" and "feeling like hitting someone," she did not *actually* attack or blame others. Instead, in common with others high in self-esteem, she tended to discuss her anger rationally. Although she was somewhat likely to experience tension, quickening pulse and faster, deeper breathing when angry, she was not very likely to have a headache, or feel nervous, shaky, or weak. Rather than feeling sad, like a failure, guilty, or depressed, she reported feeling confident, in control, and able to cope with activities of daily living.

We have looked at how self-esteem relates to women's experience and expression of anger, whether they are presenting for mental or physical health care or carrying on life in the community. We will now explore other aspects of self-esteem for women in our study.

RELATIONSHIPS OF SELF-ESTEEM WITH OTHER STUDY VARIABLES

The women we surveyed agree that self-esteem is important: 59% of them included self-esteem in their top four values (value choices will be discussed in more detail in chapter 7). When we examined correlations of self-esteem with other study variables, there was no relationship with income, but education was associated with higher self-esteem. Self-esteem varied little by occupational group; the mean score was the same for human service workers, secretaries, and professional owners/managers. Mean score for homemakers was only 1 point below the others (see Table 19, Appendix).

Women higher in self-esteem tended to see themselves as healthier; indeed, in keeping with our expectations and the findings of Antonucci and Jackson (1983), self-esteem was highest in the nonclinical group. Next were women in the medical group, followed by psychiatric outpatients. Self-esteem was lowest in women who completed our survey while inpatients on a psychiatric unit (scores are contained in Table 20, Appendix). The views of clinicians who find problems with self-esteem inherent in psychological problems are thus supported.

As mentioned earlier, our self-esteem is strongly influenced by the way we think other people—particularly those important to us—evaluate us. Thus, for all women except for the psychiatric patients the amount of perceived affection received from significant others (a component of social support) was strongly related to self-esteem. For women with medical problems this relationship was even stronger than for other women.

Two of the strongest findings held true across all groups. The first was that women high in self-esteem tended to perceive less stress in their daily lives. This supports the view of Hobfoll and Lieberman (1987) that self-esteem serves as a *resistance factor* against stress. Second, women with low self-esteem tended to be depressed, a finding in keeping with the theoretical formulations and definitions of depression. These findings are explained more fully in the chapters on stress and depression.

Thus, all our findings are congruent with Thomas's (1991) conceptualization of women's anger. In her model, appraisal concepts (self-esteem, values, perceived stress and perceived support) were proposed to directly affect anger expression modes. Women with low self-esteem in our study reported high perceived stress and either a lack of clarity regarding values or an inability to live by their values. Only one woman among those scoring lowest on the Rosenberg Self-Esteem Scale was married; most had been divorced at least once. Although an absence of spouse could result in lower perceived support, our interpretation is that this finding is more global, and these low self-esteem women felt less support from all important persons.

IMPLICATIONS

If higher self-esteem could help a woman be less prone to anger, less likely to develop anger associated physical symptoms, less likely to be troubled by recurring angry thoughts, and less likely to use maladaptive modes of expression, how might one go about helping a woman increase her self-esteem? The first step for the counselor or other health professional in implementing interventions to enhance self-esteem is to recognize that it *can* be altered. For some people the notion that basic self-esteem seems to be formed in early childhood provides a sense of hopelessness about the possibility of change. However, there is evidence that ongoing life experiences also impact self-esteem, and that new experiences can be provided to increase self-esteem (Crouch & Straub, 1983; Lerner, 1983; Sanford & Donovan, 1985; Watson & Bell, 1990; Yahne & Long, 1988).

One key area amenable to change lies in the area of cognitions, or "self-talk." This refers to the internal dialogue or thoughts running through the minds of persons in response to events of their lives. These thoughts interpret the meaning of events and in turn influence emotion and behavior (Beck, Rush, Shaw, & Emery, 1979; Burns, 1980). Faulty cognitions are often precipitants of feelings of low self-esteem. For instance, if a colleague fails to return a "good morning" a person with high self-esteem might think, "she must be distracted," whereas a person with low self-esteem might think, "she doesn't like me," or "she must be mad at me." To go a step further, if it were determined that the colleague did fail to respond out of dislike, the person with high self-esteem would tend to say to herself, "That's too bad, but I can't expect everyone to like me," whereas the low self-esteem person's interpretation would more likely be, "There must be something wrong with me," or "I'm worthless." Stanwyck (1983) attributes these tendencies to self-consistency theory, that is, people tend to behave and to interpret their experience in ways that confirm self-judgments. In other words, persons with low self-esteem tend to experience their world as saying to them, "You're not worth much." Without conscious attention, low self-esteem tends to keep reinforcing itself, even after external successes.

Another type of faulty cognition is in unrealistic expectations of oneself. Common examples are expectations of being the "perfect" wife, mother, housekeeper, student, or whatever. In William James's (1890/1950) view, self-esteem is related to how well persons are able to meet the goals they set. Making perfection the goal clearly sets one up for failure and reduction in self-esteem (Steffenhagen, 1990; Steffenhagen & Burns, 1987). Setting *realistic* goals and accomplishing them can be an avenue for enhancing self-esteem. Crouch and Straub (1983) suggest that when helping clients set goals it is useful to explore the person's ideal and perceived self-images, and discrepancies between and within them, to help avoid unrealistic expectations. To help correct faulty cognitions either regarding external events or one's own goal setting, counselors may want to assign clients to read books such as *Feeling Good* (Burns, 1980) and *Celebrate Yourself* (Briggs, 1977) to augment explanations and exercises given in person.

Behavioral changes conducive to increasing self-esteem are varied, with effectiveness primarily demonstrated through anecdotal evidence rather than in well-controlled studies. However, there does seem to be consensus that positive changes can be made (Baruch et al., 1983; Briggs, 1977; Crouch & Straub, 1983; Watson & Bell, 1990). Baruch et al. (1983), on the basis of their findings in more than 300 women, strongly advise women (especially home-makers) to develop interests outside the family and undertake activities that provide positive feedback from other sources. Even with the shifting of role expectations in our culture, there is evidence that women are still seen as the primary nurturers, both at home and on the job (Gilligan, 1982). It has been suggested that women should turn the Golden Rule around and "do unto themselves as we do unto others" (Povich, 1992, p. 68). Making sure her own needs are attended to *increases* a woman's self-esteem.

Positive self-talk (or affirmations) are also said to be useful in increasing self-esteem (Briggs, 1977; Knowles, 1981). Clients can be instructed to write affirmations about *true* positive valued attributes on small index cards and post them in places sure to catch attention such as the bathroom mirror or just inside a desk drawer. Or the client might choose one affirmation to be repeated to herself throughout the day. Another use of self-talk is in chang-ing *passive* phrases, such as "It makes me . . . ," "I can't . . . ," "I must . . . ," and so on, to *active* alternatives, such as "I choose . . . ," "I decided . . . ," and so on. Crouch and Straub (1983) encourage health care providers to model this active language in interactions with clients to reinforce the mind-set of choosing and acting rather than being passively acted on.

As was proposed earlier in this chapter, and supported through analysis of our data, anger and self-esteem seem to have a reciprocal relationship. Low self-esteem predisposes toward feeling angry, as well as anger symptoms and unhealthy anger cognitions, whereas anger symptoms and anger-out (venting of anger) contribute to low self-esteem. These findings have implications for women who themselves might learn to use the cues of physical symptoms or recurring angry thoughts to identify and to respond effectively to angry situ-ations in a manner conducive to restoring self-esteem. Lerner (1983) speaks of using anger as a clue that something is not right, clarifying the issue, then communicating clearly with the person(s) involved in a problem-solving man-ner. Two tasks are at issue here: (a) clarifying what is wrong in a particular situation, (e.g., going from anger symptoms to "I am angry because my rights are being infringed on") and (b) stating what one wants in the particular situ-ation in an assertive, nonblaming way that leads to problem solving (e.g., "When you don't want me to go out with my friends, I feel really trapped. I'm going to go because it is fun for me, but I am willing to sit down and figure out when we can do something together"). Although these skills take much work to operationalize, a patient counselor can help the client learn to be assertive about needs and wants, and thereby help increase self-esteem.

Because one of the major sources of self-esteem is positive regard from others, support groups are a logical medium for efforts to increase self-esteem. These groups often use a variety of the methods listed. Although James and Greenberg (1989) propose that some women are better at identifying feelings and may benefit more from support groups than others, Yahne and

Long (1988) reported positive results from use of support groups to raise self-esteem for graduate and undergraduate college women, aged 21 to 62. Subjects were assessed to screen out any severe pathology or crisis situations, then all participants took pretests and posttests of self-esteem. Two treatment groups each met 2 hours a week for 6 weeks; a control group was assigned to a "wait" condition. Treatment groups consisted of skills training, professional and peer counseling, and opportunities for mutual support. At the end of 6 weeks, those in treatment groups had made significant gains in self-esteem compared with the control group. These support groups were thought to be successful because they: (a) facilitated open, honest discussion; (b) alleviated social isolation; (c) decreased individual feelings of being very different from normal; (d) assisted women to explore their own uniqueness; and (e) provided peer support and peer feedback. As we have seen previously, low self-esteem includes feelings of isolation, inadequacy, and being misunderstood; thus, actions to assist in alleviating these characteristics should logically increase self-esteem. A corollary of the value of positive support from others may be that women should take care to avoid "toxic" situations (i.e., ones in which their self-esteem is chronically assaulted).

One option for a woman who needs to increase her self-esteem is intensive individual therapy; care providers such as nurse practitioners and family physicians may be instrumental in bringing this about through judicious referrals. Such a decision may well be made contingent on the amount of distress the woman is experiencing, and her openness to referral as well as available resources of time and money. If individual psychotherapy is indicated great care needs to be taken in choosing a therapist who considers women, their development, and their work as of equal importance with men's.

Bernard (1988) suggests that education of women should place first priority on assisting them in the development of a positive self-image. Women need to learn that their personal experiences are just as valuable and valid as those of men, that they do not have to be like men to be worthy, and that they have a right to define the human situation based on female experiences as much as men have a right to define them based on male experiences. As women increase their self-worth, their frustration level associated with self-deprecating thoughts and perceptions of insults to self-esteem, should be lowered, decreasing the need to become angry. The goal is *not* to stop being angry or feeling insulted completely. Situations do occur in which anger is the most appropriate response. Higher levels of self-esteem enable a person to view situations more realistically and respond more appropriately. Maintaining high self-esteem may require continuing vigilance along with practice of self-esteem enhancing behaviors to avoid falling back into lifelong patterns that lower self-esteem when new stressors arise. Hayes and Fors (1990) caution that self-esteem is resistant to change and may require repeated, continual efforts for lasting change to occur. Hope is realistic, however, in light of the possibility for change asserted by Crouch and Straub (1983), and results reported by helping professionals such as Sanford and Donovan (1985) and Yahne and Long (1988). Our study found that many women are already very high in self-esteem. Their characteristics of tending to discuss anger rationally in a problem-solving way may help provide a model for increasing self-esteem. Coming from the other perspective, efforts to increase self-esteem have potential for decreasing the tendency to become angry. Our findings support a reciprocal relationship between anger characteristics and self-esteem, giving clues to help enrich women's lives.

■ 6
Stress, Role Responsibilities, Social Support, and Anger

Sandra P. Thomas
and Madge M. Donnellan

1   cup crushed ego
1   teaspoon job discrimination
¼   teaspoon chauvinism
1   well-beaten path to the washing machine
½   teaspoon grated nerves
1   pinch from a man on the street
1   dash from the dentist and home in heavy traffic to release
    the baby sitter

*Mix all ingredients together and stir violently. Cook until you get a
slow burn and then add 1 last straw. Serves 53 percent of the population.*

**—Author of the "Stress-Anger Recipe" is unknown; in column
by Ina Hughs in the Knoxville News-Sentinel, April 30, 1992**

Although we may chuckle at the above recipe, the stress-anger connection
for contemporary women is a very real phenomenon that warrants careful
examination by scientists. Much of what we know about stress is based on
studies of men (Frankenhaeuser, 1991; Rodin & Ickovics, 1990). Although
parallels exist as more women enter the workforce and experience work-
related stress, differences are emerging in current research on women. Dur-

112

ing the past decade, women's mortality advantage over men has been steadily declining, concurrent with dramatic changes in life-style and social roles for women (Verbrugge & Wingard, 1987), although reasons for the decline are still being debated. As noted in Chapter 1, Witkin (1991) claims American women are more stressed than ever. In this chapter we explore the sources of women's stress and relationships among stress, role responsibilities, social support, and anger dimensions.

REVIEW OF LITERATURE

Caplan, who shared his thinking about stress after 30 years of study of individuals' responses, defined this phenomenon as follows: "a condition in which there is a marked discrepancy between the demands made on an organism and the organism's capability to respond, the consequences of which will be detrimental to the organism's future in respect to conditions essential to its well-being" (Caplan, 1981, p. 414). The individual's assessment of a stressor is based on his or her perceptions and expectations, which are influenced by the traditions of the cultural reference group and the "perceptive set" derived from life experiences. Caplan's Harvard group has placed particular emphasis on the erosion of a person's usual cognitive and problem-solving capacities in stressful situations. Caplan contends that the magnitude of these changes is related to the intensity of *emotional arousal* and *dysphoria*. We will have more to say a bit later in the chapter about the link of stress with anger arousal.

The consequences of stress have a profound impact on the quality and quantity of our lives. Up to 75% of all medical disorders are directly attributable to stress including cardiovascular disease and some cancers. Twenty million Americans suffer from stress-induced physical illnesses. Annual costs are estimated to be in the billions of dollars, for example, production losses of $60 billion because of physical illness and $17 billion because of mental illness (Hughes, Pearson, & Reinhart, 1984); these figures do not take into account the staggering costs of health care and treatment.

Research on stress had its roots in the work of scientists investigating stress as a response, specifically, the systemic biological response to environmental stressors (e.g., lack of oxygen). Selye's work depicted "stress as an orchestrated defense operated by physiological systems designed to protect the body from environmental challenge to bodily processes" (Hobfoll, 1989). Subsequently, researchers focused on stress as a stimulus, studying major life events such as divorce, bereavement, or debilitating illness. The pioneers in this area were Holmes and Rahe (1967), who developed a list of events, weighted in terms of severity, that yielded a cumulative score. Stressful events measured in this way were found to be correlated with physical and mental health, but the magnitude of the correlations was usually low. Improvements in measurement of life events included consideration of other pertinent factors such as the desirability, controllability, predictability, seriousness, and temporal clustering (Thoits, 1983). However, many researchers became dissatisfied with this approach to investigating stress. Some researchers moved to assessment of daily hassles (minor irritants and frustrations) which proved to be a useful approach with some groups of subjects (e.g., middle-aged) (Kanner, Coyne, Schaefer, & Lazarus, 1981). Daily hassles were a more powerful predictor of psychological symptoms than major life events for middle-aged adults in the study by Kanner et al.

Today, the most commonly used model of stress is the transactional or homeostatic model of Lazarus (Rodin & Salovey, 1989). This approach views stress as a person-environment interaction and a perceived imbalance between environmental demand and the ability of the person to respond. The person *appraises* the situation as one in which his or her resources are taxed or *exceeded,* and his well-being is endangered (Lazarus & Folkman, 1984; Lyon & Werner, 1987; Rodin & Salovey, 1989). Thus, stress is fundamentally a perceptual construct. A person's perceptions of stress are significantly related to health outcomes (Hobfoll, 1989; Rodin & Salovey, 1989).

Although most studies on stress have been done on men, a growing body of literature is available on women's stress (Frankenhaeuser, 1991). Not surprisingly, stress research on women has focused primarily on their conflicting responsibilities in the roles they enact—partner, parent, and worker. The dramatic increase in labor force participation has prompted much interest in work-related stress. In the last three decades, the number of employed women has increased from 21 million to more than 50 million (Taeuber, 1991). In 1988, 33 million women had children under 18 years of age, and 65% of women were in the labor force (U.S. Department of Labor, 1990). Early studies hypothesized that the more roles women perform, the greater the potential for stress related to role overload and role conflict. Homemaking and child care responsibilities have traditionally fallen to women, and there is little evidence that it is changing with the increasing numbers of women in the workforce (Frankenhaeuser, 1991; Sorenson & Verbrugge, 1987). Role overload may be particularly acute for women in middle adulthood, with stress of parenting teenagers *and* caring for elderly relatives. As noted in chapter 1, women experience more daily and long-term emotional distress, are less happy about life, and less satisfied with their roles than are men (Verbrugge, 1985).

Although there is no disagreement about the stressfulness of homemaking and parenting, a simple tally of the number of roles in which women are involved does not independently predict perceived stress. For example, Gove and Geerken (1977) found that married unemployed women reported more demands on them than did married employed women. Barnett and Baruch (1985) found "that role conflict and levels of role overload were significantly associated with occupying the role of mother, but were not significantly associated with occupying the role of paid worker or wife" (p. 132). Staats and Staats (1983) found that working women reported higher levels of stress and stressors, but that these were family related, not job related. Similarly, stress related to family and friendship matters was more significant than job-related stress in studies by Mansfield, Preston, and Crawford (1988) and White, Mascalo, Thomas, and Shoun (1986). In some studies, women with the most complex role configuration fared best (Baruch, Biener, & Barnett, 1987; Kandel, Davies, & Raveis, 1985). Barnett, Baruch, and Rivers (1983) reported that involvement in multiple roles actually strengthens well-being. In their sample of midlife women, *mastery* (an aggregate variable comprised of self-esteem, sense of control, and absence of anxiety and depression) was *lowest* in those who were married but unemployed and without children. Paid work best determined whether a woman ranked high or low on mastery. Enactment solely of the wife role may be less common now than it was in 1980 when the data for the Barnett, Baruch, and Rivers study was collected; there were no women in our sample in this category.

Karasek and Theorell's (1990) demand/control model, developed to predict stressful work situations, may apply to women's roles. The model proposes that jobs that have high psychological demands and low decision latitude (control) produce far more stress than high demand jobs that also have high decision latitude. A longitudinal study of 200 professional women revealed potent stressors to be lack of authority and influence on the job, heavy work load, work imposing on relaxation, and role conflict (Reifman, Biernat, & Lang, 1991). Lack of control is also a precipitant of stress in the home environments. Family roles of wife, mother, and homemaker allow little control over the welfare and happiness of the other persons for whom women are held responsible (Baruch, Biener, & Barnett, 1987).

Many studies have found adding work to family roles does *not* make women more vulnerable to stress-related illness (Baruch, Biener, & Barnett, 1987). Rather there are positive aspects such as access to others, potential for achievement and personal growth, and increased autonomy. Involvement in multiple roles expands potential resources and rewards, including alternative sources of self-esteem, control, and social support (Sorenson & Verbrugge, 1987). In almost all studies, employed women are healthier than nonemployed women (LaCroix & Haynes, 1987). Studies examining multiple roles in relation to both perceived and objective health status have shown that on the average, the more roles a woman occupies, the healthier she is likely to be (Baruch, Biener, & Barnett, 1987; Waldron & Jacobs, 1989). Possibly, married women with a family and career are able to use each role as a resource for coping with the stresses of the other (Stewart & Salt, 1981). Work may serve as a buffer against stress arising from other roles (Baruch, Biener, & Barnett, 1987).

Nevertheless, findings from the Framingham Heart Study cannot be overlooked. Certain role combinations and occupations (e.g., clerical) increased women's risk for coronary heart disease (Haynes & Feinleib, 1980). Of particular concern is a recent report documenting more "malelike" stress responses in women managers and a slower recovery time from stress compared with male counterparts (Frankenhaeuser, 1991).

Clearly, women's stress is linked to the roles they occupy. The level of stress is a complex phenomenon, made up of an interaction between the quality of roles, values and attitudes toward roles, relationships with significant others in their roles, and perceived resources to manage their responsibilities (Barnett, Davidson, & Marshall, 1991; Bolger, DeLongis, Kessler, & Schilling, 1989; Dixon, Dixon, & Spinner, 1991; Hibbard & Pope, 1987; Hirsch & Rapkin, 1986; McBride, 1988; Repetti, Matthews, & Waldron, 1989; Sorenson & Verbrugge, 1987; Verbrugge, 1982, 1986). The phenomenon of "vicarious stress," to which women appear to have particular vulnerability, has received less attention from researchers, although Kessler and McLeod (1984) found that stress for women is due not only to events in their own lives. Women tend to take on others' misfortunes. They have wider interest, concern for, and sensitivity to the well-being of others. The energy required to worry about and nurture the other members of women's social networks is considerable. In recent literature this has been termed "the cost of caring" (Turner & Avison, 1989). The added burden of vicarious stress may account for the often-noted phenomenon that women report more stress in their lives than do men (cf. Turner & Avison, 1989). This gender difference is evident as early as adolescence (Thomas, Shoffner, & Groër, 1988; Groër, Thomas, & Shoffner, 1992).

Social Support as a Stress Buffer

Numerous studies have reported the significance of perceived social support as a stress buffer, regardless of workload and number of roles (Amatea & Fong, 1991; Baruch, Biener, & Barnett, 1987; Connell & D'Augelli, 1990; Houston & Kelly, 1989; Lin & Ensel, 1989; McBride, 1988; Waldron & Jacobs, 1989). The emphasis on social support is a part of the new thrust by theorists and researchers to examine *resistance factors* in response to stress. Not all individuals become incapacitated when stress is encountered; explanatory variables such as hardiness, optimism, and various coping styles have been explored. However, the most impressive body of findings has been in the social support area.

Ornstein and Sobel (1987) proposed that solid, stable connections to a larger social group may result in improved resistance to disease. There are two "camps" of researchers, one contending that social networks exert a direct effect on reducing physical symptoms and one asserting that social ties also act to reduce symptoms by buffering the effects of stress (Cohen, Teresi, & Holmes, 1985). Caplan (1981) asserts that a person's chances of achieving mastery over stress are substantially increased when appropriate social support is given. Among the benefits of a supportive social network for the individual grappling with stressful experience are concrete help in dealing with problems, provision of information, assistance in development and implementation of a plan of action, bolstering of self-esteem, assurance that discomforts are tolerable, and encouragement to maintain hope of a satisfactory outcome. Caplan also emphasizes the role of support persons in reducing the individual's emotional arousal by "increasing nurturant input to cater to dependency needs that are being frustrated, by absorbing hostility, by counteracting hopelessness, and by dissipating shame and guilt" (p. 416).

Stress and Anger

Caplan (1981) views dysphoric emotional arousal as an inevitable response to stress. The association between stress and anger has been confirmed in several studies. Most of these, however, have dealt with college students or with men (Adams, LaPorte, Matthews, Orchard, & Kuller, 1986; Hardy & Smith, 1988; Smith & Frohm, 1985). Results of these studies may not be generalizable to women, whose stresses may be different in several respects. For example, primary concerns of highly stressed midlife women in Thomas's (1990) study were "health of a family member" and "troubling thoughts about one's future." The nature of the stressful events or circumstances could influence the arousal or expression of anger. Anger-prone persons (i.e., those high in trait anger) may be more likely to experience greater stress because of their expectations that things will go wrong; when their predictions are confirmed, they may react more readily or strongly than would a nonhostile person. As noted in chapter 1, Novaco proposed that individuals who are chronically or frequently angry may have learned to cope with stressful life demands by *becoming* angry. Of course this angry coping style serves to increase, not decrease, the level of stress.

Relationships between specific modes of anger expression and stress have not been extensively studied. Houston and Kelly (1989) studied hostility (measured by the Ho scale) and anger expression (measured by the Framingham scales) in relation to stress and social support in middle-class employed women, finding that high-hostility subjects reported more stressful job experiences and more overall stress and tension as well as greater propensity to vent anger outwardly in a blaming way. General social support was unrelated to women's hostility, but support from husbands and supervisors was negatively related to hostility.

In the Framingham study daily stress was found to be significantly correlated with all four modes of anger expression (anger-in, anger-out, anger-discuss, and anger symptoms), being most strongly related to anger symptoms (Haynes et al., 1978). In our previous study of college students, perceived stress was also related to all four modes of expression (most notably the anger symptoms mode) as well as to trait anger. All correlations were positive with the exception of an inverse correlation between stress and anger-discuss. Of the two trait anger subscales, angry reaction was correlated with stress more highly. Social support was not assessed in this project (Thomas & Williams, 1991).

If adequate social support is available to stressed individuals, might this reduce the extent of angry reactivity or maladaptive anger expression? As we have seen, Caplan (1981) contends that it would; he speaks of the support persons "absorbing" the anger. However, persons in an individual's social network can be sources of both *conflict* and support; the stress-buffering influence of social support is impaired in such cases (Sandler & Barrera, 1984). In an investigation of the negative side of social interaction, Rook (1984) found that "problematic" social ties, with persons who caused feelings of anger or took advantage, had a more powerful impact on well-being than supportive social ties.

FINDINGS OF THE STUDY

In this section of the chapter, we present findings of the study regarding relationships of women's anger to stress, role responsibilities, and social support. In keeping with the current views of stress as a perceptual construct rather than a tally of life events or daily hassles, we selected the Perceived Stress Scale (PSS) developed by Cohen, Kamarck, and Mermelstein (1983) as our measure of stress. This instrument assesses the extent to which individuals perceive their lives to be unpredictable, uncontrollable, and overloading. The reference point is the last month. Typical items are

"In the last month, how often have you felt difficulties were piling up so high that you could not overcome them?"
"In the last month, how often have you found that you could not cope with all the things that you had to do?"

There is a five-point Likert-type response format with options ranging from "never" or "almost never" to "sometimes," "fairly often," and "very often." Possible range of scores is 0 to 56. Cohen (1986) has demonstrated that the PSS provides a better measure of appraised stress than the Hassles Scale. The

Perceived Stress Scale was normed on three adult samples and has yielded Cronbach's alpha reliability coefficients of .84, .85, and .86 as well as good evidence of concurrent and predictive validity (Cohen, Kamarck, & Mermelstein, 1983).

Role responsibilities were operationalized in terms of data obtained on the demographic questionnaire regarding marital status, employment status, and parental status (mother vs. nonmother). Initially, we had intended to consider a fourth role, that of caretaking obligations for relatives or friends other than children. However, only one fifth of the sample reported that they had these responsibilities.

Five groups of women were selected for comparison: never-married workers, married workers with no children, divorced workers with children, unemployed married mothers, and employed married mothers. Our sample contained several representatives of other role combinations, such as unemployed divorced mothers, employed divorced nonmothers, and widows, but there were too few in each of these categories to permit statistical comparisons. No one fell into the category of married but unemployed and without parental responsibilities; as noted previously, we did have women in the sample who were married and unemployed, but they all had children. Because the predominant role configuration in our sample was the three-role combination of wife-worker-mother, groups in the five categories were very unequal in size. Therefore, 30 women were randomly selected from each of the five designated groups to use in ANOVA comparisons.

Social support was assessed by the Norbeck Social Support Questionnaire (Norbeck, Lindsey, & Carrieri, 1981), which includes nine items on (a) affect (feeling loved and admired by significant others); (b) affirmation (support of one's actions and thoughts); (c) aid (material help); (d) number in social network; (e) duration of relationships; (f) frequency of contact; and (g) losses of important relationships during the past year. Adequate levels of test-retest reliability (.58 to .78), internal consistency reliability ($\geq$ .89), and construct, concurrent and predictive validity have been reported (Norbeck, Lindsey, & Carrieri, 1983). Respondents list the initials of each significant person in their network and rate each of them on a 1 to 5 scale. A sample affect support item is: "How much does this person make you feel liked or loved?" A sample affirmation item is: "How much does this person agree with or support your actions or thoughts?" Aid is assessed in concrete terms, as illustrated by this item: If you needed to borrow $10, a ride to the doctor, or some other immediate help, how much could this person usually help?" The duration question ascertains the length of the relationship in categories ranging from less than 6 months to more than 5 years. Frequency of contact (defined as phone calls, visits, or letters) is assessed in categories ranging from daily to once a year or less. The questionnaire concludes with questions about

losses during the past year because of moving, job change, divorce or separation, death, or other reasons; if the response is yes, the respondent is asked
to specify the number of persons who are no longer available.

Initial examination of the data included scrutiny of the dispersion of stress
scores. Women's scores on the Perceived Stress Scale varied widely, ranging
from 4 to 49 with a mean of 25 and no problematic skewness of the data. The
mean score of this sample was almost identical to the scores obtained by the
tool developers for community (nonstudent) females (Cohen, Kamarck, &
Mermelstein, 1983). The normality of the distribution of scores negates the
presumption that *all* women, or even most, are extremely stressed. Social
support scores were not directly comparable with prior studies because of
revisions in scoring procedures. Slight negative skewness was observed on
some, but not all, of the social support variables because of the influence of
a few very low scores. Network size was relatively large; the mean number of
significant others in the networks of our subjects was seven (SD, 2.6). The
majority (70%) of the sample reported no losses during the past year, although
a few women reported as many as four, five, or six support persons lost.

Relationships Among Stress, Social Support, and Anger Variables

Correlations among stress, social support, and anger variables are presented
in Table 21 (see Appendix). Anger variables most strongly related to perceived
stress were trait anger, cognitive anger, and both somatic measures (Framingham and Contrada scales). All correlations between stress and anger
dimensions were statistically significant, but the r values for anger-in and
anger-discuss were very small. Thus, the general conclusion is that higher stress
is associated with higher anger levels, and this anger is more likely to be
somatized or vented than suppressed or discussed. Further, intense resentful
cognitions accompany the stressful experience.

The most important social support variable in relation to stress was
affect support (feeling loved and admired); women who do not have a solid
sense of being loved perceive their stress to be greater. There was also a weak
inverse relationship between duration of relationships and stress. Four social
support variables were correlated with trait anger: affect support, size of the
social network, duration of relationships, and frequency of contact with members of the social network (all inversely, indicating higher anger propensity
when less support is available). Cognitive anger was associated only with lower
affect support. There were few significant correlations between any of the
anger expression modes and the social support variables: anger-out was weakly
related (inversely) to size of network, duration, and frequency of contact;
anger-in was weakly related to duration of relationships; and anger symp-

toms was weakly related to affect support. To summarize relationships of support and anger variables, we must acknowledge that the findings are not impressive (i.e., correlations of low magnitude), but there is some association between anger and feeling unloved, smaller network size, interpersonal relationships of shorter length, and less frequent contact with one's network.

Two recent studies have examined anger variables in relation to social support. In a sample of undergraduate psychology students and their roommates, Zurawski and Richardson (1992) found higher scores on anger-in were associated with self-reports of smaller social network size and greater social isolation as well as perceptions of roommates as more hostile and unfriendly. In another sample of undergraduate psychology students, anger-in was negatively correlated with the tendency to *seek* social support (Hart, 1992). Further exploration of relationships between anger and social support in non-student samples is recommended.

Comparison of Groups Categorized by Level of Stress on Anger Dimensions

Our next set of analyses involved analysis of covariance (ANCOVA) comparisons of quartile groups categorized by level of stress (high, moderate, mild, and low) on the anger variables. There were 131 women in the highly stressed group, 105 in the moderate group, 120 in the mild group, and 123 in the low group. Because women in the sample score differently on some anger dimensions according to their age and education levels (see chapter 3), these demographic variables were used as covariates where indicated. Social support variables were also used as covariates in several comparisons; further details will be provided as we proceed. First we examined trait anger (general anger proneness), with age and affect-support (feeling loved and admired) as covariates. Highly stressed women scored significantly higher on trait anger (adjusted mean, 20.9) than did women who had low levels of stress (mean, 17.1), moderate levels (mean, 18.3) or mild levels (mean, 18.5); the difference between the latter three groups with lower levels of stress was not statistically significant. Similar results occurred when other social support variables (size of social network, duration, frequency of contact, and loss) were used as covariates. In all cases, highly stressed women were higher on trait anger than the three other groups (all model p values were .0001). Next we examined the two subscales of trait anger. Social support variables used as covariates in these comparisons were affect, network, duration and frequency of contact for the angry temperament analyses and loss for the angry reaction comparisons; we also controlled for age. In each case, highly stressed women had higher adjusted mean scores on the anger dimensions (temperament and reaction) than the low stress groups of women. In most cases mild and moderate groups did not differ from each other, and in some cases the mildly stressed and the least stressed did not differ.

Next we examined modes of anger expression. In ANCOVA comparisons, using age as a covariate because older women are more likely to be suppressors, highly stressed women differed from all other groups on *anger-in*; the remaining groups did not differ from each other. Analyses for *anger-out* (controlling for age because younger women are more prone to vent outwardly) revealed that both the highly and moderately stressed groups had higher adjusted mean scores on anger-out than the two groups with lower levels of stress. In analyses for *anger symptoms* both education and affect support were used as covariates; adjusted means of all groups differed significantly from each other except the two groups lowest in stress. Consistent with the other analyses, highly stressed women had higher anger scores. In analyses for the four modes of expression, all p values were .0001 except the model for anger-in (p = .0005). On the Contrada Somatic Anger Scale, using age as a covariate, the highly stressed women were significantly higher in the somatic manifestations of anger measured by this scale (e.g., heart pounding; body keyed up; face and mouth tight, tense, and hard) than all other groups. On the Contrada Cognitive Anger Scale, using affect support and age as covariates, the highly stressed women were higher in unhealthy cognitions (e.g., rumination, thoughts of revenge) than all other groups. Of all the anger dimensions examined in this study, only on anger-discuss were there no significant differences between groups. To summarize this section briefly, higher levels of stress were associated with higher levels of anger in virtually all of the procedures we conducted. Results were remarkably consistent. Directionality of any causal arrows is an open question, however. We cannot conclude stress causes anger or that higher anger creates more stress because we are working with cross-sectional data within a nonexperimental research design.

Comparisons of Groups Categorized by Combinations of Roles on Anger Dimensions

In the next set of comparisons, we examined women grouped according to the number of roles occupied; if the "role overload" conceptualization of stress were correct, then women with the greatest number of role responsibilities would presumably have more competing demands, more time pressures, and more anger. In these ANOVA comparisons we used five groups: never-married workers, married workers without children, divorced workers with children, unemployed married mothers, and employed married mothers. These groups did not differ in terms of expression modes but differed significantly on trait anger, in a fashion that negates the "role overload" hypothesis; the *busiest women* (those enacting the three-role combination of wife-mother-worker) scored *lowest* on anger proneness (mean = 16). *Highest* on trait anger were *never-married women* (mean = 20) followed by homemakers (enacting wife and mother roles but unemployed (mean = 19) and the remaining two groups (tied at 18.5): married workers without children and divorced workers with children. These findings support studies by Barnett, Baruch, and Rivers (1983), Waldron and Jacobs (1989), and others showing that women with the most roles display healthier profiles (lower stress, higher sense of mastery, better health status, and so forth) than those with fewer role responsibilities. Now our finding regarding anger propensity can be added to the converging evidence that occupancy of multiple roles is not problematic per se.

What is the meaning of these findings? Let us "reason backward to make educated guesses," to use a phrase from Lazarus (1991c). One plausible explanation for the lower anger proneness of the busiest woman is simply her busy-ness. It could be that the woman juggling multiple roles overlooks trivial incidents, preventing anger provocation; she doesn't have time to attend to minor hassles and frustrations. Another interpretation involves a slightly revised version of the "healthy worker effect" (a term referring to the selec- tion of individuals who are in good health into the labor force while persons in poor health are unable to work). In the revised form, we might speak of a confident, high-energy woman (Superwoman?) who is undaunted by taking on simultaneous roles of wife, mother, and worker, and therefore not very anger prone in response to the multiple demands. She may have had a dif- ferent set of early life experiences than the never-married woman who scored high in trait anger. In research by Woodall and Matthews (1989) cited ear- lier, higher trait anger in children was attributable in part to less cohesive and supportive families. As adults, women with these unhappy family back- grounds may not only retain readiness to be provoked to anger but also be less interested in taking on the roles of wife and mother. Further, their anger proneness could alienate potential intimate partners. We acknowledge that this interpretation is highly speculative. Role *quality* was not assessed in our study, so we do not know how satisfied the never-married women were with their marital status or their jobs. Future studies should take role quality into account as well as number of roles.

There is a great need for empirical examination of never-married women and the stresses of their lived experience. Demographics have noted increased numbers of never-married women over the past two decades, and a variety of reasons have been offered for this phenomenon. Among the factors cited by Stein (1981) are increased enrollment of women in graduate and profes- sional schools, expanded career opportunities, liberated sexual standards, changed attitudes about the desirability of marriage, and the excess of women in the "baby boom" generation at marriageable age (the "marriage squeeze"). One recent phenomenological study explored the meaning of singleness to nine Southern women (mean age = 41) who were involved either in human service occupations or sales (Dalton, 1992). The women frequently used the term "trade-off" to describe their singleness (speaking of the trade-off between freedom and independence on the one hand, and loneliness and lack of companionship on the other). Several participants saw being single as preferable to what they had experienced in relationships with men. Many were offended by society's assumptions about them and the implication in people's comments that their never-married state was not acceptable. Anger was not specifically examined by the interviewer but is evident in some responses. For example, one woman talked of the burden of self-reliance: "I'm responsible for all of it. I do the laundry. I wash the dishes. I cook the meals. I clean the house. I buy the clothes. I am everything in my household. I would really like not to have to do all of this all by myself all the time" (Dalton, 1992, p. 75).

What Are the Stressors Identified by our Respondents?

We turn our attention now to the qualitative data we obtained on the types of stressors experienced by our sample. Although we had used the Perceived Stress Scale to obtain a global assessment of stress level, we were also interested in the specific events occurring in women's lives. Descriptions were written in response to the question: What is your greatest stress right now? To answer this question, women's responses (n = 399) were copied onto cards and sorted into eight categories based on similarity of content by a rater who was naïve regarding the literature and then reviewed by an experienced stress researcher. The category with the largest number of responses (n = 117) was titled "Dealing with Caring for Others/Concern for Others" (title taken from the exact words of two of the responses). The basic themes of this category are (as the title indicates) women's concern for others and their need to care for others. Bearing in mind that the following statements were made in response to a question about the *woman's* greatest stress, there is certainly support for the "vicarious stress" concept identified in previous literature.

- Son's divorce
- Grandson's illness
- Nephew's car accident
- Daughter has breast cancer
- Grandchild responsibilities
- Health of family
- Turbulent adolescent son
- Husband's unemployment

- Daughter-in-law's mother terminally ill with cancer
- Friend in jail
- Pregnant unmarried daughter
- Parents have separated
- Aging parents—their change in mental capacity
- Husband's recuperation from open heart surgery

A review of the nature of these events quickly impresses on the reader that they are essentially *uncontrollable* by the woman herself. Another very important aspect of vicarious stresses such as these is the probability of very serious and long-term consequences for the woman and for others within her social network. Some traditional stress management modalities appear to be very inadequate for dealing with such stressors.

The second largest response category (*n* = 104) pertained to stresses in the work world. Examples were specific to occupations in some cases. For example, a nurse said "needle stick by HIV positive client," a teacher reported "greatest stress is encouraging pupils," and the owner of a maid service said, "that my employees show up for work." Other responses were nonspecific (e.g., "project at work") and concerned a diversity of issues including lack of full-time employment, uncooperative coworkers, and career changes.

The third category of stressors (*n* = 45) were easily categorized as "financial" (e.g., "money," "bills," "debt"); however, it is important to note that this category received less than half as many responses as the first two. Next in terms of number of responses (*n* = 31) was a category titled "love life," which included different aspects and stages of loving relationships. Illustrative data include "my love life," "dating," "marital problems," "pending divorce," "ending romantic affair," "being widowed," "trying to survive in society by myself (divorced)," and "feeling alone (divorced)." The final four categories had less than 30 responses each; they were health, school, time pressures, and "living." Stressful health problems included weight problem, addictions, allergies, surgery, and reproductive events such as "being pregnant," "recent abortion," and "menopause." The school items pertained to nonspecific stresses of graduate study, and some were one-word responses, such as "school." Time pressures included "busy lifestyle," "too much to do," "job deadlines," "keeping up with home demands," "lack of time with children," "not enough time to do things for pleasure," and "over-scheduled time." The final category comprised concerns that might be considered existential (e.g., "worry about the purpose, meaning, and brevity of life," "changing moral values," "being misunderstood").

The next stage of our analyses involved a comparison of our most highly stressed subjects (top 25% in PSS scores) with our least stressed (lower 25% on PSS) in terms of their predominant stressors. We wondered if highly stressed women were experiencing life events of a different nature than women reporting lower perceived stress. In terms of the top two categories (vicarious and job-related), the two groups were virtually identical, and there were no notable differences with respect to finances or time pressures. The two categories where differences were observed were in the areas of "love life" and "health." In the highly stressed group, more women were dealing with relationship terminations that were in process or relatively recent (death, divorce, separation), and with physical health problems (e.g., a sewing machine operator having trouble with her arm). Obviously, both of these stressors could be precipitants of considerable anger.

How Do Women Reduce their Stress?

Any discussion of stress-emotion issues is incomplete if coping has not been addressed. Do most women have a strategy for stress management? In answer to our question "What is the most helpful thing you do to reduce stress?" respondents described several coping mechanisms. We chose to collect data through this open-ended question in the belief that existing coping conceptualizations (often dichotomizing coping into "problem-focused" or "emotion-focused" strategies) were not entirely satisfactory. Analysis of the data revealed that the primary strategy used by our sample of women is exercise. This way of coping is mainly a distraction and a way to "recharge one's batteries"; it does not directly address the stressful situation in the sense of solving a problem. Let us proceed to examine the data. Four hundred fifty-one responses to our question were received, with some subjects listing more than one coping strategy, and 15 women writing the word "nothing" or saying "I don't know" or "try not to think about it." *Exercise* was specified by 95 respondents, with walking being the most frequently mentioned type. Exercise has been identified as a stress buffer in previous studies (cf. Wheeler & Frank, 1988). Further, exercise produces positive changes in mood and affect (cf. Folkins & Sime, 1981) as well as self-esteem (Sonstroem & Morgan, 1989). The second category of responses (n = 89) was labeled *dealing directly* because very direct action to deal with the stressor was described. For example, one woman who has two sets of twins wrote "get a babysitter." Another woman whose stress involved her 84-year-old father said, "try to keep him involved and enthused." A student managed school-related stress by studying more with friends. A woman whose greatest stress was her "turbulent adolescent son" reported that the most helpful thing she had done to reduce this stress was "see a therapist (family) with children and by self."

The third largest category of responses (n = 64) involved *talking with someone* or being with someone. Illustrative of this category are the following: "talk to husband," talk to friend," "be with family at home," "spend time with kids," and "be with others." This group of responses appears similar to the "social relations" stress buffer found to be more important to women than to men in Wheeler and Frank's (1988) study. Holahan and Moos (1985) also found that family interaction and support was a stress-resistance factor for women, but not for men. *Pleasurable activities* were coping strategies for many women (*n* = 59). In this category "reading" comprised the largest subcategory, followed by hobbies, music, television/movies, and shopping. Responses pertaining to women's *spirituality* constituted the fifth category (*n* = 47), including praying, meditating, and church activities. *Relaxation* (*n* = 40) included specific relaxation techniques, rocking in a rocking chair, sleep, and vacations. *Professional help* was the avenue of combatting stressful experiences for 18 women; responses mentioned "weekly psychotherapy," "12 step meeting," "take a pill," "co-dependence support group," and the like. The remaining categories were very small and included *being alone* (e.g., "isolate myself for quiet time") and *outlets* (e.g., screaming, crying, laughing, smoking, drinking, eating). On the whole, we view the coping responses of our respondents as adaptive. There is certainly no suggestion in these data that women are helpless in the face of stress or bereft of effective problem-solving strategies, as has been alleged in some literature.

Are there any strategies women might be encouraged to use more frequently? In an interesting recent paper, Repetti (1992) recommends social withdrawal as a short-term coping response to daily stressors. As proposed by Caplan (1981) and validated by our findings as well as those of other researchers, stressors immediately impact subjective well-being, increasing negative emotions such as anger. Repetti asserts that social withdrawal can assist in restoration of a more *positive* affective state. There is little research to support Repetti's assertion, because most subjects in stress and coping studies do not mention social withdrawal as a primary coping strategy; most coping inventories do not contain a social withdrawal scale. Therefore, she recommends the use of daily diaries as a data collection method. In our view, there are several obstacles to women's use of this strategy to decrease stress-induced anger. For example, child care and housecleaning responsibilities may prevent them from withdrawing after a hard day at work. Bolger et al. (1989) found that when husbands have had a demanding day at work, wives compensate by increasing their work load at home; the converse is not true, however. Perhaps more women would use this strategy if conditions were conducive to doing so.

Summary and Implications

Stress is omnipresent in women's lives, and significantly associated with anger arousal, cognitions, and somatization. What can health professionals do to assist stressed and angry women? One of the major recommendations arising from these analyses is further exploration of the phenomenon of *vicarious stress*. It is fascinating that when women were asked about their greatest stress, the largest response category pertained to stresses of *other people* in the women's social networks; the burdens of others were taken on as the women's *own*. It is not difficult to understand why spouses, children, and friends seek women when they need to share their concerns and traumas; women are empathetic, good listeners, nurturers. But how many troubled persons can a woman comfort, console, and worry about before her own energy is drained? What *is* the real "cost of caring"? Although there is no question that women are performing truly beneficial service to their friends and relatives by shoring them up during stressful times, there is some evidence in the literature that providers of social support have more health problems during the time they are heavily involved in others' stresses (Kessler, McLeod, & Wethington, 1985).

Although women in our sample were most stressed by events occurring to their significant others, involvement in multiple roles appeared to exert a protective effect in some way. Perhaps when a woman is at work, she is able to put aside temporarily her worry about her son's divorce or her daughter's financial problems. Turner and Avison (1989) found that although women in their sample were more stressed than men (especially because of vicarious stress), the paid worker role had beneficial effects. Certainly exercise and the other adaptive coping strategies reported by our respondents also assist in buffering or reducing stress.

When women are at very high levels of perceived stress, health care providers may assist them with cognitive restructuring so that the stressors can be viewed as challenges to be mastered. Even negative life events can be stimuli for psychological growth and development. For example, the first author of this chapter has worked extensively with women adjusting to divorce. In numerous cases, despite the upheaval, grief, and disorientation, tremendous personal growth was ultimately achieved. Younger's theory of mastery (1991) explains how individuals may emerge from stress states not demoralized and vulnerable, but healthy and stronger. At the conclusion of her theoretical paper she states, "the person engaged in mastery of stress may be likened to a sailor in a storm. Stress is the storm, certainty is the compass, change is the rudder, acceptance is the angle of the sail set against the wind, and growth is the progress toward a destination. Mastery suggests that the sailor may not only avoid being blown off course, but may in fact use the wind with such effectiveness as to make greater progress than was expected" (Younger, 1991, p. 87).

■7
Values and Anger

Carol Smucker, June Martin, and Dorothy Wilt

Finally . . . whatever is true, whatever is honorable, whatever is just, whatever is pure, whatever is lovely, whatever is gracious, if there is any excellence, if there is anything worthy of praise, think about these things. (Phill. 4:8)

Think, for a moment, about the values that are important to you at this time in your life. If you had to choose the four values that are most important to you, which ones would they be? Although values give meaning to and guide our daily lives, we do not often spend time thinking about them. It may be that we are not aware of what we value until we become angry and wonder why. Although there are many reasons for being angry, it is not surprising that values often play an important part in the anger experience. Both the literature and our own clinical experiences reveal that values and anger are inextricably linked.

Value has been a topic of interest to scholars for centuries. It has been studied in different ways by philosophers, sociologists, and social psychologists. The study of value has changed from trying to arrive at a broad theory of value to focusing on conceptual issues (Rescher, 1969). Axiology, the study of values in general, includes ethics, value theory, aesthetics, and social and political philosophy. Our specific concern is the relationship of values to emotion. In this chapter we will discuss the theoretical basis of the connection between values and emotion as well as the more recent inclusion of a cognitive component in conceptualizations of values.

Values have been classified as either intrinsic or extrinsic. Plato and Aristotle focused their attention on intrinsic value, as did the Austrian scholar Brentano in the late 19th century (Rescher, 1969). Intrinsic values, or end-state values, are values that are thought to be good in themselves. An extrinsic value, conversely, is a value that is used as a means to something else. Many values, such as education, have both intrinsic and extrinsic value (Barry, 1980).

We obtained information about women's values choices by including Wallston's adaptation of Rokeach's Value Survey in our test battery. This instrument is based on Rokeach's terminal values. Rokeach (1973) was a social psychologist and noted researcher on values and value changes among American men and women. He categorized values as terminal (intrinsic) and instrumental (extrinsic), and examined the relationships between the two types. Terminal values serve as goals in life or ideal end-states of existence, whereas instrumental values serve as the means to achieve these goals through ideal modes of behavior (Rokeach, 1979). For example, "a comfortable life," a terminal value, might be served by ambition, intellect, or honesty, which are instrumental values. In addition to administration of the value survey, we also obtained qualitative data about women's values. Women's write-in responses about their daily experiences with values broadened our understanding of the relationships between women's values and their anger experiences.

In this chapter values are examined in a general way as an important prelude to our specific focus on anger and values. Because there has been little research on women's values, we discuss our findings regarding the choices and their rankings before attempting to make connections to anger. Many women in our study indicated that religion is an important value to them. Thus, we will also look at the ways women's beliefs in a higher power and church attendance relate to values and anger. A brief review of pertinent literature about values precedes the discussion of findings of the study.

VALUES

Value Defined

There are as many ways to define value as there are opinions on the subject. Philosophers and social scientists haven't been able to agree on a single universal definition. According to Dossey, a value is an "affective disposition about the worth, truth, or beauty of a thought, object, person, or behavior" (Dossey, Keegan, Guzzetta, & Kolkmeier, 1988, p. 134). However, Wilberding (1985) asserted that valuing is not only an affective process but also involves critical thinking. Behavior is another element of valuing. George Lundberg states that "a thing has or is a value if and when people behave toward it so as to retain or increase their possession of it" (cited in Rescher, 1969, p. 2). Raths and colleagues define values as "those elements that show how a person has decided to use his life" (Raths, Harmin, & Simon, 1966, p. 6). For clarity and consistency, we will use the definition developed by Milton Rokeach. He defines values as "core conceptions of the desirable within every individual and society" (Rokeach, 1979, p. 2).

In summary, the weighing process called valuing has cognitive, affective, and behavioral components (Rokeach, 1973). Values are manifested, therefore, in our thinking, emotions, and actions. Valuing provides guidance and purpose in life. Values equip us to make decisions by giving us "a frame of reference" by which to assimilate, interpret, and assess new ideas, experiences, and relationships (Rescher, 1969).

Rescher writes about values as goals, contending that human nature is goal oriented. Thus, values motivate our actions and are often reflected in behavior. Knowing a person's values may tell us what a person actually will do or desires to do. However, behavior does not always reflect one's value system. Individuals who are particularly susceptible to situational stimuli or whose values are weak or conflicting, may behave in ways that contradict their values (Worthington, 1988). In fact, some women may not be aware of their values until they experience a conflict either between their behavior and values or between individual values.

An example of behavior motivated by a conflict of values is Beverly, a 33-year-old woman encountered by chapter author J. Martin while working in a hospital emergency department.

Beverly

Beverly came into the emergency department with a broken foot. She had injured herself by kicking a door in anger. This anger was the outcome of months of frustration and despair resulting from not having the freedom and happiness that she needed. Her boyfriend's possessiveness was oppressive, but this was a state that she endured because she valued the care and nurturing that he gave her son. However, her boyfriend's increasing surveillance and harassment continued. On the night Beverly came to the emergency department, her boyfriend had made another unreasonable demand, which further limited her freedom. She had kicked the door in anger and frustration.

Basic to Beverly's treatment was helping her gain insight about her values. She had taken the risk of sharing her feelings and facing the truth about her situation. She realized the conflict that had been occurring. Her value of nurturance for her son through her boyfriend had been in direct conflict with her need for freedom. It would be important to help Beverly find healthy alternatives in living out her values.

Values require personal resources of either goods, time, effort, or attention. To realize a value we make an investment of our resources. Thus, there is some "cost" to maintaining values (Rescher, 1969). In Beverly's case, one value became too costly relative to other values.

Value Development

An understanding of the development of values may be facilitated by the following imagery. Values are like the rich depths of the ocean floor. The ocean nurtures all forms of life and its floor is made up of the residue of history. One finds that at the greatest depths of the ocean, the most basic and simple life forms exist and are sustained. However, no matter how simple and basic these forms are, they are paradoxically complex in their ability to live throughout time. Such are the characteristics of values. Values are at the core of each woman. They are strong, enduring, empowering, the basis of beliefs and behavior. The "building up" of values is similar to the nurturing layers of each woman's monthly process of readiness to produce and sustain life, a phenomenon largely outside the woman's awareness.

Value choices initially are based on an infant's psychological needs. As the child continues to develop, values are formed through societal demands as well as psychological needs (Rokeach, 1979). According to Rokeach, they are "learned and determined by culture, society, society's institutions, and personal experience" (1979, p. 2). Values are developed through an individual's experiences with success, failure, love, criticism, approval, hurt, or pleasure. Core values are shaped within the family; parents traditionally use moralizing and modeling to help their children acquire values. However, messages from religions, peers, or the media may contradict rather than support parental moralizing and modeling. Some children receive insufficient guidance in value acquisition because of laissez faire parental attitudes (Wilberding, 1985).

Carl Rogers (1964), in a classic paper on values, contended that the less mature person may never question the value system received from parents and others. When persons who are less mature have difficulty living out their values, one reason may be because their values are not *their* values, but the values of *others*. If values have never been examined or tested through personal experiences, a value system tends to be rigid and unchanging. This type of system, Rogers maintained, does not serve as well as a system that is flexible and allows for change. A flexible system is more adaptive to life's contradictions and characterizes the mature individual.

A woman's health may be affected by the anxiety of trying to live out a value system that is not her own. A client of chapter author D. Wilt was referred by her physician for psychotherapy after he had diagnosed her numerous physical maladies (rash, back pain, weight gain) as anxiety related. Over time, it became evident that much of the anxiety was due to a conflict with a rigid value system. This system did not allow her to use artificial birth control. Her responsibilities of caring for five children and working outside the home had left her overwhelmed, exhausted, and terrified about getting pregnant. Although she sometimes questioned this value system, she felt that maintaining it was an important part of her faith commitment and role as a spiritual model to her 10 siblings. During therapy it became evident that the values issue was intertwined with other emotional issues. It was necessary to focus on these issues and encourage emotional growth before attending to the values conflict.

In *A Question of Values* (1990), journalist Hunter Lewis creates a framework in which personal values can be defined, compared, and contrasted. Lewis's book is based on his extensive lifelong study of philosophy. He begins by focusing on some of the simplest, most basic questions about values. Having laid the groundwork, he then examines six ways or styles of choosing values. The six styles are (a) authority, (b) deductive logic, (c) sense experience, (d) emotion, (e) intuition, and (f) science. According to Lewis, the six styles interact with each other in our daily lives. Because value choices have the power to shape lives, Lewis asserts it is critical that people be aware of the particular style of thinking by which their value judgments are made. With this awareness, a better evaluation of the validity of values can be made.

Are there some values that are better for society than others? Maslow (1964) wrote extensively about the values of persons who have achieved a level of self-actualization. He called these the B (for being) values and considered these the ideal values for society. Examples of B values are truth, honesty, justice, goodness, beauty, and wholeness. Maslow optimistically believed that if basic needs could be met, all people could experience self-actualization and exhibit these values.

Value Systems

According to Rokeach (1979), men and women across all cultures have the same *basic* values but order them differently within hierarchies. These hierarchies, called value systems, persist over time and are resistant to change. Within the hierarchy individual values may change or assume a different position (a reordering of priorities). Value systems consist of our "core" values as mentioned earlier as well as other values accumulated through life experiences. The latter type of values are more flexible and receptive to change.

Rokeach (1973) has said that value changes are a continuing maturational process. His studies were the first to measure value change over time. One way values change is through a change in self-concept. Rokeach's value change experiments were based on facilitating alterations in self-concept (1979). His findings were consistent with cognitive and behavioral change theory. When individuals were given feedback about their own and others' values and attitudes (Rokeach, 1973), the awareness of contradictions within their own value-attitude system resulted in long-term cognitive and behavioral changes. An affective state of self-dissatisfaction was aroused when a person recognized a conflict between their self-conceptions and their behavior. Values, attitudes, and behavior were reorganized to make these three components of self-concept more congruent, thus decreasing the self-dissatisfaction. Of interest to Rokeach were the changes that occurred in American's values when confronted with societal issues such as war and racism.

We conclude from the literature review that both society and experiences shape our basic values. These values stay somewhat constant but change in degree of priority with life's experiences and self-awareness. There is considerable evidence of the value change process in what women told us.

"The death of my husband 18 months ago helped clarify these values for me."

"The conflict experienced in caring for older parents restricts my independence. . . . I am enrolled in a master's program . . . this increases self-respect and a sense of accomplishment."

"I believe (I see my values) a lot clearer than when I was younger."

"Struggling much because these values have changed so much."

"Once in a while I get a real sense of feeling these things (values), a lot more often than before my divorce."

"I feel I'm living these values more now than in the past 11 years."

"These values are much more a balanced part of my life than ever before."

Research on Women's Values

Although little has been written about women's values, studies have demonstrated that women's values differ from those of men and also differ among age groups. Gender differences were found in Rokeach's research on a national sample of several hundred men and women in the late 1960s (Rokeach, 1973). Both men and women ranked the values of world at peace, family security, and freedom as the top three terminal values, while they ranked lowest an exciting life, pleasure, social recognition, and a world of beauty. For women, the value ranked fourth was salvation, while for men it was comfortable life. (Women ranked comfortable life number 13; men ranked salvation number 12). The ranking of the other values was very similar between genders except for the value "accomplishment." Men ranked it 7th;

women ranked it 10th. Perhaps this difference has disappeared with women's increasing participation in the workforce.

In a more recent investigation, Jones (1991) used Rokeach's Value Survey to compare value choices between two groups of college men and women (ages 18–22 and 23–56), which he termed "traditional" and "non-traditional" students. He predicted that the value systems of the younger students would emphasize the development of identity and intimacy, whereas the older group's emphasis would be the development of generativity (according to Erikson's theory). It was also expected that the relative importance of specific values would vary by gender regardless of age. Analyses involved converting value rankings to z scores; differences between groups were examined with discriminant analysis. Results showed that female students chose self-respect more frequently than did the males, who placed more value on pleasure and a comfortable life. Jones interpreted this to mean that males learn to value themselves through extrinsic motivators, whereas females do so through intrinsic motivators. Another significant finding was that the older females, ages 23 to 56, selected salvation and national security, whereas the males in this age group chose happiness, true friendship, and pleasure. This seemed to indicate that males in this sample were more hedonistic, whereas the females were more generative as well as intrinsically motivated. A flaw of this study was the grouping of individuals between ages 23 and 56 in one group.

In a qualitative study based on in-depth biographical interviews of 54 executive women between the ages of 35 and 60, Kintner (1983) found some interesting differences in women's value choices across the life-span. Women were asked about the meaning of entering the decades of 30, 40, and 50. Results indicated that women in their 20s and 30s were characterized by an interest in developing relationships, accelerating their careers, and making a decision on children. Self-respect was valued during the 40s. In the 50s decade, the women felt that the value "freedom" (financial, emotional, and physical independence) was more available than in earlier decades. Interestingly, all age groups perceived the 50s decade to be the most positive one.

Carol Ryff, in her studies of value change for women in transition from middle to old age (Ryff, 1982; Ryff & Baltes, 1976) supported her hypothesis that women change from instrumental to terminal value orientations with age. In the 1976 study, subjects were 119 professional women ages 40 to 50, and 65 and older. Using the Rokeach Value Survey, middle-aged women ranked values concurrently and predictively, whereas older-aged women ranked values concurrently and retrospectively. Ryff's study provides evidence for a value transition from middle age to old age. There was a main effect of class of values (F [1, 112] = 37.94, p < .01), indicating an overall preference for terminal over instrumental values. In addition, a predicted target age × desirability condition × class of values triple interaction was obtained (F [1, 112] =

6.64, $p < .01$). These results supported the hypothesized value restructuring process for women and paralleled previous findings about men.

In a later replication study Ryff (1982) extended her previous work with a sample of 80 middle-aged and 80 old-aged men and women. In this study, the educational levels were more representative of their birth cohort groups, with older persons at lower educational levels than middle-aged persons. Cohort effects need to be taken into consideration, especially in research on women, because of the recent changes in opportunities for them in life (Grambs, 1989). The findings again supported the instrumental to terminal values transition for women. For men, however, the values transition was not supported. Men preferred terminal values in both middle age and old age. Ryff (1982) states that the existing theoretical literature on sex differences in personality development provides no clear guidelines for understanding the sex differences obtained in her studies. A finding in the 1982 study that was contrary to the 1976 study (Ryff & Baltes) was that neither men nor women considered their personal values as distinct from those that were socially desirable. With this congruence, there would be less likelihood for a value conflict.

As we have seen, women are able to prioritize their values in a survey, but do they follow through and live by them? Carol Gilligan, author of *In a Different Voice* (1982), found in her research on children's values that somewhere between the ages of 11 and 15, girls stop defending their values (Gelder, 1984). Gilligan claimed that society teaches girls that "normal" values are those held by males. Girls also start to realize that if they bring their value experiences into the open, they will conflict with the male experience, causing them difficulty in life. And so, for the most part, girls go "underground" with their values and call on them only within the interpersonal sphere.

Several female scholars are currently writing to encourage women to become aware of their values. They also encourage women to appreciate the ways that these values contribute to personal development as well as to society. According to Jessie Bernard, a well-known scholar and researcher on women's relationships, women's values are the key to the future on earth (Abrams, 1981). She points out that women learn to collaborate, whereas men learn to compete. In an interview, she stated that "the important thing is for women to respect their own world. . . . Women need to become more autonomous and self-confident, stop judging everything from the male point of view. Female judgment is usually better" (Abrams, 1981, p. 29).

Margaret Hall (1990) addresses values in the context of women's identity. Like Rogers, she believes maturity involves an awareness of one's own values. She encourages women to move from patriarchal values to egalitarian values so that their identity can be more androgynous and autonomous. Women's value hierarchies, she contends, are different from men's. If women are unaware of their own value choices, they cannot make deliberate selections and tend to be subject to the contradictions and conflicts of the values in society. Because goals and commitments flow from values chosen as the core of identity, women should make these choices consciously.

STUDY RESULTS: VALUES

Value Choices

Some of the questions we had about women's values were: Which values are most important to women? Do value choices vary with age, income, or education? How clear are women about their values? Are women able to live out (enact) their values in their daily lives? What affects their ability to live out their values? What are the consequences of not being able to live out values? The women in our study were given a list of 10 values (nine of Rokeach's terminal values plus Health) and asked to choose the four most important ones in their lives at the present time. The responses women gave were both anticipated and surprising. Ranked in order by the percentage of women who chose each value, the value choices were

1. Health (86.9%)
2. Happiness (66.3%)
3. Self-respect (59.4%)
4. Inner harmony (49%)
5. Accomplishment (38.9%)
6. Freedom (36.1%)
7. Comfortable life (29.9%)
8. Excitement (14%)
9. Pleasure (14%)
10. Social recognition (5.8%)

In other words, 86.9% of our sample chose health as one of their four most important values, whereas only 5.8% of the women considered social recognition as one of their most important values.

When we compared the frequency ranking of value choices between the nonclinical, medical, and psychiatric groups of women in our sample, the only two value choices that varied among the groups were accomplishment and inner harmony. Accomplishment was chosen more often by the group receiving outpatient medical care (50%)—most of whom were homemakers—than by the psychiatric group (44%) or the nonclinical group (37%). The psychiatric group chose inner harmony more frequently (69%) than did the nonclinical group (47%) or medical group (45%). We will discuss these findings in the next section.

Value Clarity and Ability to Live Out Values

Hall (1990) has stated that the quality of our lives depends on the values we hold and our ability to express our values in everyday behavior. To help us understand this important aspect of values, we asked women to tell us (a) how clear they were about their value choices and (b) to what degree they were able to live out these choices. More than half (63%) of the women indicated they were clear or very clear about their choices, 15% said they were only somewhat clear, only 1% were not clear at all, and 21% did not respond to the question.

Because there were so many nonresponders to the two write-in questions, we examined responses to other questionnaires in the packet. We thought that there might be some common characteristics in this group related to value choices or experiences with anger. The only common element was that this group had not completed write-in sections elsewhere in the test battery. There are several plausible explanations for their failure to provide these data. Either these women did not like to write out responses or take the extra time required to do this, or the questions were unclear or too sensitive.

As far as living out their values, more than half (52%) were living out their values, whereas 30% were somewhat limited, 2.5% were unable to live out their values at all, and 15.5% did not respond. Interestingly, many women in the group "living out their values" quantified their responses saying that they were living either "all," "three-quarters," or "half" of their values. The degree of enacting values in daily life is reflected in these statements:

"I am able to live out these values more now than ever before."
"About as much as possible."
"To a limited extent, if at all—these are more strivings than realities."

We wondered if women who were having difficulty enacting their values had selected different values than women more able to act on their values. Responses to the question "How much are you able to live out your values?" were sorted into categories (not at all, limited, most, and all), and the four values selected by each woman were recorded under the appropriate category. After the entire sample's responses had been recorded, the value choices were tabulated and ranked by frequency. The only value selected more frequently by women who were having difficulty living out their values was *inner harmony*. Its ranking varied with ability to live out values. Inner harmony was chosen most often by women who were *not* able to live out their values at all and ranked second by women who were "limited" in living out their values. Women who were *able to live out at least half* of their four most important values selected inner harmony third. Inner harmony ranked fourth for women who felt they were living out *all* of their four most important values. These findings suggest that women who are unable to live according to their values experience turmoil and conflict, and the need to achieve an inner resolution.

We noted before that inner harmony was chosen more often by the psychiatric group. This choice could be related to this group's difficulty in living out their values. Only 32.3% of the psychiatric patients felt they *were* living out their values, whereas 58% were *not* living out their values at all or were *limited* in their ability; 9.7% either did not reply or the response was not clear. Lest we conclude that inner harmony is valued only by those who do not have it, inner harmony also was selected more frequently by women in our study with greater than 18 years of education. Rokeach (1973) reported a similar finding among college professors. This finding may reflect a seeking after self-knowledge in a personal as well as an intellectual sense.

Self-respect was also chosen more often by the psychiatric group than the other two groups. We suspected this choice—like the choice of "accomplishment" for the women in the medical group (mainly homemakers)—reflected unmet personal needs. We wondered what process people use when asked to rank their values. The literature did not provide answers. To enhance our understanding of individuals' rationales for their value choices we solicited feedback from a group of graduate students who completed the value instrument and then participated in an interview about the process they had used making their value choices. These students made their value choices for various reasons. Values were chosen that had always been important to the student or were of most importance to their present life circumstances. For example, one student said that self-respect had always been important to him because it had been emphasized in his family as a child, whereas a sense of accomplishment was ranked more highly at the present time because of his student status. Some students chose a value based on their desire to *acquire* the value. These students' high ranking of inner harmony seemed to reflect this. The course they were enrolled in focused on Eastern and Western belief systems about wholeness and health. To have chosen this course may have meant these students were either searching for inner harmony in their lives or desired a deeper understanding of it.

Selection of values may also be influenced by constraints; some of the women in our study said that certain values were *not* chosen because these were not *possible* at this time in their lives. For example, one woman said that as caregiver for her mother, freedom was not a value she could choose. Other women reported that their current marital status (whether married or single) did not support what they valued as an individual. Response options for the question we asked included "yes," "no," and "undecided;" whereas most (77%) women selected "yes," 11.9% chose "no," and 12% were undecided whether their marital status supported their values. In summary, values seem to be chosen for these reasons: (a) temporal, (b) recognition of need, or

(c) by default (one value chosen because another is not feasible). To illustrate value choices that appear to be based on need, we have profiled a woman from our study who we'll call Jill.

Jill

Jill is 42 years old, and has been married 22 years to the same person. She is "undecided" if her marital status supports what she values. Her children are ages 2, 15, and 21. She's employed full time as a legal secretary. She reported that she regularly attends church. Jill's value choices were health, self-respect, happiness, and freedom. Comparing these value choices to her scores and responses on the various study scales reflects a conflict between present and desired life circumstances. Jill says she has been sick "a lot" and has "lost count" of the number of visits to the doctor. She has been hospitalized "3 times" in the past year, although she claimed that she does not have any "serious" health problems. Her low score on the health scale indicates that she perceives her current health to be poor. Item responses on the self-esteem and depression questionnaires indicate global dissatisfaction with the self and unhappiness. Several of her responses were "In general I am not satisfied with myself at all," "I am sad all the time," "guilty all the time," and "I am disgusted with myself." We can only surmise Jill's reason for desiring freedom. Could it be a desire for more independence or for freedom from the conflicts between her desired values and her actual life?

Study Findings on Developmental Aspects of Value Choice

To see if value choices varied with age in our study, we divided the entire sample into four age groups: 25 to 34, 35 to 44, 45 to 54, and 55 to 66. Using a frequency distribution, we found that all groups ranked highest the values of health, happiness, and self-respect. Only the fourth most frequently chosen value varied by age group. For the 25 to 34 age group, Freedom was chosen, whereas the midlife groups (35–44 and 45–54) chose inner harmony. For the group ages 55 to 66 both inner harmony and accomplishment were chosen with the same frequency. Possible interpretations for these differing choices follow.

Freedom may have been chosen by the younger aged group because this group has limited freedom due to young children in the home. The increasing value of inner harmony to midlife women may be due to the propensity in midlife to reflect, reassess values, and choose more intrinsic values. The valuing of accomplishment by the older group suggests this group's desire to have lived a life of accomplishment, to have made a significant contribution to the world in the sense of Erikson's achievement of ego integrity.

Demographic Variables and Value Choices

We found that value choice varied more by education than income. This finding was consistent with that of Rokeach (1973). Social class, states Rokeach, accounts for most of the differences in patterns of values; education and occupation are more representative of social class than income. In our study, women who had 18 or more years of education chose inner harmony (χ^2 = 4.86, p < .03) and accomplishment (χ^2 = 17.93, p < .0001) more frequently, whereas women with a high school education chose happiness more often (χ^2 = 12.50, p < .0001).

Rokeach noted that the affluent were more likely to choose accomplishment and inner harmony, whereas the poor chose more conventional values, such as comfortable life. In our study, value choices did not vary significantly with income, although happiness was chosen slightly more often by women with household incomes of $28,000 or less per year (labeled the "low-income" group for the study). These findings are consistent with Maslow's hierarchical theory of human motivation (1954). Related to the lower order safety and security needs would be values that are concerned with material comfort, conventional forms of religion, and conformity. These values would more likely be chosen by the poor and uneducated. The affluent and educated would be more likely to choose the higher-order values, not because the other values are not considered important, but because they are taken for granted.

We have seen that value choices vary with age and education. Would they also vary according to responses to the religion question? Using frequency counts, we found that the two values that varied were freedom and accomplishment. Freedom was chosen more often by women who did not attend church regularly. These women may find religious rules confining. Women who *did* attend church regularly chose accomplishment more often than freedom. This may reflect a religious sense of responsibility or purpose in life, which is carried over into their community activities.

VALUES AND EMOTION

Theoretical Considerations

Taylor, philosopher and author of *The Values*, states that "the experience of human needs and hurts gives rise to emotions which . . . give rise to values" (1977, p. 6). It seems logical to say then, that if we are aware of our emotional arousal, we may look deeper within ourselves to understand which values have been threatened. In other words, emotion discloses value (Scheler, 1973). Indeed, values are formed based on our early emotional attachments. A child is taught to recognize value through the emotion that is expressed, recognized, and encouraged for certain actions. Values and emotion are so closely connected that a discussion of one necessarily includes a discussion of the other. The close relationship between values and anger is a common thread that runs throughout the literature. Our feelings toward an object are associated with its ascribed value. DeRivera (1977) has written about this connection in his structural theory of emotions. In anger, a person (a) perceives an object as a challenge or threat to a personal value, (b) there is a physical response, and (c) there is a motivation to remove the perceived challenge. Thus, a function of anger is to remove whatever has challenged our values.

Based on his summary of hundreds of philosophical analyses of emotion, Solomon (1976) analyzed all emotions according to categories. These categories clarify the structure and function of each emotion. In anger, the emotion's "object" *always* requires a responsible agent, someone worthy to be blamed. Anger is a judgment of personal offense. This judgmental aspect of anger often revolves around our values as projected on the world. By being angry, we are saying that the world is not turning according to our expectations. We have a desire to punish those who do not meet our demands. In anger, the self is considered as a defender of values.

Thus, anger is a personal evaluation of the significance of an incident that conflicts with our values or view of the world. We attach "worth" to certain ideas, people, and things. In other words, values arouse us to anger because we "care enough to be angry." According to Lazarus (1991b), our emotions are aroused over things we have committed ourselves to. He expands on this by saying that many of life's angry scenarios involve an assault on our values, either directly (involving self) or indirectly (other persons with whom one has identified). Likewise, DeRivera (1989) views anger and love as similar emotions based on the value of their objects. These objects are attributed not only with a sense of goodness or badness, a value relative to the needs of a person, but also are related to an "absolute value." Absolute value corresponds to intrinsic value as defined at the beginning of this chapter.

With the renewed interest in studying motivation in social science, motivational concepts such as values are being integrated with cognitive concepts. Lazarus (1991b) believes that understanding a person's values (commitments) will enhance the understanding of emotion. Our values, says Lazarus, extend to our commitment to others, and to our ideas and ideals. Though outside the self, when these projected values are assaulted, our ego identity is also assaulted. If an individual employs cognitive appraisal principles, Lazarus believes a person is better able to form accurate, reality-based, and thus healthier, emotional patterns. DeRivera (1989) also endorses a cognitive approach to understanding emotions and values. He writes that emotion that is more objective will be the most likely to reveal value. He also states that emotions not only *reveal* values, but also *preserve* or *enhance* the values to which a person is committed.

DeRivera (1989) summarizes the three different ways emotion and value are related, attributing each idea to the scholar who proposed it. The relationships are (a) emotions impart value; self-values are projected to an object (William James, 1902); (b) emotion gives form to value; value does not exist without emotion (Brentano, 1889); and (c) emotion reveals value; values of an object are revealed by the feeling one has toward the object (Scheler, 1916). DeRivera states that his view of values is closest to that of Scheler's.

In summary, the acquisition of values has an emotional component that not only forms the values but also gives them varying degrees of strength. Depending, then, on the importance of a particular value that has been violated, we react with the corresponding degree of emotion. We noted earlier that values are basic ideas about ourselves, as well as others. Values serve to maintain and enhance self-esteem (Rokeach, 1973).The emotional intensity is often quite high when values are threatened because of their close association to our identity or self-esteem (Lazarus, 1991). The implication for professionals is to be aware of what women value, the situations that often infringe on these values, and the way the anger elicited by these situations is managed. This leads us to the next section in which we discuss our analysis of the relationships between anger variables and values.

STUDY RESULTS: ANGER AND VALUES

Anger Variables

As we stated earlier in this chapter, our behavior may reflect our personal values. So then, different ways of managing our anger might relate to our value choices. Using chi-square analyses, we examined differences in value choices between women who scored high and low on two anger variables: suppression of anger (anger-in) and angry temperament (frequent anger arousal and outward expression). In other words, would women who managed their anger in different ways have different value choices? Value choices did not vary by anger-in scores. However, we found that women who scored high on angry temperament placed more value on social recognition (respect, admiration by others) ($\chi^2 = 3.68$, $p < .05$), whereas women who were low on angry temperament placed a higher value on self-respect ($\chi^2 = 5.77$, $p < .02$). Although reasons for the valuing of social recognition by the more fiery-tempered women are unclear, we suspect that they may not *receive* the admiration they seek (the deficit reason for value choice described earlier in the chapter). Being a "hot-head" is not a socially sanctioned trait for women in America.

There are several plausible explanations for the higher value placed on self-respect by those less easily aroused to anger. Displaying anger may be viewed as demeaning, lowering self-respect. These women may have learned to be "nice ladies"—that controlling anger is the "appropriate" way for women to manage their anger in our society. It is also possible that these women are able to control their feelings because of higher self-esteem (see chapter 5 for discussion of self-esteem issues).

Living Out Values

As we have seen, anger may be aroused when our values are threatened. Because of this, we surmised that if women were not able to live out their values in their daily lives, their anger might be reflected in unhealthy extremes of expression (either a greater suppression of anger or a greater outward expression of anger). A considerable number of the women receiving psychiatric treatment indicated they had difficulty enacting their values. However, this was not true for all of them. Therefore, we compared women within the psychiatric group who *were* able to live out values with those who had *difficulty* doing so; t tests were used to compare the two groups in terms of anger expression. There were no significant differences between groups on outward anger expression. However, women having difficulty enacting values were more likely to *suppress* their anger. The mean for this group on anger-in was 6.4 compared with a mean of 4.7 for the group who were able to live according to their values ($t = 2.90$, $p < .007$). Further research is needed to understand what prevents this particular group of women from expressing their anger.

Comparisons in Terms of Support for Values by Current Marital Status

As noted earlier in the chapter, 23% of study participants responded "no" or "undecided" to our question regarding support for what they valued by their current marital status (whether married or unmarried). We compared this group to a randomly selected subsample of the larger group of women who had reported support for their values, using t tests (see Table 22, Appendix). In these analyses we used all of the anger dimensions, finding significant differences between groups on four variables: trait anger, anger temperament, angry reaction, and cognitive anger. Additionally, there were differences between groups on anger-in and anger-out that approached significance ($p = .08$). The difference between the two groups in trait anger was particularly striking. In all cases, women who felt unsupported had higher anger scores. No causal inferences can be made; as noted in chapter 1, we are presenting a "snapshot" of women at one time in their lives and we do not know all of the contributing factors that led to their current circumstances. However, these findings suggest that if a woman perceives that she is not supported in enacting what she truly values in life, she has cognitions of unfairness and greater propensity to be aroused to anger.

What Women Say About Helps or Hindrances to Living Out Values

Some women gave us quite a bit of information about living out their values and things that helped or hindered this process. One respondent stated, "I've learned ways to deal with problems so I can cope. [I've] also learn[ed] to trust my intuitions in making major decisions." Another woman has used a change in schedule to her advantage. She states, "I have more time to focus on them [values] and do." Certain situations can facilitate enacting of values.

"Being single, the freedom is easy to live out."
"I am working on my inner harmony through counseling."
"I have a good husband and a nice family.
"I get a real sense of feeling these things [values], a lot more often than before my divorce."

Faith has also proved to be most beneficial to several women.

"Through my faith in Jesus Christ."
"With God's help, I can do all things."
"All things are possible through God."
"Thru my faith in Jesus Christ, I will be able to live out these values in His timing and at His pace."

Other events or factors women listed as facilitators of value enactment were: a new career, being unstressed, master's program, aging (values changing and becoming clearer), recreation and social life, exciting job, and more financial security.

Judy is an example of a woman who is able to live out her values.

Judy

Judy, age 36, works as a medical transcriptionist and is also a part-time student. She has been married to her current partner for 9 years. She has six children, four from a first marriage and two stepsons; five children live at home. Her value choices are: a comfortable life, happiness, health, and self-respect. She feels that her marital status supports what she values. She has some church involvement. Her response to living out her values was "I think my life is what I want it to be." She perceives her health to be good, with little need to seek health care in the past year; she has high self-esteem and is not depressed. Judy handles her anger by discussing it with friends and relatives. Her scores tell us that she discusses her anger more than most women in our study. She says that her greatest stress is "job and school." These life choices, however, seem to be consistent with her value choices rather than in conflict with them, based on the overall "picture" we have of Judy.

Often, the things that helped one woman live in accordance with her values were viewed as hindrances or obstacles by another. A good example is that of one's job. The following responses are illustrative:

"Due to the professional demands in my life the 'health' and 'inner harmony' and 'pleasure' I am finding very difficult to live out at this time. I must constantly strive to keep these 'professional feelings' from affecting my 'happiness' in my personal life."

"Extreme stress on the job has affected these things for the past 6 months."

"I like my job but some of the people there make it difficult to make the 'happiness' possible."

"I'm able to live out these values a great deal when my focus is kept in the right direction. Sometimes the social environment takes over and I get off track but I am aware of these times."

A lack of good health was a hindrance for these respondents.

"I'm handicapped, stuck, not much freedom!"

". . . stress from a lot of physical pain."

"Health and inner harmony are hardest for me. I'm dealing with addiction and codependency, so I'm up and down with them."

One African-American woman alluded to obstacles (in her words "stumbling blocks") to her pursuit of the value freedom.

"I'm as free as I can be as a black female living in the South. Though there are stumbling blocks I continue to strive to be the best person that I can be. I'm happy, seldom if ever depressed. I feel good about who I am."

Other obstacles that often prevented values being enacted were situations common to many individuals during a lifetime: weight problems, being single, having older parents, financial worries, the combination of a job, going to school, and having children to support and educate.

The women who provided these thoughtful comments on their life situations seemed to be in touch with their inner selves, their needs, and what was helping or blocking attainment of their values. Although it was encouraging that so many women were clear about their values, enacting them to a large extent, others were struggling with both clarity and actualization of their values. Some women seemed to be saying, "I'm floundering in the sea of life. Please help me." One can feel the distress, sadness, and tiredness of these women in the following examples as they each share their personal struggles:

"I am a long way from being able to live out these values. My life at this point is a total wreck, but is being held together by faith."
"I feel like my life is in great turmoil at this time with no chance of happiness in the future."
"I feel that I have not attained any of them [values], and probably won't ever."
"I wish my son, who is out of school, would leave and get on with his life so that I may get on with mine."
"the inner harmony and self-respect I want but can't seem to find."

Several women observed that they had little control over some of the values or that they could live out their values "only as long as my health permits." Many women were not able to live out their values to the extent that they wished but included these hopeful comments.

"I'm definitely moving closer to them."
"I am working hard at it and making progress."
"Trying to work on these values daily."

In our next profile we look at a woman named Barb, who is unable to live out her values. She is currently receiving psychiatric help.

Barb

Barb is a 41-year-old psychiatric technician. She has been married to her current husband for only 10 months (she has had three previous marriages). She has three children at home ages 7, 13, and 14, two of whom are stepchildren. Her value choices were an exciting life, inner harmony, pleasure, and self-respect. Barb commented about the values she selected: "This is what I would like now but don't see much chance of it happening the way I am. I cannot [live out my values]." She perceives her health to be poor, and her hospitalization this year and frequent sick days document this perception. Her health habit responses indicate that she does not take good care of herself. She has smoked cigarettes (a pack/day) for 25 years, does not exercise, and uses alcohol to help her stress (25 beers/week). She states that she sleeps 10 hours a night, which may be another way that she manages stress. She experiences physical symptoms when angry, although she uses all anger management modes to some extent. She scores high on depression, above average on stress, and low on self-esteem. The value she places on inner harmony and self-respect may be indicative of what she is seeking to achieve from counseling. Her other value choices of an exciting life and pleasure could be part of the conflict she is experiencing at this time. In the past month she has felt that she "could seldom cope with all the things she had to do." Along with her other responses, Barb perceives her life to be uncontrollable and overloaded. She also feels "dissatisfied or bored with everything." Barb has apparently realized that her life contains disharmony, turmoil, and lack of control. Through counseling, she will be able to reflect on her values, reevaluate the choices she has made in life, and have the opportunity to make healthy changes. She may need to reevaluate her desire to have an exciting life and pleasure if these values have been unrealistic or unhealthy.

Our last profile in this section is Trudy, a 36-year-old nurse. We present her case to illustrate the importance of listening to a client. Our perceptions of a situation may be considerably different from those of the client.

Trudy

For values, Trudy chose comfortable life, freedom, happiness, and self-respect. Trudy states that she "cannot live out these values." Although her demographic characteristics (i.e., affluence) and many of her responses give no indication of the turmoil she is experiencing, her scores indicate that she perceives her stress to be high, that her health is not good, she is depressed, and has low self-esteem. There is no indication that she does not have the resources to experience all of her values. She is employed full time as a registered nurse and has a family income of $78,000 a year. Her health is good, and she has two children, ages 2 and 4. She has been married 6 years. However, it is significant to note that Trudy states that her marital status *does not* support what she values. This may explain her depression and her desire for self-respect. The target of her anger is most commonly her husband. Although she manages her anger in a variety of ways, she employs the anger-out and anger symptoms modes most often. She states, "If my husband doesn't agree with what I have done for my family, I express my anger quickly." Her scores on anger-out are, in fact, above average. Though Trudy has realized that she is not able to live out her values, she may not be aware of the connection between this problem and her anger. She reported that her greatest stress is her "kids' education." This response seems to indicate that Trudy may not be in touch with what is really bothering her. Before intervening with Trudy, it would be important to have Trudy tell us more about the way she perceives her situation.

The part that values play in women's anger appears to be complex and not easily assessed with quantitative research methodology. Unless we ask the women themselves, we do not know the reasons for their value choices or the stories behind their experiences with value conflicts and anger. That is why we employ narrative profiles of various women throughout the chapter. These profiles allow us to put values in perspective to a woman's overall situation including that of anger. This holistic approach is also recommended for future research on women's values and anger.

RELIGIOUS FAITH: VALUING THE TRANSCENDENT

> I always think that the best way to know God is to love many things. . . . But one must love with a lofty and serious intimate sympathy, with strength, with intelligence; and one must always try to know deeper, better and more. (Vincent VanGogh, in *Sweetman*, 1990, p. 357)

Religion and Emotion

We direct our attention to religion in this chapter for several reasons. Women in our study told us that in times of despair, they often find help in their religious faith. For many women, religion not only provides the help needed at critical points in their lives but also shapes initial choices of values. Historically, religion has not been very positive about the emotion of anger. Generally, it has encouraged suppression of the emotion. For these reasons we compared women's responses to our question about religious belief and behavior to their value choices and selected anger variables. Before we share the results of these analyses, we briefly examine views of anger held by several religious groups.

Many of the ideas about anger that are held today by religions based on Judeo-Christian traditions have their origins in the philosophic writings of the Greeks and Romans. Such great scholars as Plato, Aristotle, Seneca, and Plutarch have contemplated the nature of anger. These philosophers thoroughly analyzed anger and wrote extensively about the dangers they thought were inherent in the emotion. Because of its sometimes destructive consequences, anger was often seen as evil (Schimmel, 1979). Overall, the Greeks valued emotional temperance. Aristotle acknowledged the useful purposes of anger if used *rationally*. This is reflected in his writings about anger: "Those who do not show anger at things that ought to arouse anger are regarded as fools; so too if they do not show anger in the right way, the right time, or at the right person" (Nichomachean Ethics, book 4, chapter 11). Thomas

Aquinas, a 13th-century philosopher and theologian, based his systematic theology on the writings of Aristotle. Aquinas also encouraged the rational control of anger (Encyclopedia Brittanica, 1991). In the 2nd-century A.D., the Roman Stoic, Seneca, emphasized the need for control of what he saw as a dangerous emotion. Although his views were unpopular at the time, his thinking has had a wide influence, especially within the Protestant and Catholic faiths (Schimmel, 1979). Two selections from the Bible seem to reflect these ancient philosophical viewpoints—from the wisdom literature: "A fool gives full vent to anger, but the wise quietly holds it back" (Prov. 29:11); from the New Testament: "let everyone be quick to listen, slow to speak, slow to anger" (James 1:19).

The Bible provides many examples of anger. The Old Testament shows us a God angry at his unfaithful people, the people angry at their neighbors or at God, whereas Christ in the New Testament displays anger at injustices. Although the Bible is negative about any anger expression that involves aggression (Warren, 1983), it is positive about anger directed at injustices and offers a way to learn from our anger. However, many religions today still do not differentiate between anger and aggression, continuing to equate both the *emotion* of anger, as well as its *expression*, with evil (Stearns & Stearns, 1986). For example, a recent sermon in a local church included a warning about the potential *evil* in anger. To help parishioners remember that anger is a dangerous emotion, they were told that "anger is only one letter away from *dan*ger." This negative religious stance toward anger may cause unnecessary guilt. It may also cause people to deny that they are angry or avoid taking action to resolve a situation that makes them angry.

Study Results: Religion and Anger

To see if women's anger expression varied according to religious belief and church attendance, we compared women who had the highest and lowest scores on anger-in and angry temperament in terms of their responses on the religion question. We found that women who attended church regularly had higher "anger-in" scores (χ^2 = 8.93, p < .01) and lower scores for angry temperament (χ^2 = 17.2, p < .0001). This seemed to reflect the prevailing religious advice of "don't be angry, but if you are, don't show it." Of course, a certain degree of anger control is desirable. However, not to examine and explore one's anger is not to grow. Over time, anger suppression may adversely affect mental or physical health, as a growing body of research suggests.

Admittedly, religious teachings have not always helped us to deal with our human nature in a positive manner. To live fully is to experience a range of emotions. We will sometimes be hurt and hurt others by acting on our emotions. But our emotions will also motivate us to right wrongs and live our values. And, believing in love and forgiveness, we can be thankful for our emotions rather than fearful of them.

General Religious Characteristics of the Sample

In the past, research about religion has not tapped what people actually believe, as questions usually focused only on church attendance. Although our survey questions did not ask about specific religious beliefs, we did ask about belief in a higher power as well as church attendance. Similar to previous religious surveys in which most people said they believed in a higher power, only six women in our sample (1%) answered that they had *no* belief in a higher power and had no church involvement. Thus, most women believed in a higher power but had varying degrees of church attendance. Twenty percent of the women did not have any church involvement, 26% had some church involvement, and more than half (53%) attended church regularly.

Among the women in our sample, the psychiatric group had the lowest percentage of regular church attendance. Only 24% of this group attended church regularly, whereas 57% of the nonclinical group and 50% of the medical group were regular attenders. Almost half (46%) of the psychiatric group did not attend church at all, although all but two of the women reported that they did believe in a higher power. Did the psychiatric group attend church less frequently because of their current problems, because religion is not important to them, or because they are spiritually distressed? One woman told her psychotherapist (chapter author D. Wilt) that she found it difficult to attend church because of painful memories certain hymns engendered. Carolyn (whose case is also discussed in chapter 12), had been abused during childhood by her father, who was a church deacon. Carolyn's family were members of a fundamentalist denomination, and attended church three or more times a week. As a child, she associated the imagery of the cleansing power of the blood of Christ, a common theme in their church's hymns, with her need to be cleansed of her sins. Hearing these hymns as an adult, Carolyn would become very anxious and have a desire to cut herself and bleed. She attributed this impulse in part to the visions suggested by the hymn. These images had been imbedded earlier in life in the concrete thinking of a needy child. This example illustrates the need for further research to understand why certain women do not attend church.

Although the psychiatric group exhibits less religious behavior, we cannot say that this group is not *spiritual*. Women can be spiritual without being religious, that is, without being a part of a faith community. What do we understand about spirituality—its presence and possibilities in our life? Our spirit or soul is an integral part of ourselves. It is the part of us that many believe lives on after physical death. Somehow it is that vital part that enlivens us to live a "spirited" life, literally and figuratively. Most people believe that there is a spiritual reality in the world that cannot be touched or seen, but can be experienced. People vary in the degree that they are aware of and experience this dimension. They also differ in the effort they make to nurture this dimension. Spiritual well-being is considered by several contemporary theorists to be a vital part of physical and emotional well-being (for a comprehensive summary of the most recent studies comparing spiritual well-being to health indices, see the *Journal of Psychology and Theology*, 1991, vol. 19, no. 1).

Religion, then, is the *expression* of our spirituality through established institutions or faith communities. Many people find that the expression of their beliefs in this way nurtures their faith. Religion can also be viewed as a way of being or a philosophy of life. It is a belief that is a major motive in life, and thus has intrinsic value (Jourard, 1974). For some women, like Sarah, faith and living out their values are related.

Sarah

Sarah's response to how much she was able to enact her values was: "Thru [sic] my faith in Jesus Christ, I will be able to live out these values in His timing and at His pace." Her four most important values were happiness, health, inner harmony, and a sense of accomplishment. Sarah is a 43-year-old homemaker, who has been married 22 years to the same person and has two children, ages 11 and 14. She terms herself an "Executive Director of Homefront Affairs." She states that her marital status supports what she values. She attends church regularly. Her greatest stress is "Adolescence!" "Sibling rivalry" triggers her anger. "Prayer, patience, and yelling" help her with her stress, and her anger does not last long. Sarah chooses the expression modes of "anger-out" and "anger-discuss" most often to deal with her anger. Her other scores tell us that she perceives her stress to be low and her health good. She is not depressed, but her self-esteem scores are below average. Overall, she seems content with her life, and finds the integration of her faith with her daily life a help to living out her values and managing her stress and anger.

If the spiritual is beneficial, how can women cultivate it? Theologian Matthew Fox (1972) suggests (a) increase your awareness of the mysteries of life; (b) be authentic, or true to your own self; (c) see life as a gift, appreciate and savor it; and (d) change your attitude to achieve the first three! We can choose to ignore the spiritual voice within us. However, the authors of this chapter contend that just as we have been given the sense to perceive the warmth of the sun on our skin, we have been given the sense that there is an unseen reality that can enrich and enlarge our enjoyment of life.

CONCLUSION

In this chapter we have examined the role that anger plays in shaping our values, and its relationship to our value choices and conflicts. We have also looked at spirituality and its influence on anger behavior and values. Women's own words and profiles have helped us understand how women's values guide their behavior and are an integral part of their thoughts and emotions. Women have been encouraged by authors such as Hall (1990) to become aware of their own values. As we have seen, women do have different value priorities than men. Women need to value these differences and confidently act on their valued choices in life. Remaining unaware of their values, women are more likely to follow societal values, which have traditionally been male values.

Likewise, women need to "tune in" to their anger. By becoming aware of anger, value choices can be identified and evaluated. Being angry may signal that values are blocked, violated, or are no longer the values that will serve them best. Women cannot have this knowledge unless they take the time to examine their values. We know from this study that most women *are* aware of their values. These women have demonstrated that there are key values that are held in common with other women. They also have indicated that there are particular values that are more important to one woman than another. We have seen that basic values continue through life but change in priority in response to our needs. Most women are clear about their values but sometimes have problems living them out. When enacting them becomes difficult, women may experience more anger, and some may need to seek counseling. Spirituality may guide women in their value choices and help them control their anger. Anger can be a positive motivating force. It can empower women to manage their lives and to live out their most important personal values.

Based on our findings, we recommend that future research continue to explore women's value choices. The benefits of such research are twofold. By understanding how their values develop and function in their daily lives, women will be better able to make value choices that reflect their true selves. Through greater knowledge about women's values, we should be able to learn more about the emotion of anger. We believe that qualitative research is particularly well suited to examining the relationship between anger and values.

■8
Unhealthy, Unfit, and too Angry to Care?

Mary Anne Modrcin-McCarthy and Jane Tollett

The decade of the 1980s and early 1990s has seen a proliferation of articles, books, and advertisements for exercise programs, videos, classes, and equipment; for high-fiber, low-fat, low-sugar foods and diets; for weight loss programs, classes, medications, and devices; and for gimmicks to help a person stop smoking. Apparently, the American public is buying into the health and fitness craze. In 1987 health clubs grossed $5 billion, exercise equipment grossed $738 million (up from $5 million in 1977), diet foods grossed $74 billion, and vitamin products grossed $2.7 billion (Brand, 1988). During the 1980s, exercise videos were frequently on *Billboard's* list of 10 top sellers. Magazines such as *American Health, Prevention,* and *Self* each report circulation in excess of $1 million (Morse, 1987/1988). Corporate America, in an effort to reduce insurance premiums and decrease employee days lost to illness, has succumbed to the health and fitness craze as evidenced by the increase in collaboration with health clubs and the advent of wellness programs in businesses across the country (Conrad, 1988; Glassner, 1988). Insurance providers have gotten into the act with major companies offering discounts to physically fit consumers (Breecher, 1991).

The relationship between health practices and health status has been empirically documented. Eating regular meals, maintaining ideal weight, sleeping 7 to 8 hours a day, being physically active, refraining from smoking, and consuming alcohol in moderation have all been positively associated with health status and greater longevity (Belloc & Breslow, 1972; U.S. Department of

154

Health, Education and Welfare, 1979; Wiley & Camacho, 1980). However, several studies have shown that even with the research evidence and widespread publicity regarding health behaviors, the American public is sadly deficient in the adoption of healthy life-styles. Less than half (42%) of all Americans exercise regularly, and most are not knowledgeable about the specific exercise requirements to strengthen cardiovascular and respiratory functioning (Thornberry, Wilson, & Golden, 1986). Life-style remains one of the most modifiable factors that influence health and illness in American society today with half the mortality in the United States attributable to unhealthful behaviors (*Healthy People*, 1990). According to Haggerty, the main problem is that health is not necessarily the highest value for many individuals. The real challenge is motivation to take action when there are no distressing symptoms (Haggerty, 1977). Dubos (1969) said, and it remains true, that people generally find it easier to depend on healers than to attempt the more difficult task of living well. Health care professionals continue to ask questions about what influences the choices that individuals make regarding personal health habits and about the relationship of health habits to health status. There is growing evidence of a link between certain psychosocial variables and health. Anger is one of these variables.

GENERAL ANGER PRONENESS AND HEALTH

Several studies have demonstrated the linkage of anger with disease and health (cf. Engebretson, Matthews, & Scheier, 1989; Harburg, Gleiberman, Russell, & Cooper, 1991; Johnson & Broman, 1987; Julius, Harburg, Cottington, & Johnson, 1980), but as noted in chapter 1 many of these did not include women. In a study of the relationship of resting blood pressure and heart rate to experienced anger and expressed anger in middle aged, normotensive and hypertensive, nonmedicated males (N = 21; mean age = 49.6) and females (N = 24; mean age = 53.1), Goldstein, Edelberg, Meier, and Davis (1988) found that "experienced" anger significantly contributed to the variance in systolic blood pressure in the normotensive group but not in the hypertensive group. "Experienced anger" included the frequency and intensity of experienced affects at work and in home environments. Durel, Carver, Spitzer, and Llabre (1989) found trait anger (the general propensity to become angry) positively related to blood pressure in women at work, when at rest and during the performance of laboratory tests. Anger propensity has also been linked with specific disease states such as arthritis, asthma, and CHD (Friedman & Booth-Kewley, 1987). The frequency of anginal pain was significantly correlated with trait anger in a study of cardiac patients by Smith, Follick and Korr (1984). Further, Friedman and Booth-Kewley (1987) termed anger a key component of a generic "disease-prone personality."

ANGER EXPRESSION MODES AND HEALTH

Anger expression modes have also been implicated in disease entities. Anger-in, (i.e., suppressed anger), has been linked to elevated blood pressure in several studies. In the study by Goldstein et al. (1988), anger that the patient was fully aware of, but chose not to express, played a major role in tonic elevation of blood pressure; self-expressed anger was inversely related to systolic and diastolic blood pressure. It is interesting to note gender differences in their study: expressed anger (the likelihood that others at home and at work would be aware of the anger) was a significant independent contributor for systolic and diastolic blood pressure variation among women but only for diastolic blood pressure among men.

In one of the few studies of healthy women, Broege and James (1990) examined the effects of mood (happy, angry, nervous, sad) on the blood pressure of 37 normotensive women. Women wore ambulatory blood pressure monitors over the course of a typical work day, with pressures recorded every 15 minutes. Emotional arousal was a significant source of diastolic pressure variation independent of posture and situation. Further, they found that anxiety and anger increased the blood pressure more than happiness in these women. These findings were consistent with their earlier study of borderline hypertensive women.

Some recent studies have examined lipids and lipoproteins in relation to anger variables. For example, Waldstein, Manuck, Bacher, Muldoon, and Bricker (1990) found reluctance to acknowledge or express anger associated with lower concentrations of high-density lipoprotein (HDL). However, the researchers used an exclusively male sample, and we do not know if this relationship has been examined in women.

In a subsample of the Tecumseh (Michigan) Community Health Study of anger-coping types, blood pressure, and all-cause mortality, Julius et al. (1986) found that those subjects who responded to an unjustified attack by their spouse by holding anger in were 2.4 times as likely to die over the follow-up period as those who expressed their anger to their mate. This study also found that those subjects who did not protest an unjustified attack by their spouse were 1.7 times as likely to die in the follow-up period as those who protested the attack. Furthermore, the subjects who had high overall scores on the suppressed anger index were 1.6 times as likely to have died during the follow-up period as those with moderate or low scores. Although this study included women (372 females, 324 men), the small number of deaths among women over the course of the longitudinal study precluded reliable gender-specific analysis. The researchers believe, however, that the effects of suppressed anger may be different for men and women. It is obvious from these reports that gender specific studies are needed to shed more light on the effects of gender differences in anger suppression. Greer and Morris (1975) reported on a controlled study of psychological attributes of women who develop breast cancer, which revealed that the way women handled emotion, particularly anger, was the only significant psychological attribute to differentiate between benign and malignant breast disease. In their study, "extreme suppressors" of anger (have not openly shown anger more than 1 or 2 times in their lives) and "exploders" (have frequent outbursts of temper and rarely conceal feelings) had higher rates of diagnosed breast cancer than women with "normal" emotional response patterns. Rheumatoid arthritis is yet another disease entity that has been associated with denial of hostility and, additionally, with subservient behavior among women (Solomon, 1985).

The large Framingham study (Haynes, Feinleib, & Kannel, 1980), one of the few studies of cardiovascular disease that included women subjects, found suppressed anger and Type A behaviors to be the strongest psycho-social predictors of coronary heart disease among working women. In this study, women were more likely than men to suppress their anger. Thomas (1989) found contrary evidence in a recent study of gender differences in anger expression where men and women did not differ on anger-in. Thomas's study did reveal that women were more likely than men to try discussing their anger, however. Moreover, anger-discussion was the only expression mode positively associated with health in the Framingham study (Haynes et al., 1980) and in the more recent study conducted by Thomas and Williams (1991).

Anger-out has been found to be correlated to adverse health outcomes in several studies (Williams, Haney, Lee, Kong, Blumenthal, & Whalen, 1980). In research cited by Wood (1986) outgoing aggressive behavior predicted the extent of coronary artery blockage. Another study in which anger-out was correlated with adverse health outcomes involved a national sample ($N = 1,277$) of black Americans (Johnson & Broman, 1987). The subjects who had a high level of outwardly expressed anger during a period of severe personal stress had a significantly higher number of health problems than did their counterparts with low or moderate outward expression of anger. "Potential for hostility," a construct comprised of overt behaviors such as obscenity and emotionally laden words, arrogance, rudeness, and condescension during a structured interview (clearly an anger-out style), has been identified as a risk factor for coronary heart disease (Musante, MacDougall, Dembroski, & Costa, 1989). Studies have demonstrated that expressing anger (in an attacking or blaming way) causes an arousal rather than a decrease of hostility. Kaplan's (1975) study found that subjects who expressed anger became more hostile than when they expressed the opposite of their feelings or maintained neutrality. In experiments where subjects talked about recent anger-rousing events (a) fast and loud, (b) slow and soft, and (c) normally, researchers found that speaking of the event fast and loud was associated with greater increases in blood pressure and heart rate than the other expression methods. The subjects also reported feeling more angry when they spoke fast and loud than when they talked slow and soft or normally (Siegman et al., 1990).

In another study involving recall of recent anger-provoking incidents, male patients with coronary artery disease were compared with disease-free men. The subjects were asked to describe the incidents as fully as possible, including details about what they said, did, and felt. During the anger recall task, the coronary patients (more than the control patients) had significant myocardial ischemia (as measured by left ventricular ejection fraction changes using radionuclide ventriculography). Thus anger was a particularly potent physiological stressor in the laboratory. Ambulatory studies might reveal even greater impact of anger stimuli, in view of subjects' estimation that their arousal during the laboratory recall of the angry episodes produced only one-third to one-half as much anger as the original incident (Ironson et al., 1992). Because the researchers used no women as subjects, the applicability of the study findings to women is unclear. The premorbid personality characteristics of the coronary patients are unknown. Have these men always had greater proclivity for strong reactions to anger stimuli, or has their behavior changed since they developed coronary heart disease?

ANGER AND HEALTH HABITS

It is only recently that the focus has begun to shift to the question of *how* anger actually relates to ill health. Several mechanisms have been proposed to explain the effects of anger or hostility on health. Four were listed in a recent overview by Smith and Christensen (1992). In the psychophysiological reactivity model, highly angry persons are presumed to have more frequent and extreme outbursts of anger, accompanied by exaggerated cardiovascular and neuroendocrine responses, eventually resulting in compromised health status. The psychosocial vulnerability model places considerable emphasis on social environment factors, such as high stress and less satisfactory social support. A third formulation, termed transactional, integrates the psychophysiological and psychosocial vulnerability models. In the final explanatory scheme, poor health habits are proposed to be the link between anger and deleterious health outcomes. There has been some empirical examination of all of these models, except the transactional—termed a "formidable challenge" to researchers by Smith and Christensen. Appel, Holroyd, and Gorkin (1983) believe that *indirect* pathways through which emotions influence illness may be more important than the *direct* ones.

In a study by Leiker and Hailey (1988), young adults who had high levels of hostility reported poorer health habits overall. Of the subjects in their study who scored below the median on the total Test Well score (indicating poorer health habits), 62% were in the high hostility group. Of the subjects who had better health habits (scored above the median split), 60% were in the low hostility group. The high hostility group scored significantly lower on three of the four Test Well subscales—physical fitness, self-care, drugs, and driving. The only subscale that failed to differentiate between the high and low hostility groups was nutrition.

Scherwitz and Rugulies's (1992) study of life-style variables and hostility found that among white women, hostility was inversely associated with physical activity and fitness. This relationship did not hold true for men or for black women. It is interesting to note that the researchers mention this gender difference in the results section of their paper, but in the summary section list activity and fitness as two variables not strongly associated with hostility. One can only assume that this is an example of the focus on men's health instead of women's that was mentioned in chapter 1.

Johnson-Saylor (1991) also found a relationship between hostility and healthy behaviors. For the 97 healthy women in this study, hostility (measured by the Cook and Medley Ho scale, 1954) and hardiness were the only variables significantly related to healthy behaviors (hostility was negatively and hardiness positively correlated). Anger experience and anger-in were positively associated with hostility and negatively associated with hardiness. Healthy behaviors were determined with the Personal Lifestyle Questionnaire (PLQ), which consists of 24 items related to health practices in the categories of exercise, nutrition, relaxation, health promotion, substance use, and safety. In this study, hostility accounted for 12.5% of the variance in health habits; high anger experience/high anger-out accounted for an additional 4.7% of the variance. Hardiness, although positively correlated with healthy behaviors, did not enter into the regression equation when other factors were considered. The negative relationship of a hostile attitude with healthy behaviors was strengthened by a lack of education and the tendency to experience anger frequently and to express it outwardly. Because the negative relationships of hostility, anger experience, and anger-out to healthy behaviors were much stronger than any positive relationship between hardiness and healthy behaviors, Johnson-Saylor says that, "for women, habitually experiencing anger and demonstrating it in overt behaviors seems to militate against engaging in behaviors conducive to health" (1991, p. 1169). The paucity of research using women subjects and our interest in women's health, anger, and anger expression prompted us to look at the relationship among the anger variables, health habits and health status in women. Because Johnson-Saylor's is the only study focusing specifically on anger-health habit linkages in women, much remains to be done. Our study examined additional anger dimensions in a much larger sample.

METHOD

Using data on several health habits of the study participants, we created a Health Risk Index, so called because the higher the score, the poorer the practice of the habit and the greater the risk for adverse effects on health. The index was computed by totaling the individuals' scores for the health habits. The health habit variables and their values were chosen based on the current literature and reports of empirical studies. Included were sleep, exercise, smoking, drinking, and body mass index (BMI) (an obesity indicator discussed at greater length in the next chapter).

Sleep

Studies have shown that 7 to 8 hours of sleep per day relates more favorably to physical health than sleeping 9 or more hours or less than 7 (Belloc & Breslow, 1972; Wiley & Camacho, 1980). Individuals in the 1972 (Belloc & Breslow) study who slept 6 or less hours per day were the least healthy, and sleeping less than 7 hours per day was found to be a significant health risk by Wiley and Camacho (1980) with no differences for gender. In the health-risk index we gave 7 to 8 hours of sleep per day a value of 0 and all other responses a value of 1. Data were obtained from the question: "How many hours do you sleep in a 24-hour period?"

Exercise

Regular aerobic exercise (strenuous enough to reach training heart rate and of at least 15 minutes duration) has been associated with a positive effect on psychological functioning and physical health (Folkins & Sime, 1981; Labbé, Welsh, & Delaney, 1988; McCann & Holmes, 1984). Those who exercise regularly are in better physical health than those who participate in exercise sometimes and much better than those who never exercise (Belloc & Breslow, 1972). Exercise has been found to relate to positive changes in mood and affect (Folkins & Sime, 1981; Lomranz et al., 1988; McCann & Holmes, 1984) and high levels of self-esteem (Sonstroem & Morgan, 1989). With these reports in mind, we considered at least 60 minutes of moderate to strenuous exercise per week as a good health habit with a value of 0, and less than that amount as a poor health habit with a value of 1 for the health-risk index. Exercise data were collected using the responses to the questions: "How many minutes do you spend in a week in *strenuous* activity such as jogging or running, vigorous swimming, hiking or doing heavy work around the house?" and "How many minutes do you spend in a week in *moderate* activity such as dancing, playing golf, gardening or working with tools?"

Smoking

Reports consistently indicate that nonsmokers have better health than those who smoke (Belloc & Breslow, 1972; Novotny et al., 1990; Wiley & Camacho, 1980). However, the trends in smoking habits in the United States show that the number of women who smoke in the 25 to 44-year age group increased by 15%, and by 50% in the 65 and older age group, from 1974 to 1987 (Novotny et al., 1990). For the index we classified nonsmoking as a good health habit with a value of 0, and previous and current smoking as a poor health habit with a value of 1. The subjects were asked: "How many packs of cigarettes do you smoke daily? (If non-smoker, put zero)" and the number of years they had smoked.

Alcohol

The risks of alcohol consumption for specific physical ailments such as cancer or liver disease and accidents has long been established (Laforge, Williams, & Dufour, 1990; Midanik, Klatsky, & Armstrong, 1990; Monforte et al., 1990; Stemmerman et al., 1990). There are mixed reports about how much alcohol at one time or what frequency of alcohol intake constitutes a risk for general health status. Belloc and Breslow (1972) found no significant difference in health between abstainers and moderate users among women. They did find a significant risk for general health status if the women drank five or more drinks at one time. Wiley and Camacho (1980) found that the extremes (nondrinkers and heavy drinkers) had the least favorable health scores in their study. These studies did not differentiate between the persons who were abstaining because of health problems from those who had always been abstinent. For our index, we considered abstinence as a good health habit with a value of 0 and alcohol consumption as a poor health habit with a value of 1. Responses to the question: "How many drinks of beer, wine or liquor do you usually drink in a week?" were used in data analysis.

Body Mass Index

Weight in proportion to height has been identified as a salient factor for health. Studies have shown that the most obese subjects have poorest health (Belloc & Breslow, 1972; Wiley & Camacho, 1980). Subjects who are underweight are also less healthy than average, with less than 5% underweight and less than 5% overweight as the most desirable range (Schoenborn & Cohen, 1986). Our index used the body mass index (KG/M^2) instead of weight or weight and height. For the index score a BMI of less than 27.3 was considered to be a good range with a value of 0, and all other BMI scores received a 1. Data were gathered for BMI from subjects' responses to the questions: "What is your height?" and "What is your weight?"

Rationale for Creating the Health-Risk Index

Prominent studies have shown that the benefits of practicing personal health habits are cumulative in nature (Belloc & Breslow, 1972). Subjects in the Alameda County study in every age group who followed all seven of the good health practices (7–8 hours sleep, ate breakfast, seldom ate between meals, weight in ideal range, active, no more than 4 alcoholic drinks at a time, and never smoked cigarettes) were in better physical health than those who practiced six. With the exception of the 75 and older age group there was a progression toward better health as the number of good health habits increased (Belloc & Breslow, 1972). The physical health status of those practicing all seven good habits was about the same as those 30 years younger who followed fewer or none of the health practices. This association was independent of age, gender, and socioeconomic status (Belloc & Breslow, 1972). A report of the Alameda County 9-year follow-up study of 3,892 surviving white adults indicates that certain aspects of life-style were predictive of future health status (Wiley & Camacho, 1980). The later study created a cumulative health index using five of the original seven health practices. A point was given for a current smoker, a range of 1 to 45 alcoholic drinks per month, physical activity score between 5 and 16, sleep 7 to 8 hours per day, and being within the range of –10% and +29% of ideal weight for height. Our health-risk index is a modification of this model. We reversed our scoring, however, giving the point for the absence of the good health practice, thus creating a health-risk index instead of a health index. The Wiley and Camacho study found these health practices to be significantly associated with future health status within socioeconomic level subgroups. They conclude that there is "strong support for the hypothesis that certain routine, discretionary behaviors play an important role in establishing an individual's level of resistance to illness and/or disability" (Wiley & Camacho, 1980, p. 20). These dramatic examples of the relationship between a healthy life-style and health over the life-span spurred our interest in determining if anger influences women's enactment of health habits or their general health.

Health Status

The participants' perception of their current physical health status was determined by the Current Health Scale from Ware's (1976) Health Perceptions Questionnaire (HPQ). This 9-item scale assesses perceived health status by items such as "I feel better now than I ever have before" and "I am somewhat ill." Responses are chosen on a scale of 1 to 5, from "definitely false" to "definitely true" with the range of possible scores of 9 to 45; higher scores indicate better perceived health.

Reliability and validity of the HPQ scales were established through field testing with more than 2,000 adults before administration to the 8,000 people participating in Rand's Health Insurance Study. Construct validity has been demonstrated by confirmatory factor analyses (Ward & Lindeman, 1976) and concurrent validity was established by correlations between HPQ scales and conceptually related variables. One year test-retest reliability of the HPQ was .88 (Ware, 1976).

Health Indicators

Specific health-indicator variables included in the data collection were number of days ill, number of times hospitalized, number of surgical procedures, number of prescription drugs, and number of over-the-counter drugs within the past year. Respondents were also asked to list any diagnosed conditions such as heart or lung disease, diabetes, or cancer. Because chapter 10 is devoted to substance use we do not use the data on drug-taking in our analyses. To obtain this information subjects responded to the following questions: "During the past year, how many times did you visit a doctor?" How many times did you see other health care providers, such as nurses, dentists? (Specify)"; "During the past year how many times were you hospitalized?"; "During the past year, how many days were you ill? (Illness means you were unable to work or do your activities as usual)"; "During the past year, have you had any surgical procedures (operations)? If so please specify"; During the past year, have you taken any prescription drugs? (Specify), over-the-counter drugs? (specify). Do you have any serious health problems such as heart or lung disease, diabetes, cancer? (Specify)."

RESULTS AND DISCUSSION

When we examined dispersion of scores on the health variables, we found our women reported a broad range of responses to these items. The scores on current health ranged from 10 to 45 with a mean of 32.58 and a standard deviation of 8.47. There was no problematic skewness. Dispersion of subjects' scores on smoking, alcohol, and BMI are discussed in other chapters; two health-habit variables (exercise and sleep) will be addressed here. The range for both strenuous and moderate exercise was 0 to greater than 16 hours per week with a median of 2 hours. Because of the wide range of responses there was evidence of skewness and kurtosis; this was adjusted for in the analyses.

The median number of hours sleep (per day) for our women was 7, with a range of 4 to 17 hours. Again, there was evidence of skewness and kurtosis that were adjusted for in analyses. In addition, the following health indicator variables were adjusted for skewness and kurtosis because of the large variation in responses: physician visits, visits to other health care providers, hospitalizations, days ill, and surgeries. Two was the median number of doctor visits (range, 0–80), health visits (range, 0–56), and days ill (range, 0–365). The modal number of hospitalizations (range, 0–14) and surgeries (range, 0–3) was zero, which was not surprising, given our predominantly healthy sample. Only 65 women reported any diagnosed disease condition, whereas, the remaining 414 did not. The largest reported category of disease condition was cardiovascular (n = 38), followed by endocrine (n = 16) cancer (n = 9), obesity (n = 9), musculoskeletal disorders (n = 7), pulmonary disease (n = 7), allergies (n = 4), gastrointestinal disorders (n = 4), neurological conditions (n = 3), renal disease (n = 2), hepatic disease (n = 2), psychological disorders (n = 2), gynecological disorders (n = 1), and hematological conditions (n = 1).

If women experience anger frequently or manage their anger in a maladaptive fashion, is their health compromised? To examine this question and other related hypotheses, correlations, t tests, analysis of variance, and multiple comparison procedures were performed. The results of these analyses will be presented in the following section.

How Do Trait Anger, Cognitive Anger, and Anger Expression Modes Relate to Perceived Health Status?

All anger variables were significantly correlated with perceived health status in this study, although some correlations were weak (see Table 23, Appendix). Of these, expressing anger through somatic symptoms and cognitive anger were most salient to poorer health. Consistent with findings reported by other researchers, anger discussion was the only anger variable to show a positive correlation to the level of perceived health status. It is not surprising that women with higher somatic anger (physical symptoms) and cognitive anger (a more unhealthy way of looking at situations) perceived their health as poorer than those women with lower scores (the reader is referred to chapter 3 for extensive discussion of these anger dimensions). The reader is reminded that no causal inferences can be drawn. Further investigation of all these relationships is warranted. Lazarus (1991c) contends that methodological problems make it difficult to obtain definitive answers about emotion-health relationships. Measures of emotion and measures of somatic health both depend on subjective appraisals. The "cause" (an emotion variable) overlaps with the "effect" (impaired health), and there is no completely satisfactory way to resolve the confounding. Nevertheless, the covariation of anger variables and health that is evident in our data warrants the attention and concern of health professionals.

Are There Relationships between Health-Risk Index Scores and Anger Scores?

The health-risk index positively correlated with trait anger and anger symptoms, in that, as the score increased so did the level of anger propensity and anger symptomatology (see Table 24, Appendix). Women who practiced few (or no) positive health habits, thereby increasing their risk for poor health, tended to have a higher general propensity to be angry and to express their anger through somatic symptoms than did the women who practiced good health habits (abstinence from smoking and drinking, exercising regularly, maintaining body weight in acceptable range and sleeping 7–8 hours per night). Thus, this relationship would suggest that the woman with higher trait anger and increased expression of anger through physical symptomatology may be at greater risk for health problems. The magnitude of these correlations was small, but these findings support Johnson-Saylor's (1991) proposal of a link between anger and poor health habits that may contribute to disease outcomes. Implications for professionals can be inferred; interventions would be geared toward decreasing reactivity to anger-provoking stimuli and promoting healthier modes of managing anger. To initiate this process, health care providers could ask their clients: What do you do when angry? The following responses are examples of those written by our subjects:

"I smoke."
"I lose my appetite."
"I can't sleep."
"I eat."
"I walk."
"I do intense physical activity."

As you can see, some of these behaviors are unhealthy and may contribute to poor health. If these behaviors can be modified, or replaced with new, healthier patterns of behavior, better health status may ensue. In addition, education regarding healthy modes of anger expression would be an important component to include in the treatment process.

Several studies have shown that trait anger is modifiable; significant reductions were obtained in the treatment program administered in the San Francisco Life-Style Heart Trial (Scherwitz & Rugulies, 1992). In another well-known intervention project, the Recurrent Coronary Prevention Project, subjects were taught to imagine themselves as fish; as they swim along each day, numerous "hooks" appear and offer them choices of whether or not to "bite." Eventually, subjects learned not to respond angrily to trivial daily irritations (Powell & Thoreson, 1987). Studies have also been conducted with non-diseased subjects, with positive outcomes. Deffenbacher, McNamara, Stark, and Sabadell (1990) used a combination of relaxation, cognitive, and behavioral coping-skills training in a program for university students who had scored high on Spielberger's Trait Anger Scale. Compared with controls, the counseled subjects reported greater decreases in tendency to be aroused to anger from diverse provocations and reductions in anger intensity and anger-related physiological arousal.

Examination of Individual Health Habits

In the next analyses, each health habit was examined separately. Individuals who had received the 0 (achievement of the desirable level of the health behavior) (N = 285) were compared with women who had received a 1 (failure to enact the health behavior) (N = 173); t tests were used to compare the groups. The most impressive findings pertained to exercise. The group who exercised differed significantly from the group that did not on *every anger variable* except anger-out (see Table 25, Appendix). The women who practiced good exercise habits (at least 60 minutes moderate to strenuous exercise per week) were more prone to discuss their anger than the other group. These women also reported their health as significantly better than the poor exercise group of women (t = 2.89, p = .004), which is consistent with other findings in the literature. Women who practiced poor exercise habits held anger-in, expressed their anger through somatic symptoms, and had higher levels of trait anger than did the group of good exercisers. We propose that these findings might be better understood in light of a recent paper by Pope, Wiebe, and Smith (1992).

Pope and colleagues (1992) reported hostility was inversely related to poor health behaviors in men and women. Regression analyses revealed that both self-esteem and self-efficacy were mediating variables in the "hostility-poor health behaviors relationship"—especially in women (p. 54). The researchers suggested that hostile persons directed their hostility onto themselves as well as others, thereby contributing to lack of self-care. Additionally, they proposed that "previously reported correlations between hostility and external locus of control may suggest an 'it's out of my hands' mentality in hostile individuals regarding their ability to positively impact their own health through engaging in positive health behaviors" (p. 54). It seems that some individuals are unhealthy, unfit, and too angry to care. Furthermore, the study adds support for the need to consider gender when examining anger and health linkages.

Lastly, there was a difference that almost reached significance for the smoking groups on trait anger (p = .06). When subscale analysis was performed, angry reaction scores were found to be the salient component. The women who smoked tended to have a greater propensity to "react angrily" than did nonsmokers. This relationship is discussed in greater depth in the substance use chapter of this book. No other differences between groups were found; on the remaining health habit variables (drinking, smoking, BMI), the group who practiced the desirable level did not differ significantly on any anger variables from the group who did not have the desirable level.

Do Women in Poor, Moderate, or Good Health Differ Significantly on Trait Anger and Anger Expression Mode Scores?

ANOVA and multiple comparison procedures were performed to answer this question. The sample was divided into three groups: high, medium, and low levels of perceived health. The criterion used to divide the subjects into groups was based on quartiles. Those with scores in the lower quartile of perceived health status were assigned to the "low" group, subjects with scores in the upper quartile were assigned to the "high" group; the remaining subjects (middle quartiles scores) were assigned to the "medium" health status group.

These three groups differed on *all anger variables* (anger-in, anger-out, anger discuss, anger symptoms, and trait anger) (see Table 26, Appendix). In all cases, women in the "low" group (those in poorer health) scored differently from those in the "high" group, although in a few instances the "low" and "medium" groups did not differ significantly from each other. The women whose health was reported as "poor" tended to keep their anger in and were also more likely to express their anger in somatic symptoms than either of the other two groups. Conversely, this group was less likely to discuss their anger than were the women whose health was moderate or good. Women in poorer health were also more likely to express anger outwardly and to have a greater overall propensity for anger than the group who experienced good health. These findings corroborate correlational analyses reported earlier.

Is There a Difference in Anger Scores for Women Who Have Been Hospitalized or Had Surgery Compared with Those Who Have Not?

For these analyses, the sample was dichotomized and *t* tests were used to compare those who reported hospitalizations and surgeries with those who did not. Women who had one or more hospitalizations during the past year differed significantly from those who had not been hospitalized on anger-in, anger-discuss, and anger symptoms (see Table 27, Appendix). Those women with reported hospitalizations tended to hold their anger in and express it in somatic symptoms; they were also less prone to discuss their anger than those with no hospitalizations. This same pattern held true for women with surgeries (see Table 28, Appendix). Women who had experienced surgical procedures during the previous year also held anger in or expressed it through symptoms more than those without surgeries. They were less prone to discuss their anger than their non-surgery counterparts.

Do Women Reporting High, Medium, and Low Illness Days Differ in Anger Scores?

Analysis of variance and multiple comparison procedures were done to analyze the data on days ill. The sample was divided into groups to create high (5 or more) (n = 222), medium (1–4) (n = 112), and low (zero) (n = 120) groupings. The data indicated that women who experienced illness during the past year (defined in terms of interference with work or routine activities) differed from those who reported no illness in cognitive and somatic anger (see Table 29, Appendix). Women in the "low" category were found to differ significantly from the other two groups, while the medium and high groups did not differ from each other.

Is there a difference in the anger variables for women who have high and low numbers of physician visits? High and low visits to other health care providers? For these analyses, women were grouped according to the distribution of scores for the full sample. There were 130 women who visited doctors 4 or more times within the past year (termed the "high" group), 148 who made 2 or 3 physician visits (termed the "medium" group), and 182 who made 0 to 1 visits ("low" group). ANOVA was used to compare these groups (see Tables 30 and 31, Appendix). Groups differed significantly on anger symptoms, with the "high" group having more doctor visits than either of the other two groups, and the "medium" and "low" groups scoring no differently from each other. To compare women in terms of number of visits to health professionals other than physicians, groups were created in the same fashion as previously described. There were 132 women in the "high" group who had made 3 or more visits, 159 in the "medium" group who had made 2 visits, and 162 in the "low" group who had made 0 to 1 visits to health professionals in the last year. Women who had a low number of health visits to professionals other than physicians differed on levels of trait anger from those who had a moderate number of visits but not from those with a high number of visits. There were no other significant differences between groups.

CONCLUSION

This study contributes to our knowledge because many previous studies have examined trait anger and anger expression modes in relation to specific diseases such as coronary heart disease, rather than in relation to health indicators in a nonclinical sample. Studies of individuals whose coronary arteries are already blocked do not give us adequate guidance for health promotion efforts with nondiseased individuals. When investigations are done after illness onset, we do not know what premorbid personality factors or behaviors contributed to the observed pathology. The other body of existing literature on anger-health linkages is primarily focused on college student samples that are hardly representative of the general population.

Based on our findings, it appears that some women who do not yet have diagnosable disease conditions are at risk for future pathology because of unhealthy modes of anger management and readiness to respond to provocations angrily. Furthermore, women who have recently experienced illness, hospitalizations, and/or surgeries differ from their healthier counterparts in terms of some (although certainly not all) anger dimensions. We recognize that some relationships, although statistically significant, are weak or modest; however, we do not consider this surprising in a predominantly healthy sample. Size of correlation coefficients is comparable with those reported in many widely cited studies of stress-health linkages. As Lazarus (1991c) has noted, "Health is a *multivariate* outcome, affected by a large number of powerful factors such as the genes we have inherited over which we have little or no control, accidents of living, environmental toxins, and numerous life-style variables such as smoking, drinking, drug use, diet, and exercise. After the variance in health produced by these variables has been taken into account, what remains as variance subject to the influence of the emotion process is probably modest" (p. 394).

Because all of the anger variables in our study were inversely related to health status, with discussion of anger having the only positive association, professionals may need to incorporate assessment of the frequency, intensity, and duration of anger, modes of anger expression, and other emotional parameters in initial assessment interviews. It is possible that encouraging the healthy expression of anger through discussion and promoting regular physical exercise could be the most salient services we can perform for the overall health of our women clients.

■ 9
Women's Anger and Eating

Sheryl S. Russell and Barbara Shirk

Disordered eating is not a new symptom. Today, however, it is the most obvious symptom to develop in women. In a patriarchal society that stresses perfectionism, achievement, self-control, and access to high status, the perfect body—for women, the slender body—is the symbol of all that women must adhere to in order to be accepted.

—J. H. White, "Feminism, Eating, and Mental Health"

They feel safer using their mouths to feed themselves than using them to talk and be assertive. They imagine that their fat is making the statement for them while the suffering prevents the words from coming out.

—S. Orbach, Fat Is a Feminist Issue

What role does anger play in the emotional life of the obese woman? Is it a result of the obesity or is anger a part of the cause of overeating and obesity? Or, is anger only part of the woman's natural reaction to life circumstances in general and not related to her "fatness"? The authors' clinical experience indicates that many obese people express anger about their weight, about the way they are perceived by others, and about how they feel about themselves. As discussed earlier in this book, anger is an uncomfortable emotion for many people. According to Matsakis (1990) anger has been culturally viewed as a sin, so many people eat to appease their anger in a more socially acceptable way. She contends that childhood punishment for displays of anger have further reinforced our rejection of appropriate anger expression. In one view,

170

obesity can be attributed to repressed childhood hostility; people chew constantly to sublimate this repressed hostility. Anger then, is directed inward toward the self for overeating. The weight becomes a scapegoat; it is easier to be angry and punish the self rather than insightfully deal with the real issue that provoked the anger (Burrows, 1992; Hooker & Convisser, 1983; Minirth, Meier, Hemfelt, Sneed, & Hawkins, 1990). Virtue (1989) contends that repressed anger is often confused with hunger. Based on her work with obese individuals in workshops all over the county, she claims that "anger is cited in more cases of overeating than any other emotion" (p. 34). Orbach (1990) alleged that some women choose to stuff their mouths with food rather than deal with their feelings of anger (p. 3). Viewed as a rebellion against gender stereotypes and social expectations, eating and obesity have been attributed to women's position of powerlessness. White cited MacKenzie's (1985) suggestion that "overeating and noneating are viewed as a protest against the way women are viewed in our society as objects of adornment and pleasure" (White, 1991, p. 71).

Women are often portrayed in the media as dealing with their emotions through the consumption of foods culturally defined as vices or as taboo, to be avoided by prudent persons. Popular television programs, such as "The Golden Girls" (who retreat to the kitchen and eat cheesecake when upset), and "Blossom" (a female adolescent who eats ice cream), depict women, both young and older, as responding to negative emotions such as anger by eating. McFarland and Baker-Baumann (1988) contend that eating serves as a coping mechanism to deal with painful feelings. It is "a way to stuff the feelings, to numb them, to shut them off. Focusing on food shifts the attention away from feelings" (p. 37). Minirth and colleagues (1990) elaborate, "Many people literally stuff their anger—they keep it down by putting food on top of it. The process is similar to packing in wadding when loading a cannon—and the results can be just as explosive" (p. 27). Burrows (1992), and McFarland and Baker-Baumann (1988) suggest that bingeing and then purging provide a physical release from anger by diverting the anger, avoiding the conflict, and maintaining cultural rules, such as, "Nice girls don't get angry" (McFarland & Baker-Baumann, 1988, p. 37).

Although clearly identified by women in their everyday experience, few studies have examined the relationship of anger and eating. The following discussion will give credence to our assertions that (a) obesity is a woman's issue, and (b) anger (a strong primary emotion with roots deep in the psyche) has not been given sufficient consideration in research or in assessing and treating the obese woman. In this chapter, we examine the prevalence of obesity, cultural values, and the role of emotions, (anger, specifically) in relation to eating and obesity. The voluminous literature on obesity, a complex multidimensional phenomenon, cannot be reviewed here; of necessity, we limit our discussion to emotional factors in its etiology and maintenance. References to clinical practice originate from the chapter authors' personal and professional experience.

One of the chapter author's (B. Shirk) interest in obesity began in the early 1980s as an educator involved in developing a university nursing curriculum. Intrigued by the role of obesity as a risk factor for major health problems, she conducted a research project exploring the response of obese people with hypertension to a weight loss program using behavior modification. Behavior modification did not demonstrate significance in the study, but this research led to an ongoing curiosity about obesity and its consequences. For the past 12 years, she has been involved in assisting people with weight management in an internal medicine practice.

The other chapter author's (S. Russell) interest in obesity stems from her personal struggle with weight. As a critical care nurse and educator for the past 12 years, she has witnessed the direct impact that obesity has on health and longevity. Intimately involved with the struggle of weight management, she is completing doctoral studies with a specialty focus in eating disorders. She has worked clinically with inpatients on an eating disorders unit and been involved with support groups. She has cared for patients with the usual cardiovascular complications one would expect to be associated with obesity as well as the extremes. One obese woman admitted postoperatively to the intensive care unit had bilateral mastectomies to relieve the weight on her chest to facilitate better respiratory effort. As a result of years of frustration and failure with weight loss attempts, this woman and her physicians resorted to surgery to excise part of the weight (a combined total of approximately 30 pounds). The surgery did not solve her problem with obesity. To make matters worse, no one had even thought it worthwhile preoperatively to discuss reconstructive surgery options.

REVIEW OF LITERATURE

Prevalence of Obesity

Data collected as a part of the National Health and Nutrition Examination Survey (NHANES II) from 1976 to 1980, conducted by the National Center for Health Statistics, revealed that 34 million adult Americans were overweight. Out of this group, 12.4 million were *severely* obese. Across all age groups, women were more obese than men (Van Itallie, 1985). Estimates of the percentage of overweight women in the United States vary among sources found in the scientific and popular literature. Orbach (1990) estimates that 50% of American women are overweight. Stunkard (1984) reported approximately 35% of the female population are obese. Of that group, 90.5% of obese women were 20% to 40% overweight, 9% were in the 41% to 100% category, and only 0.5% were more than 100% (estimated to be 200,000). Among young college women, 35% to 60% are estimated to be "binge eaters," and 21% of high school females, 13 to 19 years of age, report binge eating at least once per week. An additional 7% also admit to purging by vomiting or using laxatives in an attempt to control their weight (Rodin, Silberstein & Striegel-Moore, 1984). Dieting constitutes a $5 billion a year industry, which includes a variety of treatment methodologies for eating disorders with costs ranging from $25 a week to $30,000 a month (White, 1991). Women outnumber men 9 to 1 in diet clinics; the majority of overweight men do not attempt to lose weight (Bennett, 1991). Obesity is indeed a women's issue.

Ideal Body Image for Women

Obese women in the United States contend with social prejudice because of the cultural valuing of slimness. Construed as being of low social value, their self-esteem is affected dramatically. In fact, these women would prefer to talk about sexually sensitive issues than answer questions about their weight (Garrow, 1988; Rodin et al., 1984; Wadden & Strunkard, 1985). The present standard for the female body has changed considerably from the turn of the century when a full bust and large hips were in vogue. The advent of the flapper age in the 1920s began the trend to the slim, boyish figure for women. The 1960s and the "Twiggy" look propagated that image. Today, a firm muscular build is considered the ideal; an increase in the use of weights to achieve this ideal has been documented by Seid (1989). This image is made glamorous and desirable by the advertising media, which bring these slim women into our homes via television, magazines, and newspapers. Frequently, it is women from middle to upper socioeconomic levels who feel the need to conform. The lower a woman is on the socioeconomic scale, the greater the obesity (Bennett, 1991). Women striving for the "perfect" figure face biological roadblocks and emotional anguish. The normal fat distribution, in addition to changes associated with maturity, forestalls accomplishment of that "ideal" for most women. Women by nature tend to have more total body fat than men; they have twofold more fat cells in their bodies (Kraemer, Berkowitz, & Hammer, 1990). Seid (1989) noted "that only five percent of the female population are in the slimmest end of the weight distribution"; therefore, "95 percent of the women" are set up for failure (p. 261). Emotionally, many women experience feelings of low self-esteem, failure, self-deprecation, and guilt (Stunkard et al., 1986). They are in conflict and struggle with restricted eating, the abundance of food, and the biological need to eat. Frequently, they risk their health. They may develop malnutrition and other problems by diet/ binge eating, using limited food diets, using very low calorie diets, and using self induced vomiting (Orbach, 1990; Seid, 1989; Wadden & Strunkard, 1985).

Health Consequences of Obesity

Obesity is a major health risk for women to develop several serious problems. Abdominal fat (independent of total body fat) is implicated in coronary artery disease, non-insulin–dependent diabetes, elevated blood lipids, hypertension, and stroke (Pi-Sunyer, 1991). Additional problems are cancer of the uterus, of the breast, and of the gall bladder and ducts; and varicose veins. Obesity also compounds arthritis, degenerative joint disease, stress incontinence, low back pain, hypoventilation syndrome (sleep apnea), and gout (Bjorntorp, 1985; Garfinkel, 1985; Pi-Sunyer, 1991; Van Itallie, 1985). Both the Framingham and the American Cancer Society studies indicate that "the greater the degree of overweight, the higher the mortality ratio or excess death rate" (National Institutes of Health Consensus Development Panel, 1985, p. 1075). Although many obese women diet successfully, maintaining weight loss is another battle. Recidivism rates are high in terms of weight loss maintenance (*Tufts University Diet and Nutrition Letter*, Gershoff, 1991). If weight loss cannot be maintained, a woman's health may be affected. The Framingham study indicated that fluctuating body weight ("yo-yo dieting") was associated with a higher incidence of coronary heart disease. In fact, in the 30- to 44-year-old group (the group that most commonly diets), "weight fluctuation was most strongly associated with adverse health outcomes" (Lissner et al., 1991, p. 1843).

Emotion and Eating

Obesity is viewed theoretically from five different perspectives. The biological perspective involves the relationship of caloric intake to energy expenditure, the role of genetics, and the involvement of the endocrine system in altered metabolic processes. The psychoanalytic perspective basically views obesity as "an expression of an intrapsychic conflict that occurred in the oral stage of psychosexual development" (Gelazis & Kempe, 1988, p. 664). The cognitive perspective considers obesity to be the result of irrational thinking processes related to food. From the sociocultural perspective, familial and cultural values are thought to "influence the development of feelings, attitudes, and preferences about food and eating behaviors" (Gelazis & Kempe, 1988, p. 664). The fifth perspective views overeating as "a learned behavior related to environmental cues and emotional states" (Gelazis & Kempe, 1988, p. 664). Emotion and eating are conceptually linked in the psychology literature by two dominant views, the externality hypothesis and the psychodynamic (psychoanalytic) hypothesis (Slochower, 1983).

The externality hypothesis examines responsiveness to internal versus external food cues. This hypothesis looks at eating behavior as stimulated by environmental (external) cues rather than physiologic (internal) cues. In numerous studies internal versus external cues have been tested. Early studies demonstrated a significant increase in obese subjects' responses to emotionally distressing environmental stimuli. Rodin, Elman, and Schachter (1974), found that obese subjects described more distress and demonstrated greater task interference when exposed to emotionally upsetting audiotapes. The administration of painful shock while attempting to learn a complex task also was shown to affect obese subjects more dramatically. Obese subjects made greater numbers of errors and reported greater nervousness than nonobese subjects. In a study by Edelman (1984), greater weight was associated with responsiveness to external cues than to internal cues. The study also demonstrated a weak correlation between emotional responsiveness and binging, and a stronger correlation between dieting restraint and emotional responsiveness. Although both studies demonstrated a relationship between obesity and external food cues, neither examined actual eating behavior in response to external cues; rather, the association was made after obesity had already been established. Both studies used small samples.

Subsequent studies have examined this dichotomy more closely and now indicate that these external and internal cues are to some extent interdependent. Rodin (1980) explains that obese individuals have been shown to have several endocrine and metabolic abnormalities related to adiposity. The obese individuals who were most responsive to external cues (i.e., the smell, sight, and sound of a steak on the grill) also demonstrated the greatest insulin response. Oversecretion of insulin in response to food cues might induce the individual to consume an increased amount of calories to achieve a metabolic balance. The excess calories would be more inclined to be stored as fat. This phenomenon has also been demonstrated in individuals of normal weight suggesting that externality is not exclusive to obesity but instead may reflect "an underlying tendency toward hyperresponsiveness" (Rodin, 1980, p. 234). Therefore, when a person who is dieting sees, smells, or even thinks about food, a complex physiological response may be set in motion that willpower or self-restraint cannot control. In studies conducted with newborn infants, babies whose parents were overweight demonstrated a stronger preference for sweet taste than babies of normal weight parents. This study suggests that the risk of obesity may be present from birth and is compounded by an environment that, in American society, is full of food cues (Rodin, 1980).

The psychodynamic (psychoanalytic) hypothesis contends that obesity is the result of eating in response to emotional states influenced by early developmental processes (Slochower, 1983). Steven Levenkron, cited by Katherine (1991) explains.

> Our first discomfort in life is met with food. After the violent passage through the birth canal, we are given milk. And the most frequently repeated comfort given us as infants is food. The bottle is often used to stop crying regardless of the cause. (p. 15)

In fact, this very action is postulated to be related to the subsequent association of emotional states with food, resulting in confusion regarding internal physiologic hunger. The inability of a parent to distinguish between infant needs for food versus other emotional needs is thought to contribute to the infant's subsequent inability to discriminate between hunger and other states such as fear, anxiety, and anger. The continued lack of appropriate need fulfillment delays or retards progression through the oral stage resulting in fixation on oral gratification. These individuals may then learn to label any emotional state of arousal as hunger (Andrews, 1990; Bruch, 1961; Schachter, 1971; Slochower, 1983). Perlow and Shrifter (1992) suggest that this pattern continues throughout childhood in family dynamics by using food for comfort and nurturing. Eating is a response to anger, frustration, anxiety, and other distress states; this behavior is referred to in the literature as "emotional eating" (Perlow & Shifter, 1992, p. 166). Stress induces an intense emotional reaction that as an adult, elicits a return to food "in an attempt to recapture the security and comfort experienced in infancy (Slochower, 1983, p. 13). Food provides a sense of being nurtured, cared for, and interconnected.

> Shredded Wheat is not a very good substitute for Mother, but when Mother is no longer available we may try to replace her with food. In the process of growing up, girls have to do more than grow away from their dependence on Mother. They usually become Mothers themselves. They move away from being nurtured into doing the nurturing. (*Listen to the Hunger*, Elizabeth L. 1987, p. 6)

Kaplan and Kaplan (1957) have identified 27 meanings of overeating that have been proposed by psychoanalysts regarding the transformation of oral needs, thus resulting in ambiguity in terms of generalizations and research direction. Bychowski (1950), cited by Kaplan and Kaplan (1957), presents the psychoanalytic view that eating represents the "oral incorporative introjective mechanism, a type of unconscious cannibalism" that serves to express hostility in obese patients (p. 194). Woodman, in a Jungian approach, proposes that generations of young women have experienced rejection, hopelessness, bitterness, and disapproval of their mothers. Confronted with propagation of their submissive female role, many women prayed that their unborn children would be boys. Some women adopted masculine values and conducted their household management

> so the atmosphere was geared to order, to goal-oriented ideals, to success in life, success that they themselves felt they had missed. The gall of their disappointment their children drank with their mother's milk. Unrelated to their own feminine principle, these mothers could not pass on their joy in living, their faith in being, their trust in life as it is. (Woodman, 1982, pp. 16–17).

Girls, therefore, experienced rejection, not only in childhood in relation to their mothers, but their very essence of "being." Thus the maternal matrix that represents the "Great Mother" is insufficient. Unconscious conflict is manifested in psychosomatic form. Food is viewed as

> neurosis that compels women toward consciousness . . . the creative purpose of the neurosis is to bring the woman to confront within herself the negative mother which her feminine body naturally rejects. The negative mother is a foreign substance; it is alien; it does not belong to her any more than do two pounds of chocolates before she goes to sleep. Her body is demanding that she differentiate herself out from it so that she can discover who she is as a mature woman. The task her own mother may have failed to perform, she must perform. That is the new consciousness, the giant leap, the healing in her own life which she is being called upon to incorporate. (Woodman, 1982, pp. 22–23)

Overeating is conceptualized as an attempt to invoke the "positive mother" associated with nurturing, security, and comfort. Just as the unmet childhood need was inappropriately met by the "negative mother" so too, the binge results in a negative experience. "The eucharist begins sacred and ends demonic, thus repeating the child's experience of mother" (Woodman, 1982, p. 35). Associated with the consumed food, the negative mother is perceived as being trapped in the stomach resulting in bloating or swelling. Ritualistic vomiting is viewed as an attempt to purge the negative mother from the stomach. When a woman is ready to bring the unconscious identification of the negative mother to consciousness, she is able to understand that she, like her mother, was unable to fulfull her own actual needs. "Only then will she be able to nourish herself, and therefore transform a demonic ritual into a sacred one" (Woodman, 1982, p. 37). Eating may then lose its compulsive meaning.

Empirical Studies

Several studies have been done on the link of overeating and emotions, but few actually examined the experience of anger or focused specifically on women. Stress was cited by Pudel and Oetting (1977) as the cause for obese women and restrained eaters (women who controlled their weight by monitoring their food intake) to overeat. Further results from their study showed children and normal-weight adults ate less when stressed, but women were found to be more likely to overeat than men. In a more recent study of healthy, nonobese men and women, stress (operationalized by a film about accidents) resulted in markedly and significantly decreased food consumption by men but increased food consumption by women (Grunberg & Straub, 1992). Cattanach, Phil, Malley, and Rodin (1988) studied psychologic and physiologic reactivity to stressors in subjects with eating disorders and found significant effects for anger, depression, tension, and dysphoria. Although differences between the eating disordered and control groups were not significant, "eating disordered tended to report higher levels of all the negative mood states" (p. 595). Slochower, Kaplan, and Mann (1981) investigated the relationship between the stress of final exams and eating behavior for a group of obese and nonobese students. During exam week, obese students demonstrated increased eating (about 2½ times more) related to anxiety and loss of control. Following the exams, anger was correlated with eating, but this correlation was not evident during the exam week. They hypothesized that during exam week, the loss of control was understandable related to the ambiguous process of studying for and taking exams. Following exams, the continued loss of control related to the evaluation of those exams, and students did not have a target that was quite as understandable. The evaluation process of those exams was clearly beyond their control.

Emotional upset and negative moods were found to be antecedents for bingeing in two recent studies (Kristeller & Rodin, 1989; Schlundt et al., 1991). Grilo, Shiffman, and Wing (1989) analyzed relapse crises and coping among dieters using cluster analysis. One factor labeled "upset" characterized crises related to anger. Ninety-one percent of the crises related to anger resulted in relapse from the diet, although the findings of this study must be viewed with caution because of the small number of subjects in this cluster ($N = 11$). A study by Leon and Chamberlain (1973) found that dieters reported instances of emotional arousal ranging from happiness to anger to boredom as likely triggers of eating. These subjects were volunteers from a local weight loss club and were primarily white, middle aged, and middle class. Sjoberg and Persson (1979) reported anger as one of the strong emotional stressors that contributed to diet breakdowns in their weight loss patients. However, the sample size was small ($N = 9$), and only one subject specifically identified anger as the contributory stressor. Bingeing was shown to distract, effectively change the focus, and provide relief for subjects who experienced anxiety, disappointment, or anger in a study by Loro and Orleans (1978). This study included a large number of women ($N=230$) referred by physicians. Obese patients, according to studies by Rand, Stunkard, and Glucksman, were more likely to gain weight when they were depressed, anxious, or angry (Rand, 1982). Haddock and colleagues (1990) looked at the impact of obesity on the psychosocial functioning of married individuals and found that overweight females reported significantly greater anger and depression.

From the work by Schlundt et al. (1991), one is struck by the data indicating that food is used to alter moods. If any activity or substance that alters a mood is defined as addictive, then eating to alter mood may also be an addictive behavior. Looking at women with addictive problems, Rosenfield and Stevenson (1988) explored the oral behaviors of normal alcohol users who were of normal weight, those who were overweight, and recovering alcoholic women. Their perceptions of stress were evaluated. The findings were as follows: overweight women ate more spicy/salty foods, and they chose "high calorie foods regardless of their stress levels." In contrast to the other two groups, they ate more each day and even ate more on days when stress was reduced. Data about the recovering alcoholic group showed they ate more sweet, starchy, and salty/spicy foods when stressed and also smoked more, thereby substituting one addictive substance for another, food or smoking for alcohol. The normal-weight group increased eating, smoking, and alcohol intake on pleasant days with the greatest in-group variability.

Root (1989) studied women who had repeatedly failed treatment for "alcohol, substance and food abuse." These women were often labeled "resistant to treatment" or "addictive personalities." Her literature review revealed that 30% to 75% of the women who failed treatment had been either physically or sexually abused. Tice (1991) substantiated those figures; she reported 50% of the women admitted to an eating disorder clinic had been sexually assaulted. Root's subjects exhibited problems with depression, anxiety, interpersonal relationships, and *anger.* Frequently, the subject's inability to stay in treatment pertained to the surfacing of those feelings formerly covered or suppressed by the addictive behavior. Often these "stuffed" feelings were so painful that the women sought relief in the addictive behavior. In Tice's (1991) study, women who were obese and bulimic reported feeling safe and secure being overweight. Many had gained as much as 100 pounds after the abuse. She indicated that they relied on their weight to protect them against sexual advances. They described intense anger and low self-esteem. The anger was directed toward themselves and toward the abuser and frequently projected to other men, thus affecting their "normal" interpersonal relationships. Eating was also identified as a method of denying the abuse and repressing feelings including anger.

STUDY FINDINGS

Both quantitative and qualitative analyses were conducted. The first stage of data analysis involved examination of the relationship between BMI and anger variables. Obesity is defined as "a condition of excess body fat" (Shah & Jeffray, 1991, p. 73). For these analyses, obesity was operationalized as BMI, which is currently the recommended method of measurement in the scientific and professional community (NIH Consensus Development Panel, 1985; Kraemer, Burkowitz, & Hammer, 1990). For women, obesity has been defined as a BMI of greater than or equal to 27.3. BMI is calculated by weight in kilograms divided by height in meters, squared (NIH Consensus Development Panel, 1985). For example, if you are 5 feet, 4 inches tall and weigh 150 pounds, your BMI would be 25.6. The frequency of obese versus nonobese subjects in our sample was 196 or 43.4% versus 256 or 56.6%, respectively. The mean BMI was 25.6, with a standard deviation of 5.93 and a range of 17.3 to 54.0. Backward elimination stepwise regression using BMI as the criterion variable resulted in a significant model at $p < .0001$ that explained 13% of the variance of BMI with anger-in, anger-out, and current health perception as predictors. This is only a small amount of explained variance; however, when genetics, environment, and the multiplicity of other variables are considered, 13%, although a small "piece of the pie," is significant nonetheless.

There were no significant relationships of BMI with age, education, self-esteem, depression, employment, role responsibilities, marital status, or number of children, factors that have been cited in the literature as impacting women and weight. Significant negative correlations were found with BMI and other consumptive behaviors such as smoking and drinking, suggesting that some women may choose to eat instead of drink or smoke (i.e., food is the "drug of choice"). There was one significant association of BMI with a social support variable: number of losses within the past year.

Qualitative methods were employed to investigate women's experience with eating and anger in more depth. Focus groups were used to facilitate "interpretation of quantitative results and add depth to the responses obtained in the more structured survey" (Stewart & Shamdasani, 1990, p. 15). Focus group interviews gather more detailed narrative information related to real life experience. The methodology is similar to other qualitative methods such as grounded theory, ethnography, and phenomenology (Nyamathi & Shuler, 1990). These groups were used to capture the ideas, feelings, and emotional experience of women who identified food issues as problematic. Two small groups of volunteers, a clinical group from an internal medicine practice in Illinois ($N = 4$) and a self-help support group from Tennessee ($N = 5$) elected to participate. Informed consent was obtained through established procedures and policies. Open-ended questions were asked in a group interview format. Subjects were asked to share their experience with eating, their responses to strong emotional situations and the subsequent impact, the effect of eating on feelings about self, and the effect of eating on their relationships. Interviews were taped and transcribed for analysis.

Focus group responses generally revealed that eating was a response to almost every emotion; fear, anxiety, anger, sadness, and frustration were identified. Eating was described as a "medicating response to all emotions." Celebrations and holidays were identified unanimously by both groups as significant triggers for eating. Food was associated with reward. Erica, a group member, explains:

We were rewarded with food when we did something right and that has been put as a seed in our mind and I have resorted to that as if I were thanking myself for what I have done and I think that's very difficult to undo because even now, society now, even getting together it's not only for the pleasure of being together but it's, have dinner, let's have drink, it's always based around food and dinner . . . it's a total struggle plus the emotions has a lot that's struggling against.

Injustice, resentment, discrimination and rejection were common themes that triggered eating. When things don't go right, Shelley admits to using the circumstances as an excuse to eat.

Oh yeah! What the hell, I might as well eat. They don't like me, I didn't get the job, whatever. . . .

Another identified trigger was loss of control. Doris, reflects:

I think I'm discovering too that things out of my control will trigger, right [agreeing with previous speaker], and control is a big thing for me too, when I can't control situations then that triggers me to eat. When I feel like things are [struggles for words] . . . when I can't get a grip on it, make this happen or that happen, I turn to food.

Excessive self-demands, overcompensation, and perfectionism were agreed on by both groups as difficult to deal with. Erica proclaims:

Like the genie that came out of the lamp, I am everything to everybody (snapping her fingers rapidly with emphasis) and I want to just go back in the lamp and don't anybody bother me for a hundred years. I don't want anything to do with humanity in general, I'm through with everybody . . . and I feel some sort of guilt and remorse.

Susan shared her experience with self-imposed demands.

Food also is generally there all those times but then, when it comes to responsibilities, and yet the more I would get into the food to get through all those responsibilities. . . . My problem with that is that I'll get so enmeshed with food that in fact I actually flunked out of college cause I was trying to deal with the stress of college and working but the food overcame that so strongly that I couldn't function and that can happen in small ways as well. Another part of it is that, granted, it can help me cope for a while. . . .

Gladys feels that day-to-day frustration causes a stronger emotional response for her.

Just being overly busy and I feel like I'm too busy to worry about what I'm eating. That's when I get into a bad syndrome.

Hannah described her experience with an anger-producing situation.

I've been thinking about this subject of anger and all that's involved in this particular experience hurts me—realizing that I was angry at the person who . . . it's real detailed. I'm realizing that I was angry with myself because I didn't just face the situation. And I felt helpless and my husband who is in poor health and needed to have regular meals or his blood sugar would go way down and there also was a buildup of resentment against this person who is my husband's son, who for many years that, when the relationship was poor, he would frequently drop by the house right at supper and he ate a lot and we didn't have enough on hand and I offered him food, supper, and he would bring something to drink, too, where my husband wasn't supposed to have it, and they'd sit there and drink. Rather than confronting him because my husband adored him and we'd been in many battles over this stepson, I just steamed, fumed and felt helpless and hopeless and then after he finally left, I felt, what's the use, I can't deal with this and so I ate the leftovers.

Loss of control and eating had a significant impact on self-esteem. Hannah explained:

. . . every time I've been on a binge, I've been swamped with guilt. My brain tells me that I know better, that I should treat my body better. When I was through (no longer bingeing) of course, I felt a lot better about myself and that's hard to see in a mirror. I can only see my true size in a photograph. I've dieted many times and I go make pictures and then you have problems. It affects your self-esteem.

Members in both groups equated the effects of eating with a similar effect from drinking alcohol. Vickie explains:

. . . but food is acceptable and in society it's almost pushed at us. On the other hand is the tug and pull of looking beautiful, but going to McDonald's and eating three times a day, you know the people on the commercials are happy and eating has made them wonderful and on the other hand you easily gain weight and you overeat and you fall into that trap, you're not accepted into society.

Fear of rejection emerged as a result. Vickie continued:

. . . because you are rejected. Daily then you have to deal with the anger from being rejected. So it's kind of a cycle disease that takes it's toll, but I learned easily: if I ate, I felt better.

Both groups described other compulsive behaviors such as smoking and drinking as alternatives to eating. The Tennessee group admitted to compulsive shopping as a likely alternative and one member described compulsive reading. Healthy alternatives were also described and included taking bubble baths, listening to music, exercise, fresh air, talking to friends, resting, reading, and journaling. Amanda describes the benefits of journaling.

> Yeah, its getting out of yourself, not isolating it or keeping my feelings inside and then eating them. Eating my feelings, telling somebody. Writing is not really telling a person, but it's getting it out of myself.

Both groups agreed that other people affected their perception of who they are. Shelly stated she was fortunate to have a lot of good friends to reinforce her self-image positively. She says they

> help me feel that at least on one level of my self-esteem, that no matter what everybody tells you, unless you believe it yourself, its like, I know what my friends think about me and then I know what I think about myself and they say, "oh, you're so smart."

However, Shelly ruefully acknowledges that

> the support and reinforcement from the good things they say can be erased pretty quickly by two or three assholes on the street.

When asked if that affected her belief system, Shelley replied,

> "No, they reinforce my own feelings about me."

Other members' responses included the following:

> I don't think I'm near as good a person or great a person, whatever kind of adjective that describes me as a person. If I'm overweight, I diminish how good I think I am. I'm less.

> Nothing else matters. If you're overweight nothing else that you do matters.

When noticed in a restaurant eating ice cream, Amanda describes her feelings in response to "looks" as

> Rage! You bet because you stifle so much, you don't speak out nearly as much because you don't want to do anything to draw attention to yourself, absolutely nothing! You're already this big person so when you come into a room they already know you're there so why would you verbalize, or draw even further attention?

Gladys confirms this experience. She adds, "And then the feelings make you eat more and more. And you keep people at bay too because you don't want any more hurt, you've got enough." Gladys describes her isolation as "hanging in the shadows."

> I tried not to "hang in the shadows." I did a lot even when I was at my heaviest. I went to college. I graduated with a degree—I did a lot. I don't know how I did it, but I did it a lot. But, I ate over it all. I don't know, it didn't make me "hang in the shadows." I kept putting myself out there. I kept getting kicked. . . . I feel anger too. But I feel like, geez, I am fat. What they said is true. I am out of control. I'm not a very good person. I shouldn't look like this, this is ridiculous. And then I got mad at myself. There was anger, anger directed at myself mostly. What in the world am I doing? They're right. That's what I thought. Fat people are stupid people and I shouldn't be a fat person because I'm not stupid.

Eating and weight were acknowledged as having an effect on relationships. Doris lamented that relationships were affected, "very poorly." Debbie felt it has had an impact on her relationships. She ponders, "Well, I think it does because society has decided. . . ." She hesitates and then continues, "I'm not really clear about isolating myself. I mean, I didn't gain weight so that nobody would ask me out—insulating myself."

Perhaps the most succinct summary of the major interview theme can be found in these words of one of the study participants. Shelley reflects, "I've used food for so long as my damn near constant companion it's really hard to separate out the different emotions I have suppressed because of it."

The individual responses revealed the *real* impact that eating had on women's lives. These are the exact words of the women themselves. Although some words may be offensive to readers, we present unedited material from the tapes to truly reflect the pain and anger of the experience of our respondents. A model emerged from the focus groups' collective experience (see Figure 9.1).

The group consensus indicated that food was used to "medicate" as expressed by this individual's gleeful comment, "Food is such a wonderful drug. It's so easily accessible, nobody's ever gonna bust me for havin' a burger and fries in the car!" Skillfully diverting the focus away from negative emotions such as anger, food is used to cope with these uncomfortable feelings and attempt to soothe and nurture the self.

CONCLUSION

The results of this study indicate that anger is a contributing factor in women's obesity that deserves greater attention in research and treatment. Anger behavior is amenable to modification (see Chapter 12 and epilogue). Findings indicate that for some women eating may be the "drug of choice" as

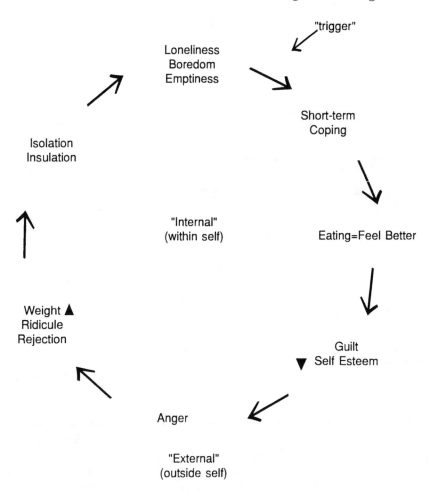

FIGURE 9.1 Model of emotion-eating linkages.

indicated by the inverse relationships between smoking and BMI and between drinking and BMI. Health professionals need information about factors that may influence choice of "drug" so that appropriate interventions can be designed. Further studies are warranted in view of the impact of obesity on health status and general well-being.

> It is important to become more aware about the true source of any anxiety or stress, more insightful about where your emotional vulnerabilities lie, and then to find ways to tolerate your feelings, to express them rather than to "swallow" them by eating. (*Tufts University Diet and Nutrition Letter*, Gershoff, 1991, p. 6)

■ 10
Women's Anger
and Substance Use

Elizabeth G. Seabrook

We asked ourselves why we were angry. In most cases it was found that our self-esteem, our pocketbooks, our ambitions, our personal relationships (including sex) were threatened. So we were sore. We were "burned up."

—Alcoholics Anonymous

This chapter is concerned with the use of mood-altering substances by women and how substance use and abuse are related to the expression of anger and anger propensity. The substances of interest in our study include alcohol, prescription drugs, over-the-counter (OTC) drugs, and nicotine (cigarette smoking). As was stated earlier in this book, when we began to look at women's anger, we found a shocking lack of research and some indication that people did not really want to address this topic. The same is generally true about substance use among women. Nellis (1980) describes women's drug and alcohol habits as being "the subject of whispered confidences, gossip-column innuendoes, and hushed family embarrassment" (p. 1). Thus, in this chapter, we will be looking at two topics that, historically, have been viewed as socially unacceptable among women and that are laden with myths and misunderstandings.

As has been the case with anger, research pertaining to substance abuse has been undertaken predominantly by male researchers studying male subjects. In the past, women who abuse substances have either been ignored by researchers or, when combined with men in studies, have been viewed as anomalies when results were not consistent with those of men. According to Hughes (1988), it is likely that male-as-norm assumptions have contributed to a lack of research in the field of substance abuse among women. In the past two decades, however, there has been a dramatic increase in research on alcohol problems in women, possibly as a result of the women's movement of the 1960s and 1970s (Wilsnack, Wilsnack, & Klassen, 1984). Most of this research, however, has been focused on women who are alcoholic and are in treatment. Interest in women who are problem drinkers can be seen in more recent research (Wilsnack et al., 1984). Predictors of drinking, onset of heavy drinking, drinking behaviors, and consequences of drinking are now being investigated with female samples. One recent longitudinal study looks at the development of women's problem drinking over a 5-year period (Wilsnack, Klassen, Schur, & Wilsnack, 1991). These studies indicate that there are important physiological, sociological, and psychological differences between men and women that influence their use and responses to alcohol and drugs. On the whole, however, information regarding etiology, theoretical explanation, and effectiveness of treatment of substance abuse among women remains scanty and unclear.

The relationship between anger and substance abuse among women has received very little attention in the literature. We will discuss research related to each substance addressed in our study later in this chapter; however, a quick look at the work of two authors gives us an idea of the continuing dearth of information on this topic. Fifteen years ago Gomberg (1978) identified the lack of data on this subject and proposed that alcoholic drinking among women might be an expression of anger toward oneself and toward others. She also suggested that women (a) may be denying their anger and covering it up with compliance and submissiveness or (b) may be frightened of their anger and incapable of expressing it. Even though Gomberg identified anger as possibly being a critical issue in understanding the etiology of alcoholism, to date few published reports specifically address alcohol and anger. In her popular book on anger, Tavris (1989) only briefly talks about alcohol. She identifies the use of alcohol as a means of soothing one's anger as well as an excuse for ventilating it. The relationship of women's anger expression and alcohol use was not discussed.

Members of Alcoholics Anonymous (AA) have recognized the link between anger and drinking for many years. The acronym HALT has been used to help recovering alcoholics recognize when they are *h*ungry, *a*ngry, *l*onely, or *t*ired. When these feelings occur, the AA program of recovery suggests that alcoholics contact a sponsor or go to a meeting to discuss their feelings instead of reverting to old, dysfunctional behaviors. One of the benefits of AA is the opportunity to discuss one's feelings. AA has been found to be one of the most successful approaches to recovery from alcoholism. The 12-step program of AA has been adopted by other groups of people who suffer from addiction to substances and behaviors (e.g., cocaine, narcotics, gambling, over-eating).

This chapter examines the use and abuse of alcohol, prescription drugs, OTC drugs, and nicotine among ordinary women and the relationship of these variables to anger. Although the use of illicit drugs is widespread in America and creates a multitude of problems for our society, we did not obtain information about the use of these drugs in our study of women's anger and will not include this topic in our discussion.

Our study attempts to answer these questions: Are there any differences in the modes of anger expression, cognitive anger, and trait anger between drinkers and nondrinkers? Smokers and nonsmokers? Prescription drug users and nonusers? OTC drug users and nonusers? What characteristics might indicate women who are at risk for substance abuse?

The questionnaire used with our sample of women asked three questions about the use of substances: (a) During the past year, have you taken any prescription drugs? (specify); OTC drugs? (specify); (b) How many packs of cigarettes do you smoke daily? (If a nonsmoker, put zero). Number of years smoked?; (c) How many drinks of beer, wine, or liquor do you usually drink in a week? (If nondrinker, put zero).

It is important to remember when looking at our questions and the information collected that we are looking at a group of ordinary women. If we had been questioning a group of women whom we suspected to have a problem with substance abuse, we would have asked more in-depth questions from which we could make more definitive conclusions or diagnoses or formulate some plan for treatment. In our research, however, we are simply trying to see if there are any relationships between the styles of anger expression that women customarily use or their overall proneness to anger (trait anger) and the amount of substances they consume on a regular basis.

It should be pointed out from the beginning that we are not attempting to prove a cause-and-effect relationship between anger and substance use or abuse. We cannot say that substance abuse *causes* women to be angry or that angry women abuse substances because they want to dampen or mask their anger. The contribution of the present study is an initial exploration of an aspect of this multifaceted problem that has largely been overlooked, given the focus on genetic and environmental influences in much of the literature.

ALCOHOL

Review of Literature

Alcohol abuse and alcoholism have historically been considered problems predominantly affecting men. Much of the early research with regard to women and alcohol focused on the effects of drinking on the fetus during pregnancy, rather than on women as individuals and the problems they experienced as a result of their use of alcohol. Women who exhibit signs of problem drinking have been perceived by our society as deviant and unfeminine. Although drinking and drunkenness have been viewed as affirmation of masculinity for men, disapproval of this type of behavior in women has led to shame and secrecy for women (Reed, 1987). Women who have problems with alcohol have been stigmatized by our society because they are considered to be unable to perform their function in life: taking care of men and children (Sandmaier, 1980). The double standard for drinking may have contributed to the invisibility of some women who are problem drinkers. Women have been found to have a tendency to drink alone and at home (Gomberg, 1974). The term "hidden drinkers" refers to those women who are generally not employed outside the home and whose drinking problems go undetected even by family members (Kilbey & Sobeck, 1988). Without early identification of drinking problems, these women are at risk for developing a dependence on alcohol as well as for premature death due to cirrhosis of the liver, suicide, and alcohol-related accidents.

Public interest in alcohol began to broaden in the 1970s when First Lady Betty Ford came forward and revealed to the nation that she had a problem with alcohol and drugs. Along with public acknowledgment of the problem of substance abuse in women has come increased interest in the differences between women and men regarding identification of the problem, issues needing attention in treatment, and effectiveness of treatment. It is important at this point to note some of the differences that have been found to define better the problem that exists for women.

Surveys consistently show that more men than women drink alcohol. According to a survey conducted in 1981 by the National Institute of Alcohol Abuse and Alcoholism, 40% of the women sampled were abstainers, whereas only 25% of the men were abstainers (Kilbey & Sobeck, 1988). A 1985 study produced similar results: 45% of women abstain from alcohol, whereas 24% of men abstain (Taeuber, 1991). Fifteen million Americans abuse or are dependent on alcohol. Nearly one third of them are women (National Institute on Alcohol Abuse and Alcoholism [NIAAA], 1990).

There has been some media concern that perhaps there has been an increase in alcohol-related problems in women. However, Wilsnack and Wilsnack (1991) found no dramatic increases in drinking or heavy drinking in women over the past two decades. In a recent Department of Health and Human Services publication, Roman (1988) also concluded that data do not support a recent sharp increase in alcohol-related problems or drinking in women. What may appear to be an increase in alcohol problems in women could possibly represent an increase in awareness of these problems. More women are out of the home and are more visible in the workplace. The media may also have influenced the increased awareness of drinking among women with advertisements for alcoholic beverages. Commercials often portray women drinking with men for fun or relaxing with a social drink after a long day at the office. Some groups of women may have become less reluctant to have a drink with professional colleagues in public places. In light of the increased social acceptance of drinking suggested by the media, women with alcohol-related problems may be more visible.

Defining alcoholism, problem drinking, and alcohol abuse is a complicated process for researchers and requires multidimensional measurements. When defining these terms, it is important to be aware of at least three factors and how they interact: alcohol consumption, social and personal alcohol-related problems, and alcohol dependence (Roman, 1988). These variables can be quantified to some extent for research purposes. The interaction between these variables is complex and not clearly understood at this time, however. Other factors including family history and personality characteristics are important but are not as easily measured.

No consensus exists among researchers regarding the classification of social drinkers, heavy drinkers, problem drinkers, or alcoholics based on the quantity of alcohol consumed. Precisely defining these terms is an impossible task in light of the physiological differences between men and women as well as individual differences. Most researchers, however, classify people who drink two or more drinks per day as heavy drinkers. According to national surveys, of the females who drink, 3% to 6% are heavy drinkers, whereas 14% to 20% of males who drink are heavy drinkers (Roman, 1988). It is estimated that 9 million women are heavy drinkers (Travis, 1988). Women who consume four or more drinks per day experience more alcohol-related problems than do men (Wilsnack, Wilsnack, & Klassen, 1984). Race and ethnic differences among women have been noted in the literature and, although not a subject of our research, bear mentioning at this point. Although black women are more likely than white women to abstain from alcohol (Clark & Midanik, 1982; Herd, 1988), an equal proportion of black and white women have been found to drink heavily (Clark & Midanik, 1982; Wilsnack, Wilsnack, & Klassen, 1984).

At least three physiological factors are known to contribute to the different response to the consumption of alcohol by women as compared with men: (a) lower total body water content causing higher concentrations alcohol in the blood; (b) hormonal fluctuation because of the menstrual cycle; and (c) the decreased activity of alcohol dehydrogenase, the enzyme responsible for the metabolism of alcohol in the stomach (National Institute on Alcohol Abuse and Alcoholism, 1990). Studies show that women who abuse alcohol tend to increase their drinking when they are premenstrual. In their study, Sutker, Libet, Albert, and Randall (cited in Sobeck & Kilbey, 1988) found that women drank more frequently to reduce tension or to relieve dysphoria during their menstrual flow. It is obvious that the physiological makeup of women influences both the consumption of alcohol as well as its biological impact.

Women also experience a phenomenon known as the *telescoping effect*. Female alcoholics have been found to experience an accelerated progression from social drinking to problem drinking. This phenomenon is measured as the time from which an individual first recognizes a drinking problem until the time of first admission to treatment (Piazza, Vrbka, & Yeager, 1989). The period in which this occurs is shorter for women than men. Women have also been found to develop alcoholic liver disease after a shorter period of heavy drinking and at lower levels of daily consumption than do men (National Institute on Alcohol Abuse and Alcoholism, 1990).

Social and Personal Problems

Social and personal problems are of particular importance in assessing alcohol problems in women. As a whole, women who use alcohol are a heterogeneous group (Pihl, 1986). Psychosocial problems that affect women vary depending on their individual differences and the context of their lives. One of the most current explanations for alcoholism in women is gender-role conflict. For some women, behavior that has been traditionally considered appropriate for women is in conflict with their individual values and personal goals. There is some evidence that female alcoholics do not feel feminine and may drink to feel more womanly (Wilsnack, 1973, 1976). In a study of alcoholic and nonalcoholic women, it was found that on an unconscious level alcoholic women have a more masculine orientation (Wilsnack, 1976). Sandmaier (1980) includes anger, independence, intellectual curiosity, and adventurousness as forbidden masculine qualities that some women may try to suppress. Socialization of women in this culture prescribes that women have the capacity to suffer in a quiet, passive, and compliant way. For women who have a more unconscious masculine orientation, drinking alcohol may provide an artificial feeling of womanliness when other coping mechanisms fail. Some studies support the idea that alcohol may become an escape for women from their internal conflict and insecurity in the female role.

There is more to be learned about gender-role conflict among women. There is some evidence that gender-role conflict is not associated with alcoholism in women but rather that the inadequate support women get for their roles from society (at home and at work) is related to alcoholism. It has been found that lack of social support, both at home and at work, is associated with heavy drinking (Metzner, 1980, cited in Sobeck & Kilbey, 1988). Some studies show that the level of social support that a substance abuser experiences may be a significant factor regarding treatment and prevention of substance abuse (Tucker, 1982). Tucker found that in the absence of social support, women tend to use dysfunctional, nonsocial strategies to deal with anger as well as depression. She points out that a woman must make social connections in order to establish a support system. Women who isolate themselves and drink, are not using or establishing social support.

Age appears to be associated with alcohol consumption by women. In their 1981 study, Wilsnack et al. (1984) found an increase in drinking among middle-aged women (ages 35 to 64) compared to findings in the 1970s. An increase in *heavy* drinking in the 35- to 49-year-old group was also noted. Whereas earlier studies of women over 55 years of age showed low rates of both drinking and problem drinking (Roman, 1988), the study by Wilsnack et al. (1984) raises concern about a trend toward an increase in problem drinking as women grow older. Recent changes in gender role socialization, multiple roles, and increased acceptance of drinking among women may affect drinking patterns in the different age groups.

Stress has been shown to be an important factor in the etiology and maintenance of alcoholism (Sobeck & Kilbey, 1988). Not only are alcoholic women more likely to have grown up in unstable family environments that produced stress and disruption of normal life, they also identify their own marital and family problems as reasons for drinking (Sobeck & Kilbey, 1988). Studies of alcoholic women show that many of these women are able to cite specific life situations that precipitated a shift to problematic drinking (Gomberg, 1978; Sandmaier, 1980). Traumatic life events include divorce, abandonment, a child leaving home, infidelity, death of a spouse, depression, hysterectomy, menopause, miscarriage, or other gynecological problems. These crises are integrally related to women's roles as wives and mothers (Sand-maier, 1980). Many of the crises mentioned previously generally occur during midlife and could be significant factors in the increase of heavy drinking seen in this age group of women.

Allan and Cooke (1985) contend that the previously mentioned research is flawed. They argue that increased alcohol consumption could precipitate the increase in frequency of stressful life events. They agree with Bowher's suggestion that women's preferred method of coping probably would be the use of prescription drugs, not alcohol (cited in Allan & Cooke, 1985). These authors also question the clinical samples used in these studies. They further cite their previous study of a nonclinical sample of women, which indicated no association between life event indices and alcohol consumption in middle-aged women or women in general.

During the 1990s, we are well aware of the increase in the number of roles that women must enact both inside and outside the home. As noted in chapter 6, grown children are returning home to live because of the economic climate in this country. In some cases elderly parents are seeking home care from adult daughters. Add these family stresses to work outside the home and some women may appear to be overloaded. (see chapter 6 for more in-depth discussion). Early research suggests that conflicting roles led to stress and lowered efficiency (Sandmaier, 1980). Risk of problem drinking, however, has *not* been associated with multiple or conflicting roles (Roman, 1988). Research indicates that women who have multiple roles (e.g., wife, worker, mother) tend to have lower rates of alcohol problems (Wilsnack et al., 1984). In fact, women who experience the loss of a role, as in the case of the loss of a spouse, may be more at risk for abusing alcohol (Wilsnack & Cheloha, 1987). Women who participate in the labor force, even when in male-dominated jobs, have *not* been found to be at greater risk for problem drinking (Wilsnack & Cheloha, 1987).

In a study of female alcoholics, Parrella and Filstead (cited in Roman, 1988) found different patterns of onset of alcoholism in men and women. Women tend to show signs of onset later in life than do men. In this study, signs of onset included regular drunkenness; thinking that alcohol gives relief; identification of problem by a significant other; trying to stop; and realizing one's own problem. Gomberg (1978) cites James's study of men and women in AA and found that women report different early signs of alcohol problems. These signs include personality changes when drinking; increased drinking before menstrual cycle; being supersensitive; feeling more capable when drinking; finding unexplained bruises; and drinking before a new situation. Men did not report these behaviors. The comparison of these two studies suggests the possible need for different assessment tools. Again, the different characteristics and needs of women call for close attention if women who have alcohol problems are to be identified and receive effective treatment.

Depression is commonly linked with alcohol abuse in women (Sobeck, & Kilbey, 1988). Sclare found that 20% of women acknowledged that depression existed before their drinking problem (Sclare, 1970, cited in Sobeck & Kilbey, 1988). Wilsnack et al. (1984) concluded that depressive symptoms are more closely related to chronic rather than episodic drinking. Of women reporting an average of one or more drinks per day (during the 30 days preceding the study), 61% reported symptoms of depression. Depression is also associated with shame that women may experience as a result of failing in any aspect of their feminine role, most especially as caretakers (Gomberg, 1988).

ANGER AND ALCOHOL

Little research has been done regarding the study of anger and alcohol use, although many counselors of alcohol abusers (including the author) can attest to the salience of anger issues for their clients. Woods and Duffy in 1966 suggested that alcohol not only provides the user with missing feelings of adequacy and acceptability, but also provides permission to release anger. Conversely, alcohol's depressant effect could be appealing to individuals who need to decrease intense angry feelings. In a recent study of midlife women, Grover and Thomas (1993) found that women who experienced higher anger symptoms (e.g., having a headache when angry) tended to drink more alcohol. Studies related to cynical hostility (which can be a factor in general anger readiness—see chapter 1) may provide some insight into anger. Some studies were found linking the cynical hostility construct with drinking. Highly hostile men and women studied by Leiker and Hailey (1988) and by Houston and Vavak (1991) tended to drink more alcohol and to drive more frequently after drinking than did subjects scoring lower on hostility. Shekelle, Gale, Ostfeld, and Paul (1983) also found that hostility scores were positively associated with alcohol use. It has been reported that for social drinkers, provocation to anger and opportunity for retaliation are determinants of alcohol consumption (Marlatt, Kostum, & Lang, 1975).

Research involving women suggests that those who turn to alcohol reported that they were more likely to do so when they felt tense or nervous, and when they wanted to relax or to forget their worries (Wilsnack, 1973). Anger has been shown to be manifested as tenseness and uneasiness (Stearns, 1972) and could represent what Wilsnack is describing. In a study of premenstrual dysphoria and alcohol consumption in 14 women, Mello, Mendelson, and Lex (1990) found that for the women whose drinking increased during the premenstrual phase, hostility/anger was also increased.

Research studying gender-role conflict among women may supply us with more information about anger in women. According to Lester (1982), those women whose personal values/goals conflict with society's view of women may experience frustration, anger, and shame. Chapter 7 in this book has addressed some pertinent value issues for women.

Although our study focuses on adult women, one recent study of adolescents is of relevance to our study of anger. This study suggests a direct effect of anger on adolescent drug use (Swaim, Oetting, Edwards, & Beauvais, 1989). It was also found that anger mediated the effect of other emotional distress variables and increased the probability that adolescents would associate with drug-using peers. Alcohol and drug problems that appear later in life are probably rooted in the adolescent years. Preadolescent and adolescent years are when most drug and alcohol use begins (Oetting & Beauvais, 1987).

Study Results Regarding Anger and Alcohol Use

In our sample of women, there were nearly twice as many nondrinkers (296) as drinkers (161). Sixty-five percent abstinence in this sample is higher than that reported in the literature. Caution should be used, however, in interpreting this finding as an indication that fewer women were drinking in 1992. It should be noted that many women in our sample are from the South, and these results may reflect religious upbringing in this "Bible Belt" region.

A subsample of nondrinkers was randomly selected from the larger group to compare with the women who drank, using t tests. No significant differences were found between drinkers and nondrinkers on any of the modes of anger expression or trait anger on these t tests. Contrary to a widespread myth that women who drink are angrier than nondrinkers, this finding suggests that ordinary women who drink are *not* anger prone, nor do they express their anger in ways that are noticeably different from other women who do not drink. There was a tendency for drinkers to score higher on angry reaction than nondrinkers, although this finding was not statistically significant ($t = -1.79$; $p = .07$). Apparently, some women who drink acknowledge that they are likely to become angry in situations of negative evaluation by others (e.g., "It makes me furious when I am criticized in front of others.") This propensity could indicate a vulnerability traceable to earlier life experiences with the family of origin. As was mentioned in chapter 3, research indicates that children who were higher in trait anger were likely to have grown up in families that were (a) not supportive, (b) not open to emotional expression, (c) displayed overt conflict, and (d) were not cohesive and warm (Woodall & Matthews, 1989). Angry reaction could represent learned behavior that was modeled in this type of family. It is also possible that early life experiences of criticism in this type of conflictual, noncaring environment may have eroded these women's self-concepts and led to a defensive stance with regard to criticism.

The family environment described earlier, from which angry children tend to come, is similar to the description of an alcoholic home. Alcoholic homes often foster an atmosphere of conflict, tension, and uncertainty (Kinney & Leaton, 1987). Emotional, security, and physical needs of the children often go unmet. A troubled child, including a child who acts out his or her anger, may be a symptom of an alcoholic problem in a family (Kinney & Leaton, 1987).

We do not have information about the use of substances in the families studied by Woodall and Matthews, and we cannot conclude that drinkers in our study came from dysfunctional families that were noncaring and emotionally unavailable. The tendency for women who drink to score higher on angry reactivity certainly warrants further investigation. Family background may be an important variable regarding the etiology of angry reaction.

Having compared the drinkers and nondrinkers, we then looked for correlations between amount of alcohol use (number of drinks consumed) and anger variables in the group of women who do admit to use of alcohol. Consistent with the findings of Grover and Thomas (1993), those women who reported higher somatic anger symptoms tended to drink more alcohol ($r = .20$, $p = .07$). Although some studies have cited stress as a factor in alcohol consumption, there was no correlation between stress and alcohol use in the present sample. Nor was an association found between depression and drinking. We did find relationships, however, between the use of alcohol and the use of other substances. Smoking was found to be significantly related to alcohol use ($r = .14$; $p = .006$ in the nonclinical sample; $r = .16$, $p = .0004$ in the full sample), and a tendency for alcohol users to use OTC drugs was also noted ($r = .10$; $p = .04$); these correlations are weak, however. From the literature we know that 68% of smokers eventually start drinking (Ray & Ksir, 1987).

Alcohol, nicotine, and the psychoactive ingredients in OTC drugs are all mood-altering and may be used by some women to dampen or excite their feelings. The fact that each of these substances is legal, readily available, and self-administered, in addition to our finding that women may be using them in combination, raises the possibility of accidental overdose or adverse drug reaction. Prospective studies of women's drug and alcohol use have shown that frequent use of one substance is highly correlated with the use of another (Lex, 1991). In our study, drinking was also inversely related with affect support (feeling loved and admired), $(r = -.19; p = .006)$, which is consistent with literature cited earlier in the chapter.

Analyses by age group were performed and yielded interesting results related to anger. Women were divided into groups as follows: (a) age 35 and younger, (b) ages 36 to 45, and (c) older than age 45. Drinking was not significantly related to any anger variables in the 35 and younger or the 36 to 45-year-old group of women. Women 36 to 45 years of age who consume alcohol did show a tendency $(r = .25; p = .09)$ to engage in unhealthy thinking and ruminating about angry incidents ("I keep thinking about what happened over and over again.") There were several associations between number of drinks and anger in the group of women older than age 45. Women older than age 45 who drink report more physical symptoms of their anger (measured by the Framingham Anger Symptoms Scale), such as headaches, shakiness, and tension $(r = .24; p = .06)$, as well as other bodily reactions to anger (measured by the Contrada Somatic Anger Scale), including quickened pulse, clenched fists, and faster respirations $(r = .52; p = .003)$. A tendency for drinking to be associated with rumination about angry incidents (cognitive anger) was also noted in this group $(r = .33; p = .07)$.

To create a profile of women who might be "at risk" of developing a problem with alcohol, we divided our sample into a "low" use group (one to four drinks per week) and a "high risk" group (five or more drinks per week). Five drinks per week was selected as the lower limit of the "at risk" group based on a review of the various parameters set in other studies. It is well known that people who use alcohol have a tendency to underreport their use. It is possible to conclude, therefore, that a woman who admitted drinking five drinks could very well have consumed more. The quantity of five drinks (two less than a drink per day) was selected to compensate for the possibility of underreporting.

Statistical comparison of the groups was not possible because of unequal sample size; therefore, descriptive data were examined for trends and patterns. Table 32 (see Appendix) presents means of groups of nondrinkers, low-level drinkers, and high-risk drinkers. From the table of means we are able to see that women who are high-risk drinkers look different in several respects from low level drinkers. Although the magnitude of these differences is not large, high risk drinkers score higher on trait anger, anger symptoms, somatic anger, and cognitive anger. Compared to low risk drinkers and nondrinkers, it appears that these women are somewhat more anger prone and experience more symptoms of anger, such as headaches and shakiness. These women also engage more in unhealthy thinking and ruminating about angry incidents. Anger-discuss was lower for high risk drinkers, indicating that these women are less likely to engage in the healthy form of anger expression—discussion of anger. High-risk drinkers also scored higher on depression than low-level and nondrinkers. A relationship between chronic drinking and depressive symptoms in women has been noted in the literature (Sobeck & Kilbey, 1988). It is not possible to establish a cause-and-effect relationship between these two variables, however. For some women, alcohol may be used as a form of self-medication for depression (Wilsnack, 1984). On the other hand, alcohol is also known to exacerbate depression.

Looking at the demographics of the high-risk drinkers we found that fewer of them were married, somewhat fewer were employed, and far fewer were regularly involved in church than the women in the low drinking group. This information gives us an idea about the support systems that may be lacking for women who are high risk drinkers. It has been noted in the literature that some women tend to isolate themselves and drink at home. We are not able to determine if these women isolate because they are drinking or if they are without social support and, therefore, drink out of loneliness. Our results are consistent with a study of adolescents in which the researchers found that religious commitment was negatively associated with adolescent alcohol use (Jessor & Jessor, 1977).

Examination of means for nondrinkers on the anger measurements reveals that these women experience more anger-in than the low and high-risk drinkers. Some of the nondrinkers may hold the stereotypic view that "nice ladies" do not drink, and they may keep their angry feelings to themselves. Interestingly, the nondrinkers scored lower as a group on the measure of self-esteem. Although these women keep their angry feelings to themselves, they may decrease their self-esteem by not being true to their feelings and values. Low-risk drinkers appear to be more verbal about their anger than high-risk and nondrinkers, as evidenced by higher scores on anger-out and anger-discuss.

Additional age group analyses were performed in order to compare nondrinkers, low risk drinkers, and high risk drinkers (see Table 33, Appendix). Some of the results of our study are contrary to what has been found in other research on the relationship between age and use of alcohol. We found that the largest percentage of drinkers were women in the age 45 and older group (37.9%). The percentage of women using alcohol in our sample increased with age. These results oppose a review of research, which indicates that percentage of drinkers is inversely related to age (Roman, 1988). As mentioned before, this may reflect a change in socialization of women as well as the more accepting attitude toward alcohol use among women.

"High-risk" drinking (5 or more drinks per week) appeared to increase with age; the number of women who consume this amount per week was higher in the older age groups, showing a peak during middle age (36 to 45 years). These results are consistent with research reviewed by Kilbey & Sobeck (1988). Thus, more women in the midlife age group were found to be "at risk" drinkers in our study. We are not able to determine from our study if these women are actually experiencing any alcohol-related problems. It is interesting to note that the highest number of drinks consumed by the 35 and younger as well as the older than 45 age groups was 14. In the middle age group, 2% of the women consumed more than 14 drinks with the maximum number reported being 25. This finding supports the literature on increased heavy use in middle age among women.

Using the parameters in the literature for heavy alcohol (defined in terms of quantity *per day*), we found that 1.6% of women under age 35, 2% of middle-aged women, and 2.5% of women older than age 45 met the criterion of two or more drinks per day. Thus, in this sample it appears that heavy use does not decrease with age. Longitudinal studies would be helpful in determining if this is a result of the movement of women who were middle-aged during the late 1970s to early 1980s (when much of the cohort research was done) into the 45 and older age group. If this is the case, it appears that heavy drinking among these women has increased slightly. These results also speak to the issue of alcohol abuse in the elderly. It is estimated that 20% of the elderly have a significant alcohol problem (Kinney & Leaton, 1987).

PRESCRIPTION DRUGS

Literature Review

Women use more prescription and nonprescription drugs than men. The higher use of prescription drugs by women in the U.S. is well documented (cf. Verbrugge & Steiner, 1985). A 1986 national survey indicated that 10.9% of the prescription drugs used by women were psychoactive (Taeuber, 1991). Nearly twice as many women as men obtain psychoactive drugs at least once per year (Cafferata, Kasper, & Bernstein, 1983; Verbrugge, 1985). Women receive 70% of psychoactive prescriptions according to recent medical literature (Ogur, 1986). A startling statistic reported in 1980 indicates that only 10% percent of the prescriptions for tranquilizers, sedatives, and stimulants were written by psychiatrists. Most prescriptions for psychoactive drugs were written by general practitioners, internists, and obstetricians-gynecologists who do not generally receive the extensive training in the effects of these drugs that psychiatrists receive (Nellis, 1980).

Psychoactive drugs can be of tremendous therapeutic value, but they also have the potential to be very destructive when used irresponsibly. Psychoactive drugs alter a person's mood by causing either arousal or relaxation. The major groups of psychoactive drugs include tranquilizers, sedatives, narcotic analgesics, antipsychotics, antidepressants, and stimulants. Addiction to any of these drugs includes the need for more and more of the substance to achieve the original level of mood alteration or relief.

For years Valium was the most prescribed psychoactive drug in the United States (Nellis, 1980). It was, and still is, prescribed to reduce anxiety. Valium, however, was found to be addictive, producing withdrawal symptoms that mimic anxiety. Xanax entered the market after Valium and was advertised as the nonaddictive answer to Valium. Xanax, however, is highly addictive and withdrawal from it has also been found to be a serious problem. Is there a connection between women's anger and their receipt of prescriptions for psychoactive drugs? Koumjian (cited in Ogur, 1986) theorizes that Valium "has served as a form of social control by containing and deflecting discontent and perhaps even dissent" (p. 108). It's possible that Koumjian is making a reference to anger in this statement. At the least, the suppression of negative affect is suggested here. Ogur (1986) also states her impression that women who use prescription drugs do so "to suppress negative emotionality, either anger, fear, or emotional pain" (p. 111).

A favorable attitude exists in the United States toward both prescription and OTC drug use. It is socially acceptable to alleviate the pain of headaches, stomach ache, and backaches as well as drowsiness, nausea, sleeplessness, and many other ailments. In this fast-paced society where these physical conditions are inconvenient, symptom relief is the choice rather than more lengthy self-exploration. Women are known to take more kinds of preventive and curative drugs than men. They also tend to take drugs that depress the central nervous system, whereas men tend to take drugs that stimulate the central nervous system (Moore, 1988). As we have seen elsewhere in this book, somatization of anger is common in women; some women may use medications to dampen the intense anger arousal as well as attenuate the physical symptoms associated with the anger. One recent study has specifically addressed the connection between the emotion of anger and the use of prescription drugs by women (Grover & Thomas, 1993).

Women tend to use the health care system more so than men. According to the biomedical model, one must be ill to receive prescription drugs, and women are more willing to report their symptoms than men (Verbrugge, 1985). Women also are more willing to discuss the psychological effects of their physical symptoms. Thus, women report symptoms and receive pills according to Ogur (1986). Some physicians may respond to women's complaints by prescribing mood-altering drugs rather than trying to determine the underlying problems causing these symptoms. Because consumers are not always warned about the addictive potential of these substances, inadvertent habituation may result. It is not uncommon for patients to receive psychoactive drugs from different doctors for different conditions. For example, a woman may receive a muscle relaxant for back pain, an analgesic for menstrual pain, and a sedative for insomnia at the same time and from three different physicians. Drug interactions and overdose are a potential risk in such cases.

According to Moore (1988), role stress for women precipitates many of the symptoms that are relieved by psychotropic drugs. Women who are married are twice as likely as unmarried women to use tranquilizers on a daily basis (Chambers, Inciardi, & Siegal, 1975, cited in Moore, 1988). Having children in the home and being unemployed outside the home increases the likelihood of daily psychotropic drug use (Pihl et al., 1982, cited in Moore, 1988). These findings suggest that even though married women have been found to have better health than unmarried women (Verbrugge, 1985), they may be moderating the stresses of their roles by taking tranquilizers. Men and women have similar prescription rates until age 45. After age 45, women use more prescription drugs than men (Moore, 1988). Older women are also more likely to combine tranquilizers or sedatives with alcohol. This increase in prescription drug use among women coincides with the time of menopause, impending retirement, and in some cases divorce or widowhood. These changes represent role and life event stresses that are potentially anger producing.

Moore (1988) proposes that as women reach middle age and come into full maturity they may experience a greater sense of psychological freedom to review the direction their lives have taken, and the selfless choices and sacrifices they have made in their nurturing roles. Some women may recognize their anger related to their life choices and lack of reward for their sacrifices. Moore (1988) suggests that it is not depression that is being treated in these women; it is anger that is being "knocked out" by psychotropic drugs.

Factors leading to prescription drug use and abuse are multidimensional and include psychological, behavioral, biomedical, and socioeconomic components. According to Ogur (1986), issues of stereotyping, various societal forces, and socially reinforced self-negation have an impact on the climate of the physician-client relationship, which favors the prescription of psychoactive drugs. Psychosocial as well as physical needs of women who abuse prescription drugs need to be addressed in treatment for these women.

Study Results Regarding Anger and Prescription Drug Use

In our total sample, 75% of the women used prescription drugs. A random sample of drug users was selected and compared using *t* tests to the 112 nonusers. The only significant difference between these two groups was in scores on anger symptoms. We found that prescription drug users were higher in somatic anger symptoms than non-users (t = –2.09, p = .04). Analyses by age groups also revealed significant relationships between prescription drug use and anger symptoms in all three age groups: age 35 and younger (r = .29; p = .05); ages 36 to 45 (r = .21; p = .007; and older than age 45 (r = .34; p = .0002). In correlational analyses of the full sample, prescription drug use was significantly related to cognitive anger (r=.15; p=.03), and anger symptoms measured by the Framingham scale (r = .25; p = .0001) as well as the Contrada scale (r = .17; p = .02). One plausible explanation for these findings could be that women who experience anger symptoms go to doctors and request medication to alleviate headaches and other physical manifestations of their emotional experience. As seen in chapter 8, women high in anger symptoms visit doctors more often. It is acceptable in our society for women to receive medication, whereas it is not as acceptable for them to be angry. As we have previously mentioned, some physicians are satisfied to treat the symptoms and neglect further exploration of psychological and sociological problems. Data indicate that once women receive prescriptions for psychotropic drugs, there is a tendency for them to continue to use these drugs for an extended period of time (Cooperstock, 1978, cited in Moore, 1988). Men, conversely, tend to take these drugs on a more time-limited basis.

Female prescription users in our sample appear to engage in unhealthy thinking about angry incidents (e.g., situations are unfair, they were deliberately provoked). As mentioned in chapter 3 high levels of cognitions such as these are associated with systolic blood pressure reactivity. Midlife women (ages 36 to 45) who use prescription drugs were particularly prone to experience unhealthy thinking about anger incidents (r = .29; p = .01) as well as physical symptoms including rapid pulse and clenched fists (r = .22, p = .06). In the women older than age 45, prescription drug use was also significantly related to suppression of anger (r = .19, p = .05). The meaning of this finding is not clear. It is possible, however, that for some women older than age 45, expressing anger is not an acceptable alternative (see discussion of anger suppression in older women in chapter 3). These women may be medicating their pain or anger related to negative life events, such as death of spouse and menopause.

In additional correlational analyses, prescription drug use by women was found to be positively associated with stress (r = .12, p = .02 in the nonclinical sample; r = .27, p = .0001 in the full sample); depression (r = .10, p = .05 in the nonclinical sample; r=.29, p=.0001 in the full sample); and OTC drug use (r = .12, p = .02 in the nonclinical sample; r = .44, p = .0001 in the full sample). Stress is a serious issue in the lives of women in our society and a serious threat to health. As noted in chapter 6, heart disease, high blood pressure, and immunological processes are known to be affected by stress. Consequently, managing stress is one of the major goals of wellness programs. For some women in our study, use of prescription drugs appears to be a means of coping with stress. In addition to prescription drugs, these women also appear to be using OTC drugs. These women are not only at risk of addiction, accidental overdose, and drug interactions, they are also buying into the attitude of reaching for a pill to solve their problems.

Health care professionals who provide prescription drugs without referral for depression or stress when indicated may be contributing to oppression of women (Moore, 1988). Minor tranquilizers such as Xanax, Valium, and Librium decrease anxiety, but they also may dull emotional and cognitive responses, and can cause lethargy. Sedation of difficult emotion can be a collusion between the physician and female patient. Moore (1988) states that women who are inappropriately prescribed drugs are deprived of the opportunity to problem solve and to take responsibility for themselves. They may increasingly see their problems as examples of their own personal failings.

OVER-THE-COUNTER DRUGS

Literature Review

OTC drugs are those drugs that can be obtained without a prescription and may be self-prescribed and self-administered (Ray & Ksir, 1987). This group of drugs include agents such as No-Doz, Vivarin, Sominex, vitamins, aspirin, laxatives, and cold tablets. If you have a headache, you can self-prescribe an aspirin or ibuprofen. All drugs have potentially harmful side effects, even drugs that most people might consider innocuous. Recently ibuprofen (Advil), an OTC drug widely used for relief of pain, was associated with visual disturbances in three women who used the drug regularly over a course of several months (Nicastro, 1989).

What makes OTC drugs different from prescription drugs? Prescription drugs are chemicals that, because of their toxicity or other harmful effects, are judged by the Federal Drug Administration (FDA) to be unsafe for use without the supervision of a physician. Generally, a prescription drug is a chemical which is not available OTC. In some cases, however, the only difference between a prescription product and an OTC product is the amount of active ingredient per dose. There are 250,000 to 300,000 OTC drugs on the market. They vary in amounts of active ingredients and mixtures of chemicals. When one considers the many possible combinations of OTC drugs that a person might ingest, the potential for overdose and drug reaction is frightening.

In many cases, when health care providers ask clients to list medications being taken, OTC drugs are not mentioned because they do not consider them to be important. Both professionals and their patients need to be aware of a history of OTC drug use because it *is* relevant to the diagnosis of some problems. The potential for drug interactions between OTC drugs and alcohol as well as prescription drugs must be considered (Moore, 1988). OTC drugs are equally available to men and women, and research indicates that there are no sex differences in the use of these drugs (Moore, 1988).

Study Results Regarding Anger and Over-the-Counter Drug Use

Eighty-two percent of all of the women in our study reported that they use OTC drugs. Because of the disproportionate size of groups of users (n = 337) and nonusers (n = 81), a smaller subsample of users was randomly selected for t-test analyses. Comparison of the means of these two groups revealed only one significant difference between groups; nonusers of OTC drugs scored higher on anger-out than did users (t = 1.96; p = .05). We have learned that anger-out, ventilation in an attacking or blaming way, tends to cause women to subsequently feel bad about themselves. This behavior is not considered that of a "nice lady" and is not socially desirable. Women who use OTC drugs may be moderating their anger with these drugs, thereby circumventing consequences of socially unacceptable behavior.

Results of correlational analyses of the nonclinical sample showed that use of OTC drugs was negatively associated with anger-in (r = −.11; p = .04. In the full sample this relationship was somewhat stronger (r = −.16; p = .001), although the magnitude of both correlations was low. This finding indicates that women who use OTC drugs are somewhat less likely to keep their angry feelings to themselves. These results might indicate that using OTC drugs is an effective way of moderating the expression of anger. The women who take OTC drugs are self-medicating and, because they make that choice, may experience a sense of control over their lives.

OTC drug use was also associated with prescription drug use and drinking as mentioned previously. Analysis by age did not reveal any significant correlations between OTC drug use and anger variables in any of the age groups of women.

SMOKING

Literature Review

Research on smoking has been performed predominantly on male subjects and, for the most part, has dealt with health problems related to smoking and smoking cessation. Since the 1970s, this country has experienced a shift in attitude towards women's smoking, however, and the trend has been toward an increase in the number of women who smoke as well as greater acceptance of smoking among women. "You've come a long way, baby" is a popular advertising slogan that reflects (or may have even contributed to) this change in attitude. In light of the fact that cigarette smoking generally begins during adolescent years, it was alarming to find that in 1976, for the first time, more female than male high school seniors reported that they smoked (Ray & Ksir, 1987). Unfortunately, the gap between the number of men and women who smoke has continued to narrow. A 1987 survey indicates that 26.5% of females smoke and 31.2% of males smoke (Taeuber, 1991). There appears to be an increase in smoking among women between the ages of 30 and 44 (34.5%), whereas fewer women 10 years older and 10 years younger smoke, (31.6% and 31.9%, respectively). Forty-one percent of separated and divorced women smoke, which Taeuber (1991) suggests is a result of stressful situations these women face. It was found that only 25.8% of married women smoke. In 1987, for the first time, more women died of lung cancer than breast cancer (U.S. Department of Health, Education and Welfare, 1990). As the percentage of smokers has been evening out between the sexes, general acceptance of this habit has decreased. Increased awareness of the health risks of smoking, as well as social undesirability of this behavior, have contributed to a decrease in smoking in the United States.

Nicotine, the active ingredient in cigarettes, is one of the most toxic drugs known (Ray & Ksir, 1987). Cigarette smoking is responsible for one in every six deaths in the United States (U.S. Department of Health, Education and Welfare, 1990). It is a psychoactive chemical and acts as a stimulant causing arousal of the cortex of the brain. Nicotine also can have depressant and tranquilizing affects, depending on the dosage (Christen & Cooper, 1979). Nicotine is addictive in that it causes dependence, increased tolerance, and withdrawal on cessation of use. Smoking can be characterized by six factors: (1) stimulation; (2) the feeling of handling the cigarette; (3) pleasurable relaxation; (4) tension reduction; (5) psychological addiction; and (6) habit (Christen & Cooper, 1979). A person may smoke for any one or a combination of the reasons mentioned. Horn (cited in Christen & Cooper, 1979) suggests that some smokers use cigarettes to manage their emotions. He states that women, because they smoke for the tranquilizing effect, have greater difficulty quitting smoking than men, who smoke for pleasure.

Tomkins (1987) suggests that there are three types of smokers: (1) people who smoke to achieve positive affect—pleasure, (2) people who smoke to cope with negative affect, and (3) people who smoke to reduce their intolerable cravings for cigarettes. The person who smokes to feel good is able to give up smoking more easily and to find other sources of positive feelings. Those people who smoke to sedate their negative feelings are more likely to go back to smoking after cessation when things do not go well. As negative affect increases, so also does frequency of smoking in this group of smokers. Addictive smokers have the greatest difficulty with cessation of smoking. For these people, the experience of negative feelings is so intense, they panic when cigarettes are unavailable. For some people smoking is a technique used to keep the lid on suppressed anger and hostility (Christen & Cooper, 1979). Many people who stop smoking experience an inability to control their emotions and may find themselves becoming a "shrew," as one housewife described herself (Christen & Cooper, 1979).

Smoking is highly addictive because of the powerful reinforcing effect of nicotine. In the case of those who are addicted, falling blood levels of nicotine cause these people to feel bad and seek relief in the form of another cigarette. When the smoker gets relief, the behavior of smoking is reinforced. This pattern of reinforcement is, perhaps, the greatest problem associated with smoking cessation. Dependent smokers seem to need to boost their brain levels of nicotine every 20 to 30 minutes while awake (Christen & Cooper, 1979).

Researchers have found that nicotine helps workers improve their performance at some types of job-related tasks (Ray & Ksir, 1987). Nicotine appears to increase functioning and the ability of a person to sustain attention, at least for a brief period of time until the effects wear off and the individual seeks more drug (another puff). Gilbert noted that while nicotine causes autonomic arousal (such as increased heart rate and increased blood pressure) it does not produce a subsequent increase in emotional behavior (cited in Ray & Ksir, 1987). To the contrary, it has been found that nicotine causes a decrease in emotions.

Most studies of anger and smoking are concerned with cessation of smoking, prevention of relapse, and coronary risk. Recently, Macnee (1991) found that smoking relapse was associated with affective states as well as social context. Affective states in this study included anger and loneliness. Smokers were also found to identify smoking as a coping behavior. No studies were found that looked at the relationship between expression of anger and smoking among women. However, one study of women found that smokers score higher than nonsmokers on anger proneness (Gilbert, 1988). Little is said about anger in the literature on smoking. Some studies related to aggression and hostility may be helpful in learning about anger and smoking, however. Occasional smokers have been found to engage in more aggressive behavior as a result of angry feelings than do nonsmokers (Witt, Kaelin, & Stoner, 1988). Shekelle, Gale, Ostfeld, and Paul (1983) also found hostility to be associated with smoking and alcohol use. Furthermore, acquisition of the smoking habit has been associated with situations of conflict and anger (Srole, 1968; Theorell & Lind, 1973).

Study Results Regarding Anger and Smoking

Twenty-three percent of the women in our total sample were smokers. Thus, slightly fewer used nicotine in comparison to national statistics. In 1983, 29.4% of women smoked, whereas in 1985 the number of women smokers decreased to 26.5% (National Center for Health Statistics, 1986; Taeuber, 1991).

Due to the preponderance of nonsmokers, a small subsample of nonsmokers was randomly selected so that t tests could be performed to compare smokers and nonsmokers. The only difference on anger variables between these two groups was found to be related to anger reaction (t = -2.17; p = .03). Smokers were found to score higher on the tendency to react angrily than nonsmokers. Thus smokers appear to be more reactive to criticism and frustrating situational circumstances than nonsmokers. A tendency toward this anger trait was found in women who used alcohol and was discussed earlier in this chapter.

In correlational analyses smoking was found to be positively associated with drinking (r = .16; p = .0004), and depression (r = .14; p = .002). The relationship between smoking and drinking was discussed earlier in this chapter. Depression during young adulthood has been associated with subsequent heavy smoking (Kandel & Davies, 1986). This relationship can be understood from the perspective of Tomkins's (1987) theory, which we reviewed earlier.

Smoking was also found to be negatively correlated to marital status (r = $-.18$; p = .0004). Women in this group who are unmarried were more likely to be smokers. This finding is consistent with recent research, which indicates that 25.8% of female smokers are married, whereas 41.4% are separated and divorced (Taeuber, 1991). Analysis by age group failed to indicate any correlations between smoking and anger variables in any of the age groups. In this sample of women, the number of cigarettes smoked increased with age.

CONCLUSION

As women's anger has begun to gather attention among researchers and the general public, interest in behaviors that may be associated with anger (such as substance use), has directed researchers into areas not yet charted. Due to the scarcity of studies on these topics, the present investigation should be considered exploratory. In this study we gathered data that gave us quantitative information. One goal was to differentiate women who may be at risk of developing substance abuse problems. Many relationships between variables were weak or moderate, but there were some useful indications of fruitful areas of further investigation. From this limited information we have been able to formulate some ideas about women's anger and use of alcohol, prescription drugs, OTC drugs, and smoking. Anger-in, angry reactivity, and anger somatization were the expression modes most salient to use of substances. As was noted in this chapter, information about other psychosocial factors is necessary to obtain a more accurate picture of women who have problems with substance abuse. Just counting the number of drinks or pills taken does not give the researcher enough information from which to make accurate assumptions about identification and treatment of potential substance abuse problems. Further study of substance abuse-related problems in women and signs of the onset of problems that might be specific to women would be helpful.

Results regarding alcohol use revealed the interesting result that women who use alcohol express their anger in ways that are similar to the general population of women. Any notion that women who use alcohol are angrier than other women was not confirmed in this study. However, a subgroup of women may be at risk for eventual alcohol abuse; this group displays several unhealthy anger management patterns. Analyses by age indicated that women older than age 45 who drink experience physical symptoms of anger as measured by both the Framingham and the Contrada scales. Further investigation of this group of women regarding their risk of alcohol-related and physical health problems is warranted.

Women in our study who experience anger symptoms such as headache and tension were found to use prescription drugs. This finding is cause for concern. Are these women and their physicians colluding to treat these symptoms rather than explore the source of distress in women's lives? As suggested earlier these women may be choosing, consciously or not, to suppress their anger chemically in a way that is acceptable and fairly commonplace in our society. This choice, however, is not a healthy choice in light of the research relating anger variables and health. As noted in chapter 8, anger-discuss is the only anger variable positively related to health. Women who are using prescription drugs are not discussing their anger, they are experiencing it as physiological distress. Another reason for concern is the combined use of OTC drugs, prescriptive drugs, and drinking found in our study, which creates risk of interactions and overdoses.

Our findings on smoking and anger give some support to the reactivity often seen in smokers. In situations in which female smokers feel frustrated, they may seek relief from a cigarette. The behavior of smoking engages the smoker and may divert attention away from an uncomfortable situation. In fact, the smoker literally creates a "smoke screen." In addition, the effect of nicotine may help tranquilize the anger being experienced.

Women who use alcohol and drugs are not a homogeneous group. Use and abuse of these substances cuts across age, sex, socioeconomic class, and education. Each woman has her own strengths, personal experiences, needs, and perspectives that determine if or when chemical dependency may occur, as well as what substance might be used. Because of the tremendous social stigma associated with substance abuse, women are in the position of being rejected and labeled deviant rather than being recognized as needing help. Confronting and admitting substance abuse problems can create intensely negative social consequences for a woman. Women are at greater risk of losing their children, spouses, jobs, and financial security when they seek help. We can no longer afford to ignore substance use and abuse among women. More research is needed to facilitate identification of women at risk for developing substance abuse problems. Perhaps anger is one variable that needs further consideration.

■ 11
Women, Depression, and Anger

Patricia Gentry Droppleman and Dorothy Wilt

> *A great Hope fell*
> *You heard no noise*
> *The Ruin was within*
> *Oh cunning wreck that told no tale*
> *and let no Witness in*
>
> *A not admitting of the wound*
> *Until it grew so wide*
> *That all my Life had entered it*
> *And there were troughs beside*
>
> —**Emily Dickinson**

All human beings feel temporarily sad and blue at various times in their lives; most people bounce back quickly and resume their usual demeanor. An intermittent, temporary sadness is not a description of clinical depression. However, an alarming trend has been surfacing over the last two generations. Growing numbers of people in the United States and indeed around the world are increasingly becoming depressed, and the rates of depression are much higher in women (Weissman & Klerman, 1977, 1985). Studies using case records as well as community surveys have found women to be at higher risk (cf. Nolen-Hoeksema, 1990), and the difference in risk holds true for white, black, and Hispanic women (Russo, Amaro, & Winter, 1987; Russo & Sobel, 1981) and across occupations, income, and education levels (Radloff, 1975). Depression in women is a complex phenomenon. What we currently know and understand about it will be presented in the following pages along with new information derived from our research. In this chapter we examine women's depression and its link to anger. We will ask and attempt to answer some of the following questions: What is depression and how are depressions classified? What are the major theories that attempt to explain depression, and what are current views regarding this phenomenon? What risk factors predispose women to depression? And what evidence is there in the literature to explain the more frequent occurrence of depression in women than in men? What are the relationships between depression and anger? Most important, we will be sharing with you the reader, what "our women" have to say about their sorrow and sadness, and we will be providing some practical ideas for health professionals regarding ways to assist women to begin to resolve their sadness.

OVERVIEW OF THE PROBLEM

In the United States depression in women is one of the most pressing health problems of the 1990s and is projected to continue into the 21st century. One fourth of all women have a depressive disorder during their lifetime. There are currently 7 million U.S. women with a diagnosable depression (McGrath et al., 1990), but many will not receive help for the following reasons: cost of treatment, lack of access to clinical services, stigma associated with receiving help, unavailability of social support, or immobilization caused by the depression, which reinforces helplessness. There are great numbers of women whose depressions go undiagnosed. Community surveys have provided evidence that untreated depression is prevalent among women of all ages (Klerman & Weissman, 1985). Depression in women is misdiagnosed 30% to 50% of the time (McGrath et al., 1990). As we will discuss at greater length later in the chapter, there was a high incidence of depression in our study, much of it undiagnosed. Because we found depression to be present in our nonclinical sample of women as well as in the clinical group who were receiving therapy, we have had a unique opportunity to examine relationships between depression and anger in both groups.

Definition and Classification

What is depression? Depression is a mood disorder that can be seriously incapacitating. The experience is one of sadness and lethargy. Classic symptoms include weight loss or gain, insomnia or hypersomnia, low self-esteem, difficulty concentrating, and slowed physical movement or increased agitation. Clients may complain of aches and pains throughout the body. Lack of interest in activities that formerly gave them pleasure (anhedonia) is evident; in fact, a general "I don't care anymore" attitude may prevail. Women have told us that they feel worthless and guilty, and they often reproach themselves. Thoughts of death or plans to attempt suicide may result from the pervasive hopelessness. Depression is not solely an either/or phenomenon but is rather a continuous variable consisting of a broad range of symptoms (Hoch, 1972). Although many readers may be familiar with the descriptions of depressive disorders that follow, we include them for the benefit of students and others who do not regularly use *Diagnostic and Statistical Manual of Mental Disorders* (3rd. ed., rev.) (DSM III-R). Further, the disturbing amount of undiagnosed depression in our sample indicates that some health care providers are overlooking symptoms of depression in their clients; most women in our sample see health care providers regularly (median number of doctor visits in last year = 2; median number of visits to other care providers=2). Therefore, let us review the classifications and diagnostic criteria.

The DSM III-R (American Psychiatric Association, 1987) categorizes depressive disorders as *major depression* and *dysthymia*; the two disorders share similar symptoms, differing only in duration and severity. Bipolar disorders (in which manic episodes alternate with depressive episodes) are described separately in the DSM III-R and are not dealt with in this chapter. For a client to be diagnosed with major depression, at least five of the following symptoms must be present during the same 2-week period and represent a change from previous functioning; further, at least one of these symptoms must be depressed mood or anhedonia.

1. Depressed mood most of the day, nearly every day
2. Markedly diminished interest or pleasure in all (or almost all) activities most of the day, nearly every day (anhedonia)
3. Significant weight loss or gain (not owing to deliberate diet alterations) or changes in appetite (decrease or increase) nearly every day
4. Insomnia or hypersomnia nearly every day
5. Psychomotor agitation or retardation nearly every day
6. Fatigue nearly every day
7. Feelings of worthlessness or guilt nearly every day
8. Decreased ability to concentrate or make decisions nearly every day
9. Recurrent thoughts of death, suicidal ideation or plans, suicide attempt

Major depression can occur in mild, moderate, or severe forms, with and without psychotic features such as delusions or hallucinations. Psychotic depression is less common. Recurrences occur in a high percentage of cases.

Dysthymia is a chronic, milder disturbance of mood (formerly called depressive neurosis); it is diagnosed when a client reports depressed mood for most of the day, more days than not, for at least 2 years. At least two of the following symptoms must accompany the depression: (a) poor appetite or overeating, (b) insomnia or hypersomnia, (c) low energy or fatigue, (d) low self-esteem, (e) poor concentration or difficulty making decisions, and (f) feelings of hopelessness. Normal fluctuations of mood are not as frequent or severe as the depressed mood in dysthymia, and there is no interference with social functioning.

Depression is a whole-body illness involving interacting biological, psychological, and sociocultural factors. There has been a phenomenal increase in knowledge about the role of neurotransmitters over the past couple of decades, with the preponderance of research focusing on norepinephrine and serotonin (although other neurotransmitters are also involved). Alterations in neuroendocrine function have also been implicated in depression (i.e., hypersecretion of cortisol) (Harris, 1982). Space does not permit review of the literature on biological factors; our focus will be on the psychological and sociocultural (for a review of literature on the pathophysiology of depressive illness, see Thomas, Wilt, and Noffsinger, 1988).

THEORETICAL FORMULATIONS OF DEPRESSION

Descriptions of depression have been around since antiquity. In the 5th-century B.C., Hippocrates first classified depression as melancholia. There have been descriptions of depression in ancient Greek, Egyptian, and biblical texts, as well as in the distinguished literature of many countries. Although there have been numerous theories proposed over the years, we will summarize only a few that have either historical importance or current application. There is no one single theory that addresses all aspects of this complex phenomenon at this point in time.

Sigmund Freud wrote a book in 1917 titled *Mourning and Melancholia*. The central theme is one of loss, loss of either a significant person or of an attraction to a person. According to Freud, melancholia and grief symptoms are similar. In both conditions the sorrowful person feels sad and lonely, has a lack of motivation, and is lethargic. The difference is that the "mourner" has a reason to be so unhappy, having really lost someone, whereas the loss experienced by the melancholy person is likely to be in the mind. Freud believed melancholics were angry and punished themselves by repressing their anger. Many subsequent psychoanalytic theorists have defined depression as anger turned inward or against oneself, and this view has prevailed for many years. Anger was viewed as the internal force behind thoughts of self-criticism, doubt, and feelings of worthlessness. It was long thought beneficial for depressed persons to express their anger. However, expression of anger does not prevent individuals from becoming depressed, nor does it necessarily produce relief from depressive symptoms.

Frameworks proposing loss of significant attachments and suppression of anger as the two factors most involved in depression prevailed during the 20th century, but other theoretical formulations were spawned. Behavioral and social learning theories developed by Skinner and Bandura were applied to depression; for example, Lewinsohn (1974) described it in terms of positive and negative reinforcers (i.e., depression was the result of too few positive reinforcers and the treatment for depression would be to increase the same). Martin Seligman's (1975) theory of learned helplessness proposed that a person became depressed because of inability to control the outcomes in his or her environment. These theories could not account for the fact that not everyone responds to situations in the same way. In other words, why do some and not others become depressed given the same set of circumstances? Perhaps cognitions and perceptions of events play a role. Aaron Beck's (1976) cognitive theory of depression evolved from his clinical practice. He noticed that depressed clients tended to exaggerate or overgeneralize their failures. They also personalized circumstances in inappropriate ways. Beck concluded that depressed people look at themselves and their world negatively, and as a result ultimately internalize a dim view of the present and the future. Seligman has reconstructed his "learned helplessness theory" with more emphasis on thinking styles (Abramson, Seligman, & Teasdale, 1978). Seligman's premise was that illogical attributions about events can influence a person's "helplessness deficits," and can place him or her at risk for depression. In a new theory Abramson has replaced the word helplessness with "hopelessness," a condition that results from not being able to control or to attain valued outcomes. Hopelessness combined with negative life events leads to depression (Abramson, Metalsky, & Alloy, 1989).

Another set of theories has to do with women's status and their work and family roles. Gilligan (1982) and Miller (1976) have argued that "nurturing," "caring," and an overabiding interest in interpersonal relationships place women at depression risk. Socialization of female children may be a crucial influence on future depression development. Women learn early that their needs are not important. They learn that they are destined to be care givers and may spend a lifetime sacrificing and giving of themselves, often without feeling appreciated. Understandably this situation may lead to anger in women which may accumulate and fester; women may find themselves in a no-win situation.

RESEARCH ON GENDER DIFFERENCES IN DEPRESSION

Research on gender differences in depression has been meager. According to Nolen-Hoeksema, "There is much we do not know. . . . Often the crucial studies for testing these explanations have yet to be carried out, and the studies that exist have often been inconclusive. In fact it is remarkable how little attention empiricists have given to such an important phenomenon" (1990, p. 2). Some research has been done on preschool children and adolescents, generally showing no gender differences in depressive symptoms before the adolescent years; when there are differences, the greater incidence is in boys, not girls (Nolen-Hoeksema, 1990). From about age 14 onward, more symptoms are reported by girls than boys (Albert & Beck, 1975) and from age 19 onward women twice as often as men report and demonstrate depressive symptoms (Myers et al., 1984). The highest rates of depressive symptoms occur between the ages of 18 and 24 (Nolen-Hoeksema, 1990). Why do adolescent and adult women experience depression more frequently than males? There are several explanations for the higher incidence of depression in women, but none is conclusive at this time. We will examine biological, psychological, and historical-sociocultural factors.

Biological

Biological events that occur in women's lives such as initiation of menses, pregnancy, childbirth, and menopause may have some role in the etiology of depression. Feminist writers have sought to minimize negative discussions of the impact of reproductive events on women's lives in light of all the clichés that smack of irrationality, helplessness, and lack of control. However, these events are realities for women, and even when viewing them from a positive perspective, some events emerge as possible contributing factors for depression. Hormonal changes may make some contribution to depression in both adolescents and older women, and the events surrounding pregnancy and childbirth enhance depressive vulnerability, especially when social support is lacking (Aaronson, 1989; Brown, 1986a; Brown, 1986b; Koniak-Griffin, 1988; Mercer & Ferketich, 1988; Norbeck & Anderson, 1989). Although there are some studies showing correlations between hormone levels and moods, no causal effects have been demonstrated (Nolen-Hoeksema, 1990).

Psychological

One theory that has been offered in an effort to explain gender differences in depression is that women are more likely to seek psychological help than men, that in fact men are as frequently as depressed but that women more often report their symptoms. It is probably true that women seek help for their depression more frequently and that women are more likely to self-disclose or discuss their troubles. Also, men may handle their depression differently (e.g., by abusing drugs and alcohol). However, these explanations are not sufficient. In an effort to outline the factors that contribute to depression in women, we were struck by how vulnerable women seem to be. There are many women who are at risk, the most obvious being the poor, the undereducated, and those who have been psychologically, physically, and sexually abused. Life stress was a central determinant of depression in a study of London working class women by Brown and Harris (1978). Caring for young children (Radloff, 1975) or adolescents (McBride, 1987), caring for aging parents (Jarvik & Small, 1988), and being in an unhappy marriage (Weissman, 1987) increase depression risk. In unhappy marriages, women are 3 times as likely as men to be depressed (Weissman, 1987). Ross and Mirowsky (1988) found that unemployed mothers of children were more depressed than employed mothers. But if employed mothers had sole responsibility for arranging child care, they also had extremely high depression levels. It makes sense that as the demands on their caregiving increased, the mothers had even less time to meet their own needs. Such women may become angry about virtually losing themselves in caring for others. Because anger is not a socially sanctioned emotion for women, they may become depressed or physically ill. This is sometimes a signal to their significant others that something is not right, therefore saying "I need help." Even "baby boomers" (Seligman, 1988) and high-achieving women (Braiker, 1987) may be at risk. Vicarious stress, that is taking on the stressors of close affiliates, is also a likely contribution. This phenomenon has been elaborated on earlier (see chapter 6).

Arieti and Bemporad (1978) pointed out the heavy emphasis in psychiatric literature on "pathologic dependency" in depressives. Based on the male-oriented cultural valuing of autonomy and self-sufficiency, women have been construed as overly dependent on others (thus more likely to become depressed because of relationship failures). In a recent book Jack (1991) argues that the concept of "dependency" requires reexamination; women in her study described their need for *intimate closeness*, a need that, when unmet, led to depression. According to Jack, this need for intimacy and connection is not *dependency* and is not pathological. Although Jack's argument is persuasive, the research presented in her book has received some criticism because of the small sample of depressed women (12 white women from rural communities) and the severe abuse many had received, limiting generalizability of the findings.

Historical-Sociocultural Perspectives

Arthur Schopenhauer (1883) wrote a treatise "On Women" in which he depicted women as being sex objects, devious, vain, and generally having arrested development. This misogynistic vision of women unfortunately has been perpetuated by other influential writers during the past 100 years, and we contend that such disparaging views have been internalized by women, greatly affecting their self-esteem. Almost 60 years later Clara Thompson (1942) wrote, "The official attitude of the culture toward women has been and still is to the effect that woman is not equal to man . . . the assumption of woman's inferiority was a part of the prevalent attitude of society and until recently was accepted by both sexes as a biological fact" (1942, pp. 331–335).

Annie Dillard, in describing her growing-up in a privileged American family in the 1950s, wrote about how little she and her friends thought about their own futures or their development separate from men.

> Ah, the boys . . . How little I understood them! How little I even glimpsed who they were . . . all along the boys had been in the process of becoming responsible members of an actual and moral world, we, small minded, and fast talking girls had never heard of. They had been learning self-control. We had failed to develop any selves worth controlling. We were enforcers of a code we never questioned; we were vigilantes of the trivial. The boys must have shared our view that we were, as girls, in the long run, negligible. (1987, p. 90)

Social discrimination of women has occurred at all levels of society and has been a generally accepted condition. It is easy to see why women might become frustrated, feel impotent and psychologically distressed; and, indeed, experience depression as a result. We did not ask questions in our study related to victimization experiences such as sexual assault, battering, or sexual harassment on the job (see epilogue for our rationale for this), but such experiences are quite common. Approximately one of every four girls is molested sexually during childhood or adolescence (Brunngraber, 1986). Acquaintance rape is in the news and seems to be much more prevalent than formerly thought. The New York Public Interest Group (1981) surveyed working women and found that as many as 71% may experience sexual harassment. These figures make sense in the context of women coming forth with their stories following the "Hill-Thomas" hearings in which Anita Hill, a former aide to Clarence Thomas, a Supreme Court nominee, claimed sexual harassment.

Obviously women experiencing victimization of any kind should be considered at high risk for a depressive disorder. Other populations reported to be at increased risk include ethnic minority women, lesbians, women living in poverty, adolescents, older women, professional women, substance abusers, and women with eating disorders; the reader is referred to the report of the APA's National Task Force on Women and Depression for further discussion about the risk factors in each of these groups (McGrath et al., 1990). Clearly, more research is needed for understanding women's greater propensity for depression. The APA task force has outlined specific detailed recommendations (McGrath et al., 1990, pp. 36-39), as primary foci for future research endeavors.

THE ANGER-DEPRESSION LINK

Several theorists have hypothesized that anger plays a significant role in depression. Abraham's (1927) postulation that manic depressive patients have repressed violence and Freud's depiction of depression as anger turned inward provided the beginning of this causal linking. Supporting these theories, some studies (cf. Lemaire & Clopton, 1981) have found greater inwardly expressed hostility among depressed individuals. Biaggio and Godwin (1987) conducted discriminant analyses to see which of nine indices of anger and hostility best discriminated between college students in the upper and lower third of scores on a depression scale; intropunitiveness scores were the strongest discriminator (i.e., inwardly directed hostility). Depressives reported less verbal hostility but significantly more resentment than nondepressed controls in a 1970 study by Friedman.

Studies by other researchers have challenged the anger-inward depression hypothesis. For example, in a study of 37 depressed patients Schless, Mendels, Kipperman, and Cochrane (1974) found that approximately equal numbers of patients showed hostility turned inward and outward. Patients who were severely depressed had higher inward *and* outward hostility. Similar findings were reported by Weissman, Klerman, and Paykel (1971). Folkman and Lazarus (1980) found that midlife women (ages 35 to 45) who were higher in depressive symptoms were more likely than those low in symptoms to express their anger in confrontive ways. Billings and Moos (1985) reported similar findings of an association between an "emotional discharge" type of coping and depression.

Weissman and Paykel (1974), in a study of 80 women (40 depressed and 40 control), found that depressed women expressed more anger in interpersonal relationships than did the control subjects. In a study of women hospitalized for depression, Gershon, Cromer, and Klerman (1968) reported that women who ventilated their anger were more depressed than those women who did not ventilate their anger. In a study comparing depressed patients with posttraumatic stress disorder (PTSD) patients and normals, Riley, Treiber, and Woods (1989) found within the depressed group a positive relationship between severity of depression and levels of anger and hostility, but severity of depression was not related to measures of anger expression. Both clinical groups showed higher levels of general anger than the normal group. Vigorously disagreeing with the notion that depression is anger turned inward, Tavris (1989) proposed that "If anything, anger is depression turned outward. Follow the trail of anger inward, and there you find the small, still voice of pain" (p. 14).

STUDY RESULTS: ANGER AND DEPRESSION

Beck Depression Inventory (BDI) Scores for the Entire Sample

Depression in our study was measured by the BDI. This instrument (Beck et al., 1961) has been used to assess depression in normal populations as well as in clinical samples of psychiatric patients. This inventory consists of 21 multiple choice items which contain specific signs and symptoms of depression;

the items are weighted in severity from 0 to 3, and total scores are obtained by addition of the weighted items selected by the respondent. Scores of 0 to 9 are considered normal; scores of 10 to 15 are considered as mild depression; scores of 16 to 19 are considered mild to moderate; 20 to 29 as moderate to severe, and 30 to 63 as severe depression (Green, 1985). The BDI has been used in numerous research studies in a wide variety of settings. In a 1988 paper, Beck, Steer, and Garbin reviewed the research on psychometric properties of the tool for the 25-year period 1961 to 1986. A meta-analysis of internal consistency estimates yielded excellent Cronbach's alpha coefficients for both psychiatric patients (.86) and nonpsychiatric subjects (.81).

We first examined BDI scores for the total sample of women as well as separating them into the three groups previously described (nonclinical, medical, psychiatric). Scores ranged from 0 to 48 (possible range 0–63). Although only 52 women in our study were receiving psychiatric treatment, 33% ($N = 152$) of all the women could be considered depressed according to their BDI scores (see Table 34, Appendix). When the clinical sample was excluded, (see Table 35, Appendix) 29.5% of ordinary or average women were depressed, some severely so. This finding is somewhat higher than the 20% to 25% of community samples that are considered by the APA to be subclinically depressed. Approximately half of individuals who score high on self-report measures of depression are said to be clinically impaired (Link & Dohrenwend, 1980). There is considerable debate about the "line" or "cutoff" separating subclinical and clinical levels of depression—which has been termed "blurry at best" by Hirschfeld and Cross (1982). There is some evidence of continuity between depressive *symptoms* and *clinical* depression (McGrath et al., 1990), and Nolen-Hoeksema (1990) argues that we do a disservice to people whose depressions do not quite meet diagnostic criteria for clinical depression by discounting their distress. She points out that even moderately depressed persons may have problems keeping up at work or school. We will examine differences between mildly, moderately, and severely depressed women a bit later in the chapter.

We turn our attention now to the complex interrelationships between depression and anger variables. Our research questions were

1. What is the relationship between levels of depression and overall tendency to experience anger arousal (trait anger)?
2. What are the relationships between depression and different modes of anger expression?
   a. Is there a relationship between suppression of anger and depression?
   b. Is there a relationship between outward expression of anger and depression?
   c. Is there a relationship between discussion of anger and depression?
   d. Is there a relationship between somatic anger and depression?
3. What is the relationship between cognitive anger and depression?

4. Are there differences on the various anger dimensions between women who score high, midrange, and low on the depression scale?
5. Are there any differences between depressed and nondepressed groups in demographic characteristics?

Trait Anger and Depression

In answer to the first research question, depression *was* correlated with overall trait anger (general propensity to become angry) in this sample (correlations are presented in Table 36, Appendix). Of the two subscales of trait anger, angry reaction was somewhat more strongly related to depression than angry temperament. In subsequent ANOVA comparison of three groups of women (highly depressed, mildly depressed, and nondepressed) there were significant differences between groups on trait anger, that is, the highly depressed and mildly depressed both scored higher than did those scoring low in depression. These results are consistent with previous research; Biaggio and Godwin (1987), also using the Spielberger Trait Anger Scale, found depressed subjects higher in trait anger. Riley, Treiber, and Woods (1989) found that depressed patients and PTSD patients scored significantly higher on the Spielberger scale than their normal comparison group. Other researchers (cf. Paykel, Weissman, Prusoff, & Tonks, 1971; Weissman, Klerman, & Paykel, 1971) have reported that depressed individuals seem to have a greater likelihood of experiencing anger than do nondepressed persons.

Linkages of Anger Expression Modes and Depression

Anger Suppression and Depression

Bivariate correlations for the total sample showed that anger-in was weakly related to depression ($r=.23$). However, when a stepwise regression was done, this variable was eliminated (results of this procedure are discussed later in the chapter). This finding directly opposes classic theory that suppressed anger is depression turned inwards, and supports the assertions of Tavris (1989) and Lerner (1987), suggesting a need to rethink this long-standing hypothesis. However, as we shall see in succeeding sections of the chapter, anger-in scores were highly salient when looking at subgroups (e.g., women in psychotherapy).

Outward Expression of Anger and Depression

There was a positive relationship between anger-out and depression ($r = .27$) in the total sample. Also using the Framingham Anger-Out Scale, Riley,

Treiber, and Woods (1989) found that depressed (and PTSD) patients scored significantly higher than normals. Lerner (1987) states that "venting anger does not offer women protection against depression . . . feelings of depression, low self-esteem, self-betrayal and even self-hatred are inevitable when women fight but continue to submit to unfair circumstances, when they complain but participate in relationships that betray their own beliefs, values, and personal goals, or when they find themselves fulfilling society's stereotypes of the bitchy, nagging, bitter, or destructive woman" (pp. 216–217).

Anger Discussion and Depression

As we predicted, there was an inverse relationship between anger-discuss and depression, although the magnitude of the correlation was small. In other words, the more women discussed their anger rationally, the less likely they were to be depressed. However, causal connections cannot be inferred; we do not know if ability to express feelings enabled some women to avoid depression. As noted in previous chapters, this choice of anger expression has been demonstrated to be related to better health status (Thomas & Williams, 1991) and has been shown to be more prevalent in women than men (Averill, 1982; Harburg, Blakelock, & Roeper, 1979; Riley, Treiber, & Woods, 1989; Thomas, 1989; Thomas & Williams, 1991). Normals were more likely to discuss their anger than depressed or PTSD patients in the study by Riley, Treiber, and Woods (1989). Louisa and Karen are women who score high on anger-discussion.

Louisa

Louisa is 52 years old, has no children, and is presently experiencing perimenopausal symptoms. She has been married to her present husband 20 years; an earlier marriage lasted 3½ years when she was a young woman. She has 15 years of education and is employed. Louisa becomes angry in situations where people "try to take advantage" of her or when someone "has shirked their responsibility." Her method of dealing with people is direct and confrontational; she discusses her anger rationally. Louisa has high self-esteem and her marital status supports her values; she is not depressed. She has a supportive husband and a network of friends. Except for menopausal symptoms, Louisa feels well and is happy.

Karen

Karen's profile might lead you to conclude that she has reason to be depressed because she has recently experienced a significant loss. Based on the battery of tests we gave her and by her own admission, she is not depressed. "I am currently going through a break-up of a relationship; anger has been expressed at my ex-partner." Karen is bisexual and has recently lost her lesbian partner. Early in her life she was married for a 3-year period. Karen has had 3 years of education postcollege and makes a fairly good living; she feels good about herself. She believes in a higher power and attends church occasionally. When we asked with whom she is likely to be angry, she responded: "With people who are not doing their assigned job." She is assertive in dealing with those causing her anger; she does not hold anger in. Karen is overweight but is generally healthy and does not somatize. She manages stress by talking to support people (of whom she has a wide network) and "writing about it." Karen appears to use healthy strategies for managing anger and stress.

Somatic Anger and Depression

Among the four expression modes, the strongest correlate of depression was somatic anger ($r = .49$ for Framingham scale, $r = .41$ for Contrada scale). The more depressed women were, the more they were likely to report physical symptoms when angry. Further research is needed on the phenomenon of anger somatization, because it has received less attention from researchers than anger-in and anger-out. As pointed out in chapter 3, anger symptoms appear to be generated and maintained by the *intensity* of the emotion, and they are strongly related to anger cognitions.

Cognitive Anger and Depression

The kind of faulty or irrational thinking assessed by the Contrada Cognitive Anger Scale logically could contribute to depression (see chapter 3 for review of item content if necessary). In particular, rumination is known to amplify depression. The relationship between cognitive anger scores and depression scores was the second strongest finding in correlational analyses using the full sample ($r = .46$). As noted previously, in Aaron Beck's (1972) cognitive theory of depression, distortions in thought process and content are postulated to be major components of depressive syndromes. In a 1985 study Clark and Teasdale made an important observation—when women were in a happy or pleasant mood, they recalled happy or pleasant words; when in a dysphoric mood, they recalled the opposite. The researchers suggested that mildly depressed women may selectively generate further cognitions that are negative, enhancing the depressed state. A cycle of negative cognition and depression may evolve, and these women are at increased risk for intensified depression and for future episodes of depression. As we will see later in the chapter, in this study the relationship between depressive and cognitive anger was stronger in the psychiatric sample than in the nonclinical sample, which is supportive of Clark and Teasdale's hypothesis.

How do relationships between depression and anger variables differ between nonclinical and psychiatric groups? Do the same relationships occur, perhaps to a different degree, for highly distressed women receiving psychotherapy? Tables 37 and 38 (see Appendix) depict separate correlational analyses for the two groups. A comparison of the figures in the two tables reveals the following: (a) there was a much stronger correlation between anger-in and depression for the clinical group than for the nonclinical (lending support to the theoretical formulations of clinicians, who probably do see more anger suppression in their clientele); (b) although important in the nonclinical group, cognitive and somatic anger (measured by the Contrada scale) were much more salient in the psychiatric sample ($r = .68$ for the relationship between cognitive anger and depression, $r = .69$ for the somatic-depression linkage); and (c) trait anger and its two subscales were essentially unrelated to depression in the psychiatric sample, as was anger-out, whereas all of these variables were significantly related to depression in the nonclinical group. These findings seem to indicate that the psychiatric group is unique in some respects. We already know from the initial comparisons on anger variables (see chapter 3) that the mean scores of the psychiatric group were higher on trait anger, angry reaction, anger-out, and anger symptoms. However, of these four variables on which psychiatric patients scored higher, only one (anger symptoms) was very pertinent to depression.

Regression Analysis

In this section we present findings of regression analysis. Depression was regressed on predictor variables found to be significant in the prior correlational analyses. Sixty-three percent of the variance in depression was explained by the following seven variables: perceived stress ($\beta = .27$), self-esteem ($\beta = -.19$), anger-out ($\beta = .14$), anger symptoms ($\beta = .14$), cognitive anger ($\beta = .07$), current health status ($\beta = -.23$), and the "affect" subscale of the social support measure ($\beta = -.14$) (which assesses feeling loved). Trait anger was not a useful predictor of depression, nor was anger-in. The more women ventilated their anger, had faulty cognitions when angry, and somatized, the more likely they were to be depressed. Consistent with previous research, lower self-esteem was predictive of depression, and the inverse relationship between poorer physical health status and depression was also expected. A major factor in depression in women of all ages is decline in physical health, whatever the cause. Our finding regarding lack of social support (or the perception that significant others do not "make you feel loved") was consistent with other studies related to social support and depression. Longitudinal research by McKinlay, McKinlay and Brambilla (1987) suggests that social support and depression either act concurrently to mutually influence each other or are influenced by a third variable (McGrath et al., 1990). Stress was the strongest predictor of depression; the more stressed a woman was, the more likely she was to be depressed. The stress that women experience has been discussed at length in chapter 6. Nolen-Hoeksema (1987) and several other investigators suggest that women are exceptionally vulnerable to depression because of female gender role socialization that initiates maladaptive styles of coping with stress, increasing their risk for developing depression and possibly contributing to maintaining this state. However, some researchers have found no evidence that women are less capable of dealing with stress. Turner and Avison (1989) demonstrated that women were more affected than men by stressful events occurring to significant others such as their spouses; their study findings supported a "cost of caring" explanation for women's greater risk of depression in connection with stressful circumstances.

Differences between Depressed and Nondepressed Women

Analysis of variance was done to see if there were any differences between women who scored high, midrange, and low (within the normal range) on depression. The groups differed in anger-in, anger-out, anger symptoms, trait anger and its anger reaction subscale (see Table 39, Appendix). They did not differ on anger discuss (although the probability was close to significance) or on angry temperament. In all cases, Tukey post hoc tests indicated that the highly depressed women scored higher, followed by the mildly depressed and then the nondepressed, with the exception of anger-discuss (where the opposite ordering occurred). Because education was related to depression in correlational analyses (inversely, indicating less educated women were more likely to be depressed), these analyses were repeated using Analysis of Covariance (ANCOVA) with education as a covariate; findings remained the same. The largest differences between the three groups were found on anger symptoms. Because the groups did not differ in angry temperament, there is no suggestion that a basic personality propensity to be more angry is involved in women's depression; the significant difference found for overall trait anger was apparently due to the scores on the angry reaction subscale. These analyses support our earlier recommendation (chapter 3) regarding careful examination of subscale scores on the Spielberger instrument.

In our final set of analyses, we sought to discover differences between depressed and nondepressed women in terms of sociodemographic characteristics and other pertinent variables. For these comparisons, the sample was divided into *depressed* (scores of 10 or above on the BDI) and *nondepressed* (scores of 0–9 on the BDI). There were no differences between groups in age or income; women of various ages and income levels were depressed. Although a slightly greater percentage of the depressed group were unemployed (19%), compared with 13% of the nondepressed group, most women were employed. Occupations of women in both groups were similar, with roughly equivalent percentages involved in the three top categories (clerical, human services, and homemaking) as well as similar percentages in the professions, management positions, sales, and teaching. Both groups included some women in lower status occupations (e.g., factory work and food services) as well as some students. Thus, there were no remarkable occupational differences between depressed and nondepressed women. Although the difference between groups in years of education was statistically significant, the nondepressed women actually had only 9 months more schooling than the depressed; this difference appears to be of little practical significance. In both groups, more women were married than unmarried, and equivalent percentages in both groups had children. There were no differences between depressed and nondepressed women in years married or number of children. Numbers of never-married women and widows were approximately equal in both groups, but the percentage of divorcees differed (26% in the depressed, 17% in the nondepressed).

Given the data reviewed thus far, we can see no striking factors that would contribute to depressive symptoms. The first clues appeared in examination of various social network variables. On the Norbeck Social Support Questionnaire, depressed and nondepressed women differed significantly in several respects: on affect support (feeling loved, respected); affirmation support (being able to obtain agreement and support of actions and thoughts); number of persons in the social network; duration of relationships with those persons in the network; and number of losses of important relationships during the past year. On all of these variables, depressed women had *less* of these important elements of social support, with the exception of *higher* number of reported *losses*. These findings are consistent with other literature, particularly the research tradition originating with Coyne (1976). In contrast to depression models emphasizing intrapsychic mechanisms, Coyne proposed that depression was, at least in part, an interpersonal phenomenon. He contended that behavior of interaction partners maintained, and exacerbated, the difficulties faced by depressed individuals. Although symptoms exhibited by the depressed person initially elicit sympathy and aid, over time the members of the social network begin to find the depressed person aversive; they begin to send mixed messages that eventually intensify the depressive symptoms. The ultimate consequence can be greater distance or relationship termination, increasing the plight of the depressive. In our sample, twice as many women (46%) in the depressed group had a loss of someone important to them compared with 23% in the nondepressed group. Although we cannot trace the chain of events that occurred in our subject's lives, Coyne's model is worthy of consideration.

Consistent with the large amount of variance explained by stress in the regression analyses, ANOVA comparisons revealed a very large difference between depressed and nondepressed women on stress; the mean of the depressed group was 31.8 compared with a mean of 21.7 for the nondepressed group. However, the stress-depression link is not a simple one; most individuals under severe stress do not develop depressive disorders. Current thinking is that individuals exposed to stressful circumstances become depressed only when other vulnerabilities are present (Monroe & Depue, 1991). Self-esteem may be such a vulnerability; in our ANOVA comparisons, there was a strongly significant difference between depressed and nondepressed women on this characteristic. Is self-esteem a precursor or a by-product of depression? Because an entire chapter of this book has been devoted to self-esteem, we elaborate no further here on this critical variable so inextricably intertwined with depression that it is a defining criterion of the disorder.

CASE STUDIES

The following case studies illustrate the complex interplay of the variables implicated in depression. We have selected one woman receiving psychotherapy (Rose), one woman receiving only medication (Claudia), and one woman as yet undiagnosed and untreated (Jessica).

Rose

A 45-year-old woman, married 28 years, with two adult children and one grandchild, Rose is currently being treated for depression (BDI score = 30) in an outpatient psychiatric clinic. As part of that treatment she is taking Prozac. Indicants of her low self-esteem are she does not have a positive self-attitude; she does not think she has any good qualities, and she wishes she could have more respect for herself. All in all she is inclined to think she is a failure . . . useless . . . she is dissatisfied with herself. Rose says this about her anger: "the trigger is frustration that builds up mostly when I have a lot of stress from dealing with my family members. I get mad at myself for not being able to say, No." Rose vents her anger at her husband and her children. She has assumed the responsibility of taking care of her grandchild since her daughter moved back into Rose's home (the "refilled nest syndrome" described in Witkin's 1991 book on women's stress). She says, "sometimes I feel like pulling my hair out." Caring for her grandchild is very stressful. She reports numerous vague physical complaints but has not been diagnosed with any serious health problems. She does not consider her support system viable. This portrait illustrates the interconnectedness of depression, decreased self-esteem, anger at the self as well as venting of anger (anger-out), somatization, lack of support, and vicarious stress.

Claudia

Claudia is a woman who does not think her current marital status (divorced) supports what she values. She is very depressed (BDI score = 35), although she is not receiving psychotherapy; her medical doctor recently placed her on Prozac. Claudia is 47 years old has been divorced 4 years from her third husband; she experienced another significant loss in the past year. Earlier marriages lasted 9 years and 3 years. She has two adult children in their 20s who do not live at home. She feels only moderately loved by her sister and one daughter and not at all loved by her second daughter, nor does she feel respected by any of them. The only two people who she thinks love and respect her are her two grandchildren. Claudia holds in her anger and rarely discusses it: "I strongly dislike confrontation." She would never express her anger to anyone in authority or to anyone who "makes me feel inferior although I am slowly learning that I allow myself to feel inferior." Claudia's sadness appears pervasive; in response to our question about number of days ill in the past year, she stated "I was ill every day at home with depression." She is also having perimenopausal symptoms and has many somatic complaints. However, she is employed full time and indicated that she had not missed any days of work in the last year; her income is very substantial. The four values in life which are most important to Claudia are self-respect, inner harmony, health, and freedom. When asked how clear she was about these values, she responded, "I am reading all the self-help material I can find to help me achieve understanding of myself, improve my self-esteem and achieve inner harmony."

Jessica

Jessica (age 31) is severely depressed according to her score on the BDI (score = 35). She has been married for the past 13 years to her current husband and has two children ages 8 and 10. Jessica is a high school graduate and works full time as a secretary; annual income is very low for a family of four ($10,000 a year). She has had thoughts about killing herself but states she would not carry this out. She feels discouraged and hopeless about the future; she does not think that her life situation can improve. Jessica does not think that she is living a life that supports her desired values, which are inner harmony, health, happiness, and a comfortable life. She does not feel inner peace, and she does not belong to a church nor does she attend one. Although she has no diagnosed or discernable physical health problems, she states that she does not feel well and smokes a pack of cigarettes per day. Because of her low income, she may not be able to realize a comfortable life. She is definitely not happy. Jessica scored low on self-esteem and primarily handles her anger by holding it in. When she is angry she usually keeps it to herself and often apologizes even though she may be right. Sometimes she takes her anger out on others. Although not quick tempered, she is "furious when her rights are violated." When she ventilates anger she does not feel good about it. Even though the ability to speak out in an assertive way could increase Jessica's self-regard, venting anger in a blaming way has not facilitated her self-esteem nor has it protected her from depression. Jessica has never been treated for depression, in fact, she has never been diagnosed as depressive.

In contrast to the women who are depressed, the following case study is a woman in charge of her life and destiny with many tools that promote well-being.

Amanda

Amanda states that she values good health, a comfortable life, freedom, and pleasure, and that she is living these values. She also says that her present marital status supports her values. She was married 12 years but is now divorced. She initiated the divorce process and is comfortable with being single. She is well educated and has no children. She confronts those with whom she is angry, and has no difficulty in expressing her anger to the person who triggers it or to "anyone else who will listen." She has had no significant relationship losses in the past year. She is employed full time as a registered nurse and is financially well compensated. She drinks moderately, and exercises vigorously every day. She does admit to smoking excessively.

The final case study describes a middle-aged woman who is coping well with experiences that could predispose her to depression. As noted previously, the midlife period for many women is characterized by losses of important supportive relationships (through death, divorce, or children leaving home).

Elizabeth

Elizabeth, age 50, has been divorced for 4 years. Her two children are adults. Even though she initiated her divorce, it is not congruent with her values. Married for 30 years, she is experiencing several stressors common to midlife women living alone after a lengthy marriage. She has 13 years of education and works as a bookkeeper at a relatively low income. She states that she is likely to become angry when "people put demands on me." Demands place her in a bind, and she finds these situations stressful. The people who are likely to make her angry are her sister, a close friend, and a coworker. However, she can talk to her best friend and express angry feelings with her. The four values that are most important to her are health, happiness, self-respect, and an exciting life. She says that she is living out her values "very well." She attends church regularly, exercises frequently, and reduces stress through swimming or walking. Elizabeth feels loved and admired by her children, her brother, and four particular friends. She considers all of them important in her life and willing to provide her with support.

TREATMENT OF DEPRESSION IN WOMEN

Even though there is a chapter of this book on treatment (see chapter 12) we believe that treatment for depression should be addressed separately because of the multiple facets of this biopsychosocial disorder. Each component (e.g., biological treatment) will be discussed individually; however, the therapist provides simultaneous treatment of these components.

Biological Treatment

The physiological changes that accompany depression (e.g., decrease in energy level, sleep disturbance, appetite loss or increase, cessation of menses, decreased libido) must be addressed initially. It is imperative to acknowledge that these changes are beyond the conscious control of the depressed person, and that expectations for the client to overcome them by "sheer willpower" only adds to a sense of defeat. Treatment begins with letting the client know that physiologic changes are a treatable part of depression. If the client's changes are mild and short term, the therapist can reassure the client that as issues regarding her depression are resolved, physiologic changes will abate. An aerobic exercise program is also useful in changing the client's depressed physiology.

In long-standing and severe depression, an exercise program may initially be very counterproductive. This client often has barely enough energy to go through the motion of daily life tasks let alone exercise. A suggestion to exercise may only increase a sense of failure. A most effective treatment is the use of antidepressants. Before 1989 the most used antidepressants were the tricyclics such as amitriptyline (Elavil) and doxepin (Sinequan). Fluoxetine (Prozac), introduced in 1987, is now the most widely prescribed antidepressant in the United States, (McGrath et al., 1990). The tricyclics act by blocking the reabsorption of the neurotransmitter norepinephrine, and fluoxetine blocks reabsorption of the neurotransmitter serotonin, thus correcting neurotransmitter deficits. Treatment with antidepressants usually results in increased energy and improved mood, appetite, and sleep patterns. Often a client's sense of worthlessness, guilt, and ambivalence is also lessened. As with all medications, there are side effects and contraindications. Overall, these antidepressants are safe and a much-needed treatment modality in facilitating a client's ability to engage in psychologic therapy. Leach (1987) states that endogenous depression may be treated successfully with antidepressants but they are not useful in exogenous or reactive depressions. Research has also found that there is little or no effect when psychopharmacological agents are used without psychological therapies.

Psychological Treatment

There are a variety of psychological treatment modalities effective in the treatment of depression, such as psychodynamic, cognitive, and behavioral therapy. The use of one or a combination of therapies should be chosen relative to the unique needs of the individual client. Initial treatment using cognitive therapy may be more successful with a highly intellectualized client before addressing emotions that accompany psychodynamic therapy. Whichever therapies are used, effectiveness will be dependent on the quality of the therapeutic relationship the therapist develops with the client. Within a strong supportive therapeutic relationship the depressed client can begin to heal the damaged self. Low self-esteem is a defining characteristic of depression, supported by the findings of this study as well as many others. For women, an integral part of the formation of self-esteem is relationship. The APA task force (McGrath et al., 1990) suggests that for women the development of the concept of self includes ego boundaries that are fluid. This fluidity allows for a high degree of empathy. Thus, a woman's self-awareness does not lead to a structure that stands alone with rigid walls or boundaries, but one that is clearly connected to emotional and interpersonal relationships. In this respect, a positive, accepting, and supportive relationship with a therapist is a potential curative experience for women with damaged or low self-esteem. Emily Dickinson (1862), the American poet, describes well some of the feelings of a depressed person.

> *This is the Hour of Lead*
> *Remembered, if outlived,*
> *as Freezing persons recollect the Snow*
> *First Chill, then Stupor, then the letting go.*

It is a challenge for the therapist to facilitate a positive connectedness with a depressed client. Often the client does not feel worthy of anyone spending time and energy, let alone genuine concern on her. An empathetic approach with acceptance of the client's feelings of unworthiness can begin the relationship. The therapist might say "I know right now you don't feel very good about yourself." When the relationship has been established and the client knows that she is accepted as she is, the therapist needs to find a part of the self that the client could perceive as positive and worthwhile. Sometimes with very depressed women the search is difficult. The therapist may need to make suggestions as to what she observes as positive, but not overwhelm the client with this support. The client may see herself as so worthless that she will have to prove it to the therapist in outward self-deprecating behavior. The therapist will need to have a deep understanding of the severe damage to the client's sense of self to provide a consistent patient, empathetic presence during this lengthy process. Small gains must be appreciated as victories. Once a client begins to regard herself in a positive way, other psychological therapies such as cognitive and behavioral therapies, and exploration of developmental experiences such as abuse and abandonment can be initiated. Assisting a client to heal from painful experiences of childhood is a highly skilled process described in chapter 12.

Cognitive therapy is used to correct distorted thinking that accompanies depression. Such thinking is most often characterized by rumination, self-criticism, negativism, and helplessness. The depressed woman usually assumes excessive responsibility for negative events in her life and underestimates the power she has to influence these events (McGrath et al., 1990). Behavioral therapies are used to assist the client to incorporate healthy behaviors into her life-style. Good judgment based on accurate knowledge of the client must be used by the therapist to insure success. The depressed client's propensity to be self critical is acute. Setting goals beyond the client's potential accentuates a sense of failure. Most often goals should be set *with* the client, so that success is felt within the client, and not in a context of dependency on the therapist. Examples of behavioral techniques are teaching assertive behavior and social skills. Because most depressed clients are anhedonic, it is important to assist them to include the experience of pleasurable activities in their lives. In D. Wilt's experience as a psychotherapist, once self-esteem begins to increase, the boundaries of the depressed client will become strengthened, and there is less fear of abandonment. Sensitivity to the responses of others as a basis for self esteem lessens as the client learns to perceive her internal strengths and unique value. As sensitivity to the needs of the self develops, less energy is put into responding to the needs of others. The client can more accurately judge, when confronted with stresses, which she will respond to or claim as hers. Though the actual number of stressors may not decrease in her life, their potential to be an antecedent to depression lessens.

Lerner (1988) speculates that depression may serve to bind anger and obscure its sources. A woman may not feel able to face the stressors in her life directly. Not until some boundary formation and a sense of self that is valued develops can the client experience herself as competent. Developing a sense of competence enables a woman to feel that something can be done about those things that are painful to her or anger her. Otherwise, she is only able to obscure, ventilate, or suppress her feelings. With competence, she is able to discuss her anger and take it seriously. "Obviously the ability to voice anger and protest on one's own behalf is essential for maintaining one's dignity and self regard and is a crucial vehicle for both personal and social change" (Lerner, 1988, p. 247).

Social Therapy

Social cultural influences often place a woman in a position of not being valued enough to be taken seriously. Feminist therapy may be a necessary part of treating the whole experience of a woman. For example, issues related to a culture in which a woman is sexually devalued need to be addressed. Also playing a part in a woman's predisposition to depression may be a perception of less power in female-male relationships. These influences can be overt or subtle, but they are powerful and can be an important part of the matrix of the distorted perception of a depressed woman. The reader will recall from chapter 2 the discussion of socialization agents influential in the formation of a woman's perception.

Case Example

Kathy

Kathy came into therapy experiencing an endogenous depression. Her thinking and responding were slow, she had become overweight, she slept no more than 2 hours at a time, and it took most of her energy just to feed her 6-month-old, her 2-year-old, and get her two stepchildren to school. Her husband and oldest stepchild (an 11-year-old) held the power in the home, and overwhelmed Kathy. Initial therapeutic interventions were to (a) assess suicide risk, (b) begin antidepressant therapy, (c) develop a supportive relationship, and (d) identify personal strengths.

As Kathy's energy increased with the antidepressant therapy, goals were set with the client for increased physical self-care. She saw nothing positive about herself but would admit that at one time she was pretty and that she had nice hair. Beginning goals were established. She was directed to go to the mall and buy one item of new clothing, and get her hair styled. These goals may seem simple to a nondepressed client, but for a severely depressed client they are a major feat. Kathy believed that she had become worthless. When she was in the mall she had to fight constant anxiety and thoughts that she must spend her money on her children. She felt undeserving of having her basic needs met, let alone anything extra. As

Kathy steadily made strides in self-care she developed awareness of how her mother, husband and oldest stepchild devalued her. At this point treatment of anger began. You will hear more about Kathy in chapter 12.

CONCLUSION

In this chapter we have examined anger-depression linkages as one aspect of a complex woman's disorder that is often overlooked or inadequately treated. We have seen that despite regular visits to health care providers, there was a significant amount of undiagnosed depression in our study participants. Whether married or unmarried, mothers or nonmothers, young or old, many women were experiencing depressive symptomatology. Depression is a treatable illness with a favorable prognosis; failure to identify it is unacceptable in 20th century America. New views of depression are being offered that deserve the attention of health professionals. For example, psychoanalyst Emmy Gut (1989) describes "productive" and "unproductive" depressions. Her thesis is that depression can potentially serve an important adaptive purpose, permitting resolution of a deadlock in functioning and leading to growth; this she calls "productive" depression. She calls on therapists to help patients *benefit* from an experience of depression, emerging more psychologically whole. Thus, we close this chapter on an optimistic note.

■ 12
Treatment of Anger

Dorothy Wilt

There are people in this world who are joyful and they always seem to have more energy than the rest of us. This is because they don't use it all up on repression and self delusion. Being miserable is not a hobby, but a full time job. . . .
—Erica Jong, How to Save Your Own Life

In this chapter we move from a focus on the everyday anger of "normal" or "average" women to issues of therapy with women whose anger is problematic. As we have seen in chapter 2, emotion is viewed in a variety of ways by different schools of psychotherapy. For example, the psychoanalytic model treats emotion as a tension state that must be manipulated and controlled in some manner. The more socially based therapies treat emotion as a culturally adaptive interpersonal function. Greenberg and Safran (1989) state, "If we are to have a comprehensive understanding of emotion in therapy, a more differentiated, multifaceted view of emotion and its function in the process of change is required" (p. 22). In this chapter, the therapeutic treatment of anger in women is discussed as a complex undertaking that requires an understanding of the formation of this emotion from developmental, biological, cultural, and feminist perspectives. Human anger is seldom experienced in isolation from other emotions, and the defensive structure of the individual is intimately tied to the way that anger is experienced and expressed. To deal with anger effectively, the therapist must understand and address this interconnectedness. Gaylin (1984) asserts that the complexity of emotions tends to be underestimated. It is most often the case that multiple feelings, sometimes confusingly contradictory, are experienced at the same time. An example could be feeling both rage and love for our children when they put themselves in a position of danger. The therapeutic engagement of anger includes identification of adaptive, maladaptive, and ego-defending responses to anger, and implementation of specific treatment approaches. For example, women who readily but aggressively express their anger may need a treatment approach that encourages initial suppression of anger, and then later in treatment use of calming techniques that allow for effective verbalization.

The treatment of anger is addressed within a relationship with a client, in which a variety of therapeutic tools are skillfully used. This is similar to the surgeon who employs a carefully chosen selection of fine instruments to excise a pathologic growth. The psychotherapist endeavors to isolate and modify the maladaptive early experience. It is imperative that the therapist accurately prepare the client before stimulation of early memory. The client is then assisted through the process of developing healthier responses and using new behaviors. The therapeutic relationship is a safe context in which the client can open herself to her anger and her pain, and begin to heal. To facilitate healing and growth the therapist must be able to accurately assess the client, use specific treatment approaches, and most importantly be able to communicate genuine care and support. The wisdom of the healing power of relationship is ancient. The Greek historian Plutarch (A.D. 46–120) stated, "For an aching mind, words are physicians."

STUDY OF CLINICAL TREATMENT OF ANGER IN WOMEN IN A PRIVATE PRACTICE

From my private practice, six women were chosen for an in-depth analysis of anger (see Figure 12.1). The women were chosen on the basis of difficulty with anger as a treatment issue and their willingness to be a part of a study. When anger was aroused in these women, three women readily expressed their anger (Maggie, Carolyn, and Helene) and three tended to withhold anger (Barbara, Marsha and Kathy). The women were seen for 1-hour psychotherapy sessions weekly or biweekly over an average of 1½ years. These women are a specific clinical sample and not a part of the larger sample discussed in other sections of the book. By the time most of the women I see seek treatment, they are in severe emotional pain. Many have suicidal thoughts and a sense of hopelessness about their situation. For this analysis, qualitative methodology (specifically in-depth interview technique) was chosen. This method has been termed by Taylor and Bogdan (1984) as flexible and dynamic, with repeated face-to-face encounters directed toward the understanding of informant perspectives. The data consisted of my notes written after each therapy session. Words spoken, and issues discussed when the client addressed anger, as well as methods used in dealing with anger were underlined. Themes

ANGER-OUT GROUP

Fictitious Name and diagnosis	Psychodynamics of the Anger	Behavioral Responses	Treatment	Specific Group Treatment Approaches
Maggie Borderline	Surface irritability severe dependency in intimate relationships. Rage and fear of abandonment depression.	Defenses worn, incapacitating depression.	Define and support clear *sense of self*. Work through abandonment depression of early childhood and relationship with mother.	1. Assist client to focus anger on real source, often family of origin. 2. Assist client to do something effective with her anger to develop a sense of control.
Carolyn Borderline	Repression and denial of rage with biological and adoptive parents. Passive relationship with husband.	Became severely suicidal "Is tired of fighting."	Medication, focus techniques, insight into internal issues, rage, calming techniques.	3. Move client to use intellect rather than emotion. 4. Decrease ventilation of anger, teach calming approaches.
Helene Obsessive-compulsive	Never individuated from father who died when child was 11. Although otherwise quite assertive, extremely passive relationship with husband.	Though loved husband of 30 years, left him.	Support during separation to develop sense of self, work through individuation from father and mother, and understanding of passivity with husband. Marital therapy.	5. Assist client to use assertive responses rather than aggressive responses.

ANGER-IN GROUP

Fictitious Name and diagnosis	Psychodynamics of the Anger	Behavioral Responses	Treatment	Specific Group Treatment Approaches
Barbara Depression	Latent grief of mother's death as a child, rage with insensitive, critical father. Cared for siblings. Severe sense of responsibility for emotional well being of others.	Intense depressive episode.	Grief work for mother and self. Worked through rage with father without severe guilt. Developed a sense of self and self nurturing.	1. Assist the client to increase awareness of anger, and all feelings. 2. Facilitate the experience and expression of anger. 3. Assist client to experience that her anger is limited, and she does not have to become out of control or thought of as a "bitch." 4. Assist client to work through own guilt responses to anger and inhibiting responses from others. 5. Assist the client to use well-established nurturing skills on self.
Marsha Obsessive-compulsive, depression	Severe sense of emotional responsibility for family of origin, own family, and the world. Rage with narcissistic father and husband.	Eight months pregnant with second child; ready to leave abusive husband.	Firm limits with abuse. Worked through rage with father and husband. Began to nurture self without guilt. Physical exercise.	
Kathy Chronic depressive	Repressed trauma as a child, felt responsible for mother's well being, no sense of self except when desperate.	Incapacitating depression.	Medication, long-term nurturing therapeutic relationship with client. Concrete goal directed sessions, role play of assertion, individuation from mother.	

Figure 12.1. Description of Clinical Cases.

and patterns emerged as the notes were read and reread. In the remainder of the chapter, these themes will be discussed, followed by presentation of two detailed case profiles.

For both groups of women (suppressors and expressors), themes of *separation* were evident. In these women, ego defenses were well established and overused. Those who readily expressed their anger most often used displacement of anger with intimate others, and those who withheld anger used denial or repression. Also, their maladaptive coping skills in response to anger had caused pathologic dysfunction in relationships. For both groups, the deepest and most intense issue was lack of individuation in relationships with intimate others and family of origin. This seemed to prevent effective expression of anger. These issues were evident with each client. Facilitation of anger was found to be *counterproductive* with clients who readily express their anger, except when assisting these clients with anger regarding intimate others. Facilitation of anger was *useful* with the group who withheld anger, except when the rage with intimate others was tapped. In this case, a skilled combination of facilitation, calming techniques, and focus was found to be most effective.

Theoretical and Philosophical Stance

Before addressing treatment of anger in the six women selected for the study, I need to share theoretical and philosophical approaches I integrate regarding treatment in general. The treatment I provide is psychotherapy using ego based developmental theory. Central to this theory is an understanding of the orderly and systematic growth of an organism resulting from physiologic maturational factors and environmental influences. My philosophy of care is based on my belief in the holistic nature of the human organism. I believe that each human being is imbued with both similar and unique physical, psychological, social, and spiritual potentials for fulfillment. The development of these potentials can be encouraged or thwarted at any stage of an individual's life. Early childhood development, however, sets the foundation for growth. If this basic foundation is faulty, later growth is unsteady and difficult. Unresolved crises later in life can also block the full development of one's potential. As long as an individual is in a conscious state there is a capacity to learn, to change, and to grow. My role as a therapist is one of partnership with the client to examine and change blocks to growth, and to build healthier emotional and cognitive structures. These structures can facilitate the client's movement toward his or her fullest potential. This process occurs within a therapeutic relationship that involves more than a cognitive understanding of thinking patterns and emotional pain. It is a dynamic interchange through which, for a while, I become a part of the client's life. I endeavor to represent a consistent, honest, positive, caring reality for the client as change and growth occur. The client is encouraged to generalize this reality to other areas in her life. One of my clients said it well: "I like who I am when I am with you. There is no reason really why I can't be the same person with everybody in my life."

Understanding Women's Anger

How the response to anger becomes complex can be understood from a developmental perspective. The infant's seeming rage in response to hunger pains is a pure, uncomplicated reaction. As the infant learns that relief or lack of relief is related to the growing complexity of his relationship with his caretakers, the experience of anger connected with hunger becomes more intricate. Symbiosis, engulfment, separation anxiety, and guilt are all powerful dynamics that serve to deepen the complexity of the experience of anger or rage. Greenberg and Safran (1989) describe this process as one in which humans engage in immediate perceptual appraisals of environmental events. These become increasingly sophisticated as individual development progresses. The concurrent phenomenon of memory storage parallels this process. If a situation occurs that is similar enough to a primary memory, a cognitive-affective network becomes activated. This creates problems such as the response to cuing that stems from memory. This response may be unconscious, leading to confusing problematic feelings that can block new adaptive responses. Judith Viorst (1986) in her book *Necessary Losses* describes this well. She says that no one suggests that we consciously remember our early childhood, for example, when our mother leaves our crib. What remains are the feelings of being powerless, needy, and alone: "Forty years later a door slams and a woman is swept away with waves of primitive terror" (p. 19).

With ego development and socialization, anxiety becomes attached to the anger that was once a primary response. The developing child learns to protect the vulnerable self from this anxiety, which is created by the experience of anger through the use of defense mechanisms, such as denial, repression, and projection. With the attachment of defenses, along with the procession of developmental issues that invariably arise, all emotional experiences become multidetermined. Because of the inherent threat involved in both the experience of and expression of anger, this emotion becomes particularly difficult to isolate.

Therefore, it is important for the therapist to use a developmental understanding. The therapist must adeptly assess the individual's developmental response and defense. Then the client must be assisted to build strength and understanding from within to adapt in a healthier manner. This needs to be done before encouraging the client to deal directly with the anger or rage.

Premature use of assertive techniques can render a client confused, or over-whelmed with a sense of guilt or failure. These responses most often occur when there has not been preparation for the emotional separation from the important other. Often, the counterresponse of others to assertion is in a form of defense or withdrawal.

Horner (1986), an object relations theorist, explains the strong response of separation. It is that sense of disorganization and dissolution of the self experienced when one separates from a person that one still feels an integral part of. For example, Carolyn, a 40-year-old participant in this study, experienced this disorganization as splitting. Early in treatment when she began to assert herself with her dominant but passive husband, she would experience a separation of herself as two selves. In one incident she ran out of the house during an argument and drove away. She then found herself calling home from a telephone booth. She saw herself talking to her husband, but felt separate as if she were really out of her body and looking down on herself. Carolyn's poor sense of self and weak ego boundaries needed to be addressed to prevent the extreme sense of vulnerability that would accompany her assertive attempts.

Therapists are additionally challenged to concomitantly support the client but disallow engulfment. Engulfment is a sense the client can develop of being lost in and controlled by the therapist. Horner (1979) states that it is important to support ego boundaries and provide a relatedness, but to avoid a sense of the client in turn being engulfed by the therapist. Support toward individuation needs to be constant. Women are especially sensitive to loss of relationship. As mentioned in chapter 2 of this book, developmental studies with children indicate marked gender differences in response to anger. Girls will abort a game to protect the relationship when anger or confrontation emerges.

I have identified the core issue of separation as a constant theme within the phenomenon of women's anger in my private practice. Women expressed what seemed to be a paralyzing fear of abandonment, or aloneness, from their significant others. This occurred as they tried to change ineffective behavioral responses to anger. Why is this fear so powerful; are these antecedents specific to women?

Regarding Women and Fear of Separation

Women may feel an overwhelming sense of responsibility for life and its quality. Thus to cut oneself off from relationships, regardless of their character, is viewed as diminishing the quality of life, and may facilitate an immediate and possibly existential sense of grief. Rainer-Maria Rilke, the 19th-century poet, states, "In women life remains and dwells in a more immediate, richer and more intimate way" (cited in Devaux's Teilhard and Womanhood, 1968,

p. 42). Father Teilhard DeChardin, a modern thinker and philosopher, sees woman as the "unitive force" in creation and in the evolution of love. According to Devaux (1968), Teilhard believed that women have a special mission in the world: not only that of bearing children but of bearing love. He contended that women are more attuned to cosmic forces, and less contained by moral legalism and the sterile logic of men.

These writers perceive that women have an awesome responsibility to what is meaningful and rich in life itself. Women are the receivers and bearers of life. They experience a cycle each month to partake of an intimate preparation for life. Consciously or unconsciously this preparation demands the woman to be intimate with herself. Biologically, psychologically, and culturally women are imbued with the patterns that set the stage for connection between themselves and others. Inevitably these intimacies and connections change. Children leave home, menopause occurs, and eventually a woman will experience change and separation.

The first experiences of separation in childhood can outline the adaptive or maladaptive patterns of separation in life. Viorst (1985) proposes that when connections are tragically disrupted, transference of that experience may occur in later relationships. For example, an individual who expects to be abandoned may desperately cling to those around her. Expecting refusal can bring about excessive aggressive demands. Viorst states that "fearful of separation we repeat without remembering our history, new sets, new actors, and a new production in our unrecollected but still so potent past" (1985, p. 22). She points out that an individual, fearful of separation, will establish what Bowlby calls anxious angry attachments. These often bring into fruition what is feared. Mahler (1981) points out that girls may have more difficulty than boys in early issues of separation from the mother. The boy has his father to support him in personal gender identity. "The girl also has to disidentify herself from part-object representations of her mother, and goes through a tortuous and complicated splitting, repressive, and re-integrative process to attain and maintain herself and gender identity" (p. 342).

Robbins (1985) warns women to be aware of the female dilemma of becoming a person thwarted by cultural developmental patterns. Cultural messages to little girls are to be ladylike, helpless, and not assertive. These behaviors are encouraged and rewarded as girls learn to imitate mothers in their care taking roles. "Nurturing others is more highly rewarded than speaking for one's needs. Clearly this dictate stifles a girl's sense of self that is separate, autonomous, differentiated and able to survive in the world" (p. 23).

Women in Therapy

A person's unique needs and strengths are an important part of a therapy that facilitates an individual to achieve his or her potential. A unique need women have is to change the thinking pattern that promotes a culturally negative connotation of feminine anger. Freud viewed the tendency to be masochistic as feminine, and a product of cultural aggression toward women. In 1933 Freud stated that "The repression of the aggressiveness which is imposed upon women by the constitution and by society, favors the development of strong masochist impulses, which have the effect of binding emotionally the destruction tendencies which have been turned inward. Masochism is then, as it were, truly feminine" (cited in Seldes, 1985, pp. 148–149). I do not agree with Freud that all anger in women converts to masochistic impulses. I do concur that there are many overt and covert messages learned by women that dictate that they should not experience or express anger. For many women, these messages scramble direct communication of anger in both the sender and the receiver.

Mary Russell (1984), a feminist therapist, states that "women are penalized in sex role socialization in many ways that men are not. Women, therefore, need a counseling approach that does not simply regard women as equal to men but rather encourages women to analyze their situation in terms of internalized sex role limitations and inhibitions" (p. 35). Women need a therapist who will move them assertively toward insight into their unique adaptations that have developed in response to society's limitations. They also need support and encouragement to identify, develop, and honor those qualities that are uniquely theirs as women, and as individuals. Gandhi (1926) identified some of women's unique characteristics and implored the world to draw upon women's strength: "if by strength is meant brute strength, then indeed is woman less brute than man. If by strength is meant moral power, then woman is immeasurably man's superior. Has she not greater intuition, is she not more self-sacrificing, has she not greater power of endurance, has she not greater courage?" (cited in Seldes, 1985, p. 156). He concludes: ". . . if nonviolence is the law of our being, the future is with women."

Treatment Approaches for the Therapeutic Management of Women's Anger

In this section of the chapter, I set forth guidelines for the therapeutic management of women's anger, ordered in chronological sequence (see Figure 12.2). The sequence reflects the timing and preparation needed for a woman to deal with the many issues attached to the experience of anger. However, as wise clinicians understand, neither this sequence nor all of the techniques listed are applicable to all clients. What will be most effective are a variety of techniques chosen from the list as well as other personally preferred techniques used by that therapist. The plan must fit specific needs of the individual client and be implemented with skillful timing. These techniques are

Treatment approaches in the therapeutic management of women's anger (same for both groups)

1. Develop a sense of self, separate from others, strengthening ego boundaries.
2. Facilitate healthy cognitive appraisal; use genogram to identify patterns of anger management and separation difficulties in family of origin.
3. Implement a social analysis.
4. Work out anger and rage issues regarding family of origin.
5. As client individuates, assist through panic, anxiety, and grief, being sensitive to the client's desire and fear of becoming engulfed with the therapist.
6. Facilitate anger where the response is avoided. Teach calming techniques when the response is overreacted.
7. Assist client to focus anger and do something about the threat experienced.
8. Teach and reinforce effective techniques in dealing with anger.

Specific group treatment approaches for women who readily express anger

1. Assist client to focus anger on real source, often family of origin, and to use calming techniques.
2. Assist client to do something effective with her anger to develop a sense of control.
3. Move client to use intellect rather than emotion.
4. Decrease ventilation of anger, teach calming approaches.
5. Assist client to use assertive responses rather than aggressive responses.

For women who hold anger in

1. Assist the client to increase awareness of anger and all feelings.
2. Facilitate the experience and expression of anger.
3. Assist client to experience that her anger is limited, and she does not have to become a "bitch."
4. Assist client to work through own guilt responses to anger and inhibiting responses from others.
5. Assist the client to use well-established nurturing skills on self.

Figure 12.2 Summary of Treatment Guidelines

used after a therapeutic relationship has been established. Also, the original crisis that has brought the client into therapy should have been managed to the point that the client can address internal issues.

Development of Self

Initially it is important to help the client to develop a sense of self separate from others. The severity of the pattern of enmeshment with others needs to be assessed and discussed with the client. In my experience it is most successful to help the client to identify strengths that are unique to her. This can be done verbally or in writing. It is important that the therapist help the client make the list or give positive feedback to the qualities identified. The woman is encouraged to use and develop these strengths in everyday practical situations. At this time the client needs to feel the positive support from the therapist. I also find it useful to help a client identify themes in her life based on her past and present values that bring her meaning. For instance, her relationship with God and her spirituality may be an important source of strength, identity, and sense of unique self. These techniques help the client's formation of identity, and enable her to feel that she is an individual and is respected. This feeling should be established before the identification of her problems with enmeshment or separation issues. This sets a supportive solid relationship as the basis of treatment before the confrontation of the maladaptions and defenses she uses in managing of anger. At this point the need for psychotropic medication should also be assessed.

Cognitive Tools

A genogram is an excellent tool to use with the client to help her visualize patterns of difficulty with separation and anger issues within her family of origin. The genogram can also diffuse the client's self-criticism, which comes from the misperception that her problems are solely her inadequacies. The genogram also elucidates healthy and adaptive patterns that can serve as models. The use of the genogram is one technique that may be useful in setting the stage for isolating irrational beliefs and working with cognitive reconstruction. Greenberg and Safran (1989) suggest that cognitive reconstruction begin after the evocation of emotional experiences. I find that starting the reconstruction before the stimulation of memory provides a beginning structure, like a safety net, as the client reexperiences emotionally implosive memories. This need is, of course, most specific to treatment of clients in a private practice setting versus the hospital. Often, in private practice the last part of an emotionally intense interview must be used to shore up the client and prepare her to deal with the real world she must face after she leaves the session. Many women go back to the office, school, hospital, or home and resume their roles as professionals, wives, or mothers, within the hour after the session. An adaptive cognitive focus at the end of the session can at times offer an intellectual organizational structure to focus on. It is, however, a structure that takes time to develop. Therefore, I like to begin the process early in treatment. For example, through the use of a genogram, one client and I discovered that there was a subtle but strong pattern in her family of origin. The women in her family would only be direct in confronting other female members of the family. Male members were treated with a sense of protection. The belief system was that the men were too busy with business matters and would only "blow up" if confronted. The women accepted that men had no other way to communicate their displeasure or differences. The client could see how irrational and nonproductive this belief system was. She also could see how she reenacted this belief with her husband and how it set the stage for her resentment. Techniques were used to provide the client with success experiences and opportunities to practice new ways to communicate with her husband. This was done before evoking memories of her father's abuse. I knew she would need her husband's support during that period.

It is also helpful to facilitate a client's understanding of anger within a useful conceptual framework. There are several concepts that I share with clients. One is that anger is a biologically adaptive system. Another is that anger has both cognitive and affective components. Then we augment and develop from these basic facts a structure for understanding anger, based on her own cognitive and affective responses to anger. We also project considerations for change. I use a form of the threefold division of emotion developed by Greenberg and Safran (1989). The first division is that of primary emotion. This emotion is pure. Often there are body responses and images such as in the following expression by a client of mine: "My rage consumes me, I see and feel intense explosive bursts of red." Secondary emotions are learned dysfunctional responses that interrupt therapeutic resolution. For example, instead of experiencing anger a woman may automatically and unconsciously experience a sense of helplessness about her situation. Instrumental emotion is that which is driven by secondary gain such as attempts to blame, or punish others. This type is used to achieve a sense of security. For example, a client may have incorporated a deep belief that she must be a good person, and that anger is unfeminine and bad. When she experiences anger (which she cannot consciously allow herself) she quickly projects messages to the outside world that she is unappreciated and her "goodness" to others is taken advantage of. She is saying that if others were as thoughtful as she, they would not treat her this way. For example Carolyn, a client of mine in this study, would come home from a long day's work and find the dishes not done and the dogs not fed or let out, although these chores were supposed to be completed by her children and husband by 6:00 p.m. She would proceed to tell her family how hard she had worked and that all she expected was a little consideration. She would become tearful and list all of her responsibilities in the home, in contrast to how little she asked of them.

Social Analysis

Another cognitive tool to use along with the genogram is a social analysis. This analysis addresses social and cultural restraints that have affected a woman's thinking about herself and the world. Clients are helped to restructure their thinking to recognize social influences. Women are helped to look at such feelings of helplessness and powerlessness, and the possibility that a part of these feelings stem from their social conditioning rather than their personal inadequacy (Russell, 1984).

For example, Marsha, another client in this study, grew up in a competitive and rigid southern community. Within her family it was understood and accepted that financial and emotional preference would be given toward the success of her brother. Marsha sought treatment with me when she was 8 months pregnant. At this time she was being physically abused by her successful professional husband. Though Marsha was an honors graduate from her master's program and was brilliant, she believed that her role as a wife was to be an example of Christian womanhood, which included full support of her husband. She also felt it was her duty to her family to represent to the community a successful happy home.

Family of Origin Issues

Once a client's relationship with her therapist is strong enough, and the client's own strengths are established, anger and rage issues with the family of origin need to be addressed, if they indeed have been denied or repressed. This can be done through what Safran and Greenberg (1991) suggest as the stimulation of emotion. They state that "the therapeutic situation needs to be used as a laboratory for evoking and re-processing reactions in order to restructure the cognitive/affective/behavioral network or scheme" (p. 24). Techniques that I find effective in stimulation of emotions are (a) reinforcement or restatement of a client's words in the session that allude to a strong emotional response; (b) stated observations of nonverbal expressions of anger such as a clenched jaw; and (c) use of dreams, music, drawing, journals, books, and movies. What I ask my clients to do while reading, or after viewing an emotionally intense scene, is to take notes or describe their feelings and compare these feelings with personal events that they experienced. In the next session we recreate the experience and move to their memory and affective response.

The goal of the experience is to create what primal therapists view as a forceful upheaval of a neurotic system of defenses. These defenses, by blocking a full affective response, enable a client to function better externally but cause pathologic inner tension. Janov (1970) (the founder of primal therapy) describes this anger expressed in overreaction to minor incidents as "anger being siphoned off in bits and pieces" (p. 71). It removes the focus from the primal source of anger, aborts the feeling, and thus mitigates the hurt. He sees anger as a response to early hurt, the hurt being not receiving the love one needed. The anger serves the purpose of easing the hurt. He states that "in primal groups there is almost never the hostile interchange among members, nor anger at the therapist, there is just a great deal of hurt" (p. 71). This accurately describes years of my similar experience in dealing with anger in my clients. After the original situations of deep anger are remembered, refelt, and reworked there comes a sense of grief for the real issue of loss and hurt. Clinicians must be prepared to assist a client through grief toward resolution. Again this is most often not completed in one 1-hour session but continues during subsequent sessions. Therapeutic techniques specific to treatment of grief and loss need to be used with this stage of growth.

Pierce, Nichols, and Dubrin (1983) found not only that clients who do not express feelings do not change, but also those who demonstrated the *most* catharsis didn't necessarily demonstrate the greatest change: "The significant criteria for change appeared to be expression of previously avoided conflict-laden or unconscious feelings, accompanied by cognitive understanding of the work, and a clear increase above the baseline amount of expressiveness" (cited in Safran & Greenberg, 1991, p. 176). It cannot be emphasized enough that in treatment this emotional experience must only take place within the context of an established positive, supportive relationship. Rice and Greenberg (1984) emphasize the healing effect of expressing painful, disavowed emotions in the presence of an accepting validating therapist (cited in Safran & Greenberg, 1991). Reality dictates, of course, that when emotional events or conflict laden memories occur, the therapist will not always be there. I reinforce to my clients that one of the treatment goals I have for them is that they become their own therapist. I find that once emotions are tapped, like opening Pandora's box, they begin to take wing outside of the confinement of the therapeutic office. I work with clients to develop helpful techniques to deal with their emotions in between sessions. Regarding the physiologic response to anger, energy channeling methods are identified. However, methods that require fine movements become costly and should be avoided. For example, dusting the china cabinet is not a good choice. Better choices are vacuuming, raking, screaming in the bathroom or car with the radio on full blast, cleaning house, and running. These are the healthy methods most often chosen by my clients to channel the energy and urges felt when experiencing anger. They are especially needed when a woman has not yet developed fully adequate skills of effective verbalization of feelings.

After the physiological "fight or flight" response has abated, journaling, writing letters about the anger, or talking with a supportive friend seems most helpful. The poet William Blake addresses the need to verbalize anger, in his poem "A Poison Tree."

> I was angry with my friend:
> I told my wrath, my wrath did end.
> I was angry with my foe:
> I told it not, my wrath did grow.

(cited in The Great Thoughts, 1985, p. 44)

I also tell the client to contact me in intense situations when she feels her anger is destructive to herself or others. I do not want to encourage dependency, but I realize the depth of panic or fear that anger release can trigger. The cognitive reconstructions set in treatment sessions may not always hold the emotions to a feeling of safe containment. An experience of personal reassurance may be imperative. Assessment by the therapist can be important in evaluating the potential of harm and to provide judicious guidance. When anger is assessed to be destructive to the client or others near the client, restructuring of action is necessary. If possible, it is helpful to direct the client to back away from the anger producing person or situation. I suggest the use of distraction or calming techniques, at the same time acknowledging that her response is a response to a very real concern. I also explain that her anger will not be denied or repressed, but it will be set aside to work with later. Distracting techniques that have a usual positive strong emotional response from this particular client should be identified by the therapist. Examples of distracting techniques my clients have used include going for a walk, visualization of being in the mountains or at the beach, gardening, playing with their dogs or cats, shopping, going to movies, or painting.

Calming Techniques

Calming techniques are also helpful methods of distracting clients, as well as being helpful in decreasing some of the physiological responses to anger. Calming techniques have the potential of decreasing blood pressure, brain wave activity, and muscle tension. Some calming techniques are taking a hot bath, meditation or deep prayer, quieting oneself and listening to soothing music, and using progressive muscle relaxation exercises. The calm soothing presence or voice of the therapist cannot be underestimated in its potential to calm or soothe a client. Johnson (1991) addresses its particular usefulness with borderline clients. "One view of borderline behavior is caused by a deficit in the ability to hold or soothe oneself from early developmental failure. Thus, healing occurs through the therapist being a stable, consistent, caring, nonpunitive person, who survives the patient's rage and destructive impulses" (p. 168).

Stimulation of anger, evoking memories of repressed anger, distraction, and calming techniques are often used in various combinations during the treatment of a client in this experiential period of therapy. The therapist wants the client eventually to be able to integrate the experience of unblocked anger without the use of various defenses or maladaptations while maintaining her emotional integrity. The therapist may have to point this out to the client, saying something to this effect: "Your anger has not shocked or harmed me in any way"; "I'm fine, as a matter of fact you also seem quite fine to me." After the client is more comfortable with the experience of anger, she then may be ready to increase her repertoire of adaptive behaviors. It is hoped at this point she has started to view anger as an adaptive internal healthy system.

Assertiveness Techniques

The Assertive Woman, an excellent book written by Nancy Phelps, addresses difficulties women face in being assertive. It provides various clear techniques for change. There are many other books on the market that are quite helpful to use in teaching the client adaptive responses to anger. As mentioned previously, full use of assertion techniques should not be strongly encouraged until the client has dealt with the blocks to her healthy experience of anger. In addition to discussing various assertive techniques the client can role play anticipated difficult situations with the therapist. It is best for the clinician to guide the client to start with less threatening or personally costly situations, and to begin with small attainable goals to experience success. Kathy (referred to in chapter 11) started her assertion practicum in the grocery supermarket. She found assertion difficult with her family, but the supermarket provided many situations in which she could express her feelings and needs without intense fear of reprisal. She said, "I will probably never see most of these people again. What can they do to me?" She felt triumphant when she asked the checkout person to check her receipt. She thought she was overcharged, and she was!

Specific Treatment Approaches for Women Who Tend to Hold Anger in

The general techniques listed earlier are all applicable to women who suppress anger. However, more time is often needed to nurture the client's positive sense of self and experience of her unique strengths. A more in-depth social analysis may be needed to explore those cultural influences that have facilitated her fear of expression. Women who hold anger in often hold in other feelings. Before the stimulation of anger, the therapist should encourage acknowledgement of less threatening feelings such as pleasure, satisfaction, and a sense of safety. One client of mine found that sitting in a chaise lounge under a large maple tree in her back yard would bring an incredible sense of safety, peace, and pleasure. For most of her life she was too busy caring for others to take time for herself.

Once areas of safety are established, a focus on the situation that initially brought the client to treatment is helpful in terms of exploring areas of rage or anger. This client will most probably not initially use such a strong word as anger. Other less negative words like "irritation" and "upset" may be used but often represent what are actually dormant volcanoes of rage. The therapist might use cognitive restructuring techniques to assist clients to build a healthy perception of anger. Very carefully the client should then be stimulated to experience anger. These initial experiences will often be shrouded with a feeling of being "out of control" or engender a deep sense of guilt for her response. It is important that the therapist verify the reality that she was and is not out of control. The therapist might repeat words and actions the client expressed while angry and point out that they were tame compared with what she *could* have said. After this session the therapist should be well aware that the client may cancel or be very guarded in the next session for fear that she would have to reexperience her anger. If she is guarded, the session should focus on her feelings in a cognitive manner with reassurance that this learning process of working with her anger will be gradual. To feel that she is a partner in the process of her growth, feedback from her is imperative in safely controlling the process. One of my clients would initially raise her hand, as if to tell me *"stop"* when she wanted to end the exploration of her anger. Later she was able to verbalize what she was feeling and articulated what she wanted from me in a more sophisticated manner. For example, she would tell me that feeling angry toward her former lover felt like a black cloud was lifting around her. But she felt panicky as we began to identify patterns of behavior in her former lover that were similar to those of her mother.

The anger from repressed memories may be so powerful that the therapist should use calming techniques and reintroduce the client's intellectual adaptations. For example, the therapist might help the client to make a list of those things she will do after the session to "shore" up her feelings. One of the most important maneuvers is to include a list of those things that the client does for others when they are upset. The client often has well-developed nurturing skills that she has only used in the care of those around her. The client needs to know that *she* is the one who now needs caring for, and that it is essential that she learns to "mother" herself. When the client has learned to weather the storm of her emotions, new assertive techniques could be introduced, as suggestions (not expectations!). The client is often prone to please others and be self-critical if she falls short of the expectations of herself and others. Clinically, much support and reinforcement should be given to the client for her positive changes. Eventually the therapist needs to facilitate ways in which the client finds encouragement and support from within herself. We will now examine one client in the anger-in group.

ANGER-IN GROUP

Barbara

History/Psychodynamics

Barbara, the oldest of four children, grew up in a working class family. Significant to her early development was the constant illness of her mother and her father's inability to fill in emotionally during the mother's periods of incapacitation. Barbara's early memories of her mother centered around her being chronically sick and taking medicine. Her father was an alcoholic who was immature, boorish, and extremely emotionally insensitive. There was considerable fighting in the home over the father's extravagances and his impulsivity. In this tense environment, Barbara came to worry constantly about her mother's health. She would leave school, walk home to check on her mother, only to be scolded by her mother. Barbara was constantly afraid that her mother would die and that she would be hurt by her father's anger. Barbara developed early on into a very good, compliant, and responsible child. She never received praise, however, from either her mother or father; from her father because of his insensitivity, or from her mother because of her focus on her chronic health problems, and the overwhelming needs of Barbara's three younger siblings.

When Barbara was 10 years old her mother died. She related that the children were sent to school the day their mother died because her father didn't know what to do with them. Within 2 months, Barbara's father had moved another woman into the home. Barbara said that she never had the time to grieve, and that there was no one around to help her with her grief. After her mother died, Barbara was relegated to the care of her siblings. She strongly felt the loss experienced by her siblings, and she felt responsible for their entire welfare. She made a vow to herself that she would never let *that* woman be their mother. Barbara set up the stance that she was the only person that could care for her siblings adequately, and she became hyperresponsible to the task of mothering. She never wanted to be caught in a position of not being able to care for her siblings in the proper way. This sense of caretaking prompted Barbara in her choice of career. After high school she found a way to attend nursing school where she was a very dedicated student. Barbara was, however, very emotionally underde-veloped, and she had difficulty making friends. She had resigned herself to never being attractive to a man, and essentially did not date until she met her future husband at the age of 25.

The adaptations that Barbara made early in life led to some prominent difficulties. She had never developed a real sense of self except in regard to taking care of others (i.e., the care of her siblings and her choice of pro-fession). She would typically feel guilty about giving to herself. Barbara told me in the first interview that she knew she needed help when she did not respond with anger when her husband told her he was interested in another woman. She said that she didn't blame him because she saw her-self as being ugly. Barbara gave herself the name "the mother superior of perpetual responsibility." In her job, she had difficulty taking a break at lunch to eat. If she allowed herself to do this she would also do charting or be thinking about other details to take care of. It took 6 months of working with Barbara before she was able to ask her husband to help with dinner after work. Asking for help triggered a sense of annihilation; she had no sense of self except to serve others. Barbara was isolated from her own emo-tions, but she was sensitive to the feelings of others—especially their pain. She was particularly afraid of the experience of anger. Barbara felt that if she began to experience it she would be unable to turn it off, and she would become a "bitch."

Treatment

Barbara came into treatment at a time when her marriage was in dif-ficulty, and she had become depressed. Her husband had emotionally with-drawn from her, and she felt that he no longer loved her. The consistent themes in working with her involved the development of a sense of self and helping her to accept the concept that she was a deserving person. Bar-bara came into treatment feeling that she deserved whatever criticism or abuse that she gave herself or that she allowed from others. The initial therapeutic focus, therefore, was on Barbara's strengths and the experi-ence of allowing some sense of pleasure. Barbara loved to read, and she contracted to read for one afternoon every other week, without getting up every 5 minutes to clean. We spent much time nurturing responses to her feelings. This beginning sense of recognizing herself helped to stabilize Barbara, as we began the difficult task of working through her grief over the loss of her mother and her childhood, and the anger that she felt to-ward her mother, father, and her husband. A concept of anger as a healthy adaptive system was developed with Barbara.

The issue of assertiveness was central to Barbara's development of a stronger sense of her own importance. She initially practiced being more assertive at work and had to confront the strong sense of guilt that she felt when setting limits on others. She had the most difficulty asserting herself at home. Barbara had particular difficulty tolerating her husband's emotional withdrawal when she began to express her needs. As she began to recognize this as separation anxiety, Barbara found that just being able to label these feelings helped her to have more control over them. Within time, Barbara was able to develop some techniques for dealing with her husband's distancing responses. She also allowed herself to join a women's book group, where she received a feeling of warmth and sharing along with emotional support for her assertiveness. The women became emotionally available to Barbara as she worked toward changing the dysfunction in her home.

Barbara had a very difficult decision to make when her husband wanted to move away from the area to get new employment. Barbara had established a support system at work and in her church, and she had become strong enough to realize that she could function independently, both emotionally and financially. Through therapy, Barbara had developed some life goals, and she was able to make the decision to move with her husband, provided that he agree to continue their work on their marriage and commit to trying to have a second child. She had finally been able to recognize her needs as being as important as the needs of her husband, and she acted on her feelings. As a postscript, following Barbara's move, I received a letter from her in which she told me that her marriage was more fulfilling than ever, and that she and her husband were the proud parents of a new daughter.

Specific Treatment Approaches for Those Women Who Readily Express Anger

Most of the general techniques mentioned earlier are applicable to this group of women. However, some of the approaches will need adapting. Because these clients readily express their anger, conscious anger stimulation is not needed or recommended early in therapy. What will be needed early in treatment is *focus*. Tavris (1982) describes what often occurs with women who readily express anger. She describes emotions as flying about without focus to change. The person is often labeled bitch, hysterical, or negative, and her anger is not taken seriously.

The therapist may have to interrupt the client in the first sessions to redirect her to what seems to be the current source of her anger. A very firm cognitive approach would be most useful, along with a step-by-step plan developed with the client, outlining an effective manner to deal with her anger and its recent source. A sense of control within the client needs to be established. Distracting and calming techniques also need to be introduced early in treatment. A skilled, firm approach must be presented along with support and a sense of respect for the client and her feelings.

The clinician may find it helpful to suggest to the client that the real source of anger may come from past experiences. The client may feel a sense of relief that there is a reason for her overreaction. This suggestion may also unconsciously begin the process of insight into her repressed anger. Safran and Greenberg (1991) caution against the use of focused expressive psychotherapy "with those whose expression of anger is undercontrolled." They state that "uncontrolled patients indiscriminately express their anger at indirect targets or in inappropriate ways such as physical abuse" (p. 177). It is my experience that a sense of internal control is a vital need for this group of women. Also helpful is the use of a cognitive understanding of anger and its management. The client needs to be introduced to an understandable form of the concept of *boundaries.* In my practice I have found that this group of women is so frequently stimulated by any threat or hassle that they are constantly responding. To visualize and feel a self strong and separate from others, a woman must be helped to understand that she has emotional boundaries. Within these boundaries she can shut out stimuli, listen, and use her intellect and judgment. She can also decide whether an issue is important enough to respond to. Eventually she will learn that instead of displacing her anger she has the choice to deal directly with its source. Fritz Perls (1951) took the view that emotion needed to be discharged but was careful to state that senselessly discharged emotion would not bring satisfaction: "Beneficial discharge must occur in the context of contact with an appropriate object in the environment" (cited in Safran & Greenberg, 1991, p. 170). Another cognitive insight to be developed is that there may be cultural impediments to the healthy adaption of anger. With my clients who readily expressed anger, each felt that she was different than other women. Helene said, "I enjoy talking with men. They are more direct, I've always been different, it's sad, I just don't fit in with most women, even though I want to." A social analysis was helpful with Helene. Cultural influences (especially those influencing women living in the south) effected the greatest part of her perception of being "different."

Once cognitive structures are in place and the client has developed a solid beginning sense of control, focus, and boundary formation, stimulation of repressed anger may be safely initiated. As in any situation of tapping into repressed anger, the therapist must provide a calming safe presence. This is done with skill and judgment to allow only as much exposure of the anger, and accompanying feelings, as the client and the therapist can safely and effectively manage. Structure, calming techniques, and distraction are interwoven into this process.

When the intensity of the anger response from early memory and external stimuli has decreased, the client is most amenable to learning. She can then practice new adaptive and assertive responses to anger, and can give up her aggressive behavior without feeling vulnerable. At this point teaching, role playing, and support of the use of assertion is most helpful, and integrates quickly. In my experience, assertion comes quite naturally to this group of women. In many situations they were clear about their needs, but would overreact because of a repressed sense of vulnerability, lack of boundaries, and separation from intimate others, and long-standing internal anger. We will now examine one client in the anger out group.

ANGER OUT GROUP

Carolyn

History/Psychodynamics

Carolyn is the adopted child of a very passive mother and an extremely overbearing, intrusive, and critical father. She was adopted at the age of 6 weeks. She grew up in a home where the father was extremely controlling and possessive, and a strict disciplinarian who used humiliation to punish even the most minor infractions. Carolyn described her mother as being passive and cold, and also controlled by the intensity of the father's demeanor. Carolyn never felt defended by her mother, regardless of the severity of the father's punishment. Both the mother and father were very religious, and the father tended to glory in his unselfishness for raising an unwanted child. Carolyn always felt that there was something wrong with her for her anger toward this man. She was terrified of her rage with her father but also felt that she owed him her love because she was adopted. Carolyn has one sibling, an adoptive sister 6 years younger, who was placed under Carolyn's responsibility while she was at home.

Carolyn described her home life as being very sterile. She fell into the role of the "good child" and said that she felt like a "performing poodle." She developed a functioning external personality. She was a very good student and obedient daughter, but was affectively blunted. Carolyn related having thoughts of suicide since the age of 6 years, and early in her childhood she developed a sense of a split self (good child/bad child). Early on she tried to think of plans to get away from home, but she felt trapped because her father was such a pillar in the church and community. There is suspicion that Carolyn was a victim of sexual abuse by her father, but her memory of clear encounters is blocked.

Carolyn physically separated from home when she went away to college. During the first year, however, she became pregnant and was sent to a home for unwed mothers. While there her parents never visited her, and the pregnancy was treated as though it had never occurred. Carolyn surrendered the baby for adoption. At the age of 23, Carolyn entered into a brief and disastrous marriage from which she had another child. She was divorced after 2 years. Carolyn subsequently married her present husband, a kind and supportive man (opposite from her father). She has two children by this marriage.

Dynamically, Carolyn is caught in the bind of having feelings of rage while being terrified of abandonment depression, which is characteristic of a borderline disorder. Although Carolyn tends to be passive with those to whom she is close, she has an aggressive edge toward her external environment. Her anger is triggered by minor irritations, and it tends to be without focus or direction. Because of this, she has been viewed negatively by some people, and her anger has often not been taken seriously. When Carolyn came into treatment she was still feeling the control of her father, and she was unable to set limits on him. She was agitated, unfocused, and emotionally labile. Her emotional status in the recent past before treatment was marked by periods of severe depression agitation, with intermittent periods of relative calmness. Although she had been quite emotionally distressed, Carolyn had been able to function well in her job, and she is a very caring, effective mother.

Treatment

Early in Carolyn's treatment various focusing techniques were employed to help her bring organization and definition to her thoughts and feelings. Otherwise, sessions would be used up with an hour of ranting and raving. Maneuvers were used to identify what was really threatening her in her multiple crises, and at the same time we tried to identify strengths from which to establish some sense of self. In one crisis Carolyn said that she hated everything about herself, but she would admit that she was quite intelligent. I gradually moved Carolyn to use her intellect rather than her emotions. Key treatment issues involved the nurturing of her strengths and her self-esteem, while building a sense of self with boundaries. She is a talented artist, seamstress, and a very competent professional. She loved to sing in the church choir. We are moving toward involvement with the church, but God has been defined by her father. The concept of Church brings on much ambivalence.

The second stage of Carolyn's treatment involved the development of insight into the over-reaction of anger or rage that she experienced in response to rather minor irritations. Here the focus is being placed on the real source of her anger—her father. As an example, Carolyn called one evening frantic, guilt ridden, and suicidal. She had been at her 9-year-old daughter's baseball game and an umpire had made a bad call on her daughter. Carolyn began to scream and had to restrain herself from hitting the umpire. She was thrown off the baseball field, and both she and her daughter felt humiliated. An analysis of the real problem uncovered that Carolyn's father had called her 2 days earlier; he had criticized her for a misspelled word on a letter that she had written him. Through talking about situations such as this one, Carolyn developed techniques to maintain a workable distance from her father. This allowed her growth, without the constant exacerbation of her rage. For example, Carolyn's husband would quickly get on the phone when her father called, or Carolyn would change the subject when critical issues were approached. We next established together techniques in which she would set limits on her father. *Together* is a key concept that would be supported by object relations theorists. Carolyn really wanted me to tell her what to do. It was important that I supported her individuation and that she not feel engulfed by me. Individuation was supported by (a) encouraging her to think through scenarios of how she would respond to her father in an assertive way and (b) helping her to establish limit-setting goals. It was interesting that Carolyn expected me to reproach her when she didn't follow through with the goals developed. She was amazed that I didn't criticize her, and that I would support her assertions to become independent and trust her own judgment.

I have shared with you how I have used and developed treatment approaches in working with women's anger. I feel privileged to be allowed to know these women so well and to have permission to share their lives with you. A client of mine gave me permission to publish her essay "The Evening Miracle." She beautifully describes the depths of various emotions that can flow with the phenomenon of anger. She gave this to me in the session in which she said in tears "I feel like my spirit has been battered" and that "it was me I had been killing, I did it. I was killing myself because I didn't feel safe. They didn't know, my mother, my father and my husband what they were doing to me." Crying she said "I would kill the best of what I am, just to be safe."

She came to this painful insight when, for what seemed like the first time in her life, she started to realize and enjoy that she was very bright, creative, well educated, attractive, and knowledgeable. It was interesting that this session occurred several days after she directly, effectively, and very clearly expressed her anger to her former husband, and set limits on his criticism of her. I believe she shared "The Evening Miracle" with me because she finally decided to choose to live, not just for her children, but for herself.

THE EVENING MIRACLE

The sea threw itself against the rock walls with all the forces of nature behind it. It had an angry feeling to it as if the wall and the land behind were encroaching on its territory, instead of the other way around.

Far out to sea a storm slowed its way toward the quiet waiting land. Its fury was invisible yet and the full moon imbued the quiet beauty of the coast with a whiteness never seen in daylight.

The beauty of this scene will be forever etched on my soul for it was in direct opposition to the turmoil in my mind. It's odd that such beauty should seem out-of-place, unfitting somehow, at any time. And serenity would seem to be a welcome relief at a time like this. Instead, the loveliness only made me angry.

I had come to this spot in a vain attempt to escape the hell that my life had become. How I generally dealt with problems was to run away. I knew no other way.

So here I was, watching the distant storm approach, wondering how I got here and where to go and what to do now. My life was a mess. I had cut myself off from my old friends and left the comfort of my relatives. And, alone, I watched the sea.

I'd been here before. Before my insanity led me down so many wrong paths. Before I became so adept at making all the wrong choices.

Youth is no excuse. So what if I was young and naive when I met him? Is that a reason for abandoning myself for someone else? Is that a decent excuse for abdicating my position as a human being as a barter for paltry offering of affection? What choices could I have changed? What now?

Here, in this beautiful place with the sea pounding at my feet, I find myself with another choice. I could now choose the coward's way out and join my agony with that of the rolling waves, or I could face my pain and somehow calm the troubled seas of my mind.

Oh how does one make choices when one is in such turmoil? Can the sea decide to ignore the storm and calm itself? And how much more able am I in the whirlpool of my being to make this decision to either quit this life or to fight back?

I see the glow of the moon off the wet rocks below. And I glance around me at the tall grasses blowing in the rising wind. Such beauty as the near white sparkle of sand shows itself as the water recedes, only to return crashing with a roar and receding again. I see down the length of the shoreline this activity repeating itself again as it has for centuries.

The sounds of the water, the flow of the breeze against my skin and the beautiful shimmer of the waves are entering my mind, consuming my pain, allaying the fear. The storm approaches, rumbling in the distance, coming inexorably to greet the great rocky cliffs. I feel the electricity in the air, pricking me like a million tiny needles, making me feel exuberant, exhilarated, suddenly very much alive.

How could I have even considered giving up, leaving my life, as if it were a discarded newspaper? I'm unfinished, a diamond in the rough. Whatever force that created the magnificence before me, also created me. And just as the sea is a living, growing thing, so am I.

I had come here to end my pain by ending my life. I had lifted my soul like a searching hand toward heaven and asked for help to decide what to do. And I have my answer.

The wind is rising quickly now, whipping my hair across my face. The distant rumble of the storm speaks of its increasing intensity. It's coming and I should leave, find shelter. But I can't just yet. I've just experienced a rebirth, a miracle, a feeling of joy in the midst of despair and I want to remain a few moments longer . . . with my evening miracle.

Epilogue

It would be impossible to summarize all of the study findings that have been presented in this book neatly. We have examined why women become angry, with whom, and what they do with this anger once it has been aroused. We have seen that there is covariation between many anger variables and crucial aspects of a woman's identity, such as her self-esteem and values, as well as several physical and mental health indicators. We have captured women's anger in a way that laboratory research could not. Researchers could never duplicate in experimental conditions the anger a woman feels when her husband stays out late, her son lies to her, and her coworkers fail to do what they are responsible for. However, by moving out into the world to collect data, we have relinquished the control that can be achieved in the laboratory. There are many limitations of our study, of which we are fully cognizant. Obviously, we could only examine the anger that was within women's conscious awareness; no survey could access deeply repressed mental contents. This brings us to an interesting question. Can emotions exist outside of conscious awareness? Is repressed emotion truly a tenable concept? Certainly, when one's *memory* of painful and anger-provoking incidents is stimulated, strong emotion is created and experienced somatically in the *now*, in the person that has lived and grown and evolved over time since the original event occurred. The author has observed women in consciousness-raising groups who became very angry when they brought forth memories of prior life events in which they were put down or harassed on the basis of gender. Are they uncovering repressed anger or is this entirely fresh new emotion, grounded in an enlightened conscious appraisal that would not have even been possible at the time of the original incident? We leave this question for you to ponder also.

Another limitation of the study is the use of self-report data, not "validated" by objective observations of behavior, physiological measurements, and the like. This is a real limitation, but we also question the use of observational methods to study emotion, a very private personal experience. Here we cite Lazarus (1991c): "If we can't depend to some extent on what humans tell us, we lose important information about emotions, because behavior alone is not easy to interpret" (p. 29).

Some may question our decision to include intervention implications throughout the book, given the descriptive-correlational nature of our data. We believe that there is enough converging evidence that frequently recurring anger, and expression of anger through modes such as blaming and somatizing, are not beneficial to individuals in the short term, and are likely to produce health consequences in the long term, that to omit suggestions for intervention would be remiss. We hope professionals will conduct research on the outcomes of their interventions with angry women.

The purpose of these final comments will be to answer the question: Where do we go from here? Although it may sound like the researcher's obligatory disclaimer, we must make the often-heard recommendation for further research—because we have only scratched the surface of women's anger. Clearly, anger is a factor to consider when assessing and treating female clients. But our knowledge base remains limited. We are aware that our cross-sectional study does not permit any causal conclusions. We also acknowledge that factors unexplored in this study undoubtedly affect women's anger. Although we examined stress, self-esteem, social support, values/spirituality, and role responsibilities, there are several other variables worthy of scrutiny. Having the benefit of hindsight, we know that measures of quality of experience in major roles (e.g., marital satisfaction and job satisfaction) would have been useful additions to the test battery. Several times we have wished we had access to more information about family of origin data (e.g., alcohol abuse by parents). Although the research team had deliberately chosen not to ask questions about sexual abuse (based on our belief that such questioning should occur in a one-on-one interview with a sensitive listener rather than in a self-report test battery), one woman revealed her abuse in response to our open-ended questions. Had we chosen to ask specific questions about such experiences, we would have veered from our primary focus on typical everyday anger. However, we know from national statistics on sexual abuse that many other women in the sample may have had such experiences, influencing their current patterns of anger arousal and expression.

Because the authors of this book are nurses and counselors, we are especially interested in investigative work going forward in the areas of anger propensity and anger expression in specific physical and mental disorders. At this point, we do not know if some anger patterns are precursors or by-products of disease. So many questions remain unanswered. For example, how do anger cognitions and behaviors change over the course of chronic, non-fatal conditions? Do fluctuations in anger levels correlate with disease exacerbations? What anger dimensions are most salient in diseases known to be more prevalent in women, such as arthritis, lupus erythematosus, hypertension, and diabetes? If an anger-prone personality or certain ways of handling anger seem to predispose women to disease conditions such as heart disease and cancer, what preventive interventions could be introduced, and when? What therapeutic interventions are most effective with women whose high anger proneness or maladaptive anger management has already resulted in pathology?

Another fruitful area of investigation would be cultural influences on the acquisition and maintenance of women's anger expression styles. We made a very small beginning with our comparison of predominantly middle-class whites, blacks, and Chinese-Americans. Much more needs to be done to examine other ethnocultural groups, such as Native Americans, Chicanos, and Mexican Americans, just to mention a few. There are a few cultures with no sex difference in depression (e.g., the Amish). Do the cultural rules regarding anger have any influence on this interesting aberration from the preponderance of studies across the world? Thomas and Atakan, a professor at Bogazici University in Istanbul, have recently completed a study comparing Turkish and American women using many of the instruments employed in the present investigation (i.e., Spielberger's Trait Anger Scale, the Framingham Anger Scales), which were translated into Turkish (Thomas & Atakan, in press). A few caveats are in order concerning cross-cultural comparisons. Translation across languages may be difficult in many cases, and there is still the problem of the connotative *meanings* of emotion words. Researchers indigenous to the cultures should assume leadership in these efforts whenever possible.

Greater attention should be given to anger cognitions in future studies. Cognitions play a crucial role in women's anger experience; unhealthy attributions and rumination were related to stress, depression, physical health, and overall anger propensity in our study. Cognitions such as those we measured have been termed "resentful" by Harburg's group (Harburg, Gleiberman, Russell, & Cooper, 1991) and appear similar to the "brood" concept discussed by Siegel (1985) and Kahn et al. (1972). In an interview study of resentment, Johnson-Saylor's (1986) subjects used terms such as "simmering," "stewing," or "festering," implying long-term cognitive awareness of their anger. There is also some overlap between resentful cognitions and the cynical hostility construct that has dominated the literature in recent years. A moderate association has been found between scores on the Contrada Cognitive Anger scale and cynical hostility (Ho scale) scores of white, but not black, women (Durel et al., 1989). We also recommend further investigation of somatic anger symptoms. Are women who score high on anger symptoms measures more anxious or conflicted about their anger? If so why?

In future studies, the intrapsychic and social *consequences* of using various modes of anger expression should be investigated. What behaviors lead to resolution of the issues that provoked the anger? What behaviors create prolonged resentment, impede problem solving, or escalate interpersonal conflicts? What behaviors are more likely to produce guilt, self-recrimination, and lowered self-esteem? Although the present study produced evidence of a reciprocal relationship between some anger expression modes and self-esteem, we did not examine issues of guilt.

Among the implications for further research, we suggest that instrument development be given a high priority. Women in our sample identified responses to anger that were not assessed by the scales we used (e.g., try to understand the other person's motivation, try to look at the situation rationally). Many of the anger tools in current use were developed by men (e.g., Spielberger et al., 1983), and a common method of tool development was borrowing items from previously developed tools. For example, the item pool for Spielberger's Anger Expression Scale (Spielberger, Johnson, Russell, Crane, Jacobs, & Worden, 1985) contained items adapted from Zelin's Anger Self-Report Scale (Zelin, Adler, & Myerson, 1972) and the Buss-Durkee Hostility Inventory (Buss & Durkee, 1957). We know of no tool developed on the basis of interviews with women about their behavior when angry. In designing our project, we deliberately selected widely used instruments with well-established reliability and validity, but the write-in responses of our respondents illuminated the deficiencies in these measures. For example, many women cry when angry. Although hitting (or the impulse to hit) is an anger behavior mentioned in most tools, crying is not. The male orientation is evident. Therefore, we are not convinced that the questionnaires we used have adequately captured the constructs of anger proneness and anger expression. Instruments that depict anger-in and anger-out on a continuum should be abandoned. Findings of this study support those of Spielberger et al. (1985) and other investigators regarding the independence of the two anger dimensions. With improved instrumentation and replication of the analyses we conducted, researchers will be able to place greater confidence in the important relationships between anger variables and various mental and physical health indicators.

As we concluded our study, women's anger catapulted into media prominence in discussions of the Hill-Thomas confrontation. In a front-page newspaper story, Lynn Yeakel, who won the Democratic nomination for the U.S. Senate in the Pennsylvania primary, was said to have "made women's anger a keystone of her campaign . . . like Carol Mosely Braun in Illinois before her, Ms. Yeakel mined women's anger over the grilling of Anita Hill during the

Clarence Thomas Supreme Court hearings" (*The Cincinnati Post*, April 29, 1992, p. 1A). Other newspapers and magazines are spotlighting women's anger, taking note of various signs of that anger, such as (a) cheers for the actions of Thelma and Louise in the movie of the same name; (b) public opinion polls showing women were "fed up" and "angrier at men than they were twenty years ago"; and (c) movements in several parts of the country to draft women into politics (Tevlin, 1992). In an article in a popular women's magazine, "Why Women are Mad as Hell," Tevlin (1992) asserted that American women are angry about their relationships, their work, their lack of political representation, and "the hundreds of frustrations and roadblocks . . . in a male-dominated culture" (p. 208). Another popular magazine recently conducted a survey of its readers regarding anger and ways of expressing it. (*Self*, February, 1992, p. 17). Thus, greater attention is finally being given to the "topic most people really do not want to hear about" (Miller, 1991, p. 182). It is our hope that this attention will produce positive results. One of the functions of anger is to convey protest when conditions need to be corrected. The ultimate outcomes may be empowerment of women, and improved physical and mental health.

There is presently a great deal of momentum building to promote women's health, according to Bernadine Healy, director of the National Institutes of Health. In the inaugural issue of the new *Journal of Women's Health* (published by a female publisher with female editors), Healy (1992) asserts her resolve to close the knowledge gaps that exist because of the paucity of research about many women's health issues. NIH has established (a) a Research Agenda for Women's Health, (b) an ambitious program to recruit (and retain) women in biomedical careers, and (c) the Women's Health Initiative, a study of the major causes of death and disability in older women. The new Office of Research on Women's Health is monitoring NIH-supported studies to ensure that women are included. Interestingly, because there has been so much media attention to some of these activities in Washington, Healy reports she has been asked if women's health is "just a fad." To this, she answers, "women certainly aren't a fad! How could women's health be a fad?" (Healy, 1992, p. XVII). Our hope is that the funding climate will be more favorable for women's health researchers, and that emotion-health linkages for *women* will receive the attention that formerly was paid only to men.

Several groups have formed within the past decade to promote scholarship and research on women's health. The Society for the Advancement of Women's Health Research was established in 1990 and has convened several meetings of scientific, medical, and health experts as well as involving consumers. Another organization, the International Council on Women's Health Issues, has brought together representatives of many disciplines and many nations at conferences in Canada, the United States, New Zealand, and Denmark, with meetings in Botswana and Thailand scheduled for the future. *Health Care for Women International* is the official journal of this organization. Another organization dedicated to advancing knowledge, understanding and practice in the area of women's health care is the Jacobs Institute of Women's Health, established in 1990 by the American College of Obstetricians and Gynecologists; this nonprofit organization has both individual and institutional members, and publishes its own journal, *Women's Health Issues*. Groups such as these will help ensure that women's health is not a passing fad. Euripides once said, "Woman is woman's natural ally" (cited in Healy, 1992). Together, we can find the answers to the questions that remain.

References

Abrams, M. (1981). The woman's world. *Graduate Woman, 75*(4), 24–29.

Aaronson, L. (1989). Perceived and received support: Effects on health behavior during pregnancy. *Nursing Research, 38*, 4–9.

Abraham, K. (1927). Notes on the psychoanalytical investigation and treatment of manic depressive insanity and allied conditions. In *Selected papers* (pp. 137–156). London: Hogarth.

Abramson, L., Metalsky, G., & Alloy, L. (1989). Hopelessness depression: A theory-based subtype of depression. *Psychological Review, 96*, 358–372.

Abramson, L., Seligman, M., & Teasdale, J. (1978). Learned helplessness in humans: Critique and reformulation. *Journal of Abnormal Psychology, 87*(1), 49–74.

Adams, L., La Porte, R., Matthews, K., Orchard, T., & Kuller, L. (1986). Blood pressure determinants in a middle-class black population: The University of Pittsburgh experience. *Preventive Medicine, 15*, 232–243.

Adler, T. (1989). Responses to emotion both innate and social. *APA Monitor, 20*(4), 10.

Albert, N., & Beck, A. (1975). Incidence of depression in early adolescence: A preliminary study. *Journal of Youth and Adolescence, 4*, 301–307.

Alcoholics Anonymous (1976). New York: Alcoholics Anonymous World Services, Inc.

Allan, C. A., & Cooke, D. J. (1985). Stressful life events and alcohol misuse in women: A critical review. *Journal of Studies on Alcohol, 46*, 147–152.

Allport, G. (1961). *Pattern and growth in personality.* New York: Holt, Rinehart & Winston.

Amatea, E. S., & Fong, M. L. (1991). The impact of role stressors and personal resources on the stress experience of professional women. *Psychology of Women Quarterly, 15*, 419–430.

American Psychiatric Association. (1987). *Diagnostic and statistical manual of mental disorders* (3rd ed., rev.). Washington, DC: Author.

Anastasi, A., Cohen, N., & Spatz, D. (1948). A study of fear and anger in college students through the controlled diary method. *Journal of Genetic Psychology, 73,* 243–249.

Andrews, H. B., & Jones, S. (1990). Eating behavior in obese women: A test of two hypotheses. *Australian Psychologist,* 25(3), 351–357.

Antonucci, T. J., & Jackson, J. S. (1983). Physical health and self-esteem. *Family and Community Health,* 6(2), 1–9.

Appel, M. A., Holroyd, K. A., & Gorkin, L. (1983). Anger and the etiology and progression of physical illness. In L. Temoshok, C. Van Dyke, & L. S. Zegans (Eds.), *Emotions in health and illness: Theoretical and research foundations* (pp. 73–87). New York: Grune & Stratton.

Arieti, S., & Bemporad, J. (1978). *Severe and mild depression: The psychotherapeutic approach.* New York: Basic Books.

Armstead, C. A., Lawler, K. A., Gorden, G., Cross, J., & Gibbons, J. (1989). Relationship of racial stressors to blood pressure responses and anger expression in black college students. *Health Psychology,* 8, 541–556.

Arnold, M. B. (1960). *Emotion and personality.* New York: Columbia University Press.

Asplund, G. (1988). *Women Managers.* New York: Wiley.

Atakan, S. (1989). *Relationship of anger variables and menopausal symptoms.* Paper presented at the American Nurses' Association Research Conference, Chicago.

Averill, J. R. (1980). A constructivist view of emotion. In R. Plutchik & H. Kellerman (Eds.), *Emotion: Theory, research, and experience: Vol. 1. Theories of emotion* (pp. 305–339). New York: Academic Press.

Averill, J. R. (1982). *Anger and aggression: An essay on emotion.* New York: Springer-Verlag.

Averill, J. R. (1983). Studies on anger and aggression: Implications for theories of emotion. *American Psychologist,* 38, 1145–1160.

Averill, J. R. (1984). The acquisition of emotions during adulthood. In C. Malatesta & C. Izard (Eds.), *Emotion in adult development* (pp. 23–43). Beverly Hills: Sage.

Ax, A. (1953). The physiological differentiation between fear and anger in humans. *Psychosomatic Medicine,* 15, 433–442.

Bach, G., & Goldberg, H. (1974). *Creative aggression.* Garden City, NY: Anchor Books.

Bardwick, J. M. (1971). *Psychology of women.* New York: Harper & Row.

Bardwick, J. M. (1979). *In transition.* New York: Holt, Rinehart & Winston.

Barefoot, J. C., Peterson, B. L., Dahlstrom, W. G., Siegler, I. C., Anderson, N. B., & Williams, R. B., Jr. (1991). Hostility patterns and health implications: Correlates of Cook-Medley Hostility Scale Scores in a national survey. *Health Psychology,* 10, 18–24.

Barnett, R. C., Davidson, H., & Marshall, N. L. (1991). Physical symptoms and the interplay of work and family roles. *Health Psychology,* 10, 94–101.

Barnett, R. C., & Baruch, G. K. (1985). Women's involvement in multiple roles and psychological distress. *Journal of Personality and Social Psychology,* 51, 578–585.

Baron, R. (1983). Social influence theory and aggression. In R. G. Geen & E. L. Donnerstein (Eds.), *Aggression: Theoretical and empirical reviews: Vol. 2. Issues in research* (pp. 173–190). New York: Academic Press.

Barron, C. (1987). Succeeding in a man's world: Women's expectations for success and perceptions of ability. *Journal of Nursing Education,* 26, 310–316.

Barry, V. (1980). *Philosophy*. Belmont, CA: Wadsworth.

Baruch, G. K., Biener, L., & Barnett, R. C. (1987). Women and gender in research on work and family stress. *American Psychologist, 42*, 130–136.

Baruch, G., Barnett, R., & Rivers, C. (1983). *Life prints: New patterns of love and work for today's women*. New York: McGraw-Hill.

Bateson, M. C. (1990). *Composing a life*. New York: Plume.

Beatty, J., Gutkowski, M., Moleti, C., & Yeransian-Nassery, L. (1985). Anger generated by unmet expectations. *MCN, 10*, 324–327.

Beck, A. (1972). *Depression: Causes and treatment*. Philadelphia: University of Pennsylvania Press.

Beck, A. (1976). *Cognitive therapy and the emotional disorders*. New York: International Universities Press.

Beck, A, Rush, A. J., Shaw, B. F., & Emery, G. (1979). *Cognitive therapy of depression*. New York: Guilford.

Beck, A., Steer, R., & Garbin, M. (1988). Psychometric properties of the Beck Depression Inventory: Twenty-five years of evaluation. *Clinical Psychology Review, 8*, 77–100.

Beck, A., Ward, C., Mendelson, M., Mock, J., & Erbaugh, J. (1961). An inventory for measuring depression. *Archives of General Psychiatry, 4*, 561–570.

Belloc, N. B., & Breslow, L. (1972). Relationships of physical health status and health practices. *Preventive Medicine, 2*(1), 67–81.

Ben-Zur, H., & Zeidner, M. (1988). Sex differences in anxiety, curiosity, and anger: A cross-cultural study. *Sex Roles, 19*, 335–347.

Bennett, G. (1988). Stress, social support, and self-esteem of young alcoholics in recovery. *Issues in Mental Health Nursing, 9*, 151–167.

Bennett, E. M. (1991). Weight loss practices of overweight adults. *American Journal of Clinical Nutrition, 53*, 1519S–1521S.

Berkowitz, L. (1990). On the formation and regulation of anger and aggression: A cognitive neoassociationistic analysis. *American Psychologist, 45*, 494–503.

Bernard, J. (1981). *The female world*. New York: Free Press.

Bernard, J. (1982). *The future of marriage* (2nd ed.) New Haven: Yale University Press.

Bernard, J. (1988). The inferiority curriculum. *Psychology of Women Quarterly, 12*, 261–268.

Bernardez-Bonesatti, T. (1978). Women and anger: Conflicts with aggression in contemporary women. *Journal of the American Medical Women's Association, 33*, 215–219.

Bernardy, R. (1987, Spring). An important new family issue. *Gray Panther Network*, pp. 4–5, 11.

Biaggio, M. & Godwin, W. (1987). Relation of depression to anger and hostility constructs. *Psychological Reports, 61*, 87–90.

Billings, A. G., & Moos, R. H. (1985). Psychosocial processes of remission in unipolar depression: Comparing depressed patients with matched community controls. *Journal of Consulting and Clinical Psychology, 53*, 314–325.

Birnbaum, D. W., & Croll, W. L. (1984). The etiology of children's stereotypes about sex differences in emotionality. *Sex Roles, 10*, 677–691.

Bjorntrop, P. (1985). Regional patterns of fat distribution. *Annals of Internal Medicine, 103*, 994–995.

Blake, W. (1794). A poison tree. In G. Seldes (Ed.), *Great thoughts* (p. 44). New York: Ballantine Books.

Bolger, N., DeLongis, A., Kessler, R. C., & Schilling, E. A. (1989). Effects of daily stress on negative mood. *Journal of Personality and Social Psychology, 57*, 808–818.

Bolger, N., DeLongis, A., Kessler, R., & Wethington, E. (1989). The contagion of stress across multiple roles. *Journal of Marriage and the Family, 51*, 175–183.

Boyd, J. A. (1981). Ethnic and cultural diversity: Keys to power. In Brown, L. (Ed.), *Diversity and complexity in feminist therapy* (pp. 151–167). Hawthorne Press.

Braiker, H. (1987, December). Why depression is different for high-achieving women. *Working Woman*, 79–83.

Brand, D. (1988, July 25). A nation of health worrywarts? *Time*, p. 66.

Branden, N. (1971). *The psychology of self-esteem*. New York: Bantam Books.

Brazelton, T. B. (1976). Early parent-infant reciprocity. In V. C. Vaughn & T. B. Brazelton (Eds.), *The family—can it be saved?* (pp. 133–141). Chicago: Year Book Medical.

Breecher, M. M. (1991). The hidden value of being fit. *Cooking Light, 5*(6), 16–18.

Briggs, D. C. (1977). *Celebrate yourself*. Garden City, NY: Doubleday.

Broege, P. A., & James, G. D. (1990). *The effects of mood on the blood pressure of normotensive women*. Paper presented at Society of Behavioral Medicine, Chicago.

Brondolo, E. (1992, March). *Confiding versus confronting: Gender differences in anger expression among children and adolescents*. Paper presented at the meeting of the Society of Behavioral Medicine, New York.

Brown, G. W., & Harris, T. (1978). *Social origins of depression*. London: Tavistock.

Brown, M. (1986a). Social support during pregnancy: A unidimensional or multidimensional construct? *Nursing Research, 35*, 4–9.

Brown, M. (1986b). Marital support during pregnancy. *Journal of Obstetric and Gynecological Nursing*, 475–482.

Bruch, H. (1961). Transformation of oral impulses in eating disorders: A conceptual approach. *Psychiatric Quarterly, 35*, 458–481.

Brunngraber, L. (1986). Father–daughter incest: Immediate and long-term effects of sexual abuse. *Advances in Nursing Science, 8*(4), 15–35.

Burns, D. (1980). *Feeling good: The new mood therapy*. New York: Signet.

Burrows, B. A. (1992). Research on the etiology and maintenance of eating disorders. In E. M. Freeman (Ed.), *The Addiction Process: Effective Social Work Approaches* (pp. 149–160). White Plains, NY: Longman.

Bush, D., Simmons, R., Hutchinson, B., & Blyth, D. (1977-1978). Adolescent perception of sex roles in 1968 and 1975. *Public Opinion Quarterly, 41*, 459–474.

Bush, J. (1988). Job satisfaction, powerlessness, and locus of control. *Western Journal of Nursing Research, 10*, 718–731.

Buss, A. H., & Durkee, A. (1957). An inventory for assessing different kinds of hostility. *Journal of Consulting Psychology, 21*, 343–349.

Buss, A. H. (1987). Personality: Primate heritage and human distinctiveness. In J. Aronoff, A. Rabin, & R. Zucker (Eds.), *The emergence of personality* (pp. 13–48). New York: Springer.

Bychowski, G. (1950). On neurotic obesity. *Psychoanalytical Review, 37*, 301.

Byers, P. H., Raven, L. M., Hill, J. D., & Robyak, J. E. (1990). Enhancing the self-esteem of inpatient alcoholics. *Issues in Mental Health Nursing, 11*, 337–346.

Cafferata, G. L., Kasper, J., & Bernstein, A. (1983, June). Family roles, structure, and stressors in relation to sex differences in obtaining psychotropic drugs. *Journal of Health and Social Behavior, 24*, 132–143.

Campbell, D. T., & Fiske, D. W. (1959). Convergent and discriminant validation by the multitrait-multimethod matrix. *Psychological Bulletin, 56*, 81–105.

Campbell, J. D. (1990). Self-esteem and clarity of the self-concept. *Journal of Personality and Social Psychology, 59*, 538–549.

Cannon, W. B. (1932). *The wisdom of the body*. New York: Norton.

Caplan, G. (1981). Mastery of stress: Psychosocial aspects. *American Journal of Psychiatry, 138*, 413–420.

Carey, W. B. (1970). A simplified method for measuring infant temperament. *Journal of Pediatrics, 77*, 188–194.

Carmines, E. G. & Zeller, R. A. (1974). On establishing the empirical dimensionality of theoretical terms: An analytical example. *Political Methodology, 1*, 75–96.

Cates, D., Houston, B., Vavak, C., Crawford, M., & Utley, M. (1990, April). *Heritability of anger, hostility and aggression in women*. Paper presented at the meeting of the Society of Behavioral Medicine, Chicago.

Cattanach, L., Phil, M., Malley, R. & Rodin, J. (1988). Psychologic and physiologic reactivity to stressors in eating disordered individuals. *Psychosomatic Medicine, 50*(6), 591–599.

Centers for Disease Control (1989, July 28). Trends in lung cancer incidence-United States, 1973–1986. *Morbidity and Mortality Weekly Report, 38*, 505-506, 511–513.

Chesler, P. (1971). Patient and patriarch: Women in the psychotherapeutic relationship. In V. Gornick & B. Moran (Eds.) *Woman in sexist society* (pp. 362–392). New York: Basic Books.

Chess, S., Thomas, A. & Birch, H. (1965). *Your child is a person*. New York: Viking.

Christen, A. G., & Cooper, K. H. (1979). *Strategic withdrawal from cigarette smoking*. New York: American Cancer Society.

Clark, W. B., & Midanik, L. (1982). Alcohol use and alcohol problems among U.S. adults: Results of the 1979 national survey. In *Alcohol consumption and related problems*. National Institute on Alcohol Abuse and Alcoholism. Alcohol and Health Monograph No. 1. DHHS Pub. No. (ADM) 82-1190. Washington, DC: U.S. Govt. Printing Office.

Clark, D., & Teasdale, J. (1985). Constraints in the effects of mood and memory. *Journal of Personality and Social Psychology, 48*, 1–13.

Cohen, C. I., Teresi, J., & Holmes, D. (1985). Social networks, stress, and physical health: A longitudinal study of an inner-city elderly population. *Journal of Gerontology, 40*, 478–486.

Cohen, S. (1986). Contrasting the Hassles Scale and the Perceived Stress Scale: Who's really measuring appraised stress? *American Psychologist, 41*, 716–718.

Cohen, S., Kamarck, T., & Mermelstein, R. (1983). A global measure of perceived stress. *Journal of Health and Social Behavior, 24*, 385–396.

Coleman, L. M. & Antonucci, T. C. (1983). Impact of work on women at midlife. *Developmental Psychology, 19*(2), 290–294.

Collins, S. K. (1988). Women at the top of women's fields: Social work, nursing, and education. In A. Statham, E. M. Miller, & H. O. Mauksch (Eds.), *The worth of women's work* (pp. 187–204.) New York: State University of New York Press.

Connell, C. M., & D'Augelli, A.R. (1990). The contribution of personality characteristics to the relationship between social support and perceived physical health. *Health Psychology, 9,* 132–207.

Conrad, P. (1988). Health and wealth: Notes on the rise of worksite wellness programs. *Millbank Quarterly, 65,* 255–75.

Contrada, R. J., Hill, D. R., Krantz, D. S., Durel, L. A., & Wright, R. A. (1986, August). *Measuring cognitive and somatic anger and anxiety: Preliminary report.* Paper presented at the meeting of the American Psychological Association, Washington, DC.

Coopersmith, S. (1967). *The antecedents of self-esteem.* San Francisco: Freeman.

Costa, P. T., Zonderman, A. B., McCrae, R. R., & Williams, R. B., Jr. (1986). Cynicism and paranoid alienation in the Cook and Medley Ho Scale. *Psychosomatic Medicine, 48,* 283–285.

Coward, D. D. (1990). Critical multiplism: A research strategy for nursing science. *Image: Journal of Nursing Scholarship, 22,* 163–167.

Coyne, J. C. (1976). Toward an interactional description of depression. *Psychiatry, 39,* 28–40.

Crawford, J., Kippax, S., Onyx, J., Gault, U., & Benton, P. (1990). Women theorizing their experiences of anger: A study using memory-work. *Australian Psychologist, 25,* 333–350.

Crouch, M. A. & Straub, V. (1983). Enhancement of self-esteem in adults. *Family and Community Health, 6*(2), 65–78.

Cummings, E. M. (1987). Coping with background anger in early childhood. *Child Development, 58,* 976–984.

Cummings, E. M., Zahn-Waxler, C., & Radke-Yarrow, M. (1981). Young children's responses to expressions of anger and affection by others in the family. *Child Development, 52,* 1274–1282.

Dalton, S. T. (1992). Lived experience of never-married women. *Issues in Mental Health Nursing, 13,* 69–80.

Darwin, C. R. (1872). *The expression of emotions in man and animals.* London: John Murray.

Deffenbacher, J., McNamara, K., Stark, R., & Sabadell, P. (1990). Combination of cognitive, relaxation, and behavioral coping skills in the reduction of general anger. *Journal of College Student Development, 31,* 351–358.

Dembroski, T. M., & Costa, P. J. (1987). Coronary-prone behavior: Components of the Type A pattern and hostility. *Journal of Personality, 55,* 211–235.

Demo, D. H. (1985). The measurement of self-esteem: Refining our methods. *Journal of Personality and Social Psychology, 48,* 1490–1502.

DeRivera, J. (1984). Development and the full range of emotional experience. In C. Malatesta & C. Izard (Eds.), *Emotion in adult development* (pp. 45–63). Beverly Hills: Sage.

DeRivera, J. (1989). Choice of emotion in ideal development. In L. Cirillo, B. Kaplan, & S. Wapner (Eds.), *Emotions in ideal human development* (pp. 7–34). Hillsdale, NY: Erlbaum.

Derogatis, L., Abeloff, M., & Mellisaratos, N. (1979). Psychological coping mechanisms and survival time in metastatic breast cancer. *Journal of the American Medical Association, 242,* 1504–1508.

Devaux, A. A. (1968). *Teilhard and womanhood*. New York: Deus Books/Paulist Press.

Dickinson, E. (1976). In T. H. Johnson (Ed.), *The complete poems of Emily Dickinson*. Little, Brown.

Dillard, A. (1987). *An American childhood*. New York: Harper & Row.

Dixon, J. P., Dixon, J. K., & Spinner, J. C. (1991). Tensions between career and interpersonal commitments as a risk factor for cardiovascular disease among women. *Women & Health, 17*(3), 30–57.

Dossey, B., Keegan, L., Guzzetta, C., & Kolkmeier, L. (1988). *Holistic nursing: A handbook for practice*. Rockville, MD: Aspen.

Doyal, L. (1990). Waged work and women's well being. *Women's Studies International Forum, 13*(6), 587–604.

Dubos, R. (1961). *The mirage of health: Utopia, progress and biological change*. New York: Doubleday.

Duerk, J. (1990). *Circle of stones: Woman's journey to herself*. San Diego: LuraMedia.

Durel, L. A., Carver, C. S., Spitzer, S. B., Llabre, M. M., Weintraub, J. K., Saab, P. G., & Schneiderman, N. (1989). Associations of blood pressure with self-report measures of anger and hostility among black and white men and women. *Health Psychology, 8*, 557–575.

Dykema, L. (1985). Gaventa's theory of power and powerlessness: Application to nursing. *Occupational Health Nursing*, 443–446.

Edelman, B. (1984). A multiple factor study of body weight control. *Journal of General Psychology, 110*, 99–114.

Ekman, P. (1972). Universals and cultural differences in facial expressions of emotion. In J. R. Cole (Ed.), *Nebraska Symposium on Motivation, 1971* (pp. 207–283). Lincoln: University of Nebraska Press.

Ekman, P. Friesen, W. V., & Ellsworth, P. (1982). Research foundations. In P. Ekman (Ed.), *Emotion in the human face* (2nd ed.) (pp. 1–143). New York: Cambridge University Press.

El-Sheikh, M., Cummings, E.M., & Goetsch, V. (1989). Coping with adults' angry behavior: Behavioral, physiological, and verbal responses in preschoolers. *Developmental Psychology, 25*, 490–498.

Ellis-Ordway, N. (1992). The impact of family dynamics on anorexia: A transactional view of treatment. In E. M. Freeman (Ed.), *The Addiction Process: Effective Social Work Approaches* (pp. 149-160). White Plains, NY: Longman.

Engebretson, T., Matthews, K., & Scheier, M. (1989). Relations between anger expression and cardiovascular reactivity: Reconciling inconsistent findings through a matching hypothesis. *Journal of Personality and Social Psychology, 57*, 513–521.

Engle, D., Beutler, L. E., & Daldrup, R. J. (1991). Focused expressed psycho-therapy: Treating blocked emotions. In J. D. Safran & L. S. Greenbergs (Eds.), *Emotion, psychotherapy, and change* (pp. 169–196). New York: Guilford.

Ewart, C.K. (1991). Familial transmission of essential hypertension: Genes, environments, and chronic anger. *Annals of Behavioral Medicine, 13*(1), 40–47.

Feldman, J. (1987). Alternative therapies. In J. Haber, P. Hoskins, A. Leach, & B. Sideleau (Eds.), *Comprehensive psychiatric nursing* (3rd ed., pp. 485–504). New York: McGraw-Hill.

Fine, B. J., & Sweeney, D. R. (1968). Personality traits, and situational factors, and catecholamine excretion. *Journal of Experimental Research in Personality, 3*, 15–27.

Fischman, J. (1987). Type A on trial. *Psychology Today, 21*(2), 42–50.

Folkenberg, J. (1991). Adolescent boys view the world differently than adolescent girls. *American Health, 10*(6), 97.

Folkins, C. H., & Sime, W. E. (1981). Physical fitness training and mental health. *American Psychologist, 36,* 373–389.

Folkman, S., & Lazarus, R. S. (1980). An analysis of coping in a middle-aged community sample. *Journal of Health and Social Behavior, 21,* 219–239.

Fox, M. (1972). *On becoming a musical, mystical bear: Spirituality American style.* New York: Paulist Press/Deus Book.

Fox, N. A. (1991). If it's not left, it's right: Electroencephalograph asymmetry and the development of emotion. *American Psychologist, 46,* 863–872.

Frankenhaeuser, M. (1971). Behavior and circulating catecholamines. *Brain Research, 31,* 241–262.

Frankenhaeuser, M. (1991). The psychophysiology of workload, stress, and health: Comparison between the sexes. *Annals of Behavioral Medicine, 13,* 197–204.

Frankenhaeuser, M., Lundberg, U., & Fredrikson, M. (1989). Stress on and off the job as related to sex and occupational status in white-collar workers. *Journal of Organizational Behavior, 10,* 321–346.

Frankenhaeuser, M., Lundberg, U., & Mardberg, B. (1990). *The total workload of men and women as related to occupational level and number and age of children.* Reports from the Department of Psychology, Stockholm University, No. 726.

Franks, F., & Faux, S. (1990). Depression, stress, mastery, and social resources in four ethnocultural women's groups. *Research in Nursing and Health, 13,* 283–292.

Freeman, M., Csikszentmihalyi, M., & Larson, R. (1986). Adolescence and its recollection: Toward an interpretive model of development. *Merrill Palmer Quarterly, 32,* 167–185.

Freeman, S. J. M. (1990). *Managing lives: Corporate women and social change.* Amherst: The University of Massachusetts Press.

Freud, S. (1917/1961). Mourning and melancholia. In J. Strachey (Ed.), *The standard edition of the complete psychological works of Sigmund Freud* (Vol. 14, pp. 237–258). London: Hogarth.

Freud, S. (1946). Instincts and their vicissitudes. In *Collected papers* (Vol. 4, pp. 60–83). London: Hogarth. (Original work published 1921)

Frey, W., & Langseth, M. (1985). *Crying: The mystery of tears.* Minneapolis: Winston.

Friedman, A. (1970). Hostility factors and clinical improvement in depressed patients. *Archives of General Psychiatry, 23,* 524–537.

Friedman, H. S. & Booth-Kewley, S. (1987). The "disease-prone personality": A meta-analytic view of the construct. *American Psychologist, 42,* 539–555.

Friedman, M., St. George, S., Byers, S., & Rosenman, R. (1960). Excretion of catecholamines, 17-ketosteroids, 17-hydroxy-corticoids, and 5 hydroxyindole in men exhibiting a particular behavior pattern (A) associated with high incidence of clinical coronary artery disease. *Journal of Clinical Investigation, 39,* 758–764.

Frijda, N. (1987). *The emotions.* New York: Cambridge University Press.

Frijda, N. H. (1988). The laws of emotion. *American Psychologist, 43,* 349–358.

Froberg, D., Gjerdingen, D., & Preston, M. (1986). Multiple roles and women's mental and physical health: What have we learned? *Women and Health, 11,* 79–96.

Fujita, F., Diener, E., & Sandvik, E. (1991). Gender differences in negative affect and well-being: The case for emotional intensity. *Journal of Personality and Social Psychology, 61,* 427–434.

Funkenstein, D. H., King, S. H., & Drolette, M. E. (1954). The direction of anger during a laboratory stress-inducing situation. *Psychosomatic Medicine, 16,* 404–413.

Ganley, R. M. (1989). Emotion and eating in obesity: A review of the literature. *International Journal of Eating Disorders, 8,* 343–361.

Garfinkel, L. (1985). Overweight and cancer. *Annals of Internal Medicine, 103,* 1034–1036.

Garrow, J. (1988). *Obesity and related diseases.* New York: Churchill Livingstone.

Gates, G. S. (1926). An observational study of anger. *Journal of Experimental Psychology, 9,* 325–331.

Gaventa, J. (1980). *Power and powerlessness: Quiescence and rebellion in an Appalachian valley.* Urbana: University of Illinois Press.

Gaylin, W. (1984). *The rage within: Anger in modern life.* New York: Simon & Schuster.

Gelazis, R. S., & Kempe, A. (1988). Therapy with clients with eating disorders. In C. K. Beck, R. P. Rawlins, & S. R. Williams (Eds.), *Mental health-psychiatric nursing* (pp. 662–680). St. Louis: Mosby.

Gelder, L. (1984, January). Carol Gilligan: Leader for a different kind of future. *Ms.,* pp. 37–38, 40, 101.

Gentry, W. D., Chesney, A. P., Gary, H., Hall, R. P., & Harburg, E. (1982). Habitual anger-coping styles: Effect on mean blood pressure and risk for essential hypertension. *Psychosomatic Medicine, 44,* 195–202.

Gershoff, S. N. (1991). At what price the quest for thinness? *Tufts University Diet and Nutrition Letter, 9*(6), 3–6.

Gershon, E., Cromer, M., & Klerman, G. (1968). Hostility and depression. *Psychiatry, 31,* 224–235.

Gilbert, D. G. (1988). EEG and personality difference between smokers and non-drinkers. *Personality and Individual Differences, 9,* 659–665.

Gilligan, C. (1982). *In a different voice: Psychological theory and women's development.* Cambridge, MA: Harvard University Press.

Glassner, B. (1988). *Bodies.* New York: G. P. Putman.

Goldin, C. (1990). *Understanding the gender gap.* New York: Oxford University Press.

Goldstein, H. S., Edelberg, R., Meier, C. F., & Davis, L. (1988). Relationship of resting blood pressure and heart rate to experienced anger and expressed anger. *Psychosomatic Medicine, 50,* 321–327.

Gomberg, E. S. L. (1974). Women and alcoholism. In V. Franks & V. Bartle (Eds.), *Women in therapy* (pp. 169–190). New York: Brunner/Mazel.

Gomberg, E. S. L. (1978). Introduction: Risk factors. In *Alcoholism and alcohol abuse among women: Research Issues* (pp. 83–106). Rockville, MD: National Institute on Alcohol Abuse and Alcoholism.

Gomberg, E. S. L. (1988). Shame and guilt issues among women alcoholics. *Alcoholism Treatment Quarterly, 4,* 139–155.

Goodrich, T. J. (1991). *Women and power.* New York: Norton.

Gormley, A. V. & Gormley, J. B. (1984). Research studies: A psychological study of emotions. *Transactional Analysis Journal, 14,* 74–79.

Gove, W. R., & Geerken, M. R. (1977). The effect of children and employment on the mental health of married men and women. *Social Forces, 56,* 66–76.

Grambs, J. (1989). *Women over forty: Visions and realities.* New York: Springer.

Green, C. J. (1985). The use of psychodiagnostic questionnaires in predicting risk factors and health outcomes. In P. Karoly (Ed.), *Measurement strategies in health psychology* (pp. 301–333). New York: Wiley.

Greenberg, L., & Safran, J. (1989). Emotion in psychotherapy. *American Psychologist, 44,* 19–29.

Greenglass, E. R., & Julkunen, J. (1989). Construct validity and sex differences in Cook-Medley hostility. *Personality and Individual Differences, 10,* 209–218.

Greenspan, Miriam (1983). *A New Approach to Women and Therapy.* New York: McGraw-Hill.

Greer, S., & Morris, T. (1975). Psychological attitudes of women who develop breast cancer: A controlled study. *Journal of Psychosomatic Research, 19,* 147–153.

Greer, S., & Morris, T. (1978). The study of psychological factors in breast cancer: Problems of method. *Social Science and Medicine, 12,* 129–134.

Grilo, C. M., Shiffman, S., & Wing, R. (1989). Relapse crises and coping among dieters. *Journal of Consulting and Clinical Psychology, 57,* 488–495.

Groër, M. W., Thomas, S. P., & Shoffner, D. (1992). Adolescent stress and coping: A longitudinal study. *Research in Nursing and Health, 15,* 209–217.

Grover, S. M., & Thomas, S. P. (1993). Substance use and anger in mid-life women. *Issues in Mental Health Nursing, 14,* 19–29.

Grunberg, N., & Straub, R. (1992). The role of gender and taste class in the effects of stress on eating. *Health Psychology, 11,* 97–100.

Gut, E. (1989). *Productive and unproductive depression.* New York: Basic Books.

Haddock, C. K., Stein, R. J., Klesges, R. C., Eck, L. H., & Hanson, C. L. (1990). *An examination of the impact of obesity on the psychosocial functioning of married individuals.* Paper presented at the Society of Behavioral Medicine, Eleventh Annual Meeting, Chicago, IL.

Haggerty, R. J. (1977). Changing lifestyle to improve health. *Preventive Medicine, 6,* 276–289.

Hall, M. (1990). *Women and identity: Value choices in a changing world.* New York: Hemisphere.

Hamilton, P. (1989). *The interaction of depressed mothers and their 3-month-old infants.* Unpublished doctoral dissertation, Boston University.

Harburg, E., Blakelock, E., & Roeper, P. (1979). Resentful and reflective coping with arbitrary authority and blood pressure: Detroit. *Psychosomatic Medicine, 41,* 189–199.

Harburg, E., Erfurt, J., Hauenstein, L., Chape, C., Schull, W., & Schork, M. (1973). Socio-ecological stress, suppressed hostility, skin color, and black-white male blood pressure: Detroit. *Psychosomatic Medicine, 35,* 276–296.

Harburg, E., Gleiberman, L., Russell, M., & Cooper, M. (1991). Anger-coping styles and blood pressure in black and white males: Buffalo, New York. *Psychosomatic Medicine, 53,* 153–164.

Hardy, J., & Smith, T. (1988). Cynical hostility and vulnerability to disease: Social support, life stress, and physiological response to conflict. *Health Psychology, 7,* 447–459.

Hare-Mustin, R. T. (1991). Sex, lies, and headaches: The problem is power. In T. J. Goodrich (Ed.), *Women and power* (pp. 63–85). New York: Norton.

Hare-Mustin, R. T., & Marecek, J. (1990). *Making a difference.* New Haven: Yale University Press.

Hart, K. E. (1992, March). *Psychological and behavioral effects of exposure to anger provocation: Influence of anger-in and anger-out coping styles.* Paper presented at the meeting of the Society of Behavioral Medicine, New York.

Haviland, J. M. & Malatesta, C. Z. (1981). The development of sex differences in nonverbal signals: Fallacies, facts and fantasies. In C. Mayo & N. Henley (Eds.), *Gender and nonverbal behavior.* New York: Springer-Verlag.

Hayes, D. M., & Fors, S. W. (1990). Self-esteem and health instruction: Challenges for curriculum development. *Journal of School Health, 60,* 208–211.

Haynes, S. G., & Feinleib, M. (1980). Women, work and coronary heart disease: Prospective findings from the Framingham Heart Study. *American Journal of Public Health, 70,* 133–141.

Haynes, S., Feinleib, M., & Kannel, W. B. (1980). The relationship of psychosocial factors to coronary heart disease in the Framingham Study: III. Eight-year incidence of coronary heart disease. *American Journal of Epidemiology, 111,* 37–58.

Haynes, S. G., Feinleib, M., Levine, S., Scotch, N., & Kannel, W. B. (1978). The relationship of psychosocial factors to coronary heart disease in the Framingham Study: II. Prevalence of coronary heart disease. *American Journal of Epidemiology, 107,* 384–402.

Haynes, S. G., Levine, S., Scotch, N., Feinleib, M., & Kannel, W. B. (1978). The relationship of psychosocial factors to coronary heart disease in the Framingham Study: I. Methods and risk factors. *American Journal of Epidemiology, 107,* 362–383.

Hazaleus, S. L. (1985, January). Irrational beliefs and anger arousal. *Journal of College Student Personnel,* 47–52.

Healy, B. (1992). A celebration and new resolve. *Journal of Women's Health, 1*(1), XVII.

Helson, R., Elliott, T., & Leigh, J. (1990). Number and quality of roles. *Psychology of Women Quarterly, 14,* 83–101.

Herd, D. (1988). Drinking by black and white women: Results from a national survey. *Social Problems, 35,* 493–505.

Hibbard, J. H., & Pope, C. R. (1987). Employment characteristics and health status among men and women. *Women and Health, 12,* 85–102.

Hirsch, B. J., & Rapkin, B. D. (1986). Multiple roles, social networks, and women's well-being. *Journal of Personality and Social Psychology, 51,* 1237–1247.

Hirschfeld, R., & Cross, C. (1982). Epidemiology of affective disorders: Psychosocial risk factors. *Archives of General Psychiatry, 39,* 35–46.

Hobfoll, S. (1988). *The ecology of stress.* New York: Hemisphere.

Hobfoll, S. E. (1989). Conservation of resources. *American Psychologist, 44,* 513–524.

Hobfoll, S., & Leiberman, J. R. (1987). Personality and social resources in immediate and continued stress resistance in women. *Journal of Personality and Social Psychology, 52,* 18–26.

Hoch, P. A. (1972). *Differential diagnosis in clinical psychiatry.* New York: Aronson.

Hockett, C. A. (1990, June). *Women and anger: The relationship between sex role, self-esteem and awareness, expression and condemnation of anger* (University Microfilm No. DA9012001). *Dissertation Abstracts International, 50*(12), 3852-A.

Hokanson, J. E., & Burgess, M. (1962). The effects of status, type of frustration, and aggression on vascular processes. *Journal of Abnormal and Social Psychology, 65,* 232–237.

Hokanson, J. E., Burgess, M., & Cohen, M. (1963). Effects of displaced aggression on systolic blood pressure. *Journal of Abnormal and Social Psychology, 67,* 214–218.

Hokanson, J. E., & Edelman, R. (1966). Effects of three social responses on vascular processes. *Journal of Personality and Social Psychology, 3,* 442–447.

Holahan, C., & Moos, R. (1985). Life stress and health: Personality, coping, and family support in stress resistance. *Journal of Personality and Social Psychology, 49,* 739–747.

The Holy Bible (rev. standard version). (1953). New York: Thomas Nelson.

Hooker, D., & Convisser, E. (1983). Women's eating problems: An analysis of a coping mechanism. *The Personnel and Guidance Journal, 62,* 236–239.

Hoover-Dempsey, K. V., Plas, J. M., & Wallston, B. S. (1986). Tears and weeping among professional women: In search of new understanding. *Psychology of Women Quarterly, 10,* 19–34.

Horner, A. J. (1979). *Object relations and the developing ego in therapy.* New York: Jason Aronson.

Houston, B. K., & Kelly, K. E. (1989). Hostility in employed women: Relation to work and marital experiences, social support, stress, and anger expression. *Personality and Social Psychology Bulletin, 15,* 175–182.

Houston, B. K. & Vavak, C. (1991). Cynical hostility: Developmental factors, psychosocial correlates, and health behaviors. *Health Psychology, 10,* 9–17.

Hoyenga, K. B., & Hoyenga, K. T. (1979). *The question of sex differences: Psychological, cultural, and biological issues.* Boston: Little, Brown.

Hoyenga, K. B., & Hoyenga, K. T. (1984). *Motivational explanations of behavior: Evolutionary, physiological, and cognitive ideas.* Monterey: Brooks/Cole.

Hughes, G. H., Pearson, M. A., & Reinhart, G. R. (1984). Stress: Sources, effects, and management. *Family & Community Health, 7*(1), 47–58.

Hughes, T. (1988). Women, alcohol, and drugs. In C. J. Leppa & C. Miller (Eds.), *Women's health perspectives: An annual review* (pp. 54–70). Phoenix, AZ: Oryx.

Ironson, G., Taylor, C., Boltwood, M., Bartzokis, T., Dennis, C., Chesney, M., Spitzer, S., & Segall, G. (1992). Effects of anger on left ventricular ejection fraction in coronary artery disease. *American Journal of Cardiology, 70,* 281–285.

Izard, C. E. (1971). *The face of emotion.* New York: Appleton-Century-Crofts.

Izard, C. E. (1990). Facial expressions and the regulation of emotions. *Journal of Personality and Social Psychology, 58,* 487–498.

Izard, C. E., & Buechler, S. (1980). Aspects of consciousness and personality in terms of differential emotions theory. In R. Plutchik & H. Kellerman (Eds.), *Emotion: Theory, research, and experience: Vol. 1. Theories of emotion* (pp. 165–187). New York: Academic Press.

Jack, D. (1991). *Silencing the self: Women and depression.* Cambridge: Harvard University Press.

James, K., & Greenberg, J. (1989). In-group salience, intergroup comparison, and individual performance and self-esteem. *Personality and Social Psychology Bulletin, 15,* 604–616.

James, W. (1884). What is an emotion? *Mind, 9,* 188–205.

James, W. (1890). *The principles of psychology* (Vol. 2). New York: Holt.

James, W. (1890/1950). *The principles of psychology.* New York: Dover.

Janov, A. (1970). *The Primal Scream.* New York: Putnam's.

Jarvik, L. F., & Small, G. (1988). *Parent care: A common sense guide for adult children.* New York: Crown.

Jessor, R. & Jessor, S. L. (1977). *Problem behavior and psychosocial development: A longitudinal study of youth.* New York: Academic Press.

Johnson, E., & Broman, C. (1987). The relationship of anger expression to health problems among Black Americans in a national survey. *Journal of Behavioral Medicine, 10,* 103–116.

Johnson, H. C. (1991). Borderline clients: Practice implications of recent research. *Social Work, 36,* 166–173.

Johnson-Saylor, M. (1986). An exploratory study of the experience of resentment. *Western Journal of Nursing Research, 8*(1), 49–62.

Johnson-Saylor, M. T. (1991). Psychological predictors of healthy behaviors in women. *Journal of Advanced Nursing, 16,* 1164–1171.

Jones, C. (1991). Age related differences in college students' values. *College Student Journal, 24,* 292–295.

Jones, R. G. (1969). *The Irrational Beliefs Test.* Wichita: Test Systems.

Jong, E. (1977). *How to save your own life.* New York: Holt, Rinehart & Winston.

Jourard, S. (1974). *Healthy personality.* New York: MacMillan.

Julius, M., Harburg, E., Cottington, E., & Johnson, E. (1986). Anger coping types, blood pressure and all-cause mortality: A follow-up in Tecumseh, Michigan (1971–1983). *American Journal of Epidemiology, 124,* 220–233.

Jung, C. G. (1940). *The integration of the personality.* London: Routledge.

Kagan, J. (1989). Temperamental contributions to social behavior. *American Psychologist, 44,* 668-674.

Kagan, J., & Snidman, N. (1991). Temperamental factors in human development. *American Psychologist, 46,* 856–862.

Kahn, H. A., Medalie, J. H., Neufeld, H. N., Riss, E., & Goldbourt, U. (1972). The incidence of hypertension and associated factors: The Israeli ischemic heart disease study. *American Heart Journal, 84,* 171–182.

Kandel, D. B., & Davies, M. (1986). Adult sequelae of adolescent depressive symptoms. *Archives of General Psychiatry, 43,* 255–262.

Kandel, D. B., Davies, M., & Raveis, V. H. (1985). The stressfulness of daily social roles for women: Marital, occupational and household roles. *Journal of Health and Social Behavior, 26,* 64–78.

Kaplan, H. B. (1975). *Self attitudes and deviant behavior.* Pacific Palisades, CA: Goodyear.

Kaplan, H., & Kaplan, H. S. (1957). The psychosomatic concept of obesity. *Journal of Nervous and Mental Disease, 125,* 181–201.

Kaplan, H. B., Robbins, C., & Martin, S. S. (1983). Antecedents of psychological distress in young adults: Self-rejection, deprivation of social support, and life events. *Journal of Health and Social Behavior, 24,* 230–244.

Kaplan, R. (1975). The cathartic value of self-expression: Testing catharsis, dissonance, and interference explanations. *Journal of Social Psychology, 97,* 195–208.

Karasek, R., & Theorell, T. (1990). *Healthy work.* New York: Basic Books.

Katherine, A. (1991). *Anatomy of a food addiction: The brain chemistry of overeating.* New York: Prentice Hall Press.

Kernis, M. H., Grannemann, B. D., & Barclay, L. C. (1989). Stability and level of self-esteem as predictors of anger arousal and hostility. *Journal of Personality and Social Psychology, 56,* 1013–1022.

Kessler, R. C., & McLeod, J. D. (1984). Sex differences in vulnerability to undesirable life events. *American Sociological Review, 46,* 443–452.

Kessler, R., McLeod, J., & Wethington, E. (1985). The costs of caring: A perspective on the relationship between sex and psychological distress. In I. G. Sarason & B. R. Sarason (Eds.), *Social support: Theory, research, and applications* (pp. 491–506). Dordrecht, the Netherlands: Martinus Nijhoff.

Kessler-Harris, A. (1981). *Women have always worked: A historical overview.* New York: The Feminist Press.

Kilbey, M. M., & Sobeck, J. P. (1988). Epidemiology of alcoholism. In C. B. Travis (Ed.), *Women and health psychology: Mental health issues* (pp. 92–107). Hillsdale, NJ: Erlbaum.

Kinney, J., & Leaton, G. (1987). *Loosening the grip* (3rd ed.). St. Louis: Times Mirror/ Mosby College.

Kintner, S. (1983). Older is better. *Women and Therapy, 2*(4), 61–67.

Klauber, J. (1966). An attempt to differentiate a typical form of transference in neurotic depression. *International Journal of Psychoanalysis, 47,* 539–545.

Klerman, G., & Weissman, M. (1985b). Depressions among women: Their nature and causes. In J. H. Williams (Ed.), *Psychology of women: Selected readings.* New York: Norton.

Knafl, K., & Howard, M. (1986). Interpreting, reporting, and evaluating qualitative research. In P. Munhall & C. Oiler (Eds.), *Nursing research: A qualitative perspective* (pp. 265–278). Norwalk: Appleton-Century-Crofts.

Knowles, R. D. (1981). Positive self-talk. *American Journal of Nursing, 81*(3), 535.

Knox, A. B. (1977). *Adult Development and Learning.* San Francisco: Jossey-Bass.

Knoxville News-Sentinel (1991, August 23). Drinking aids heart, study says.

Kohlberg, L. (1969). Stage and sequence: The cognitive developmental approach to socialization. In D. Goslin (Ed.), *The handbook of socialization theory and research* (pp. 347–480). Chicago: Rand McNally.

Kohlberg, L. (1984). *The psychology of moral development.* New York: Harper & Row.

Kollar, M., Groër, M., Thomas, S., & Cunningham, J. (1991). Adolescent anger: A developmental study. *Journal of Child and Adolescent Psychiatric Nursing, 4,* 9–15.

Koniak-Griffin, (1988). The relationship between social support, self-esteem and maternal-fetal attachment in adolescents. *Research in Nursing and Health, 11,* 269–278.

Kopper, B. A., & Epperson, D. L. (1991). Women and anger: Sex and sex-role comparisons in the expression of anger. *Psychology of Women Quarterly, 15*, 7–14.

Kövecses, Z. (1989). *Emotion concepts.* New York: Springer-Verlag.

Kraemer, H. C., Berkowitz, R. I., & Hammer, L. D. (1990). Methodological difficulties in studies of obesity. I. Measurement Issues. *Annals of Behavioral Medicine, 12*, 112–118.

Kristeller, J. L., & Rodin, J. (1989). Identifying eating patterns in male and female undergraduates using cluster analysis. *Addictive Behaviors, 14*, 631–642.

L., Elizabeth. (1987). *Listen to the hunger.* Center City, MN: Hazeldon Foundation.

Labbé, E. E., Welsh, M. C., & Delaney, D. (1988). Effects of consistent aerobic exercise on the psychological functioning of women. *Perceptual and Motor Skills, 67*, 919–925.

LaCroix, A. Z., & Haynes, S. G. (1987). Gender differences in the health effects of workplace roles. In R. C. Barnett, L. Biener, & G. K. Baruch (Eds.), *Gender and stress* (pp. 96–121). New York: Free Press.

LaForge, R., Williams, G. D., & Dufour, M. C. (1990). Alcohol consumption, gender and self-reported hypertension. *Drug and Alcohol Dependence, 26*, 235–249.

Lazarus, R. S. (1991a). Cognition and motivation in emotion. *American Psychologist, 46*, 352–367.

Lazarus, R. S. (1991b). Progress on a cognitive-motivational-relational theory of emotion. *American Psychologist, 46*, 819–834.

Lazarus, R. S. (1991c). *Emotion and adaptation.* New York: Oxford University Press.

Leach, A. (1987). Somatic therapy. In J. Haber, P. Hoskins, A. Leach, & B. Sideleau (Eds.), *Comprehensive psychiatric nursing* (3rd ed.) (pp. 505–535). New York: McGraw Hill.

Leiker, M., & Hailey, B. J. (1988). A link between hostility and disease: Poor health habits? *Behavioral Medicine, 14*, 129–133.

Lemaire, T., & Clopton, J. (1981). Expressions of hostility in mild depression. *Psychological Reports, 48*, 259–262.

Leon, G., & Chamberlain, K. (1973). Emotional arousal, eating patterns, and body image as differential factors associated with varying success in maintaining a weight loss. *Journal of Consulting and Clinical Psychology, 40*, 474–480.

Lerner, H. G. (1985). *The dance of anger: A woman's guide to changing the patterns of intimate relationships.* New York: Harper & Row.

Lerner, H. G. (1987). Female depression: Self-sacrifice and self-betrayal in relationships. In R. Formanek & A. Gurian (Eds.), *Women and depression: A lifespan perspective* (pp. 200–221). New York: Springer.

Lerner, H. (1988). *Women in therapy.* Northvale, NJ: Aronson.

Lester, L. (1982). The special needs of the female alcoholic. *Social Casework: The Journal of Contemporary Social Work, 63*, 451–456.

Lever, J. (1976). Sex differences in the games children play. *Social Problems, 23*, 478–487.

Levinger, G. (1976). A social psychological perspective on marital dissolution. *Journal of Social Issues, 32*, 21–47.

Lewinsohn, P. (1974). A behavioral approach to depression. In R. J. Friedman & M. M. Katz (Ed.), *The psychology of depression: Contemporary theory and research* (pp. 157–178). Washington, DC: Winston-Wiley.

Lewis, H. (1990). *A question of values*. New York: Harper & Row.

Lex, B. W. (1991). Some gender differences in alcohol and polysubstance users. *Health Psychology, 10*, 121–132.

Lin, N., & Ensel, W.M. (1989). Life stress and health: Stressors and resources. *American Sociological Review, 54*, 382–399.

Link, B,. & Dohrenwend, B. (1980). Formulation of hypotheses about the true prevalence of demoralization in the U.S. In B. P. Dohrenwend & M. Schwartz-Gould et al. (Eds.), *Mental illness*. New York: Praeger.

Lissner, L., Odell, P. M., D'Agostino, R. B., Stokes III, J., Kreger, B. E., Belanger, A. J. & Brownell, K. D. (1991). Variability of body weight and health outcomes in the Framingham population. *The New England Journal of Medicine, 324*, 1839–1844.

Lohr, J. M., Hamberger, L. K., & Bonge, D. (1988). The relationship of factorially validated measures of anger-proneness and irrational beliefs. *Motivation and Emotion, 12*, 171–183.

Lomranz, J., Bergman, S., Eyal, N., & Shmotkin, D. (1988). Indoor and outdoor activities of aged women and men as related to depression and well-being. *International Journal of Aging and Human Development, 26*, 303–314.

Lorenz, K. (1966). *On aggression*. New York: Harcourt, Brace, & World.

Loro, A. D., & Orleans, C. S. (1981). Binge eating in obesity: Preliminary findings and guidelines for behavioral analysis and treatment. *Addictive Behavior, 6*, 155–166.

Lyon, B. L., & Werner, J. S. (1987). Stress. In J. Fitzpatrick & R. Taunton (Eds.), *Annual Review of Nursing Research Vol. 5* (pp. 3–22). New York: Springer.

Maccoby, E. E., & Jacklin, C. N. (1974). *The psychology of sex differences*. Stanford, CA: Stanford University Press.

MacDougall, J. M., Dembroski, T. M., Dimsdale, J. E., & Hackett, T. P. (1985). Components of Type A, hostility, and anger-in: Further relationships to angiographic findings. *Health Psychology, 4*, 137–152.

MacKenzie, M. (1985). The pursuit of slenderness and addiction to self-control: An anthropological interpretation of eating disorders. *Nutrition Update, 5*, 174–194.

Macnee, C. L. (1991). Perceived well-being of persons quitting smoking. *Nursing Research, 40*, 200–203.

Mainiero, L. (1986). Coping with powerlessness: The relationship of gender and job dependency to empowerment-strategy usage. *Administrative Science Quarterly, 31*, 633–653.

Malatesta, C., & Culver, L. (1984). Thematic and affective content in the lives of adult women: Patterns of change and continuity. In C. Malatesta & C. Izard (Eds.), *Emotion in adult development* (pp. 175–193). Beverly Hills: Sage.

Malatesta, C. A., & Izard, C. E. (1984a). Introduction: Conceptualizing emotional development in adults. In C. Malatesta & C. Izard (Eds.), *Emotion in adult development* (pp. 13–21). Beverly Hills: Sage.

Malatesta, C. A., & Izard, C. E. (1984b). The ontogenesis of human social signals: From biological imperative to symbol utilization. In N. A. Fox & R. J. Davidson (Eds.), *The psychobiology of affective development* (pp. 161–206). Hillsdale, NJ: Erlbaum.

Mansfield, P., Preston, D., & Crawford, C. (1988). Rural-urban differences in women's psychological well-being. *Health Care for Women International, 9*, 289–304.

Marlatt, G. A., Kostum, C. F., & Lang, A. R. (1975). Provocation to anger and opportunity for retaliation as determinants of alcohol consumption in social drinkers. *Journal of Abnormal Psychology, 84,* 652–659.

Martin, S., Housley, K., McCoy, H., Greenhouse, P., Stigger, F., Kenney, M. A., Shoffner, S., Fu, V., Karslund, M., Ercanli-Huffman, F. G., Carter, E., Chopin, L., Hegsted, M., Clark, A. J., Disney, G., Moak, S., Wakefield, T., & Stallings, S. (1988). Self-esteem of adolescent girls as related to weight. *Perceptual and Motor Skills, 67,* 879–884.

Maslow, A. (1964). *Religions, values, and peak experiences.* Columbus: Ohio State.

Matsakis, A. (1990). *Compulsive eaters and relationship.* New York: Random House.

Matthews, K. A., Glass, D. C., Rosenman, R. H., & Bortner, R. W. (1977). Competitive drive, Pattern A, and coronary heart disease: A further analysis of some data from the Western Collaborative Group Study. *Journal of Chronic Diseases, 30,* 489–498.

May, R. (1940). *The springs of creative living.* New York: Abington-Cokesbury.

McBride, A. B. (1987). *The secret of a good life with your teenager.* New York: Times Books.

McBride, A.B. (1988). Mental health effects of women's multiple roles. *Image: Journal of Nursing Scholarship, 20*(1), 41–47.

McCann, I. L. & Holmes, D. S. (1984). Influence of aerobic exercise on depression. *Journal of Personality and Social Psychology, 46,* 1142–1147.

McCord, W., McCord, J., & Howard, A. (1961). Familial correlates of aggression in nondelinquent male children. *Journal of Abnormal and Social Psychology, 62,* 79–93.

McDougall, W. (1926). *An introduction to social psychology.* Boston: Luce.

McFarland, B., & Baker-Baumann, T. (1988). *Feeding the empty heart.* Center City, MN: Hazeldon Foundation.

McGrath, E., Keita, G., Strickland, B., & Russo, N. (Eds.). (1990). *Women and depression: Risk factors and treatment issues.* Washington, DC: American Psychological Association.

McGuire, K. (1991). Treating blocked emotions. In J. D. Safran & L. S. Greenberg (Eds.), *Emotion, psychotherapy, and change* (pp. 227–251). New York: Guilford.

McKinlay, J., McKinlay, S., & Brambilla, D. (1987). The relative contributions of endocrine changes and social circumstances to depression in mid-aged women. *Journal of Health and Social Behavior, 28,* 345–363.

Mead, G. (1934). *Mind, self and society.* Chicago: University of Chicago Press.

Mecca, A. M., Smelser, N. J., & Vasconcellos, J. (Eds.) (1989). *The social importance of self-esteem.* Los Angeles, CA: University of California Press.

Meisenhelder, J. B. (1986). Self-esteem in women: The influence of employment and perception of husband's appraisals. *Image: Journal of Nursing Scholarship, 18*(1), 8–14.

Mello, N. K., Mendelson, J. H., & Lex, B. W. (1990). Alcohol use and premenstrual symptoms in social drinkers. *Psychopharmacology, 101,* 448–455.

Mercer, R., & Ferketich, S. (1988). Stress and social support as predictors of anxiety and depression during pregnancy. *Advances in Nursing Science, 10,* 26–39.

Meyer, W. S. (1988). On the mishandling of "anger" in psychotherapy. *Clinical Social Work Journal, 16,* 406–417.

Midanik, L. T., Klatsky, A. L., & Armstrong, M. A. (1990). Changes in drinking behavior: Demographic, psychosocial, and biomedical factors. *The International Journal of the Addictions, 25,* 599–619.

Miller, C., & Crouch, J. (1990). Gender differences in problem solving: Expectancy and problem context. *The Journal of Psychology, 125,* 327–336.

Miller, J. B. (1976). *Toward a new psychology of women.* Boston: Beacon Press.

Miller, J. B. (1983). The construction of anger in women and men. *Work in progress: Stone Center for Developmental Services and Studies.* Wellesley, MA: Wellesley College, Stone Center.

Miller, J. B. (1991). The construction of anger in women and men. In J. Jordan, A. Kaplan, J. B. Miller, I. Stiver, & J. Surrey (Eds.), *Women's growth in connection: Writings from the Stone Center* (pp. 181–196). New York: Guilford.

Minirth, F., Meier, P., Hemfelt, R., Sneed, S., & Hawkins, D. (1990). *Love hunger.* Nashville: Thomas Nelson.

Monforte, R., Estruch, R., Graus, F., Nicolas, J. M., & Urbano-Marquez, A. (1990). High ethanol consumption as risk factor for intercerebral hemorrhage in young and middle-aged people. *Stroke, 21,* 1529–1532.

Monroe, S., & Depue, R. (1991). Life stress and depression. In J. Becker & A. Kleinman (Eds.), *Psychosocial aspects of depression* (pp. 101–130). Hillsdale, NJ: Erlbaum.

Moore, P. L. (1988). Psychotropic drugs. In C. B. Travis (Ed.), *Women and health psychology: Mental health issues* (pp. 68–90). Hillsdale, NJ: Erlbaum.

Morse, M. (1987/1988). Artemis aging: Exercise and the female body on video. *Discourse, 10,* 19–53.

Moses, S., (1990). Teen girls can have "crisis of connection." *APA Monitor, 21*(11), 26.

Mulford, H. A., & Salisbury, W. W. (1964). Self conceptions in a general population. *Sociological Quarterly, 5,* 35–46.

Musante, L., MacDougall, J., Dembroski, T., & Costa, P., Jr. (1989). Potential for hostility and dimensions of anger. *Health Psychology, 8,* 343–354.

Myers, J., Weissman, M., Tischler, G., Holzer, C., Leaf, P., Orvaschel, H., Anthony, J., Boyd, J., Burke, J., Kramer, M., & Stoltzman, R. (1984). Six month prevalence of psychiatric disorders in three communities: 1980–1982. *Archives of General Psychiatry, 41,* 959–967.

Nasby, W., Hayden, B., & DePaulo, B. (1980). Attributional bias among aggressive boys to interpret ambiguous social stimuli as displays of hostility. *Journal of Abnormal Psychology, 89,* 459–468.

Nathanson, C. (1977). Sex, illness, and medical care: A review of data, theory, and method. *Social Science and Medicine, 11,* 13–25.

National Institute on Alcohol Abuse and Alcoholism (1990). *Alcohol and women.* U.S. Department of Health and Human Services. Rockville, MD: Public Health Service.

National Institutes of Health Consensus Development Panel on the Health Implications of Obesity, (1985). Health implications of obesity. *Annals of Internal Medicine, 103*(6 pt. 2), 1073–1077.

Needleman, R., & Nelson, A. (1988). Policy implications: The worth of women's work. In A. Statham, E. M. Miller, & H. O. Mauksch (Eds.), *The worth of women's work: A qualitative synthesis* (pp. 293–308). New York: State University of New York Press.

Nellis, M. (1980). *The female fix.* Boston: Houghton Mifflin.

The New Encyclopedia Brittanica. (1991). Chicago: Encyclopaedia Brittanica.

Newman, B., & Newman, P. (1979). *An introduction to the psychology of adolescence.* Homewood, IL: Dorsey.

Nicastro, N. J. (1989). Visual disturbances associated with over-the-counter Ibuprofen in three patients. *Annals of Ophthalmology, 29,* 447–450.

Nolen-Hoeksema, S. (1987). Sex differences in unipolar depression: Evidence and theory. *Psychological Bulletin, 101,* 259–282.

Nolen-Hoeksema, S. (1990). *Sex differences in depression.* Stanford, CA: Stanford University Press.

Norbeck, J., & Anderson, N. (1989). Life stress, social support, and anxiety in mid-and-late-pregnancy among low-income women. *Research in Nursing and Health, 12,* 281–287.

Norbeck, J., Lindsey, A., & Carrieri, V. (1981). The development of an instrument to measure social support. *Nursing Research, 30,* 264–269.

Norbeck, J., Lindsey, A., & Carrieri, V. (1983). Further development of the Norbeck Social Support Questionnaire. *Nursing Research, 32,* 4–9.

Novaco, R. W. (1975). *Anger control: The development and evaluation of an experimental treatment.* Lexington, MA: Lexington Books.

Novaco, R. W. (1985). Anger and its therapeutic regulation. In M. A. Chesney & R. H. Rosenman (Eds.), *Anger and hostility in cardiovascular and behavioral disorders* (pp. 203–226). New York: Hemisphere.

Novotny, T. E., Fiore, M. C., Hatziandreu, E. J., Giovino, G. A., Mills, S. L., & Pierce, J. P. (1990). Trends in smoking by age and sex, United States, 1974–1987: The implications for disease impact. *Preventive Medicine, 19,* 552–561.

Nyamathi, A., & Shuter, P. (1990). Focus group interview: A research technique for informed nursing practice. *Journal of Advanced Nursing, 15,* 1281–1288.

Oatley, K., & Johnson-Laird, P. N. (1987). Towards a cognitive theory of emotions. *Cognition and emotion, 1,* 29–50.

Oetting, E. R., & Beauvais, F. (1987, spring). Common elements in youth drug abuse: Peer clusters and other psychosocial factors. *Journal of Drug Issues,* 133–151.

Ogur, B. (1986). Long day's journey into night: Women and prescription drug abuse. *Women and Health, 11*(1), 99–115.

Olweus, D. (1980). Familial determinants of aggressive behavior in adolescent boys— A causal analysis. *Developmental Psychology, 16,* 644–660.

Orbach, S. (1990). *Fat is a feminist issue.* New York: Berkley.

Ornstein, R., & Sobel, D. (1987). The healing brain. *Psychology Today, 21*(3), 48–52.

Ortony, A., Clore, G. L., & Collins, A. (1988). *The cognitive structure of emotions.* New York: Cambridge University Press.

Papp, P. (1991). It's the same all over. In T. J. Goodrich (Ed.), *Women and power* (pp. 249–256). New York: Norton.

Parker, R. S. (1990). Measuring nurses' moral judgments. *Image: Journal of Nursing Scholarship, 22*(4), 213–218.

Patterson, G. R. (1985). A microsocial analysis of anger and irritable behavior. In M. A. Chesney and R. H. Rosenman (Eds.), *Anger and hostility in cardiovascular and behavioral disorders* (pp. 83–100). New York: Hemisphere.

Paykel, E., Weissman, M., Prusoff, B., & Tonks, C. (1971). Dimensions of social adjustment in depressed women. *Journal of Nervous and Mental Disease, 152,* 158–172.

Perlow, S., & Shrifter, S. (1992). Obesity and overeating: The value of mutual goal setting in social work treatment. In E. Freeman (Ed.), *The addiction process: Effective social work approaches* (pp. 161–179). White Plains, NY: Longman, Publishers Group.

Pi-Sunyer, F. X. (1991). Health implications of obesity. *American Journal of Clinical Nutrition, 1*(53), 1595S–1603S.

Piazza, N. J., Vrbka, J. L., & Yeager, R. D. (1989). Telescoping of alcoholism in women alcoholics. *The International Journal of the Addictions, 24*(1), 19–28.

Pihl, R. (1986). Psychotrope and alcohol use by women: One or two populations? *Journal of Clinical Psychology, 42,* 991–999.

Pines, M. (1984). Resilient children. *Psychology Today, 18*(3), 57–65.

Pleck, J., & Rustad, M. (1980). *Husbands' and wives' time in family work and pay work: A 1975-76 study of time use.* Unpublished paper, Wellesley College Research Center for Women.

Plutchik, R. (1980). A general psychoevolutionary theory of emotion. In R. Plutchik & H. Kellerman (Eds.), *Emotion: Theory, research, and experience: Vol. 1: Theories of emotion* (pp. 3–33). New York: Academic Press.

Polivy, J., Herman, C. P., & Warsh, S. (1978). Internal and external components of emotionality in restrained and unrestrained eaters. *Journal of Abnormal Psychology, 87,* 497–504.

Pope, M. K., Wiebe, D. J., & Smith, T. W. (1992, March). *The cynical hostility and poor health behaviors relationship: Mediating variables.* Paper presented at the Society of Behavioral Medicine Annual Meeting, New York.

Povich, L. (1992, January). Gloria Steinem talks about what you'd least expect. *Working Woman,* pp. 66–68, 81.

Powell, L., & Thoreson, C. (1987). Modifying the type A pattern: A small group treatment approach. In J. A. Blumenthal & D. C. McKee (Eds.), *Applications in behavioral medicine and health psychology: A clinician's source book* (pp. 171–207). Sarasota, FL: Professional Resource Exchange.

Pribram, K. (1980). The biology of emotions and other feelings. In R. Plutchik & H. Kellerman (Eds.), *Emotion: Theory, research, and experience: Vol. 1. Theories of emotion* (pp. 245–269). New York: Academic Press.

Pudel, V. E. & Oetting, M. (1977). Eating in the laboratory: Behavioral aspects of the positive energy balance. *International Journal of Obesity, 1,* 369–386.

Purvis, A. (1990). A perilous gap. *Time Magazine Special Issue, "Women: The Road Ahead," 136*(19), 66–67.

Radloff, L. (1975). Sex differences in depression: The effects of occupation and marital status. *Sex Roles, 1,* 249–265.

Rakowski, W., Lefebvre, R. C., Assaf, A. R., Lasater, T. M., & Carleton, R. A. (1990). Health practice correlates in three adult age groups: Results from two community surveys. *Public Health Reports, 105,* 481–491.

Rampage, C. (1991). Personal authority and women's self-stories. In T. J. Goodrich (Ed.), *Women and power* (pp. 109–122). New York: Norton.

Rand, C. S. W. (1982). Psychoanalytic treatment of obesity. In B. B. Wolman (Ed.), *Psychological Aspects of Obesity: A Handbook* (pp. 177–191). New York: Van Nostrand Reinhold.

Rapaport, D. (1971). *Emotions and memory.* New York: International University Press.

Raths, L. E., Harmin, M., & Simon, S. B. (1966). *Values and teaching: Working with values in the classroom.* Columbus, OH: Merrill.

Rawl, S. M. (1992). Perspectives on nursing care of Chinese Americans. *Journal of Holistic Nursing, 10,* 6–17.

Ray, O. & Ksir, C. (1987). *Drugs, society, and human behavior.* St. Louis: Times Mirror/ Mosby College.

Reed, B. G. (1987). Developing women-sensitive drug dependence treatment services: Why so difficult? *Journal of Psychoactive Drugs, 19,* 151–164.

Reifman, A., Biernat, M., & Lang, E. L. (1991). Stress, social support, and health in married professional women with small children. *Psychology of Women Quarterly, 15,* 431–445.

Reisenzein, R., & Schönpflug, W. (1992). Stumpf's cognitive-evaluative theory of emotion. *American Psychologist, 47,* 34–45.

Repetti, R. (1992). Social withdrawal as a short-term coping response to daily stressors. In H. S. Friedman (Ed.), *Hostility, coping and health* (pp. 151–165). Washington, DC: American Psychological Association.

Repetti, R. L., Matthews, K. A., & Waldron, I. (1989). Effects of paid employment on women's mental and physical health. *American Psychologist, 44,* 1394–1401.

Rescher, N. (1969). *Introduction to value theory.* Englewood Cliffs, NJ: Prentice Hall.

Rickman, R. L., & Spielberger, C. D. (1990). *Gender differences in the experience and expression of anger in persons with essential hypertension.* Paper presented at the Society of Behaviorial Medicine, Chicago.

Riley, W., & Treiber, F. (1989). The validity of multidimensional self-report anger and hostility measures. *Journal of Clinical Psychology, 45,* 397–404.

Riley, W., Treiber, F., & Woods, M. (1989). Anger and hostility in depression. *The Journal of Nervous and Mental Disease, 177,* 668–674.

Robbins, J. H. (1985). The appointment hassle: Clues about women's themes of separation-individuation. In L. B. Rosewater & L. E. A. Walker (Eds). *Handbook of feminist therapy: Women's issues in psychotherapy* (pp. 22–31). New York: Springer.

Robbins, T. W., & Fray, P. J. (1980). Stress-induced eating: Fact, fiction or misunderstanding? *Appetite, 1,* 103–133.

Robins, L. N., Helzer, J. E., Weissman, M. M., Orvaschel, H., Gruenberg, E., Burke, J. D., & Regier, D. A. (1984). Lifetime prevalence of specific psychiatric disorders in three sites. *Archives of General Psychiatry, 41,* 949–958.

Rodin, J., Elman, D., & Schachter, S. (1974). Emotionality and obesity. In S. Schachter & J. Rodin (Eds.), *Obese humans and rats* (pp. 15–20). Potomac, MD: Erlbaum.

Rodin, J. (1980). The externality theory today. In A. J. Strunkard (Ed.) *Obesity* (pp. 226–239). Philadelphia: Saunders.

Rodin, J., & Ickovics, J.R. (1990). Women's health: Review and research agenda as we approach the 21st century. *American Psychologist, 45*(9), 1018–1034.

Rodin, J., & Salovey, P. (1989). Health psychology. *Annual Review of Psychology, 40,* 533–579.

Rodin, J., Silberstein, L., & Striegel-Moore, R. (1984). Women and weight: A normative discontent. In T. B. Sonderegger (Ed.), *Nebraska symposium on motivation, psychology and gender: Vol. 32* (pp. 267–307). Lincoln: University of Nebraska Press.

Rogers, C. (1959). A theory of therapy, personality, and interpersonal relationships, as developed in the client-centered framework. In S. Koch (Ed.), *Psychology: A study of a science* (Vol. 3, pp. 184–256). New York: McGraw-Hill.

Rogers, C. (1964). Toward a modern approach to values: The valuing process in the mature person. *Journal of Abnormal and Social Psychology, 68,* 160–167.

Rokeach, M. (1973). *The nature of human values.* New York: Free Press.

Rokeach, M. (1979). Change and stability in American value systems. In M. Rokeach (Ed.), *Understanding human values: Individual and societal* (pp. 129–147). New York: Free Press.

Roman, P. M. (1988). *Women and alcohol use: A review of the research literature.* (DHHS Publication No. ADM 88-1574). Rockville, MD: U.S. Department of Health and Human Services.

Rook, K. (1984). The negative side of social interaction: Impact on psychological well-being. *Journal of Personality and Social Psychology, 46,* 1097–1108.

Root, M. (1989). Treatment failures: The role of sexual victimization in women's addictive behaviors. *American Journal of Orthopsychiatry, 59,* 542–549.

Roseman, I. J. (1979, September). *Cognitive aspects of emotion and emotional behavior.* Paper presented at the 87th Annual Convention of the American Psychological Association, New York.

Roseman, I. J. (1983). Cognitive determinants of emotions (Doctoral dissertation, Yale University, 1982). *Dissertation Abstracts International, 43,* 4200B.

Roseman, I. J. (1984). Cognitive determinants of emotions: A structural theory. In P. Shaver (Ed.), *Review of personality and social psychology* (Vol. 5, pp. 11–36). Beverly Hills, CA: Sage.

Roseman, I. J., Spindel, M. S., & Jose, P. E. (1990). Appraisals of emotion-eliciting events: Testing a theory of discrete emotions. *Journal of Personality and Social Psychology, 59,* 899–915.

Rosenbaum, M. E., & deCharms, R. (1960). Direct and vicarious reduction of hostility. *Journal of Abnormal and Social Psychology, 60*(1), 105–111.

Rosenberg, F., & Simmons, R. G. (1975). Sex differences in the self concept in adolescence. *Sex Roles: A Journal of Research, 1,* 147–159.

Rosenberg, M. (1965). *Society and the adolescent self-image.* Princeton: Princeton University Press.

Rosenberg, M. (1979). *Conceiving the self.* New York: Basic Books.

Rosenberg, M. (1986). Self-concept from middle childhood through adolescence. In J. Suls & A. G. Greenwald (Eds.), *Psychological perspectives on the self* (Vol. 3, pp. 107–135). Hillsdale, NJ: Erlbaum.

Rosenfield, S. N., & Stevenson, J. S. (1988). Perceptions of daily stress and oral coping behavior in normal, overweight and recovering alcoholic women. *Research in Nursing and Health, 1,* 165-174.

Ross, C., & Mirowsky, J. (1988). Child care and emotional adjustment to wives' employment. *Journal of Health and Social Behavior, 29,* 127–128.

Rotenberg, K. J. (1983). Causes, intensity, motives, and consequences of children's anger from self-reports. *The Journal of Genetic Psychology, 146,* 101–106.

Rothenberg, A. (1971). On anger. *American Journal of Psychiatry, 128*(4), 86–92.

Rubin, T. I. (1970). *The angry book.* New York: Collier.

Ruderman, E. B. (1986). Creative and reparative uses of countertransference by women psychotherapists treating women patients: A clinical research study. In T. Bernay & D. W. Cantor (Eds.) *The psychology of today's woman: New psychoanalytic visions* (pp. 339–363). Hillsdale, New Jersey: The Analytic Press.

Russell, M. N. (1984). *Skills in counseling women, the feminist approach.* Springfield, IL: Thomas.

Russo, N., Amaro, H., & Winter, M. (1987). The use of inpatient mental health services by Hispanic women. *Psychology of Women Quarterly, 11,* 427–442.

Russo, N., & Sobel, S. (1981). Sex differences in the utilization of mental health facilities. *Professional Psychology, 12,* 7–19.

Ryff, C., & Baltes, P. (1976). Value transition and adult development in women: The instrumentality-terminality sequence hypothesis. *Developmental Psychology, 12,* 567–568.

Ryff, C. (1982). Self perceived personality change in adulthood and aging. *Journal of Personality and Social Psychology, 42*(1), 108–115.

Safran, J., & Greenberg, L. (1991). *Emotion, psychotherapy, and change.* New York: Guilford.

Sandler, I., & Barrera, M. (1984). Toward a multimethod approach to assessing the effects of social support. *American Journal of Community Psychology, 12,* 37–52.

Sandmaier, M. (1980). *The invisible alcoholics.* New York: McGraw-Hill.

Sanford, L. T., & Donovan, M. E. (1985). *Women and self-esteem.* New York: Penguin.

Scarr, S. (1987). Personality and experience: Individual encounters with the world. In J. Aronoff, A. Robin, & R. Zucker (Eds.), *The emergence of personality* (pp. 49–78). New York: Springer.

Schachter, S. (1971). *Emotion, obesity, and crime.* New York: Academic Press.

Schachter, S., & Singer, J. E. (1962). Cognitive, social, and physiological determinants of emotional state. *Psychological Review, 69,* 379–399.

Schaefer, C. (1990). Self-concepts of creative girls: A twenty-five year follow-up. *Psychological Reports, 67,* 683–686.

Scherer, K. R. (1982). Emotion as process: Function, origin and regulation. *Social Science Information, 21,* 555–570.

Scherer, K. R. (1984). On the nature and function of emotion: A component process approach. In K. R. Scherer & P. Ekman (Eds.), *Approaches to emotion* (pp. 293–317). Hillsdale, NJ: Erlbaum.

Scherer, K. R. (1988). Criteria for emotion-antecedent appraisal: A review. In V. Hamilton, G. H. Bower, & N. H. Frijda (Eds.), *Cognitive perspectives on emotion and motivation* (pp. 89–126). Norwell, MA: Kluwer Academic.

Scherwitz, L., & Rugulies, R. (1992). Life-style and hostility. In H. S. Friedman (Ed.), *Hostility, coping and health* (pp. 77–98). Washington, DC: American Psychological Association.

Scherwitz, L., Perkins, L., Chesney, M., & Hughes, G. (1991). Cook-Medley Hostility Scale and subsets: Relationship to demographic and psychological characteristics in young adults in the CARDIA study. *Psychosomatic Medicine, 53,* 36–49.

Schimmel, S. (1979). Anger and its control in Graeco-Roman and modern psychology. *Psychiatry, 42,* 320–337.

Schless, A., Mendels, J., Kipperman, A., & Cochrane, C. (1974). Depression and hostility. *Journal of Nervous and Mental Disease, 159,* 91–100.

Schlundt, D. G., Taylor, D., Hill, J. O., Sbrocco, T., Pope-Cordle, J. Kasser, T., & Arnold, D. (1991). A behavioral taxonomy of obese female participants in a weight loss program. *American Journal of Clinical Nutrition, 53*(5), 1151–1158.

Schoenborn, C. A., & Cohen, B. H. (1986, June 30). Trends in smoking, alcohol consumption and other health practices among U.S. adults, 1977 and 1983. *Advance Data from Vital and Health Statistics* (No. 118) (DHHS Publication No. [PHS] 86-1250). Hyattsville, MD: Public Health Service.

Scholte, D. E., Cools, J. & McNally, R. J. (1990). Film induced negative affect triggers overeating in restrained eaters. *Journal of Abnormal Psychology, 99*(3), 317–320.

Schopenhauer, A. (1942). In A. Johnson (Ed.), *The complete essays of Arthur Schopenhauer.* New York: Wiley.

Schwartz, G. E., Weinberger, D. A., & Singer, J. A. (1981). Cardiovascular differentiation of happiness, sadness, anger and fear following imagery and exercise. *Psychosomatic Medicine, 43,* 343–364.

Seid, R. P. (1989). *Never too thin.* New York: Prentice Hall.

Seldes, G. (1985). *The great thoughts.* New York: Ballantine Books.

Seligman, M. (1975). *Helplessness: On depression, development, and death.* San Francisco: Freeman.

Seligman, M. (1988, October). Boomer blues. *Psychology Today, 22*(10), 50–55.

Shearer, L. (1991, August 18). Poor image. *Parade,* p. 8.

Shekelle, R. B., Gale, M., Ostfeld, A. M., & Paul, O. (1983). Hostility, risk of coronary heart disease, and mortality. *Psychosomatic Medicine, 45,* 109–114.

Siegel, J. M. (1985). The measurement of anger as a multidimensional construct. In M. A. Chesney and R. Rosenman (Eds.), *Anger and hostility in cardiovascular and behavioral disorders* (pp. 59–81). New York: Hemisphere.

Siegman, A., Anderson, R., & Berger, T. (1990). The angry voice: Its effects on the experience of anger and cardiovascular reactivity. *Psychosomatic Medicine, 52,* 631–643.

Sjöberg, L,. & Persson, L. O. (1979). A study of attempts by obese patients to regulate eating. *Addictive Behaviors, 4,* 349–359.

Slochower, J. A. (1983). *Excessive eating: The role of emotions and environment.* New York: Human Sciences Press.

Slochower, J., Kaplan, S., & Mann, L. (1981). The effects of life stress and weight on mood and eating. *Appetite, 2,* 115–125.

Smelser, N. J. (1989). Self-esteem and social problems: An introduction. In A. M. Mecca, N. J. Smelser, & J. Vasconcellos (Eds.), *The social importance of self-esteem.* Los Angeles, CA: University of California Press.

Smith, T., & Christensen, A. (1992). Hostility, health, and social contexts. In H. S. Friedman (Ed.), *Hostility, coping and health* (pp. 33–48). Washington, DC: American Psychological Association.

Smith, T., & Frohm, K. D. (1985). What's so unhealthy about hostility? Construct validity and psychosocial correlates of the Cook and Medley Ho Scale. *Health Psychology, 4,* 503–520.

Smith, T. W., Follick, M. J., & Korr, K. S. (1984). Anger, neuroticism, Type A behavior and the experience of angina. *British Journal of Medical Psychology, 57,* 249–252.

Smith, T., Pope, M., Sanders, J., Allred, K., & O'Keeffe, J. (1988). Cynical hostility at home and work: Psychosocial vulnerability across domains. *Journal of Research in Personality, 22,* 525–548.

Snygg, D. & Combs, A. W. (1949). *Individual behavior: A new frame of reference for psychology.* New York: Harper & Row.

Sobeck, J. P., & Kilbey, M. M. (1988). Etiology and treatment of alcoholism among women. In C. B. Travis (Ed.), *Women and health psychology: Mental health issues* (pp. 110–131). Hillsdale, NJ: Erlbaum.

Solomon, G. F. (1985). The emerging field of psychoneuroimmunology. *Advances, 2*(1), 6–19.

Solomon, R. C. (1976). *The passions.* Garden City, NY: Anchor Doubleday.

Solomon, R. C. (1989). Emotions, philosophy, and the self. In L. Cirillo, B. Kaplan, & S. Wapner (Eds.), *Emotions in ideal human development* (pp. 135-149). Hillsdale, NJ: Erlbaum.

Sommers, S. (1984). Adults evaluating their emotions: A cross-cultural perspective. In C. Malatesta & C. Izard (Eds.), *Emotion in adult development* (pp. 319–338). Beverly Hills, CA: Sage.

Sonstroem, R. J., & Morgan, W. P. (1989). Exercise and self-esteem: Rationale and model. *Medicine and Science in Sports and Exercise, 21*(3), 329–337.

Sorensen, G., & Verbrugge, L. M. (1987). Women, work, and health. *Annual Review of Public Health, 8,* 235–251.

Spielberger, C. D., Barke, L., Russell, S., Silva de Crane, R., Westberry, L., Knight, J., & Marks, E. (1979). *Preliminary manual for the State-Trait Personality Inventory (STPI).* Tampa: University of South Florida.

Spielberger, C. D., Jacobs, G., Russell, S., & Crane, R. (1983). Assessment of anger: The State-Trait Anger Scale. In J. N. Butcher & C. D. Spielberger (Eds.) *Advances in personality assessment* (Vol. 2, pp. 161–189). Hillsdale, NJ: Erlbaum.

Spielberger, C. D., Johnson, E. H., Russell, S. F., Crane, R. J., Jacobs, G. A., & Worden, T. J. (1985). The experience and expression of anger: Construction and validation of an anger expression scale. In M. Chesney & R. Rosenman (Eds.), *Anger and hostility in cardiovascular and behavioral disorders* (pp. 5–30). New York: Hemisphere.

Staats, M., & Staats, T. (1983). Differences in stress levels, stressors, and stress responses between managerial and professional males and females on the Stress Vector Analysis, Research Edition. *Issues in Health Care of Women, 5,* 165–176.

Stanwyck, D. J. (1983). Self-esteem through the life span. *Family and Community Health, 6*(2), 11–28.

Stapley, J., & Haviland, J. (1989). Beyond depression: Gender differences in normal adolescents' emotional experiences. *Sex Roles, 20,* 295–308.

Statham, A. (1988). Woman working for women: The manager and her secretary. In A. Statham, E. M. Miller, & H. O. Mauksch (Eds.), *The worth of women's work* (pp. 225–244). New York: State University New York Press.

Stearns, C. Z., & Stearns, P. N. (1986). *Anger: The struggle for emotional control in America's history.* Chicago: The University of Chicago Press.

Steffenhagen, R. A., & Burns, J. D. (1987). *The social dynamics of self-esteem.* New York: Praeger.

Steffenhagen, R. A. (1990). *Self-esteem therapy.* New York: Praeger.

Stein, P. J. (1981). *Single life: Unmarried adults in social context.* New York: St. Martin's.

Steinem, G. (1991a). Gross national self-esteem. *Ms, 2*(3), 24–34.

Steinem, G. (1991b). *Revolution from within: A book of self-esteem.* Boston: Little, Brown.

Stemmermann, G. N., Nomura, A. M. Y., Chyou, P. & Yoshizawa, C. (1990). Prospective study of alcohol intake and large bowel cancer. *Digestive Diseases and Sciences, 35,* 1414–1420.

Stenberg, C. R., & Campos, J. J. (1990). The development of anger expressions in infancy. In N. Stein, B. Leventhal, & T. Trabasso (Eds.), *Psychological and biological approaches to emotion* (pp. 247–282). Hillsdale, NJ: Erlbaum.

Stewart, A. J., & Salt, P. (1981). Life stress, life-styles, depression, and illness in adult women. *Journal of Personality and Social Psychology, 40,* 1063–1069.

Stewart, D. W. & Shamdasani, P. N. (1990). Focus groups: Theory and practice. *Applied Social Research Methods Series* (Vol. 20). Newbury Park, CA: Sage.

Stone, A. A. (1981). The associations between perceptions of daily experiences and self- and spouse-rated mood. *Journal of Research in Personality, 15,* 510–522.

Stone, A. A., Cox, D., Valdimarsdottir, H., Jandorf, L., & Neale, J. M. (1987). Evidence that secretory IgA antibody is associated with daily mood. *Journal of Personality and Social Psychology, 52,* 988–993.

Stone, A. A., & Neale, J. M. (1984). The effects of "severe" daily events on mood. *Journal of Personality and Social Psychology, 46,* 137–144.

Storr, A. (1983). *The essential Jung.* Princeton, NJ: Princeton University Press.

Stott, D. H. (1973). Follow-up study from birth of the effects of prenatal stresses. *Developmental Medicine and Child Neurology, 15,* 770–787.

Stott, D. H., & Latchford, S. A. (1976). Prenatal antecedents of child health, development, and behavior: An epidemiological report of incidence and association. *Journal of Child Psychology, 15,* 161–191.

Strickland, B. R. (1988). Sex-related differences in health and illness. *Psychology of Women Quarterly, 12,* 381–399.

Stunkard, A. J. (1984). The current status of treatment of obesity in adults. In A. J. Stunkard & E. Stellar (Eds.), *Eating and its disorders.* New York: Raven.

Sue, D. W., & Sue, D. (1990). *Counseling the culturally different: Theory and practice* (2nd ed.). New York: Wiley.

Sullivan, H. S. (1953). *The interpersonal theory of psychiatry.* New York: Norton.

Surrey, J. L. (1984). Self-in-relation: A theory of women's development. *Work in progress: Stone Center for Developmental Services and Studies, No. 13.* Wellesley, MA: Wellesley College, Stone Center.

Swain, R. C., Oetting, E. R., Edwards, R., & Beauvais, F. (1989). Links from emotional distress to adolescent drug use. *Journal of Consulting and Clinical Psychology, 57,* 227–231.

Sweetman, D. (1990). *VanGogh—his life and his art.* New York: Simon & Schuster.

Taeuber, C. (Ed.). (1991). *Statistical handbook on women.* Phoenix, AZ: Oryx.

Taffel, R. (1991). Why is daddy so grumpy? In T. J. Goodrich (Ed.), *Women and power* (pp. 257–262). New York: Norton.

Tavris, C. (1982). *Anger: The misunderstood emotion.* New York: Touchstone/Simon & Schuster.

Tavris, C. (1989). *Anger: The misunderstood emotion* (rev. ed.). New York: Simon & Schuster.

Taylor, C. (1977). *The values.* New York: Philosophical Library.

Taylor, E. (1988). Anger intervention. *The American Journal of Occupational Therapy, 42,* 147–155.

Tevlin, J. (1992, March). Why women are mad as hell. *Glamour,* pp. 206–209, 265–266.

Thoits, P. A. (1983). Dimensions of life events that influence psychological distress: An evaluation and synthesis of the literature. In H. B. Kaplan (Ed.), *Psychological stress: Trends in theory and research.* New York: Academic Press.

Thoits, P. (1986). Multiple identities: Examining gender and marital status differences in distress. *American Sociological Review, 51,* 259–272.

Thomas, C. B. (1988). Cancer and the youthful mind: A 40-year perspective. *Advances, 5*(2), 42–59.

Thomas, S. P. (1989). Gender differences in anger expression: Health implications. *Research in Nursing and Health, 12,* 389–398.

Thomas, S. P. (1990). Theoretical and empirical perspectives on anger. *Issues in Mental Health Nursing, 11,* 203–216.

Thomas, S. P. (1991). Toward a new conceptualization of women's anger. *Issues in Mental Health Nursing, 12,* 31–49.

Thomas, S. P., & Donnellan, M. M. (1991). Correlates of anger symptoms in women in middle adulthood. *American Journal of Health Promotion, 5,* 266–272.

Thomas, S. P., Shoffner, D. H., & Groër, M. W. (1988). Adolescent stress factors: Implications for the nurse practitioner. *The Nurse Practitioner: The American Journal of Primary Health Care, 13*(6), 20–29.

Thomas, S. P., & Williams, R. (1991). Perceived stress, trait anger, modes of anger expression and health status of college men and women. *Nursing Research, 40,* 303–307.

Thomas, S. P., Wilt, D., & Noffsinger, A. (1988). Pathophysiology of depressive illness: Review of the literature and case example. *Issues in Mental Health Nursing, 9,* 271–284.

Thomas, S. P., & Atakan, S. (in press). Trait anger, anger expression, stress, and health status of American and Turkish mid-life women. *Health Care for Women International.*

Thompson, C. (1942). Cultural pressures in the psychology of women. *Psychiatry, 5,* 331–339.

Thoreson, C. E., & Mahoney, M. J. (1974). *Behavioral self control.* New York: Holt, Rinehart & Winston.

Thornberry, O. T., Wilson, R. W., & Golden, P. (1986, May 14). Health promotion and disease prevention: provisional data from the National Health Interview Survey: United States, January-June 1985. *Advance Data from Vital and Health Statistics* (No. 119). Hyattsville, MD: Public Health Service.

Tice, L., Hall, R. C. W., Beresford, T. P., Quimones, J. & Hall, A. K. (1989). Sexual abuse in patients with eating disorders. *Psychiatric Medicine, 7,* 257–267.

Tomkins, S. S. (1963). *Affect, imagery, and consciousness.* New York: Springer.

Tomkins, S. S. (1980). Affect as amplification: Some modifications in theory. In R. Plutchik, & H. Kellerman (Eds.), *Emotion: Theory, research, and experience: Vol. 1. Theories of emotion* (pp. 141–164). New York: Academic Press.

Tomkins, S. S. (1984). Affect theory. In K. R. Scherer & P. Ekman (Eds.), *Approaches to emotion* (pp. 163–195). Hillsdale, NJ: Erlbaum.

Tomkins, S. (1987). Script theory. In J. Aronoff, A. Rabin, & R. Zucker, (Eds.) *The emergence of personality* (pp. 147–216). New York: Springer.

Tomkins, S. (1991). *Affect, imagery, and consciousness: Vol. 30, The negative affects: Anger and fear.* New York: Springer.

Torestad, B. (1990a). What is anger provoking? A psychophysical study of perceived causes of anger. *Aggressive Behavior, 16,* 9–26.

Torestad, B. (1990b). What is anger provoking? Provokers and provoked in anger situations: Developmental trends and sex differences. *Aggressive Behavior, 16,* 353–359.

Travis, C. B. (1988). *Women and health psychology: Biomedical issues.* Hillsdale, NJ: Erlbaum.

Tronick, E. Z. (1989). Emotions and emotional communication in infants. *American Psychologist, 44,* 112–119.

Tronick, E. Z., & Cohn, J. F. (1989). Infant-mother face-to-face interaction: Age and gender differences in coordination and the occurrence of miscoordination. *Child Development, 60,* 85–92.

Tucker, M. B. (1982). Social support and coping: Applications for the study of female drug abuse. *Journal of Social Issues, 38*(2), 117–137.

Turkington, C. (1985). What price friendship? The darker side of social networks. *American Psychological Association Monitor, 16,* 38, 41.

Turner, R. J., & Avison, W. R. (1989). Gender and depression: Assessing exposure and vulnerability to life events in a chronically strained population. *The Journal of Nervous and Mental Disease, 177,* 443–455.

U.N. finds women lag in power, opportunity. (1991, June 22). *The Knoxville News Sentinel,* pp. A-1, A12.

U.S. Department of Health, Education and Welfare (1979). *Healthy people: The surgeon general's report on health promotion and disease prevention* (DHEW Publication [PHS] No. 79-55-71). Washington, DC: U.S. Government Printing Office.

U.S. Department of Health, Education and Welfare (1990). *Healthy People: 2000.* Washington, DC: U.S. Government Printing Office.

U.S. Department of Labor, Bureau of Labor Statistics (1990). *Employee benefits in medium and large firms, 1989* (Bulletin 2363). Washington, DC: U.S. Government Printing Office.

Van Itallie, T. (1985). Health implications of overweight and obesity in the United States. *Annals of Internal Medicine, 103*(6 pt. 2), 983–988.

Van der Ploeg, H. M. (1988). The factor structure of the State-Trait Anger Sclae. *Psychological Reports, 63,* 978.

Van Egeren, L., Abelson, J., & Thornton, D. (1978). Cardiovascular consequences of expressing anger in a mutually-dependent relationship. *Journal of Psychosomatic Research, 22,* 537–548.

Table 22. t Test Comparisons of Women Whose Marital Status Supports, or Fails to Support, Their Values

Anger Variable	Supported Mean	Not Supported Mean	t	p
Anger-in	4.77	5.27	1.74	.08 (NS)
Anger-out	2.58	2.90	1.74	.08 (NS)
Anger-discuss	4.50	4.17	-1.57	.12 (NS)
Anger-symptoms	8.77	9.36	1.27	.20 (NS)
Trait anger	17.88	20.97	3.63	.0004
Somatic anger	20.12	21.61	1.28	.20 (NS)
Cognitive anger	19.97	22.46	2.39	.02
Angry reaction	9.17	10.20	2.09	.04
Angry temperament	5.98	7.05	2.49	.01

Verbrugge, L. M. (1985). Gender and health: An update on hypotheses and evidence. *Journal of Health and Social Behavior, 26,* 156–182.

Verbrugge, L. M. (1986). Role burdens and physical health of women and men. *Women & Health, 11*(1), 47–77.

Verbrugge, L. M. (1989). The twain meet: Empirical explanations of sex differences in health and mortality. *Journal of Health and Social Behavior, 30,* 282–304.

Verbrugge, L. M., & Steiner, R. P. (1985). Prescribing drugs to men and women. *Health Psychology, 4*(1), 79–98.

Verbrugge, L. M., & Wingard, D. L. (1987). Sex differentials in health and mortality. *Women and Health, 12*(2), 103–145.

Viorst, Judith (1986). *Necessary Losses.* New York: Fawcett Gold Medal/Ballantine.

Virtue, D. L. (1989). *The yo-yo syndrome diet.* New York: Harper & Row.

Voydanoff, P. (1988). Women, work, and family: Bernard's perspective on the past, present, and future. *Psychology of Women Quarterly, 12,* 269–280.

Wadden, T. A,. & Strunkard, A. J. (1985). Social and psychological consequences of obesity. *Annals of Internal Medicine , 103*(6 pt. 2), 1062–1067.

Waldron, I., & Jacobs, J. A. (1989). Effects of multiple roles on women's health—evidence from a national longitudinal study. *Women & Health, 15*(1), 3–19.

Waldstein, S., Manuck, S., Bachen, E., Muldoon, M., & Bricker, P. (1990, April). *Anger expression, lipids and lipoproteins.* Paper presented at the Society of Behavioral Medicine, Chicago.

Ward, M. J. & Lindeman, C. (Eds.) (1978). *Instruments for measuring nursing practice and other health care variables* (Vol. 1, p. 159). (DHEW Publication No. HRA78-53). Washington DC: U.S. Government Printing Office.

Ware, J. E. (1976). Scales for measuring general health perceptions. *Health Services Research, 11,* 396–415.

Warren, N. (1983). *Make anger your ally: Harnessing our most baffling emotion.* New York: Doubleday.

Watson, V. M. (1989). Minorities and the legacy of anger. *APA Monitor, 20*(11), 30–31.

Watson, W. L., & Bell, J. M. (1990). Who are we? Low self-esteem and marital identity. *Journal of Psychosocial Nursing, 28*(4), 15–20.

Webster's new collegiate dictionary (1976). Springfield, MA: G. & C. Merriam Company.

Webster's ninth new collegiate dictionary (1989). Springfield: Merriam-Webster.

Weiner, B. (1991). Metaphors in motivation and attribution. *American Psychologist, 46,* 921–930.

Weinstein, R. (1986). The patient experiencing marital conflict. In J. D. Durham & S. B. Hardin (Eds.), *The nurse psychotherapist in private practice* (pp. 285–296). New York: Springer.

Weiss, A. (1977). Characteristics of successful weight reducers: A brief review of prediction variables. *Addictive Behavior, 2,* 193–201.

Weissman, M. (1987). Advances in psychiatric epidemiology: Rates and risks for major depression. *American Journal of Public Health, 77,* 445–451.

Weissman, M., & Klerman, G. (1977). Gender and depression. *Trends in Neurosciences, 8,* 416–420.

Weissman, M., & Klerman, G. (1985). Sex differences in the epidemiology of depression. *Archives of General Psychiatry, 34,* 98–111.

Weissman, M., Klerman, G., & Paykel, E. (1971). Clinical evaluation of hostility in depression. *American Journal of Psychiatry, 128,* 41–46.

Weissman, M., & Paykel, E. (1974). *The depressed woman.* Chicago: The University of Chicago Press.

Wentz, A. C., & Haseltine, F. P. (1992). Editorial. *Journal of Women's Health, 1*(1), xv.

Wheeler, R. J., & Frank, M. A. (1988). Identification of stress buffers. *Behavioral Medicine, 14,* 78–89.

White, J. H. (1991). Feminism, eating and mental health. *Advances in Nursing Science, 13,* 68–80.

White, P., Mascalo, A., Thomas, S., & Shoun, S. (1986). Husbands' and wives' perceptions of marital intimacy and wives' stresses in dual-career marriages. *Family Perspective, 20,* 27–35.

White, R. B. (1977). Current psychoanalytic concepts of depression. In W. E. Fann, I. Karacan, A. D. Pokorny, & R. L. Williams (Eds.), *Phenomenology and treatment of depression* (pp. 127–141). New York: Spectrum.

Wilberding, J. Z. (1985). Values clarification. In G. Bulechek & J. McCloskey (Eds.), *Nursing interventions: Treatments for nursing diagnoses* (pp. 173–184). Philadelphia: Saunders.

Wiley, J. A., & Camacho, T. C. (1980). Life-style and future health: Evidence from the Alameda County Study. *Preventive Medicine, 9,* 1–21.

Williams, R. B., Jr., & Barefoot, J. C. (1988). Coronary-prone behavior: The emerging role of the hostility complex. In B. K. Houston & C. R. Snyder (Eds.), *Type A behavior pattern: Research, theory, and intervention* (pp. 189–211). New York: Wiley.

Williams, R. B., Jr., Barefoot, J. C., & Shekelle, R. B. (1985). The health consequences of hostility. In M. A. Chesney & R. H. Rosenman (Eds.), *Anger and hostility in cardiovascular and behavioral disorders* (pp. 173–185). New York: Hemisphere.

Williams, R. B., Haney, T. L., Lee, K. L., Kong, Y., Blumenthal, J. A., & Whalen, R. E. (1980). Type A behavior, hostility, and coronary artery disease. *Psychosomatic Medicine, 42,* 539–549.

Wilsnack, R. W., & Cheloha, R. (1987). Women's roles and problem drinking across the life span. *Social Problems, 34,* 231–248.

Wilsnack, R. W., Wilsnack, S. C., & Klassen, A. D. (1984). Women's drinking and drinking problems: Patterns from a 1981 national survey. *American Journal of Public Health, 74,* 1231–1238.

Wilsnack, S. C. (1973). Sex role identity in female alcoholism. *Journal of Abnormal Psychology, 82,* 253–261.

Wilsnack, S. C. (1976). The impact of sex roles on women's alcohol use and abuse. In M. Greenblatt & M. A. Schuckit (Eds.), *Alcoholism problems in women and children* (pp. 37–64). New York: Grune & Stratton.

Wilsnack, S. C., Klassen, A. D., Schur, B. E., & Wilsnack, R. W. (1991). Predicting onset and chronicity of women's problem drinking: A five-year longitudinal analysis. *American Journal of Public Health, 81,* 305–317.

Wilsnack, S. C., & Wilsnack, R. W. (1991). Epidemiology of women's drinking. *Journal of Substance Abuse, 3*, 133–157.

Wilt, D. (1989, September). *Treatment of anger in mid-life women*. Paper presented at the American Nurses' Association Research Conference, Chicago, IL.

Witkin, G. (1991). *The female stress syndrome* (2nd ed.). New York: Newmarket Press.

Witt, E. M., Kaelin, J. A., Stoner, S. B. (1988). Smoking behavior and anger. *Psychological Reports, 63*(1), 117–118.

Wood, N. (1986). Self care practices among young adult married women. *Research in Nursing & Health, 8*, 227–234.

Wood, H. D., & Duffy, E. L. (1966). Psychological factors in alcoholic women. *American Journal of Psychiatry, 123*, 341–345.

Woodall, K. L., & Matthews, K. A. (1989). Familial environment associated with Type A behaviors and psychophysiological responses to stress in children. *Health Psychology, 8*, 403–426.

Woodman, M. (1982). *Addiction to perfection: The still unravished bride*. Toronto, Canada: Inner City Books.

Worchel, P. (1961). Status restoration and the reduction of hostility. *Journal of Abnormal and Social Psychology, 63*, 443–445.

Worchel, S., & Worchel, J. (1985). Aggression and psychodynamic therapy: From theory to practice. In G. Stricker & R. H. Keisner (Eds.), *From research to clinical practice: The implications of social and developmental research for psychotherapy* (pp. 113–138). New York: Plenum.

Worthington, E. (1988). Understanding the values of religious clients: A model and its application to counseling. *Journal of Counseling Psychology, 35*(2), 166–174.

Wylie, R. C. (1989). *Measures of self concept*. Lincoln, NE: University of Nebraska Press.

Yacichak, A. J. (1978). A study of the self-concept evaluations of alcoholics and non-alcoholics. *Journal of Drug Education, 8*(1), 41–49.

Yahne, C. E., & Long, V. O. (1988). The use of support groups to raise self-esteem for women clients. *College Health, 37*, 79–83.

Yeung, W. H., & Schwartz, M. A. (1986). Emotional disturbance in Chinese obstetrical patients: A pilot study. *General Hospital Psychiatry, 8*, 258–262.

Younger, J. (1991). A theory of mastery. *Advances in Nursing Science, 14*, 76–89.

Zajonc, R. B. (1984). On the primacy of affect. *American Psychologist, 39*, 117–123.

Zegans, L. (1983). Emotions in health and illness: An attempt at integration. In L. Temoshok, C. Van Dyke, & L. Zegans (Eds.), *Emotions in health and illness: Theoretical and research foundations* (pp. 235–254). New York: Grune & Stratton.

Zelin, M. L., Adler, G., & Myerson, P. G. (1972). Anger Self-Report: An objective questionnaire for the measurement of aggression. *Journal of Consulting and Clinical Psychology, 39*, 340.

Zurawski, R., & Richardson, S. (1992, March). *Psychosocial and psychophysiological correlates of the Multidimensional Anger Inventory*. Paper presented at the annual meeting of the Society of Behavioral Medicine, New York.

Appendix

Table 1. Percentage Distributions for Categorical Demographic Variables (N = 479)*

VARIABLE	PERCENTAGE
RACE	
Caucasian	84.7
African-American	13.2
Asian	1.7
Other	0.4
MARITAL STATUS	
Never married	6.7
Married	69.2
Divorced/Sep.	19.9
Widowed	4.2
EMPLOYMENT STATUS	
Unemployed	13.7
Full-time	73.8
Part-time	12.5
OCCUPATION	
Professional practice	6.2
Owner of business	1.6
Clerical	19.5
Teaching	5.3
Human Services	30.8
Sales	2.0
Technical/engineering	4.7
Management	7.5
Homemaking	10.0
Finance/banking	1.6
Factory/production	1.6
Other	5.3
Student	3.3
Retired	0.7

*Note: This table does not include 56 Chinese-American women whose data were only used in selected crosscultural comparisons.

Table 2. Means and Standard Deviations for Continuous Demographic Variables

Variable	Mean	SD	Range
Age	43.5	7.3	25-66
Number of children	2.0	1.3	0-7
Years of education	15.3	2.6	7-24
Annual household income	$46,317.21	$31,386.42	$1,700-$300,000

Table 3. Cronbach's Alpha Reliability Coefficients for Instruments

Scale	Coefficient
Beck Depression	.91
Perceived Stress	.89
Current Health	.92
Trait Anger	.82
Rosenberg Self-Esteem	.89
Cognitive Anger	.87
Somatic Anger	.90
Anger Symptoms	.81
Anger-in	.64

Note: Cronbach's alpha was not computed for the anger-out and anger-discuss scales due to the small number of items. Inter-item correlation for anger-out was .40, for anger discuss .36.

Table 4. Means and Standard Deviations for Anger Variables

VARIABLE	Mean	S.D.	RANGE
Anger-in	5.20	1.69	3-9
Anger-out	2.62	0.93	2-6
Anger-discuss	4.50	1.16	2-6
Anger-symptoms	8.92	2.71	5-15
Trait anger	18.26	4.90	10-40
Angry temperament	6.16	2.43	4-16
Angry reaction	9.07	2.71	4-16
Cognitive anger	20.59	5.86	10-35
Somatic anger	20.07	6.52	10-40

Table 5. t test Comparisons of Women in Upper and Lower Quartiles of Education on Anger Dimensions

Anger Variable	Highly Educated (upper 25% of sample, n = 135) Mean	Less Educated (lower 25% of Sample, n = 133) Mean	t	p
Anger-in	4.94	5.56	-3.06	.0025
Anger-out	2.60	2.62	-0.21	NS
Anger-discuss	4.43	4.47	-0.31	NS
Anger-symptoms	8.49	9.75	-3.85	.0002
Trait anger	17.99	17.93	0.11	NS
Angry temperament	5.96	6.02	-0.23	NS
Angry reaction	9.15	8.83	0.32	NS
Cognitive anger	19.89	21.93	-1.79	NS
Somatic anger	19.53	20.86	-1.11	NS

300

Table 6. ANOVA Comparisons of Women Grouped by Age on Anger Dimensions

Age	34 or less	35-39	40-44	45-49	50-54	55 or more	F	p
Anger Variable	Mean	Mean	Mean	Mean	Mean	Mean	F	p
Anger-in	5.15	4.87	5.27	5.17	5.51	5.79	2.48	.03
Anger-out	2.79	2.77	2.72	2.48	2.41	2.34	2.94	.01
Anger-discuss	4.60	4.60	4.46	4.57	4.32	4.34	0.79	NS
Anger-symptoms	8.76	8.84	9.39	8.99	8.92	7.66	2.51	.03
Trait anger	20.64	19.66	18.02	17.90	16.92	15.13	8.61	.0001
Angry temperament	6.88	6.91	5.87	6.20	5.51	4.89	6.89	.0001
Angry reaction	10.03	9.40	9.15	8.90	8.66	7.87	3.18	.0078
Cognitive anger	23.94	21.01	21.08	19.84	17.83	19.15	2.71	.02
Somatic anger	21.71	20.65	20.40	19.74	18.04	18.08	1.09	NS

Table 7. ANOVA Comparsions of Psychiatric Patients ($\underline{n}$ = 52), Medical Patients ($\underline{n}$ = 40), and 50 Randomly Selected Women from the Nonclinical Sample on Anger Dimensions*

ANGER VARIABLE	Psych Group Mean	Medical Group Mean	Nonclin. Group Mean	$\underline{F}$	$\underline{p}$
Anger-in	5.35	5.13	5.12	0.24	NS
Anger-out	2.98	2.45	2.48	4.42	.01
Anger-discuss	4.36	4.23	4.76	2.49	NS
Anger symptoms	10.86	8.60	8.40	12.93	.0001
Trait anger	20.31	17.33	17.06	8.29	.0004
Angry temperament	6.88	5.80	6.14	2.45	NS
Angry reaction	9.88	8.50	8.18	7.42	.0009

*Note: Data were available on too few subjects to conduct comparisons on cognitive anger and somatic anger.

302

Table 8. ANOVA Comparisons of Women Grouped by Race on Anger Dimensions*

RACE	Caucasian American*	African American	Chinese American		
ANGER VARIABLE	Mean	Mean	Mean	F	p
Anger-in	5.23	5.08	4.55	4.27	.01
Anger-out	2.57	2.56	3.05	7.05	.001
Anger-discuss	4.54	4.62	4.50	0.19	NS
Anger-symptoms	8.77	8.21	8.86	1.41	NS
Trait anger	17.98	18.32	21.07	9.70	.0001
Angry temperament	6.04	6.11	7.82	13.91	.0001
Angry reaction	9.04	8.98	9.84	2.12	NS
Cognitive anger	20.50	20.20	21.43	0.69	NS
Somatic anger	20.46	18.65	19.70	1.30	NS

*Note: These analyses involved only the nonclinical sample.

303

Table 9. Correlations Among Anger Variables for Full Sample

	Anger-in	Anger-out	Anger discuss	Anger symptoms	Angry temperament	Angry reaction	Trait anger	Cognitive anger	Somatic anger
Anger-in	—	-0.06	-0.38***	0.20***	-0.23***	-0.01	-0.14*	0.04	-0.02
Anger-out		—	0.04	0.24***	0.38***	0.20***	0.39***	0.40***	0.34***
Anger-discuss			—	-0.06	0.15**	0.15**	0.16**	0.02	0.02
Anger-symptoms				—	0.19***	0.33***	0.33***	0.56***	0.58***
Angry temperament					—	0.34***	0.79***	0.39***	0.32***
Angry reaction						—	0.80***	0.61***	0.52***
Trait anger							—	0.65***	0.54***
Cognitive anger								—	0.77***
Somatic anger									—

* $p < .01$ ** $p < .001$ *** $p < .0001$

Note: Angry temperament and angry reaction are subscales of the trait anger instrument.

Table 10. Situational Triggers of Women's Anger

The frequency with which women reported anger situations analyzed by realms (intrapersonal, interpersonal, and extrapersonal) follows:

Intrapersonal	16.20%	(29/179)
Interpersonal		
work	13.42%	(24/179)
family/friends	17.32%	(31/179)
others	35.75%	(64/179)
Extrapersonal	2.79%	(5/179)
situational	11.17%	(20/179)
No Anger	3.35%	(6/179)

Table 11. Targets of Women's Anger

Intrapersonal	5.44%	(19/349
Interpersonal		
work	30.96%	(108/349)
family	42.69%	(149/349)
people	17.19%	(60/349)
Extrapersonal	3.15%	(11/349)
No response	.57%	(2/349)

305

Table 12. Individuals to Whom Women Express Anger

Intrapersonal	4.65%	(15/323)
Interpersonal	91.33%	(295/323)
co-workers	12.69%	(41/323)
family	46.75%	(151/323)
friends	15.48%	(50/323)
people	6.19%	(20/323)
person who caused	9.60%	(31/323)
Extrapersonal		
no one	3.4%	(11/323)
spiritual	.62%	(2/323)
No response	.62%	(2/323)

Table 13. Individuals to Whom Women Would Not Express Anger

Intrapersonal	0	
Interpersonal		
co-worker	35.4%	(74/209)
family	24.88%	(52/209)
friends	8.61%	(18/209)
authority figures	10.53%	(22/209)
Extrapersonal		
no one	10.05%	(21/209)
No answer	10.53%	(22/209)

Table 14. Duration of Women's Anger

Seconds	.54%	(1/186)
Minutes	40.85%	(76/186)
a few		15
1-2 minutes		5
5 minutes		12
5-10 minutes		3
10 minutes		8
10-15 minutes		3
15 minutes		10
30 minutes		15
30-60 minutes		3
Hours	23.12%	(43/186)
Days	10.75%	(20/186)
Weeks	.54%	(1/186)
Brief	12.90%	(24/186)
Varies	7.53%	(14/186)
Miscellaneous	2.69%	(5/186)
Never angry	.54%	(1/186)
No response	.54%	(1/186)

Table 15. Anger and Self-Esteem Correlations

Variable	Entire Sample	Non Clinical	Medical	Psych
Anger Symptoms	-.46 $p<.0001$	-.43 $p<.0001$	-.32 $p<.042$	-.45 $p<.0008$
Cognitive Anger	-.34 $p<.0001$	-.34 $p<.0001$	NS	-.53 $p<.05$
Trait Anger	-.28 $p<.0001$	-.27 $p<.0001$	NS	NS
Anger Out	-.27 $p<.0001$	-.27 $p<.0001$	NS	NS
Somatic Anger	-.26 $p<.0001$	-.25 $p<.0008$	NS	-.65 $p<.01$
Angry Temperament	-.22 $p<.0001$	-.23 $p<.0001$	NS	NS
Anger In	-.18 $p<.0001$	-.18 $p<.0005$	NS	-.35 $p<.01$
Anger Discuss	.19 $p<.0001$	.21 $p<.0001$	.30 $p<.064$	NS
Angry Reaction	-.19 $p<.0001$	-.17 $p<.001$	NS	-.26 $p<.07$

Table 16. Prediction of Anger Variables by Step-Wise Multiple Regression

Anger Symptoms

   Self-esteem accounted for 22% of variance (- relationship)
   $p = .0001$
   Years of education added 1% (- relationship)
   Together the two variables accounted for 23% of variance
   $p = .0397$

Anger Cognitions

   Self-esteem accounted for 12.6% of the variance (-
   relationship) $p = .0001$

Trait Anger

   Self-esteem accounted for 8% of the variance (-
   relationship) $p = .0001$

Anger Out

   Self-esteem accounted for 7% of the variance (-
   relationship) $p = .0001$
   Age added 1.6% (-relationship) $p = .0055$
   Non-married status added .9% (- relationship)
   The three variables together accounted for 9.7% of
   variance $p = .0415$

Angry Temperament

   (a component of trait anger)
   Self-esteem accounted for 5% of the variance $p = .0001$

Table 17. Prediction of Self-Esteem by Multiple Regression

Beck Depression accounted for 36% of variance (- relationship)
Perceived stress added 6% (- relationship)
Anger symptoms added 1% (- relationship)
Anger out added .5% (- relationship)
Combination of four variables accounted for 43.6% of the variance in self-esteem

Table 18. t Test Comparisons of High and Low Self-Esteem Women on Anger Variables

Anger Variable	Non-Clinical t	Non-Clinical p	Entire Sample t	Entire Sample p
Anger-in	-4.6	<.0001	-3.8<	.0002
Anger-out	-5.0	<.0001	-5.0	<.0001
Anger Discuss	4.3	<.0001	3.8	<.0002
Anger Symptoms	-10.3	<.0001	-10.6	<.0001
Trait Anger	-5.0	<.0001	-5.3	<.0001
Anger Cognitions	-5.0	<.0001	-4.99	<.0001
Somatic Anger	-3.93	<.0001	-3.69	<.0003
Angry Temperament	-4.21	<.0001	-4.43	<.0001
Angry Reaction	-3.94	<.0001	-3.87	<.0001

Table 19. Self-Esteem by Occupation

Occupation	RES Mean	S.D.	Range
Human Service Workers (N = 125)	32.3	5.36	15-40
Secretaries (N = 86)	32.1	4.89	21-40
Prof. owners/managers (N = 63)	32.0	5.71	19-40
Homemakers (N = 43)	31.0	5.06	19-40

Table 20. Self-Esteem Among Clinical and Nonclinical Groups

Group	RES Mean	S.D.	Range
Non-clinical (N = 364)	32.4	4.96	20-40
Medical (N = 40)	31.6	4.13	22-40
Psychiatric out-pt. (N = 28)	28.4	5.83	18-40
Psychiatric in-pt. (N = 21)	24.9	5.78	12-36

Table 21. Intercorrelations of Stress, Anger, and Social Support

	TA	AI	AO	AD	AS	CA	SA	PS	AF	FI	AID	SIZE	DUR	FRE
TA	--	-.14	.39	.16	.33	.65	.54	.42	-.19	NS	NS	-.16	-.17	-.15
AI		--	NS	-.38	.20	NS	NS	.10	NS	NS	NS	NS	-.14	NS
AO			--	NS	.24	.40	.34	.28	NS	NS	NS	-.14	-.14	-.14
AD				--	NS	NS	NS	-.10	NS	NS	NS	NS	NS	NS
AS					--	.56	.58	.55	-.19	NS	NS	NS	NS	NS
CA						--	.77	.48	-.17	NS	NS	NS	NS	NS
SA							--	.41	NS	NS	NS	NS	NS	NS
PS								--	-.35	NS	NS	NS	-.14	NS
AF									--	.55	.45	NS	NS	NS
FI										--	.50	-.15	NS	NS
AID											--	-.23	-.17	NS
SIZE												--	.97	.92
DUR													--	.92
FRE														--

Note: All correlations shown are statistically significant at p = .05 or less
TA = TRAIT ANGER, AI = ANGER-IN, AO = ANGER-OUT, AD = ANGER-DISCUSS, AS = ANGER SYMPTOMS, CA = COGNATIVE ANGER, SA = SOMATIC ANGER, PS = PERCEIVED STRESS, AF = AFFECT SUPPORT, FI = AFFIRMATION SUPPORT, AID = AID SUPPORT, SIZE = NUMBER IN NETWORK, DUR = DURATION OF RELATIONSHIP, FRE = FREQUENCY OF CONTACT

Table 23. Relationships of Perceived Health and Anger Variables (N = 479)

Variable	r	p
Anger-in	-0.14	.003
Anger-out	-0.12	.007
Anger-discuss	0.13	.006
Anger symptoms	-0.36	.0001
Trait anger	-0.13	.006
Cognitive anger	-0.18	.008
Somatic anger	-0.15	.02

Table 24. Correlations of Health Risk Index Scores and Anger Variables

Variable	r	p
Trait anger	.10	.03
Anger symptoms	.12	.01

Table 25. Comparison of Groups with Low and High Levels of Exercise on Anger Variables

Variable	Mean for low group (N = 173)	Mean for high group (N = 285)	t	p
Anger-in	5.50	5.06	-2.59	.01
Anger-out	2.59	2.62	0.32	NS
Anger discuss	4.27	4.66	3.47	.0006
Anger symptoms	9.53	8.59	-3.50	.0005
Trait anger	18.79	17.77	-2.23	.03

315

Table 26. ANOVA Comparisons of Women Reporting Low, Medium and High Levels of Health on Anger Variables

Variable	F	p
Anger-in	8.41	.0003
Anger-out	3.18	.04
Anger discuss	5.59	.004
Anger symptoms	25.93	.0001
Trait anger	3.32	.04

Table 27. t-Test Comparisons of Women Reporting Hospitalizations to Those with No Hospitalizations

Variable	t	p
Anger-in	3.46	.0008
Anger-discuss	-2.25	.03
Anger symptoms	3.21	.002

316

Table 28. $\underline{t}$-Test Comparisons of Women Reporting Surgeries to Those with No Surgeries

Variable	$\underline{t}$	$\underline{p}$
Anger-in	3.18	.002
Anger discuss	-1.94	.05
Anger symptoms	2.49	.01

Table 29. ANOVA Comparisons of Women Reporting Low, Medium and High Levels of Days III on Anger Variables

Variable	F	$\underline{p}$
Cognitive anger	4.12	.02
Somatic anger	4.46	.01

Table 30. ANOVA Comparisons of Women Reporting Low, Medium and High Numbers of Physician Visits

Variable	F	$\underline{p}$
Anger symptoms	9.09	.0001

Table 31. ANOVA Comparisons of Women Reporting Low, Medium and High Numbers of Health Visits

Variable	F	$\underline{p}$
Trait anger	3.70	.03

Table 32. Comparison of Means of Non-drinkers, Low Risk, and High Risk
Drinkers

	Non-drinkers (n = 159)	Low Risk (n = 114)	High Risk (n = 49)
Anger-in	5.27	5.04	5.18
Anger-out	2.51	2.67	2.57
Anger-discuss	4.41	4.61	4.35
Anger-symptom	8.78	8.50	9.08
Trait anger	17.67	17.86	19.16
Somatic anger	20.00	19.03	21.19
Cognitive anger	20.73	19.20	21.04
Depression	8.35	7.72	9.02
Self-esteem	31.32	32.04	32.18
Health	31.79	34.78	34.63
Stress	24.81	24.18	24.37

Table 33. Percentage of Women Who Use Alcohol by Age

	35 and under (n = 64)	36 to 45 (n = 245)	over 45 (n = 161)
Abstain	68.8	66.5	62.1
1-4/week	23.4	22.5	27.3
5 + /week	7.8	11.0	10.6

318

Table 34. Categorization of Study Participants According to BDI Scores

Category*	Frequency	Percent
severe depression (scores $\geq$ 30)	13	2.9%
moderate to severe depression (scores 20-29)	30	6.6%
mild to moderate depression (scores 16-19)	22	4.8%
mild depression (scores 10-15)	87	19.1%
normal (nondepressed) (scores 0-9)	303	66.6%

*Categorization based on Green [Green, C. J. (1985). The use of psychodiagnostic questionnaires in predicting risk factors and health outcomes. In P. Karoly (Ed.), Measurement strategies in health psychology (pp. 301-333). New York: John Wiley.]

Table 35. Categorization of Women in Nonclinical Sample According to BDI Scores

Category*	Frequency	Percent
severe depression	7	1.9%
moderate to severe depression	16	4.4%
mild to moderate depression	13	3.6%
mild depression	71	19.6%
normal (nondepressed)	256	70.5%

Table 36. Relationships between Depression and Anger Variables in Nonclinical Sample

Variable	r	p
Trait anger	.34	.0001
Angry reaction	.28	.0001
Angry temperament	.22	.0001
Anger-in	.19	.0003
Anger-out	.31	.0001
Anger-discuss	-.13	.0172
Anger symptoms	.52	.0001
Cognitive anger	.44	.0001
Somatic anger	.40	.0001

Note: A shortened anger symptoms scale (omitting the "feel depressed" item) was used in all correlations with Beck Inventory Scores, to avoid inflation of correlations

Table 37. Relationships between Depression and Anger Variables in the Psychiatric Sample

Variable	r	p
Trait anger	.24	.09
Angry reaction	.21	NS
Angry temperament	.15	NS
Anger-in	.41	.003
Anger-out	.10	NS
Anger-discuss	-.27	.05
Anger symptoms	.38	.0055
Cognitive anger	.68	.0073
Somatic anger	.69	.0063

Table 38. Relationships between Depression and Anger Variables in Total Sample of Women

Variable	r	p
Trait anger	.31	.0001
Angry reaction subscale	.24	.0001
Angry temperament subscale	.20	.0001
Anger-in	.23	.0001
Anger-out	.27	.0001
Anger-discuss	-.16	.0009
Anger symptoms	.49	.0001
Cognitive anger	.46	.0001
Somatic anger	.41	.0001

Table 39. ANOVA Comparisons of Highly Depressed (n = 65), Mildly Depressed (n = 87), and a Randomly Selected Subsample of Nondepressed (n = 75) Women on Anger Variables

Variable	F	p
Anger-in	4.87	.0085
Anger-out	9.29	.0001
Anger-discuss	2.78	.0640
Anger symptoms	37.39	.0001
Trait anger	6.74	.0014
Angry temperament	2.10	.1245
Angry reaction	3.94	.0209

Notes:

- Data were available on too few subjects to conduct comparisons on cognitive anger and somatic anger

Index

323

⑤ *Springer Publishing Company*

FEMINIST ETHICS
IN PSYCHOTHERAPY

Hannah Lerman, PhD,*Clinical Psychologist, Los Angeles*
Natalie Porter, PhD,*University of New Mexico School of
Medicine,* Editors

*"From the very beginning, it was clear that ethics was a very
significant issue for most of us...We began to think deeply about
some of the ethical issues that were raised. It became increasingly
clear that our thinking was not the same as that of the mental health
professionals from whom we has received our training. We then
decided to devote a book to ethics, one of our major and central
concerns."* —**From the Preface**

Focusing on the Feminist Therapy Institute's Code of Ethics,
this important volume addresses a variety of issues—
including ethics of power differentials • therapist
accountability • specific cultural diversities and oppressions •
the therapist-society relationship.

Partial Contents: The Contribution of Feminism to Ethics in Psychotherapy,
H. Lerman and N. Porter. The Need for an integrated Analysis of Opression
in Feminist Therapy Ethics, *V. Kanuha.* Empowerment as an Ethical
Imperative, *A.J. Smith and M.A. Douglas.* Boundary Violations: Misuse of
the Power of the Therapist, *H. Lerman and D.N. Rigby.* How To Be a Failure
as a Family Therapist: A Feminist Perspective, *E. Kaschak.* Working Within
the Lesbian Community: The Dilemma of Overlapping Relationships, *A.J.
Smith.* On Being an "Only One," *V.L. Sears.* The Self-Care and Wellness of
Feminist Therapists, *P.S. Faunce.* Women in Poverty: Ethical Dimensions
in Therapy, *P.S. Faunce.* Therapy, Feminist Ethics and the Community of
Color with Particular Emphasis on the Treatment of Black Women, *E.K.
Childs.* Feminist Ethics with Victims of Violence, *L.E.A. Walker.* Public
Advocacy, *L.B. Rosewater.* Feminist Therapy Ethics in the Media, *K.E. Peres.*

1990   267pp   0-8261-6290-8   *hardcover*

$ *Springer Publishing Company*

WOMEN AS THERAPISTS
A Multitheoretical Casebook

Dorothy W. Cantor, PsyD,
New Jersey Psychological Association, Editor

A concise, carefully edited work providing key explanations of why certain clients (both male and female) prefer working with a woman therapist, and how the therapist's gender affects client relationships. The text also examines how therapists of different theoretical orientations would handle a specific case.

"It is our hope that this book will advance the understanding of women who bring to their work as therapists the empathy and caring that are the cornerstone of successful treatment, regardless of their theoretical orientation." **—From the Introduction**

Contents

1990   250pp   0-8261-6910-4   hardcover